# Windows® 98 Administrator's Handbook

# Windows® 98 Administrator's Handbook

*Jerry Honeycutt*

## IDG Books Worldwide, Inc.
An International Data Group Company

Foster City, CA ■ Chicago, IL ■ Indianapolis, IN ■ New York, NY

**Windows® 98 Administrator's Handbook**
Published by
**IDG Books Worldwide, Inc.**
An International Data Group Company
919 E. Hillsdale Blvd., Suite 400
Foster City, CA 94404
www.idgbooks.com (IDG Books Worldwide Web site)

ISBN: 0-7645-3316-9

Printed in the United States of America

10 9 8 7 6 5 4 3 2 1

1P/RX/QT/ZZ/FC

Distributed in the United States by IDG Books Worldwide, Inc.

Distributed by CDG Books Canada Inc. for Canada; by Transworld Publishers Limited in the United Kingdom; by IDG Norge Books for Norway; by IDG Sweden Books for Sweden; by Woodslane Pty. Ltd. for Australia; by Woodslane (NZ) Ltd. for New Zealand; by TransQuest Publishers Pte Ltd. for Singapore, Malaysia, Thailand, Indonesia, and Hong Kong; by ICG Muse, Inc., for Japan; by Norma Comunicaciones S.A. for Colombia; by Intersoft for South Africa; by Le Monde en Tique for France; by International Thomson Publishing for Germany, Austria, and Switzerland; by Distribuidora Cuspide for Argentina; by Livraria Cultura for Brazil; by Ediciones ZETA S.C.R. Ltda. for Peru; by WS Computer Publishing Corporation, Inc., for the Philippines; by Contemporanea de Ediciones for Venezuela; by Express Computer Distributors for the Caribbean and West Indies; by Micronesia Media Distributor, Inc., for Micronesia; by Grupo Editorial Norma S.A. for Guatemala; by Chips Computadoras S.A. de C.V. for Mexico; by Editorial Norma de Panama S.A. for Panama; by American Bookshops for Finland. Authorized Sales Agent: Anthony Rudkin Associates for the Middle East and North Africa.

For general information on IDG Books Worldwide's books in the U.S., please call our Consumer Customer Service department at 800-762-2974. For reseller information, including discounts and premium sales, pl ease call our Reseller Customer Service department at 800-434-3422.

For information on where to purchase IDG Books Worldwide's books outside the U.S., please contact our International Sales department at 317-596-5530 or fax 317-596-5692.

For consumer information on foreign language translations, please contact our Customer Service department at 800-434-3422, fax 317-596-5692, or e-mail rights@idgbooks.com.

For information on licensing foreign or domestic rights, please phone +1-650-655-3109.

For sales inquiries and special prices for bulk quantities, please contact our Sales department at 650-655-3200 or write to the address above.

For information on using IDG Books Worldwide's books in the classroom or for ordering examination copies, please contact our Educational Sales department at 800-434-2086 or fax 317-596-5499.

For press review copies, author interviews, or other publicity information, please contact our Public Relations department at 650-655-3000 or fax 650-655-3299.

For authorization to photocopy items for corporate, personal, or educational use, please contact Copyright Clearance Center, 222 Rosewood Drive, Danvers, MA 01923, or fax 978-750-4470.

Library of Congress Cataloging-in-Publication Data

Honeycutt, Jerry.
  Windows 98 administrator's handbook / Jerry Honeycutt.
     p.  cm.
  ISBN 0-7645-3316-9 (alk. paper)
  1. Microsoft Windows (Computer file)
  2. Operating systems (Computers)  I. Title.
  QA76.76.063H667   1999
  005.4'469—dc21                          99-13764
                                          CIP

is a registered trademark or trademark under exclusive license to IDG Books Worldwide, Inc., from International Data Group, Inc., in the United States and/or other countries.

# ABOUT IDG BOOKS WORLDWIDE

Welcome to the world of IDG Books Worldwide.

IDG Books Worldwide, Inc., is a subsidiary of International Data Group, the world's largest publisher of computer-related information and the leading global provider of information services on information technology. IDG was founded more than 30 years ago by Patrick J. McGovern and now employs more than 9,000 people worldwide. IDG publishes more than 290 computer publications in over 75 countries. More than 90 million people read one or more IDG publications each month.

Launched in 1990, IDG Books Worldwide is today the #1 publisher of best-selling computer books in the United States. We are proud to have received eight awards from the Computer Press Association in recognition of editorial excellence and three from Computer Currents' First Annual Readers' Choice Awards. Our best-selling ...For Dummies® series has more than 50 million copies in print with translations in 31 languages. IDG Books Worldwide, through a joint venture with IDG's Hi-Tech Beijing, became the first U.S. publisher to publish a computer book in the People's Republic of China. In record time, IDG Books Worldwide has become the first choice for millions of readers around the world who want to learn how to better manage their businesses.

Our mission is simple: Every one of our books is designed to bring extra value and skill-building instructions to the reader. Our books are written by experts who understand and care about our readers. The knowledge base of our editorial staff comes from years of experience in publishing, education, and journalism — experience we use to produce books to carry us into the new millennium. In short, we care about books, so we attract the best people. We devote special attention to details such as audience, interior design, use of icons, and illustrations. And because we use an efficient process of authoring, editing, and desktop publishing our books electronically, we can spend more time ensuring superior content and less time on the technicalities of making books.

You can count on our commitment to deliver high-quality books at competitive prices on topics you want to read about. At IDG Books Worldwide, we continue in the IDG tradition of delivering quality for more than 30 years. You'll find no better book on a subject than one from IDG Books Worldwide.

John Kilcullen
Chairman and CEO
IDG Books Worldwide, Inc.

Steven Berkowitz
President and Publisher
IDG Books Worldwide, Inc.

*Eighth Annual Computer Press Awards ≥1992*

*Ninth Annual Computer Press Awards ≥1993*

*Tenth Annual Computer Press Awards ≥1994*

*Eleventh Annual Computer Press Awards ≥1995*

# Credits

**Acquisitions Editor**
Tracy Thomsic

**Development Editor**
Eric Newman

**Technical Editor**
Curtis A. Knight

**Copy Editors**
Amy Eoff
Vicky Nuttall
Dennis Weaver

**Project Coordinator**
Tom Debolski

**Book Designer**
Kurt Krames

**Graphics and Production Specialist**
Jude Levinson

**Quality Control Specialists**
Mick Arellano
Mark Schumann

**Proofreading and Indexing**
York Production Services

**Cover Designer**
Peter Kowaleszyn

# About the Author

**Jerry Honeycutt** provides business-oriented technical leadership to the Internet and end-user communities and the software development industry. His clients include companies such as The Travelers, IBM, Nielsen Norton America, IRM, Howard Systems International, and NCR. He continues to serve a variety of organizations via independent consulting, speaking, training, and other activities.

Jerry is a leading author in the Internet and operating system categories. He is the author of 19 other books through various publishers. Most of Jerry's books are sold internationally and have been translated into a variety of languages. His work has been published in *Computer Language* magazine, and he is a regular speaker at Windows World, COMDEX, and other industry trade shows on topics related to software development, the Windows product family, and the Internet. He also writes a bimonthly column for *Frisco Style* magazine.

Jerry graduated from the University of Texas at Dallas in 1992 with a B.S. degree in Computer Science. He lives in the Dallas suburb of Frisco, Texas, with Bones, his loyal Jack Russell terrier, and has a passion for golf, fine photography, and international travel. Feel free to visit Jerry's Web site at `http://www.honeycutt.com`.

*For David Rogelberg*

# Preface

Windows 98 is the sequel to Windows 95, Microsoft's popular desktop operating system. It represents the natural evolution of Windows and incorporates a variety of improvements, including

- **User interface**. Microsoft has enhanced the Windows user interface so that Windows Explorer and the desktop both behave similarly to a Web browser. By introducing HTML into the user interface, Microsoft makes the user interface more customizable than ever before.

- **Internet support**. The Internet support built into Windows 98 rivals that of any other product available today. It has a variety of side effects, such as making the disk easier to browse, that you learn about in this book.

- **Administration**. Windows 98 includes new administrative tools designed to lower the total cost of ownership. With these tools, the administrator has a better shot at keeping each workstation up-to-date and running healthily.

- **Hardware support**. Windows 98 includes support for new hardware standards such as MMX, USB, IEEE 1394, and DVD.

## Why You Should Read This Book

Technical professionals, such as administrators and field consultants, will appreciate the range of topics that this book covers. *Windows 98 Administrator's Handbook* is a guide that you can keep by your side while you work. It covers advanced installation and networking with sufficient detail so that you can do your job better and faster. Here are some of the assumptions I've made, while writing this book, about your day-to-day job:

- You have a highly technical job.
- You work with varieties of hardware, software, and networks and tend to go far beyond the ordinary to the esoteric features of an operating system.
- You take responsibility for the deployment and maintenance of Windows 98 within your organization — typically on a network.
- You rely on the information you learn in books to better your job performance and further your career.

# How This Book Is Organized

*Windows 98 Administrator's Handbook* has 18 chapters, contained in four parts, and two appendixes. The following sections describe what you find in each part of the book.

## Part I: Installation

Part I, "Installation," helps you understand what's new in Windows 98 and how to deploy Windows 98 in your organization. It contains chapters on installing and removing Windows 98 as well as on automating and debugging the installation process.

## Part II: Configuration

Part II, "Configuration," shows you how to configure Windows 98. This part contains chapters on configuring hardware and the Windows 98 desktop; managing your disks, files, printers, and fonts; connecting to the Internet; and installing and using applications.

# Part III: Networking

Part III, "Networking," is for the administrator responsible for rolling out and maintaining Windows 98 on the network. In this part, you find chapters on using network resources, installing adapters and protocols, installing the Client for Microsoft Networks and the Client for NetWare Networks, and supporting remote network connections.

# Part IV: Administration

Part IV, "Administration," shows you how to administer Windows 98 in an enterprise environment. This part contains chapters on enabling remote administration, implementing profiles and policies, scheduling tasks and running scripts, and using the Windows Registry.

## Appendixes

In the back of this book, you find two useful appendixes. Appendix A, "Command Lines," is a quick reference to the command lines for many of the Windows 98 utilities. This reference is handy when you schedule tasks with the Task Scheduler. Appendix B, "Keyboard Shortcuts," contains lists of keyboard shortcuts that you can use in a variety of situations, such as when you are browsing folders in Windows Explorer.

# Conventions

This book uses some special conventions that make the material easier to follow and understand:

- Key combinations such as Ctrl+Alt+Delete are joined by plus signs.
- Menu choices use a notation such as File ⇨ Edit, which means choose File from the menu bar, and then choose Edit.

- *Italic text* indicates new terms or placeholders and is sometimes used for emphasis.
- **Bold text** indicates text you type.
- `Monotype text` indicates code, on-screen text, or Internet addresses.

# Contacting the Author

The good folks at IDG Books Worldwide and I have made every attempt to provide you with accurate, timely, and useful information. In the unlikely event that you find a mistake in *Windows 98 Administrator's Handbook* or this book leaves you with unanswered questions, please feel free to contact me at `jerry@honeycutt.com`. Put a brief description of your question in the subject line, and provide complete instructions for duplicating the situation as well as a description of the hardware and software installed on the computer.

# Acknowledgments

It's an uncommon statement, but this book was a breeze. One of the reasons is the determination of Eric Newman, this book's development editor. Development editors are responsible for checking the content and organization of a book, keeping one eye on the big picture and the other on minute details. Thanks, Eric.

The other reason is that this book is based on another title I wrote for IDG Books Worldwide: *Windows 98 Administrator's Bible*. Without the hard work of the people who contributed to that book, this handbook would have been much more difficult. First, Tracy Thomsic was the acquisitions editor for this handbook and the *Bible* on which it's based. I must thank her for her endless support and encouragement on both. I also thank the development editors who worked on the *Bible*, Janet Andrews and Deborah Craig. Other folks who played equally important roles in the previous book include BC, Bill, Nicole, Art, and Serdar. Thanks, one and all.

Last, a handful of other folks contributed chapters to the original *Bible*, and you find chapters based on those in this book. Bob Johnson contributed Chapter 11. Barry Lewis contributed portions of Chapter 7. Art Brieva contributed Chapters 13 and 14. Portions of Chapter 7 come from *Windows 98 Secrets*, another great IDG Books Worldwide title, which was written by Brian Livingston and Davis Straub.

# Contents at a Glance

# Contents

# Part I

## Installation

# Chapter 1

# Installing and Removing Windows 98

## Preparing for Installation

To run the Windows 98 Setup program, your computer must have at least 16MB of memory and the following amount of free disk space:

- 130MB for upgrading from Windows 95
- 170MB for creating a new installation
- 170MB for upgrading from Windows 3.1 or Windows for Workgroups

The minimum requirements for running Windows 98 itself are a 486 CPU with 16MB of memory and a 256-color VGA adapter. Even though Windows 98 runs on that configuration, *Microsoft recommends a minimum of a Pentium processor with 24MB of memory and a 16-bit or 24-bit super VGA adapter.* Microsoft strongly recommends the following few additional pieces of hardware, too:

- Mouse or other pointing device.
- An 8x or faster CD-ROM drive.

- Sound Blaster–compatible audio card and speakers. Microsoft further recommends that you use a full-duplex sound card or external digital audio provided by a USB- or IEEE 1394–compatible device.

Optional hardware includes the following:

- Modem.
- Network adapter with NDIS 2.0 or MAC drive support. Microsoft recommends NDIS 4.0 or 5.0 support with OnNow power management support.
- DVD-ROM and decoder card. Microsoft recommends a device that supports MPEG-2 playback.
- Scanner or digital camera that's Plug and Play compatible. Microsoft recommends a device that supports IEEE 1394.
- Second monitor and video adapter. Microsoft recommends a PCI or AGP adapter.
- IEEE 1394 bus. Microsoft recommends a controller that supports Plug and Play and OnNow power management.
- USB bus and HID hardware. Microsoft recommends a controller that supports OnNow power management.

## Get Ready to Coexist: Dual-Booting

Windows 98 can peacefully coexist with OS/2, when using MS-DOS, and any other version of Windows except Windows 95. You can even switch between Windows 98 and MS-DOS version 5.0, Windows 3.1*x*, Windows for Workgroups 3.1*x*, or Windows NT with MS-DOS. However, the following requirements apply:

- **Windows NT.** You must install Windows 98 in a different folder from Windows NT, and drive C must be a FAT16 partition that has enough free disk space. Note that you must configure your applications twice, once in each operating system, because neither registry is compatible with the other.

Also note that NT can't access FAT32 drives, and Windows 98 can't access NTFS drives.

- **Windows 3.1x or MS-DOS 5.x.** You can dual-boot with any other version of Windows except Windows 95 as long as you're using MS-DOS version 5.x or later. To boot to the previous operating system when dual-booting, press F4 as Windows 98 starts. The C drive must be FAT16.

- **Windows 95.** Windows 98 is not supported in a dual-boot configuration with Windows 95.

## Preparing the Workstation for Installation

Before running the Windows 98 Setup program, prepare each computer as follows:

- **Disable any software that might cause problems with the Setup program.** In particular, disable any virus protection software (after scanning the hard drive for viruses, of course) and any running MS-DOS programs. In many cases, the Setup program detects when a problematic program is running and gives you instructions to close it. Disable any TSR programs that aren't required to operate the computer, too, because these have a tendency to interfere with the Setup program.

- **Back up your existing configuration.** The Windows 98 Setup program prompts you to back up your existing configuration, which you can restore by uninstalling Windows 98. The Windows 98 Setup program requires an additional 50MB of disk space if you choose to save the uninstall information. This configuration backup is no substitute, however, for a full system backup, which assures you that you can restore the system to its original state if the installation fails.

**Caution**

To uninstall Windows 98, thereby restoring Windows 95, you must make sure the workstation meets a few requirements. First, you must save uninstall information when prompted during the Setup program. Second, you must not compress the hard drive or convert the drive to FAT32 *after* installing Windows 98. If you compress or convert the drive to FAT32 *before* installing Windows 98, you're okay.

# Choosing an Installation Type

The Windows 98 Setup program offers four different installation options: typical, portable, compact, and custom. Table 1-1 indicates with a *yes* under each column the components included in each of the following options:

- **Typical**. This is the default and recommended option for most users, per Microsoft. It automatically installs the most commonly used options, requiring little input from the user. It almost never is suitable, however, because it leaves out some of the most useful programs.

- **Portable**. For mobile users, this option installs files useful for portable computers, such as Briefcase and Direct Cable Connection. Likewise, this option usually isn't suitable because it leaves out useful applications.

- **Compact**. This option installs only the minimum files required to run Windows 98. Use this option only if disk space is severely limited.

- **Custom**. This option enables the user to pick and choose which components Windows 98 installs. For most administrators and power users, this is the appropriate option to choose.

**Table 1-1**  *Components for Each Installation Type*

| Set | Component | Typical | Portable | Compact | Custom |
|---|---|---|---|---|---|
| Accessibility | Options | | | | |
| | Tools | | | | |
| Accessories | Briefcase | | Yes | | |
| | Calculator | Yes | | | Yes |
| | Character Map | | | | |
| | Clipboard Viewer | | | | |
| | Desktop Wallpaper | | | | |
| | Document Templates | | | | Yes |
| | Games | | | | |
| | Imaging | | | | Yes |
| | Mouse Pointers | | | | |
| | Net Watcher | | | | |
| | Paint | | | | Yes |
| | Quick View | | | | |
| | Screen Savers | | | | Yes |
| | System Monitor | | | | |
| | System Resource Meter | | | | |
| | Windows Scripting Host | | | | Yes |
| | WordPad | | | | Yes |
| Communications | Dial-Up Networking | | | | Yes |
| | Dial-Up Server | | | | |
| | Direct Cable Connection | Yes | | | |
| | HyperTerminal | | | | |
| | Infrared | | | | |
| | Microsoft Chat 2.0 | | | | Yes |
| | Microsoft NetMeeting | | | | yes |
| | Phone Dialer | Yes | Yes | | Yes |
| | Virtual Private Networking | | | | |

*Continued*

**Table 1-1** *Continued*

| Set | Component | Typical | Portable | Compact | Custom |
|-----|-----------|---------|----------|---------|--------|
| Disk Tools | Backup | | | | |
| | Disk Compression | | Yes | Yes | Yes |
| | FAT32 Converter | Yes | Yes | | Yes |
| Internet Tools | FrontPage Express | | | | Yes |
| | VRML 2.0 Viewer | | | | Yes |
| | Microsoft Wallet | | | | |
| Outlook Express | | | | | Yes |
| Multilanguage-Support | Baltic | | | | |
| | Central European | | | | |
| | Cyrillic | | | | |
| | Greek | | | | |
| | Turkish | | | | |
| Multimedia | Audio Compression | | | | Yes |
| | CD Player | | | | Yes |
| | DVD Player | | | | |
| | Media Player | | | | Yes |
| | Microsoft Agent 1.5 | | | | Yes |
| | Microsoft NetShow Player 2.0 | | | | |
| | Multimedia Sound Schemes | | | | |
| | Sample Sounds | | | | |
| | Sound Recorder | | | | Yes |
| | Video Compression | | | | Yes |
| | Volume Control | | | | Yes |
| Online Services | AOL | | | | Yes |
| | AT&T WorldNet Service | | | | Yes |
| | CompuServe | | | | Yes |
| | Prodigy Internet | | | | Yes |
| | The Microsoft Network | | | | Yes |
| TV Viewer | Broadcast Data Services | | | | |
| | TV Viewer | | | | |

# Running the Setup Program

Windows 98 Setup has a bar along its left side that contains information showing Setup's progress. The top part of this sidebar indicates the step on which Setup is working. The middle shows the approximate time remaining, which is seldom accurate, and the bottom part of the sidebar contains additional useful information. As usual, the rest of the screen is dedicated to useful Windows 98 tips and, in some cases, marketing hype.

You can start the Setup program from any location that contains the Windows 98 source files:

- **Floppy**. Microsoft ships Windows 98 on CD-ROM, but a floppy-disk version is available on request. Setup.exe is on the first disk in the set.

- **CD-ROM**. Setup.exe is in the root folder of the CD-ROM.

- **Network**. If you copy the source files to a central network location, Setup.exe is in the root folder of that network location. In most cases, the source files on the network should reflect the contents of \Win98 on the Windows 98 CD-ROM.

- **Local Hard Disk**. Copying the Windows 98 source files to the computer's hard disk has a certain advantage: the source files are always available. To do so, copy the entire contents of \Win98 from the CD-ROM to a folder on the computer's disk — \Windows\Install is a good location. Setup.exe should be in the folder to which you copied those files.

You can start the Setup program from the previous version of Windows or from an MS-DOS command prompt. If you start the Setup program from the command prompt, you must have any real-mode drivers that are required to access the Windows 98 source files loaded. If you're installing from a CD-ROM, for instance, you must have the real-mode CD-ROM device driver and Mscdex.exe loaded. If you're installing from the network, you must have any real-mode device drivers that are required to access the network loaded. Two notes here: When Setup detects these real-mode device drivers, it installs their protected-mode counterparts after the first reboot, removing the drivers from Config.sys and Autoexec.bat. Also, copying the Windows 98 source files to the local hard disk removes this necessity altogether, greatly simplifying the installation.

To start the Windows 98 Setup program, follow these instructions:

- **From Windows 95,** open the Run dialog box from the Start menu and locate Setup.exe in the folder that contains the source files. Press Enter. A dialog box that describes the process appears; click Continue.

- **From Windows 3.1, Windows for Workgroups, and so on,** launch Setup.exe from File Manager. You find Setup.exe in the folder that contains the source files. A dialog box that describes the process appears; click Continue.

- **From MS-DOS,** change directories to the folder containing the source files. Type setup.exe at the command prompt, and then press Enter. A dialog box that describes the process appears; click Continue.

**Tip**

If you're installing from a Windows 98 upgrade disk, the Setup program asks you to verify that you have the qualifying product. Usually, you simply need to provide a disk or CD-ROM containing a previous version of Windows, including Windows 3.1 and Windows 95. If you don't have either the disk or CD-ROM handy, you can trick the Windows 98 Setup program into installing anyway. In the root folder of your hard disk, create a text file called Ntldr (no file extension). Enter only one line in this file: Rem. The Setup program won't ask for a qualifying product if it finds this file.

# Controlling the Setup Process with Command Line Options

The Windows 98 Setup program provides several command line options that you can use to control the installation process. Table 1-2 describes the command line options that are available. The first column shows the switch (any arguments are italicized), and the second column describes the switch. Table 1-3 describes command line options that are available only in some localized versions of Windows 98. The second column indicates the language version to which the switch applies.

Of all the switches that Setup supports, the most useful for normal use are /ID, /IE, /is, and /IW, depending on your situation. /ID prevents Setup from checking for available disk space, and /is prevents Windows 98 from running ScanDisk, which is a waste of time if you're absolutely sure you have enough space and your drives are healthy. /IE prevents Setup from creating the Emergency Startup Disk, thus enabling you to get Windows 98 up and running quickly and create the Emergency Startup Disk later. /IW prevents Setup from displaying the End User License Agreement — a nuisance at best. Thus, the following command line knocks a small bit of time out of the total installation process:

```
Setup /ID /IE /is /IW
```

**Table 1-2** *Setup Command Line Options*

| Switch | Description |
|---|---|
| /? | Gives help for Setup's command line options. |
| /c | Prevents Setup from loading the SmartDrive disk cache. |
| /d | Prevents Setup from using the existing version of Windows for the early portions of the process. Use this option if you believe you're unable to start the Setup program because of problems with your current Windows configuration. |
| /domain *name* | Points Setup to the security provider for Client for Microsoft Networks. This domain validates the user's logon credentials. |

*Continued*

**Table 1-2** *Continued*

| Switch | Description |
| --- | --- |
| /IA | Instructs Setup to disable the *after providers* list in Setupc.inf. This is a list of functions in DLLs to invoke after copying the files to the hard disk and before restarting the computer. |
| /IB | Instructs Setup to disable the *before providers* list in Setupc.inf. This is a list of functions in DLLs to invoke before coping the files to the hard disk. |
| /IC | Prevents Windows 98 from loading drivers in Config.sys or Autoexec.bat, forcing it to do a clean boot. If the setting called **KeepRMDrives** in the Registry is equal to 1, this command line switch has no effect. |
| /ID | Prevents the Setup program from checking for the minimum disk space required to install Windows 98. |
| /IE | Skips the Emergency Startup Disk screen during setup. |
| /IF | Performs a Fast setup. |
| /ih | Runs ScanDisk in the foreground, enabling you to see the results. |
| /iL | Loads the Logitech mouse device driver, which you need if you're using a Logitech Series C mouse. |
| /iN | Skips the networking setup. |
| /iq | Prevents Setup from running the ScanDisk quick check when installing from MS-DOS. Use this switch if you're using disk compression software other than DriveSpace or DoubleSpace. |
| /is | Prevents Setup from running the ScanDisk quick check when installing from Windows. Use this switch if you're using disk compression software other than DriveSpace or DoubleSpace. |
| /nostart | Copies the minimum Windows 3.*x* DLLs used by Setup and exits to MS-DOS without installing Windows 98. |
| /IR | Prevents Windows 98 from updating the master boot records. |
| *script* | Causes the Setup program to use the settings found in the setup script called *script*, which allows unattended installation. |
| /SrcDir | Specifies the location of the Windows 98 source files. |
| /S *filename* | Causes the Setup program to use the Setup.inf file called *filename* when starting. |
| /t:*tempfolder* | Specifies a location for the Setup program's temporary files. The folder *tempfolder* must already exist; the Setup program will delete its contents. |

| Switch | Description |
|---|---|
| /U:*UPI* | Specifies the *UPI*. |
| /IX | Prevents Windows 98 from doing a character-set check. |
| /IW | Prevents Windows 98 from displaying the End User License Agreement. |

**Table 1-3** *Additional Command Line Options for International Versions*

| Switch | Flavor | Description |
|---|---|---|
| /IJ | Japanese NEC | Prevents Setup from prompting the user for a boot drive. |
| /IO | Japanese NEC | Causes Setup to call the exit Windows executable. |
| /IF | Japanese NEC | Prevents Setup from creating a bootable setup. Setup does not put `BootMulti=1` in Msdos.sys if you're doing a clean install on a drive other than an AT drive. |
| /A | Japanese NEC | Requires Setup to use AT drive mode. |
| /IY | Pan European | Ignores language mismatches. |

# Understanding Each Step of the Setup Program

The Windows 98 Setup program has five steps, each of which is described in the following sections, respectively:

1. Preparing to run Windows 98 Setup
2. Collecting information about your computer
3. Copying Windows 98 files to your computer
4. Restarting your computer
5. Setting up hardware and finalizing settings

Running Setup from within Windows is very similar to running it from MS-DOS. Some differences do exist, however, especially in Step 2. Each section that follows points out these differences. Remember, if you're installing Windows 98 from MS-DOS, you must load any real-mode device drivers required to access the source files. If you've copied the source files to the local hard disk, so much the better.

## Preparing to Run Windows 98 Setup

This step of the installation process prepares the computer for Windows 98. It creates a folder called \Wininst0.400 and copies the following files into it:

- Precopy1.cab
- Precopy2.cab

At the end of this step, Setup prompts you to close any running applications if it detects any. Microsoft strongly recommends that you do this because some applications might interfere with the setup process. Moreover, you might lose data if the Setup program restarts your computer without the application's first giving you the opportunity to save your open documents.

## Collecting Information about Your Computer

Next, Setup collects information about the user and the computer. It does so in a number of smaller subphases:

1. **Confirm license agreement.** Setup confirms your acceptance of the End User License Agreement. You can avoid this phase by using the /IW command line switch.

2. **Select a folder (MS-DOS only).** Select a folder into which you want to install Windows 98. This step occurs only if you're installing from MS-DOS. Otherwise, Setup installs Windows 98 in the same folder as Windows 95.

3. **Run ScanDisk to check for errors.** Setup checks the disk for errors by using ScanDisk. You can avoid this phase by using the /iq switch if you're installing from MS-DOS or the /is switch if you're installing from Windows 95. You don't see ScanDisk unless you use the /ih command line switch.

4. **Run Registry Checker to scan for Registry errors.** Setup launches Registry Checker to scan the existing Registry for errors. It uses Scanregw.exe in Windows 95 or Scanreg.exe in MS-DOS. If it finds an error, it prompts you to restart your computer to MS-DOS and run Scanreg.exe at the command prompt to fix the error.

5. **Prepare the folder for Windows 98.** In this phase, Setup creates the directory structure: \Program Files and \Windows. It checks for installed components and makes sure enough disk space is available. You can skip the disk space check by using the /ID command line switch. If Setup doesn't find enough space, it prompts you to restart your computer and free up additional disk space.

6. **Prompts you for setup options (MS-DOS only).** Setup prompts you to specify the installation option you want to use: typical, portable, compact, or custom. If you're installing from Windows 95, Setup repeats the installation option you used to install Windows 95.

7. **Prompts for user information (MS-DOS only).** Setup asks you for a user name, a company name, and a product ID. You can find the product ID on the Windows 98 disks or the Certificate of Authenticity. If you're installing from Windows 95, Setup uses the information already provided in the Registry.

8. **Prompts for components to install (MS-DOS only).** You can add or remove components at this point, or you can do so later by using the Add/Remove Programs Properties dialog box.

9. **Prompts for identification information (MS-DOS only).** Setup asks for the computer name, workgroup, and computer description, all of which describe how to identify your computer on a network. If you're installing from Windows 95, Setup takes this information from the Registry.

10. **Prompts for your computer's settings (MS-DOS only).** If you run Setup from within Windows 95, it automatically migrates these settings. Otherwise, a dialog box prompts you for basic hardware information, such as keyboard layout, machine type, and regional settings.

11. **Prompts to save important configuration files (Windows 95 only).** If you choose Yes, Setup creates the files described after this paragraph in the root folder of your boot disk. If you choose No, you won't be able to uninstall Windows 98 and restore your original configuration. If you convert your disk to FAT32 or compress the disk, you won't be able to uninstall Windows 98, regardless of whether you saved the configuration files or not. You don't see this dialog box if you're installing from MS-DOS. This option creates the following two files:

    • Winundo.dat—Contains all files required to restore Windows 95 and can be up to 75MB in size

    • Winundo.ini—Contains information about the original location of each file stored in Winundo.dat

12. **Prompts for Internet channels.** Setup prompts you for the location of the channel set, which determines the channels that it initially sets up for Internet Explorer.

13. **Prompts you to create an Emergency Startup Disk.** You can avoid this by using the /IE command line switch. Make sure you create this disk eventually, however, so that you can recover your system if you run into problems. This disk contains a generic real-mode ATAPI CD-ROM driver that works with most ATAPI CD-ROM drives, so it's a great thing to have around. It doesn't work with SCSI CD-ROMs, though, or a CD-ROM connected via a sound card.

## Copying Windows 98 Files to Your Computer

If you start Setup from a CD-ROM, a network location, or any other device that requires a device driver, Setup copies the appropriate files to your hard disk, enabling itself to access that device after Setup restarts your computer.

**Caution**

Setup copies the required files to your hard disk, requiring no input from the user. Interrupting this phase can prevent your computer from restarting, so don't do it.

## Restarting Your Computer

Setup prompts you to restart the computer. You can either click Restart Now or wait 15 seconds for Setup to restart the computer automatically. This ensures that you can install Windows 98 unattended. After the computer restarts, the message `Getting ready to start Windows 98 for the first time` appears. Windows 98 also updates your configuration files as follows:

- It updates Win.ini, System.ini, and the Registry with changes required by Windows 98.

- It removes incompatible device drivers and TSR programs from Autoexec.bat and Config.sys by commenting them out with REM statements. Entries in Setupc.inf determine what device drivers and TSRs Windows 98 considers incompatible.

## Setting Up Hardware and Finalizing Settings

In the last phase, Windows 98 runs hardware detection after the computer restarts. Running hardware detection after the first reboot is more reliable than performing hardware detection beforehand. The extent to which Windows 98 detects hardware on the computer depends on how you started Setup:

- **From Windows 95**. Windows 98 detects only Plug and Play devices. It keeps all other settings for the existing legacy hardware. It doesn't prompt for any additional settings, such as printer information or time zone settings, either.

- **From MS-DOS**. Windows 98 detects both Plug and Play and legacy hardware when you launch it from MS-DOS. It prompts you for additional settings, such as printer settings and time zone settings, too.

## Recovering from a Previous Attempt

If Setup fails or you stop Setup before it finishes, you can recover any previous attempt. Before starting Step 2 in the previous section, Setup displays the Safe Recovery dialog box, which asks you whether you want to proceed with the previous setup. Click Use Safe Recovery to continue with the previous attempt. In many cases, Setup can determine what caused the failure and avoid it on the next attempt.

# Upgrading to Windows 98

If you're upgrading to Windows 98 from a previous version of Windows — Windows 3.1, Windows for Workgroups, or Windows 95 — you can choose to keep your existing settings or change them as follows:

- **Keeping your existing settings**. Run the Setup program from within Windows, which installs Windows 98 in the same folder as the previous version and also uses the existing configuration information. This option requires less user interaction because it migrates the previous settings to Windows 98.

- **Changing your existing settings**. Run the Setup program from MS-DOS. That is, boot your computer to MS-DOS as opposed to starting the Setup program from within an MS-DOS window. You must provide the installation folder, network information, and so forth. If you are upgrading and not trying to set up a dual-boot configuration, make sure you install Windows 98 in the same folder as the previous version of Windows.

If you're currently running an operating system other than a previous version of Windows, you must start the Setup program from MS-DOS, and you can't necessarily *upgrade* to Windows 98. For instance, installing Windows 98 with Windows NT or OS/2 creates a dual-boot configuration.

To upgrade to Windows 98, keeping the existing settings, follow these steps:

1. Start your computer to the previous version of Windows. If Windows 95 is installed on the computer, for instance, start Windows 95 instead of booting to MS-DOS.

2. Launch the Setup program. Setup.exe is in the root folder of the location that contains the Windows 98 source files. You conveniently use the Run dialog box to start Setup.exe.

3. Follow the instructions you see on the screen.

To upgrade to Windows 98, without keeping existing settings, follow these steps:

1. Start your computer to MS-DOS. Don't start Windows and then try to run the Setup program from an MS-DOS window.

2. At the command prompt, change to the folder that contains the Windows 98 source files, and then run Setup.exe.

3. Follow the instructions you see on the screen.

You can install Windows 98 on compressed volumes. Windows 98 supports Microsoft DriveSpace and DoubleSpace, Stacker versions 3.0 and 4.*x*, and AddStor's SuperStor. You might have to resize the host drive to accommodate the Windows 98 swap file, however, because Windows 98 stores the swap file on the host drive. See the Readme.txt file that comes with Windows 98 to learn more about installing Windows 98 on compressed volumes.

# Installing Windows 98 on a Newly Formatted Disk

Before you're ready to run the Setup program, you're going to have an empty hard drive. You're not going to have access to the CD-ROM or network; thus, you need to create a boot disk that contains the system files required to start MS-DOS, as well as a few other files:

- **Real-mode device drivers**. If you're installing Windows 98 from a CD-ROM, copy the device driver and Mscdex.exe files to the boot floppy. Create Config.sys and Autoexec.bat files that load these device drivers. If you're installing Windows 98 from a network, copy the appropriate drivers to the boot disk and modify Config.sys and Autoexec.bat accordingly. You might be able to find these files on a similarly configured Windows 98 computer.

- **Fdisk.exe and Format.com**. Both of these programs are required to partition and format the hard disk. If the disk is already partitioned, you need only Format.com. Copying both files is still a good idea, however.

- **Edit.com and Edit.hlp**. These files are purely optional, but you'll be thankful that they're on the boot disk if you have to tweak the Config.sys or Autoexec.bat files. Otherwise, you'll have to resort to `copy con: config.sys` and `copy con: autoexec.bat` to recreate each file from scratch.

- **Himem.sys and Emm386.exe**. Both of these files provide the memory management necessary to give your system enough memory to format the hard disk and transfer the system files if you choose to do so. In many cases, you can't format the disk without loading Himem.sys and Emm386.exe because Format.com reports that your system doesn't have enough free memory.

- **Autoexec.bat and Config.sys**. Listing 1-1 shows a typical Config.sys file for a boot disk that loads the real-mode device driver for a CD-ROM drive. The only necessary line in the Autoexec.bat file is the following:

```
MSCDEX /D:MSCD001
```

**Listing 1-1** *Example Config.sys for the Boot Disk*
```
FILES=99
BUFFERS=99
DEVICE=HIMEM.SYS
DEVICE=EMM386.EXE NOEMS
DEVICEHIGH=TEAC_CDI.SYS /D:MSCD001
DOS=HIGH,UMB
```

To give you an example, the boot disk that starts my portable computer with the appropriate real-mode CD-ROM device driver contains the following files:

| | |
|---|---|
| Autoexec.bat | Fdisk.exe |
| Config.sys | Format.com |
| Edit.com | Himem.sys |
| Edit.hlp | Mscdex.exe |
| Emm386.exe | Teac_cdi.sys |

To install Windows 98 on a newly formatted disk, follow these steps:

1. Create a boot disk that you can use to start your computer with support for the CD-ROM or network, whichever contains the source files. This section describes the files that you need to put on the disk.

2. Restart the computer by using the boot disk. Technically, you don't need the boot disk to restart the computer — you can boot to the previous version of MS-DOS — but the boot disk offers extra protection in case the Setup program fails and you have to start over.

3. Format the hard disk. You don't need to lay down the system files when you format the hard disk. Thus, you can use the command line `format c:` without the `/s` command line switch.

4. Copy the Windows 98 source files from the CD-ROM or network location to the hard disk. You find the source files on the CD-ROM in \Win98. This step isn't required, but it makes the installation go a bit faster and enables you to install additional Windows 98 components later without having to drag out the Windows 98 CD-ROM. This does chew up a bit of disk space, however, so don't copy the Windows 98 files if space is at a premium.

5. Start the Setup program.

# Using Windows 98 with Other Operating Systems

To dual-boot Windows 98, *drive C must be FAT16*. Although you can install Windows 98 on any FAT partition that has enough free space, drive C must be FAT16 because previous versions of Windows — Windows 3.1, Windows for Workgroups, and Windows NT — don't understand FAT32. You can't install Windows 98 on an NTFS or HPFS partition, either. To give you another example, you can install Windows 98 on drive D, even if it's a FAT32 partition, as long as the previous version of Windows is on drive C and drive C is a FAT16 partition.

If you want to dual-boot Windows 98 with another operating system, install it into a different folder; then, to start the previous operating system, press F4 while Windows 98 starts. Make sure you've put the line BootMulti=1 in Msdos.sys. If you didn't install Windows 98 so that it dual-boots with your previous operating system, you can still do so. On a bootable floppy disk, rename Io.sys, Msdos.sys, Command.com, Config.sys, and Autoexec.bat to Io.dos, Msdos.dos, Command.dos, Config.dos, and Autoexec.dos, respectively. Then, copy these files to the root folder of the boot drive.

To configure Windows 98 to dual-boot after installing it, follow these steps:

1. Create a bootable floppy that starts MS-DOS version 5.0 or greater. This floppy should contain appropriate Config.sys and Autoexec.bat files.

2. *On the floppy*, rename the files as shown in the following list. Io.sys and Msdos.sys usually have the hidden, read-only, and system attributes enabled, so you'll have to use Attrib to reset these attributes.

   - **Io.sys** — Rename to Io.dos
   - **Msdos.sys** — Rename to Msdos.dos
   - **Command.com** — Rename to Command.dos
   - **Config.sys** — Rename to Config.dos
   - **Autoexec.bat** — Rename to Autoexec.dos

3. Copy the files you renamed to the root folder of the boot drive. If you're using disk compression, you must also copy all five files to the host drive.

4. Restart the computer.

**Caution**

Don't copy Io.sys, Msdos.sys, Command.com, Config.sys, or Autoexec.bat to the boot drive before renaming them with the DOS file extension. Copying these files without renaming them prevents Windows 98 from working properly. If you accidentally do this, start Windows 98 Setup from MS-DOS, and run the Setup program again to repair your installation.

## Windows 95

You can't configure Windows 98 to dual-boot with Windows 95. This is a major problem for some folks who want to test Windows 98 before completely giving up their Windows 95 configurations. The reason you can't is that Windows 95 and Windows 98 share boot files; thus, when you install Windows 98, it wipes out the files required to start Windows 95. Microsoft considers Windows 98 an upgrade to Windows 95 and thus doesn't allow this dual-boot.

## MS-DOS 5.x, Windows 3.1x, and So Forth

You can dual-boot Windows 98 with MS-DOS 5.x or later and any other version of Windows that boots using MS-DOS 5.x or later. This includes Windows 3.1x and Windows for Workgroups. To boot to the previous operating system, press F4 when the computer starts. Here are notes for dual-booting Windows 98 and MS-DOS 5.x or any version of Windows that starts from MS-DOS:

- Drive C must be FAT16 to support the previous OS.
- Install Windows 98 on any FAT partition (FAT16 or FAT32), including on a removable drive, such as Iomega JAZ drives.
- The line BootMulti=1 must be in Msdos.sys, which you find in the root folder. This file enables you to choose the operating system you want to start each time you boot the computer.

- Windows 98 works well with third-party partition schemes, such as Disk Manager and Storage Dimensions' SpeedStor.

 **Tip**

After configuring the computer to dual-boot Windows 98 with MS-DOS, you can install a previous version of Windows, including Windows 3.1 and Windows for Workgroups. This excludes Windows 95, of course, which can't dual-boot with Windows 98. Start the computer to the previous version of MS-DOS. Then, run the Windows Setup program as normal, installing it into a different folder from the one in which Windows 98 is installed.

## Windows NT

You can install Windows 98 on any FAT16 partition available on a Windows NT system. You can use an existing FAT16 partition or create a new one. Remember, though, that Windows NT doesn't know what to do with FAT32 partitions, so you can't create a FAT32 partition for Windows 98. The following are some additional items that you should consider when creating a dual-boot configuration between Windows 98 and Windows NT:

- Install Windows 98 in a different folder from Windows NT.

- Drive C must be a FAT16 partition and have enough disk space available for Windows 98 and its swap file. A typical installation requires about 170MB of disk space.

- The Windows 98 and Windows NT registries are not compatible with each other; therefore, you must install each application twice in a dual-boot configuration — once in Windows 98 and once in Windows NT. Regardless, you can install the application in the same folder, cutting down on wasted disk space.

- Windows 98 can't access an NTFS partition, and, likewise, Windows NT can't access FAT32 partitions; thus, the only partition scheme both operating systems have in common is FAT16 — for now.

- If you want to dual-boot MS-DOS, Windows 98, and Windows NT, first configure the system to dual-boot MS-DOS and Windows NT before trying to install Windows 98.

To start Windows 98 on a Windows NT system, do the following:

- Choose Windows 98 from the NT Boot Loader Operating System Selection menu. If you don't see Windows 98, choose MS-DOS.

### Caution

If you start the computer by using an MS-DOS floppy disk and then install Windows 98, you won't be able to start NT again. You can restore NT's multiboot configuration, however, by using the Windows NT Emergency Repair Disk. Therefore, just in case, updating your emergency repair disk before trying to create a dual-boot configuration with Windows 98 is a good idea.

## OS/2

You can't start the Windows 98 Setup program from OS/2. You must start MS-DOS first, and then run Setup from the command prompt. If MS-DOS isn't installed on the OS/2 system, install MS-DOS; then, configure the system to dual-boot OS/2 and MS-DOS. After doing so, install Windows 98 from MS-DOS on a FAT16 partition. Here are some additional notes for creating a dual-boot configuration with OS/2:

- Install Windows 98 into a folder other than OS/2.

- Windows 98 won't migrate any settings from OS/2.

- Make sure you enable OS/2's boot manager before trying to install Windows 98. Windows 98 disables the boot manager, however, so that it can restart and finish the installation. You can reenable the boot manager by using the Fdisk utility that comes with Windows 98.

- Don't boot an OS/2 system by using an MS-DOS floppy disk and then try to install Windows 98. Doing so prevents OS/2 from starting.

- You have to reinstall any Windows-based applications because their settings don't migrate over to Windows 98.

# Removing Windows 98

In most cases, you can remove Windows 98, restoring the previous operating system. Doing so restores the previous operating system only if you configured Windows 98 to dual-boot with it. Otherwise, you'll have to reinstall the previous operating system after removing Windows 98. Before removing Windows 98 from your computer, make sure your computer meets the following conditions:

- **Saved system files are available**. If you chose to save system files during setup, Windows 98 Setup prompts you to save your system files before proceeding with the installation. As a result, it creates two files, Winundo.dat and Winundo.ini, in the root folder of the boot drive.

- **File system has not changed**. If you compressed the boot drive or converted the file system to FAT 32 *after* installing Windows 98, you can't restore the previous operating system. Note that if you converted the boot drive to FAT32 *before* installing Windows 98, which you might have done if you were running Windows 95 OSR2, you can still restore the previous operating system.

To remove Windows 98 from your computer, restoring the previous OS, follow these steps:

1. Open the Add/Remove Programs dialog box from the Control Panel.

2. Select Uninstall Windows 98 on the Install/Uninstall tab, and click Add/Remove. When prompted, click Yes to continue.

3. Click Yes to confirm that you want to scan the disk for errors.

4. Click Yes to continue removing Windows 98.

5. Windows 98 restarts your computer and boots to MS-DOS mode, running Uninstall.exe after it starts. Uninstall.exe restores the previous operating system from Winundo.dat and prompts you to restart the computer.

**Tip**

If you're certain that you don't want to go back to Windows 95, you can remove the system files that Setup saved to restore some lost disk space – up to 75MB. Don't remove Winundo.dat and Winundo.ini from the root folder, however. Open the Add/Remove Programs Properties dialog box, choose Delete Windows 98 Uninstall Information, and click Add/Remove.

After removing Windows 98, you'll lose any configuration changes made after installing it. If you customized your desktop, for instance, those customizations will be gone. If you installed any programs after installing Windows 98, you'll have to reinstall those programs after restoring the previous operating system.

## Restoring Windows 95 from the MS-DOS Prompt

Create an MS-DOS boot disk before trying to remove Windows 98. The steps described in this section prevent your computer from booting off the hard disk. Make sure you put Sys.com on this disk as well so that you can restore the system files on your hard disk. Aside from the boot disk, you need a few other programs that make removal a bit easier. You can get the following from \Windows\ Command or from the Windows 98 CD-ROM:

- **Deltree.exe** helps you remove entire folders at one time.

- **Scandisk.exe** removes information that might confuse earlier versions of MS-DOS, including spaces in long filenames, from the hard disk.

To remove Windows 98 at the MS-DOS command prompt, follow these steps:

1. Restart your computer to the command prompt.

2. Change Scandisk.ini, which you find in \Windows, by adding the following lines:

   - `labelcheck=on` forces ScanDisk to check for invalid characters in volume labels.

   - `spacecheck=on` forces ScanDisk to check for spaces in filenames.

3. Run ScanDisk on the drive containing Windows 98. For instance, type `scandisk d:`.

4. Remove the Windows 98 folder. To do so, use Deltree.exe like this: `deltree \windows`. Before doing so, make sure you've copied any data files you want from within \Windows. In particular, check the \Desktop and \Favorites folders.

5. Remove the following files from the root folder of the boot drive (some of these files are hidden, so you must use the Attrib command to show them):

   - Autoexec.bat
   - Bootlog.*
   - Command.com
   - Config.sys
   - Dblspace.bin

- Detlog.*
- Drvspace.bin
- Io.sys
- Msdos.sys
- Setuplog.*
- Winboot.*

6. Restore MS-DOS to the hard disk. To do so, put the boot disk you made earlier in drive A and restart the computer. After MS-DOS starts, use Sys.com to restore MS-DOS to the hard disk: Sys C:\.

If you configured Windows 98 to dual-boot with a previous version of MS-DOS, you can restore your original configuration files by renaming them as follows:

- **Config.dos** — Rename to Config.sys
- **Autoexec.dos** — Rename to Autoexec.bat

In all likelihood, you'll still need to reinstall the previous operating system — MS-DOS, Windows 3.1, Windows for Workgroups, and so forth — after removing Windows 98. This is particularly true if you didn't install Windows 98 to dual-boot with the previous operating system.

## Removing Windows 98 When Using Windows NT

Before removing Windows 98 from a shared Windows NT installation, create or update a Windows NT Emergency Repair Disk. You'll need this disk to enable Windows NT to start after you remove Windows 98. The steps for removing Windows 98 from Windows NT are the same as those listed in the previous section. The one exception is that the files you must remove from the root folder of the boot drive are different. The reason for this is that when you boot Windows NT, the Windows 98 system files are renamed with the W40 file extension.

To remove Windows 98 from a shared Windows NT installation, follow these steps:

1. Restart your computer to the command prompt.

2. Change Scandisk.ini, which you find in \Windows, by adding the following lines:

   - `labelcheck=on` forces ScanDisk to check for invalid characters in volume labels.

   - `spacecheck=on` forces ScanDisk to check for spaces in filenames.

3. Run ScanDisk on the drive containing Windows 98. For instance, type `scandisk d:`.

4. Remove the Windows 98 folder. To do so, use Deltree.exe like this: `deltree \windows`. Before doing so, make sure you've copied any data files you want from within \Windows. In particular, check the \Desktop and \Favorites folders.

5. Remove the following files from the root folder of the boot drive:

   - Autoexec.w40
   - Bootlog.*
   - Command.w40
   - Config.w40
   - Dblspace.bin
   - Detlog.*
   - Drvspace.bin
   - Io.w40
   - Msdos.w40
   - Setuplog.*
   - Winboot.*

6. Restart your computer using the first Windows NT Setup disk.

7. Choose Repair when prompted, insert your Emergency Repair Disk, and choose to repair the boot files.

After removing the system files, you must repair Windows NT using the Emergency Repair Disk. Make sure you have an updated repair disk before removing Windows 98.

# Chapter 2

# Deploying Windows 98 with Setup Scripts

Installing Windows 98 individually on a large number of computers is not practical. Custom setup scripts, combined with network-based installation, enable the administrator to make short work of a very difficult job.

This chapter describes the process used to install Windows 98 via setup scripts. This process includes creating the script, posting the Windows 98 source files to the network server, and then providing a means by which the user can launch the Setup program with the script. It also discusses two different ways you can create a script: by using the Batch 98 or by creating a script by hand. Last, it shows you how to automate installation by pushing the setup script to each individual user or allowing the users to launch the setup script on their own.

## Understanding Setup Scripts

Customized setup scripts enable you to spend less time installing Windows 98 and more time managing your network. You develop a script that reliably repeats a predefined installation, which is based on a test installation containing all the appropriate settings. You can push the setup script to each user, as well, by using the user's login script, a batch file embedded in an e-mail message or stored in a central network location, or by using a network management system, such as Microsoft's Systems Management Server. Thus, after you create the script and make it available to each user, you're hands-off; but each user is installing Windows 98 with the configuration you sanctioned.

Creating a script is easy enough. The script is in Msbatch.inf format, which is the language that the Setup program uses for specifying installation options. You can create a script two different ways. First, you can use the Batch 98 program, which is Batch.exe in \Tools\Reskit\Batch on the *Windows 98 Resource Kit*. If you don't have the Resource Kit handy, you can build a setup script based on a template. This chapter provides a few examples.

To roll out Windows 98 by using a custom setup script, follow these steps:

1. Install and configure Windows 98 in a test installation.

2. Create a setup script based on the settings in the test installation.

3. Publish the Windows 98 source files and the setup script on the network.

4. Push the installation by using the login script, a batch file, and so forth.

System policies are an alternative to using a setup script for controlling the user's setup. Although system policies don't automatically answer each prompt as the user installs Windows 98, they do give you rather complete control over the user's working environment, including networking configuration, desktop access, and so forth. Note that you might still want to use a custom setup script to make sure that each user's workstation is configured such that it supports system policies, but from then on you can use policies dynamically to control the user's desktop.

# Creating a Setup Script Using Batch 98

Batch 98 comes with the *Windows 98 Resource Kit*. As a bonus, Microsoft also includes Batch 98 on the Resource Kit sampler that you find on the Windows 98 CD-ROM. Run the installation program from the Resource Kit's CD-ROM or from the Windows 98 CD-ROM, in \Tools\Reskit, to install Batch 98. After the program is installed, you launch it from the Start menu by choosing Programs ➪ Microsoft Batch 98. To create a custom setup script using Batch 98, follow these steps:

1. Install Windows 98 on a test machine, configuring it so that it represents the configuration you want to use on each user's workstation.

2. Install Batch 98 from the Windows 98 CD-ROM or *Windows 98 Resource Kit* and launch it from the Start menu. You see Microsoft Batch 98, as shown in Figure 2-1.

3. Click Gather now to collect information about the test machine from the Registry. Batch 98 uses this information to prefill each prompt with the configuration data it finds on the workstation, eliminating the guesswork. This is why you must make sure your test machine works and is configured correctly before running Batch 98. After you complete this step, you see Complete below the button.

4. Click each of the buttons — General Setup Options, Network Options, Optional Components, and Advanced Options — to change the settings contained in the setup script. The subsections in this section describe in more detail the settings for each of these dialog boxes.

5. Click Save settings to INF to save your custom setup script. Batch 98 prompts you for a filename, but you should consider accepting the default filename, Msbatch.inf.

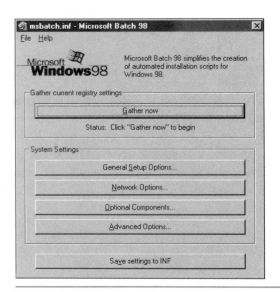

**Figure 2-1** *Batch 98 scripts a script based on the configuration of the test machine and the prompts that you answer.*

# General Setup Options

The General Setup Options dialog box collects a variety of configuration information, including user information, regional settings, and display settings. Here are the settings you find on each tab:

- **Install Info**. Specify the product ID and installation folder on this tab. This tab also enables you to determine whether Setup displays a warning if the previous version of Windows is installed in a folder other than \Windows, and whether Setup saves uninstall information.

- **User Info**. Specify the user name and company name, and identify the computer on the network by providing a computer name, workgroup, and description.

- **Setup Prompts**. Specify the level of user interaction that is required during Setup. You can control whether the user sees the End User License Agreement, whether the user is prompted to create the Emergency Startup Disk, and so forth. You must check all the boxes on this tab if you want a completely unattended installation.

- **Regional Settings**. Specify regional settings, such as the time zone, keyboard layout, and locale.

- **Desktop**. Specify what the user sees on the desktop when Setup finishes. You can control which of the following icons the user sees on the desktop: My Documents, Internet Explorer, Network Neighborhood, Outlook Express, Recycle Bin, and Setup the Microsoft Network. You can also disable the Online Services folder, the Windows 98 welcome screen, and Registration Wizard.

- **Printers**. Specify the printers to install during Setup. You can add multiple printers. For each printer, you specify the name, type, and port. The port can point to a local printer port or to a printer share on the network.

- **MRU Locations**. Specify a list of recently used paths. The only suitable use for this tab is to make locating files easier during the Setup program.

- **Display Settings**. Specify the display settings for the user's computer. You can control the display and color resolutions.

- **User Profiles**. Specify whether the machine uses user profiles.

# Network Options

The Network Options dialog box configures the computer's network connections. If you configure the test machine so that it properly connects to the network, the required settings for this dialog box should already be filled in for you. Here's a description of each tab on this dialog box:

- **Protocols**. Specify the protocols that Setup installs. You can install one or all of the following: IPX/SPX-compatible, NetBEUI, Microsoft 32-bit DLC, and TCP/IP. If you're installing TCP/IP, click TCP/IP Settings to configure the machine's IP address, WIN settings, Gateway, and DNS settings.

- **Services**. Specify the services that Setup installs. You can choose to install File and Printer Sharing for Microsoft Networks or for NetWare Networks.

- **Clients**. Specify the networking clients that Setup installs. You can choose between Client for Microsoft Networks and Client for NetWare 3.*x*/4.*x* Networks. If you select Client for NetWare 3.*x*/4.*x* Networks, you can also choose to install NetWare Directory Service. Both clients provide additional fields on this tab that enable you to further configure them.

- **Access Control**. Specify whether the machine uses share-level or user-level security. If you specify user-level security, you must also provide a security provider, to provide a list of users to Windows 98.

- **Additional Clients**. Specify any additional clients you want Setup to install. You can choose between Banyan DOS/Windows 3.1 Client, Novell NetWare NETX, and Novell NetWare VLM.

## Optional Components

You use the Optional Components dialog box to add components to and remove them from the installation. No, you don't choose between typical, portable, compact, or custom. You choose the exact components to install in this case.

The list of available areas and components matches that which you find in the Setup program or in the Add/Remove Programs Properties dialog box. You choose an area in the left-hand list and select the components in the right-hand list. Batch 98 prefills this form with the same settings used to install Windows 98 on the test machine.

To add, remove, and configure optional components by using Batch 98, follow these steps:

1. In Batch 98, click Optional Components.

2. Select an area in Available Areas to display the matching components in Available Components. In Available Components, select each component that you want to include in the setup script.

3. Repeat Step 2 for each area in Available Areas.

4. Close the Optional Components dialog box to save your changes.

## Advanced Options

The Advanced Options dialog box enables you to customize each user's computer even further. You can distribute REG files with the setup script, for instance, that Setup merges into the user's Registry. You can also specify whether Windows 98 uses automatic system policies, which it downloads from a central location on the server, or manual system policies, which points to an exact path to a policy file. To further customize the installation by distributing REG files, follow these steps:

1. Create a REG file containing the settings that you want to customize. You can export a key from the Registry or, more appropriately in this case, you can create a REG file by hand.

2. Type the path and filename of the REG file in the space provided and then click Add. You can repeat this step for each REG file that you want to distribute with the setup script.

3. Close the Advanced Options dialog box to save your changes.

You must copy the REG files to the path indicated in Step 2. This should be a shared network location, preferably the same path that contains the setup script, so that Setup has easy access to the REG files. If you're distributing the setup script on a floppy disk, include the REG files on the floppy. If you're distributing the setup script in an e-mail message, post the REG files to a network share and use the appropriate path in the script.

# Writing a Setup Script Manually

A setup script looks much like any INF or INI file:

- The setup script is divided into sections, each of which starts with a unique name enclosed in square brackets—for instance, [Setup].

- Each section contains one or more items. Each item contains a keyword, followed by an equal sign (=) and a value—for instance, Name=Jerry.

- You can add comments to Msbatch.inf by preceding each comment with a semicolon (;). Setup ignores anything after the semicolon.

- Msbatch.inf files are limited to a certain set of section and item names, otherwise known as keywords. These are the only keywords that Setup understands. "Understanding the Available Keywords for Msbatch.inf," later in this chapter, describes these keywords.

Every setup script contains a least two sections: [Setup] and [Optional Components]. [Setup] controls the overall installation process, determining how much user interaction Setup requires, and [Optional Components] determines which components, such as Accessories and System Tools, that Setup installs.

Listing 2-1 shows you a minimal setup script, which you can expand to fulfill your purposes. This script contains only the [Setup] and [Optional Components] sections. The [Setup] section is configured to provide a completely automated installation in my working environment—you must customize it for your own environment. The [Optional Components] section is configured to install all the optional components. To prevent any component from being installed, assign 0 to the component instead of 1: "Accessibility Options"=0.

**Listing 2-1** *A Minimal Setup Script*

```
[Setup]
Express=1
InstallDir="C:\WINDOWS"
InstallType=3
ProductID=XXXXXXXXXXXXXXXXXXXXX
EBD=0
ShowEula=0
ChangeDir=0
OptionalComponents=1
Network=1
System=0
CCP=0
CleanBoot=0
Display=0
DevicePath=0
NoDirWarn=1
TimeZone="Central"
Uninstall=0
VRC=0
NoPrompt2Boot=1

[OptionalComponents]
"Accessibility Options"=1
"Enhanced Accessibility"=1
"Briefcase"=1
"Calculator"=1
"Desktop Wallpaper"=1
"Document Templates"=1
"Games"=1
```

```
"Imaging"=1
"Mouse Pointers"=1
"Paint"=1
"Quick View"=1
"Windows Scripting Host"=1
"WordPad"=1
"Dial-Up Networking"=1
"Dial-Up Server"=1
"Direct Cable Connection"=1
"HyperTerminal"=1
"Infrared"=1
"Microsoft Chat 2.0"=1
"Microsoft NetMeeting"=1
"Phone Dialer"=1
"Virtual Private Networking"=1
"Baseball"=1
"Dangerous Creatures"=1
"Inside your Computer"=1
"Jungle"=1
"Leonardo de Vinci"=1
"More Windows"=1
"Mystery"=1
"Nature"=1
"Science"=1
"Space"=1
"Sports"=1
"The 60's USA"=1
"The Golden Era"=1
"Travel"=1
"Underwater"=1
"Windows 95"=1
"Desktop Themes Support"=1
"Microsoft FrontPage Express"=1
"Microsoft VRML 2.0 Viewer"=1
"Microsoft Wallet"=1
```

```
"Personal Web Server"=1
"Web Publishing Wizard"=1
"Web-Based Enterprise Mgmt"=1
"Microsoft Outlook Express"=1
"Baltic"=1
"Central European"=1
"Cyrillic"=1
"Greek"=1
"Turkish"=1
"Audio Compression"=1
"CD Player"=1
"DVD Player"=1
"Macromedia Shockwave Director"=1
"Macromedia Shockwave Flash"=1
"Media Player"=1
"Microsoft NetShow Player 2.0"=1
"Multimedia Sound Schemes"=1
"Sample Sounds"=1
"Sound Recorder"=1
"Video Compression"=1
"Volume Control"=1
"AOL"=1
"T WorldNet Service"=1
"CompuServe"=1
"Prodigy Internet"=1
"The Microsoft Network"=1
"Additional Screen Savers"=1
"Flying Windows"=1
"OpenGL Screen Savers"=1
"Backup"=1
"Character Map"=1
"Clipboard Viewer"=1
"Disk compression tools"=1
"Drive Converter (FAT32)"=1
"Group policies"=1
```

```
"Net Watcher"=1
"System Monitor"=1
"System Resource Meter"=1
"WinPopup"=1
"TV Viewer"=1
```

# Understanding the Available Keywords for Msbatch.inf

The following table describes the sections available for use in your custom setup script and the keywords for each section. You find a more detailed description of each keyword in the following sections.

| Section | Keyword |
|---------|---------|
| [Setup] | Devicepath |
|  | EBD |
|  | Express |
|  | InstallDir |
|  | InstallType |
|  | PenWinWarning |
|  | ProductType |
|  | ProductID |
|  | SaveSUBoot |
|  | TimeZone |
|  | Uninstall (with BackupDir) |
|  | Verify |
|  | VRC |
| [System] | Display |
|  | DisplChar |
|  | Keyboard |
|  | Locale |
|  | Machine |

| Section | Keyword |
|---------|---------|
| | Monitor |
| | Mouse |
| | Multilanguage |
| | PenWindows |
| | Power |
| | Tablet |
| `[NameAndOrg]` | Name |
| | Org |
| | Display |
| `[InstallLocationsMRU]` | List of paths |
| `[OptionalComponents]` | List of descriptions |
| `[Network]` | Clients |
| | ComputerName |
| | Description |
| | DefaultProtocol |
| | Display |
| | DisplayWorkstationSetup |
| | HDBoot |
| | IgnoreDetectedNetcards |
| | NetCards |
| | PassThroughAgent |
| | Protocols |
| | RemoveBinding |
| | RPLSetup |
| | Services |
| | Security |
| | ValidateNetcardResources |
| | Workgroup |
| | WorkstationSetup |

*Continued*

*Continued*

| Section | Keyword |
|---|---|
| `[netcard_ID]` | Values taken from INF file for network adapter |
| `[MSTCP]` | DHCP |
| | DNS |
| | DNSServers |
| | Domain |
| | DomainOrder |
| | Gateways |
| | Hostname |
| | IPAddress |
| | IPMask |
| | LMHostPath |
| | PrimaryWINS |
| | ScopeID |
| | SecondaryWINS |
| | WINS |
| `[NWLink]` | Frame_Type |
| | NetBIOS |
| `[NWRedir]` | FirstNetDrive |
| | ProcessLoginScript |
| | PreferredServer |
| | SearchMode |
| `[NWRedir4]` | PreferredTree |
| | NameContext |
| `[NWServer]` | BrowseMaster |
| | Use_SAP |
| `[VRedir]` | LogonDomain |
| | ValidatedLogon |
| `[VServer]` | LMAnnounce |
| | MaintainServerList |

| Section | Keyword |
|---------|---------|
| [Printers] | List of printers to install |
| [Strings] | List of strings for INF file |
| [Install] | List of files to copy to the user's computer |

You can copy the appropriate settings for most of these keywords from Setuplog.txt, which you find in the root folder of your test machine. Make sure the test machine's configuration comes fairly close to the machine on which you're installing Windows 98. This file contains a large number of entries that have little or nothing to do with a setup script. Your best bet is to search Setuplog.txt for an entry's name; then, copy that entry to your setup script by using the clipboard. A perfect section to copy from Setuplog.txt is [Optional Components], for instance, and you can grab the entire section at one time.

## [Setup]

The following table describes parameters that control how much Setup interacts with the user.

| Keyword | Description |
|---------|-------------|
| Devicepath | Specifies whether Windows 98 should use the location containing the installation source files for finding INF files. The default value is 0. |
|  | 0    Don't use installation source path to locate INF files. |
|  | 1    Use installation source path to locate INF files. |
| EBD | Specifies whether to prompt the user to create an Emergency Startup Disk. The default value is 1. |
|  | 0    Don't prompt user to create an Emergency Startup Disk. |
|  | 1    Prompt the user to create an Emergency Startup Disk. |

*Continued*

*Continued*

| Keyword | Description |
|---------|-------------|
| Express | Specifies whether the user is asked to provide input during the setup process. The default value is 0.<br><br>0   Allow user input.<br><br>1   Use only values from the setup script and current configuration. |
| InstallDir | Specifies the path into which Setup installs Windows 98. The default value is the current Windows path or \Windows, if a previous Windows installation exists. |
| InstallType | Specifies the installation option used for Setup. The default value is 1.<br><br>0   Compact.<br><br>1   Typical.<br><br>2   Portable.<br><br>3   Custom. |
| PenWinWarning | Specifies whether Setup displays a warning if an unknown version of Pen Windows is installed on the machine. The default value is 1.<br><br>0   Don't display a warning.<br><br>1   Display a warning. |
| ProductType | Specifies the product type. |
| ProductID | Specifies the product ID for your site. You find the product ID on the CD-ROM or Certificate of Authenticity. No default value exists for this parameter. |
| SaveSUBoot | Specifies whether to save the SUBOOT folder when performing a server-based setup. The default value is 0.<br><br>0   Delete the SUBoot folder.<br><br>1   Save the SUBoot folder. |
| TimeZone | Specifies the time zone for the computer's location. The default value is the time zone already set on the computer. You can use any of the following time zone strings: |

| | | |
|---|---|---|
| Afghanistan | Eastern | Romanian |
| Alaskan | Egypt | Russian |
| Arabian | Fiji | SA Eastern |
| Atlantic | GFT | SA Pacific |
| AUS Central | GMT | SA Western |

| Keyword | Description |
|---|---|
| | Azores   Greenwich   Samoa<br>Bangkok   Hawaiian   Saudi Arabia<br>Canada Central   India   South Africa<br>Cen. Australia   Iran   Sydney<br>Central   Israel   Taipei<br>Central Asia   Lisbon   Tasmania<br>   Warsaw<br>Central   Mexico   Tokyo<br>Pacific<br>China   Mid-   US Eastern<br>   Atlantic<br>Czech   Mountain   US Mountain<br>Dateline   New Zealand   W. Europe<br>E. Europe   Newfoundland   West Asia<br>E. South   Pacific   West Pacific<br>America |
| `Uninstall` | Specifies whether Setup creates a compressed backup of the existing Windows and MS-DOS folders that can be used to automatically uninstall Windows 98. If you set `Uninstall` to 5, you must also set `BackupDir` to the path to copy the uninstall information. The default value is 1.<br><br>0    Do not create uninstall information.<br>1    Show uninstall information and allow user to choose.<br>5    Automatically create uninstall information. |
| `Verify` | Specifies whether Setup is to actually install Windows 98 or just verify the existing Windows 98 installation. The default value is 0.<br><br>0    Do a full installation.<br>1    Verify the Windows 98 installation. |
| `VRC` | Specifies whether Setup overwrites existing files automatically, even if the existing file is newer. The default value is 0.<br><br>0    Confirm before overwriting newer files.<br>1    Overwrite existing files without confirming. |

## [System]

The following table describes parameters for changing the Windows 98 system settings.

| Keyword | Description |
| --- | --- |
| Display | Specifies an INF description from Msdisp.inf. |
| DisplChar | Specifies the initial configuration of the display. Assign a string value to `DisplChar` that looks like `ColorDepth,x,y`. The default value is `4,640,480`. |
| | `ColorDepth`    Bits per pixel (BPS) |
| | $x$    Horizontal resolution |
| | $y$    Vertical resolution |
| Keyboard | Specifies an INF description from Keyboard.inf. |
| Locale | Specifies an INF section name from Locale.inf. |
| Machine | Specifies an INF section name from Machine.inf. |
| Monitor | Specifies an INF description from Monitor.inf. |
| Mouse | Specifies an INF description from Mouse.inf. |
| Multilanguage | Specifies the type of multilanguage support to install in Windows 98. The default value is `English_M`. |
| | `English_M`    English and Western European |
| | `Greek_M`    Additional support for Greek |
| | `Cyrillic_M`    Additional support for Cyrillic |
| | `CE_M`    Additional support for Eastern European |
| PenWindows | Specifies an INF section name from Penwin.inf. |
| Power | Specifies an INF section name from Machine.inf. |
| SelectedKeyboard | Specifies a keyboard from any of the values contained in the `[KeyboardList]` section of Multilng.inf. |
| Tablet | Specifies an INF section name from Pendrv.inf. |

## [NameAndOrg]

The following table describes the parameters available for identifying the user and organization.

| Keyword | Description |
| --- | --- |
| Name | Specifies the full user name for this installation of Windows 98. No default value exists for this parameter. |
| Org | Specifies the organization to which Windows 98 is registered. No default value exists for this parameter. |
| Display | Specifies whether Setup displays the name and organization dialog box. The default value is 1.<br><br>0    Don't display the dialog box.<br><br>1    Display the name and organization dialog box. |

## [InstallLocationsMRU]

This section contains a list of paths to add to the list of folders from which the user can choose when Setup prompts for a path. Listing 2-2 shows you an example.

**Listing 2-2** *Example [InstallLocationsMRU] Section*

```
[InstallLocationsMRU]
mru1=\\server\Win98\folder
mru2=D:\Win98
mru3=\\server\WinSource
```

## [OptionalComponents]

This section contains a list of components, explicitly indicating whether Setup is to install each component. The components in this section correspond to the components you see during a custom setup or in the Add/Remove Programs Properties dialog box. Type the name of the component and enclose it in quotation marks. Then, assign a 1 to a component to explicitly install it. Assign a 0 to a component to explicitly prevent installation. If you leave out the component altogether, Setup uses the default action. The following list describes the component strings you can use in this section:

| | |
|---|---|
| Accessibility Options | Disk Compression Tools |
| Accessories | Disk Tools |
| Additional Screen Savers | Document Templates |
| AOL | DVD Player |
| AT&T WorldNet | Fat32 Converter |
| Audio Compression | Flying Windows |
| Backup | Games |
| Baltic_M | Greek_M |
| Blank Screen | Group Policies |
| Briefcase | HyperTerminal |
| Broadcast Data Services | Imaging |
| Broadcast PC | Infrared |
| Calculator | Internet Tools |
| CD Player | Macromedia Shockwave Director |
| CE_M | |
| Character Map | Macromedia Shockwave Flash |
| Clipboard Viewer | Media Player |
| Communications | Microsoft Chat 2.0 |
| CompuServe | Microsoft Fax Services |
| Cyrillic_M | Microsoft FrontPage Express |
| Desktop Wallpaper | Microsoft NetMeeting |
| Dial-Up Networking | Microsoft NetShow Player 2.0 |
| Direct Cable Connection | Microsoft Outlook Express |

Microsoft VRML 2.0 Viewer          Quick Viewer

Microsoft Wallet                   Sample Sounds

Mouse Pointers                     Screen Savers

Multilanguage Support              System Monitor

Multimedia                         System Resource Meter

Multimedia Sound Schemes          Task Scheduler

Mystify Your Mind                  The Microsoft Network

Net Watcher                        Turkish_M

Online Services                    TV Viewer

OpenGL Screen Savers               Volume Control

Paint                              Windows Scripting Host

Phone Dialer                       WordPad

Prodigy Internet

Three component strings that were previously available in Windows 95 have now been redefined. `Extra Cursors` is now `Mouse Pointers`. `Windows Accessories` is now `Accessories`. `Microsoft Fax` is now `Microsoft Fax Services`.

You can copy this entire section from Setuplog.txt, which you find in the root folder of the test machine.

## [Network]

The following table describes the parameters available for defining the machine's network configuration within the [Network] section of your setup script. Many of these parameters accept a comma-separated list of values that looks like this:

```
clients=vredir,nwredir
```

| Keyword | Description |
|---|---|
| Clients | Specifies the device ID to use from Netcli.inf, Netcli3.inf, or any other INF file provided by a third-party vendor. If you list more than one device ID for this parameter, by separating each client with a comma, the first client listed always starts first when the user starts the computer: |
| | lant5 — Artisoft LANtastic 5.*x* or 6.*x*. |
| | netware3 — Novell NetWare 3.*x*. |
| | netware4 — Novell NetWare 4.*x*. |
| | nwredir — Microsoft Client for NetWare Networks. |
| | vines552 — Banyan VINES 5.52 or greater. |
| | vredir — Client for Microsoft Networks |
| ComputerName | Specifies the computer's name on the network. The name can be a string of up to 15 alphanumeric characters and can include these characters: ! @ # $ % ^ & ( ) - _ ' { } . ~. If the computer's name is not specified, Setup creates a default name based on the first 8 characters of the user's name. |
| Description | Specifies the computer's description on the network. The description can be a string of up to 48 characters, with no spaces, and can include the following special characters: ! @ # $ % ^ & ( ) - _ ' { } . ~. By default, Setup uses the user's full name. |
| DefaultProtocol | Sets a default protocol, optionally binding it to a particular network adapter. You assign one of the protocols defined in **Protocols** to this parameter. You can also add a network adapter defined in **NetCards** to the end of this value, separating them with a comma, which binds that protocol to the adapter: |
| | DefaultProtocol=mstcp,*pnp80F6 |
| Display | Specifies whether Setup displays any network configuration dialog boxes during the process. The default value is **1**. |
| | 0 — Don't display network configuration dialog boxes. |
| | 1 — Display network configuration dialog boxes. |

| Keyword | Description |
|---|---|
| `NetCards` | Specifies the network card drivers to install. This is a comma-separated list of device IDs taken from the appropriate INF files, or an INF file provided by your vendor. Microsoft strongly recommends that you don't specify network adapters by using this parameter, however, but instead let Windows 98 detect the hardware, to properly configure it. |
| `PassThroughAgent` | Specifies the pass-through agent (security provider) for use with user-level security. Assign the name of the server that is providing security to this parameter. The default value depends on the value assigned to `Security`. If you assign `domain` to `Security`, Setup uses the value contained in `Workgroup`. If you assign `nwserver`, Setup uses the value contained in `Preferred Server`. In every other case, Setup doesn't assign a value to this parameter. |
| `Protocols` | Specifies the protocols to install in Windows 98. This is a comma-separated list of device IDs taken from the appropriate INF files. You can use either the following device IDs, which are from Nettrans.inf, or device IDs from an INF file provided by your vendor: |

|  |  |
|---|---|
| `dec40` | DECnet 4.1 Ethernet protocol. |
| `dec40t` | DECnet 4.1 token-ring protocol. |
| `dec50` | DECnet 5.0a Ethernet protocol. |
| `dec50t` | DECnet 5.0a token-ring protocol. |
| `ipxodi` | Novell-supplied IPXODI protocol. |
| `msdlc` | Microsoft real-mode DLC. |
| `mstcp` | Microsoft TCP/IP. |
| `ndisban` | Banyan VINES NDIS Ethernet protocol. |
| `ndtokban` | Banyan VINES NDIS token-ring protocol. |
| `netbeui` | Microsoft NetBEUI. |
| `nwlink` | IPX/SPX-compatible protocol. |
| `nwnblink` | NetBIOS support for IPX/SPX. |

| Keyword | Description |
|---|---|
| `RemoveBinding` | Specifies a binding between two devices to remove. This is a comma-separated list of devices IDs. See `DefaultProtocol`. |

*Continued*

*Continued*

| Keyword | Description |
|---------|-------------|
| Security | Specifies the type of security to use. The default value is `share`. |
| | `share` Share-level security. |
| | `nwserver` User-level security through NetWare. |
| | `domain` User-level security through an NT domain. |
| | `msserver` User-level security via NT server or workstation. |
| Services | Specifies the services to install in Windows 98. This is a comma-separated list of device IDs taken either from the appropriate INF files or from an INF file provided by your vendor. The following values come from a variety of INF files found in \Windows\Inf, including Bakupagnt.inf, Cheyenne.inf, Hpnetprn.inf, Nmagent.inf, Msbatch.inf, Netsrvr.inf, Mspsrv.inf, Regsrv.inf, and Snmp.inf: |
| | `bkupagnt` Arcada Backup Exec agent. |
| | `cheyagnt` Cheyenne ARCserver agent. |
| | `jadm` HP Network Printer service for Microsoft. |
| | `janw` HP Network Printer service for NetWare. |
| | `nmagent` Microsoft Network Monitor agent. |
| | `nwredir4` NetWare Directory Services. |
| | `nwserver` File and Printer Sharing for NetWare Networks. |
| | `pserver` Microsoft Print service for NetWare Networks. |
| | `remotereg` Microsoft Remote Registry Service |
| | `snmp` Microsoft SNMP agent. |
| | `vserver` File and Printer Sharing for Microsoft Networks. |
| ValidateNetcard Resources | Specifies whether Setup displays a dialog box if it detects a hardware conflict or a partial installation. The default value is `1`. |
| | 0    Don't display the dialog box. |
| | 1    Display the dialog box to resolve conflicts. |

| Keyword | Description |
|---------|-------------|
| `Workgroup` | Specifies the workgroup to which the computer belongs. The workgroup name can be a string of up to 15 characters, with no spaces, and can contain the following special characters: ! @ # $ % ^ & ( ) - _ ' { } . ~. By default, Setup uses the workgroup name previously configured on the computer or, if none is configured, it creates a workgroup from the first 15 nonspace characters in the organization's name. |

## [*netcard_*ID]

The name of this section depends on the actual name of the network adapter, which is defined in the card manufacturer's INF file. It sets additional parameters for the adapter, which you find in the [`netcard.NDI`] section of its INF file.

**Caution**

The values you can define in this section depend entirely on the adapter's INF file. Given the variations from adapter to adapter, you should rely on Windows 98 to detect automatically the network adapter that's installed in the computer and configure it appropriately. Optionally, you can look in the adapter's [`netcard.ndi.reg`] section to determine what parameters are available.

For your convenience, the following table lists the parameters available for some common network adapters. It also tells you the name of the adapter's INF file.

| Adapter | INF File | Parameters |
|---------|----------|------------|
| 3COM | Net3com.inf | Interrupt |
|  |  | IOAddress |
|  |  | DMAChannel |
|  |  | MaxTransmits |

*Continued*

*Continued*

| Adapter | INF File | Parameters |
| --- | --- | --- |
| DIC DE201 Etherworks Turbo TP | Netdec.inf | DataTransfer<br>XmitBufs<br>Transceiver<br>Interrupt<br>IOAddress<br>RamAddress<br>MaxMulticasts<br>Maxtransmits<br>AdapterName |
| IBM Token Ring | Netibm.inf | MaxTransmits<br>Primary<br>Alternate<br>RecvBufs<br>XmitBufs<br>MaxPacketSize<br>ProductID<br>NetworkAddress<br>Iobase<br>RecvBufSize<br>XmitBufSize |
| Intel Etherexpress 16 or 16TP | Netee16.inf | IOBaseAddress<br>IRQ<br>IOAddress<br>Transceiver<br>IOChrdy<br>IOChannelReady |
| SMC 9000 | Netsmc.inf | Interrupt<br>Port_Num<br>Xt_Type<br>Microsoft_Channel |

| Adapter | INF File | Parameters |
|---------|----------|------------|
| Thomas-Conrad | Nettcc.inf | `Interrupt` |
|  |  | `IOBase` |
|  |  | `MemoryBase` |
|  |  | `PackSize` |

## [MSTCP]

The following table describes the parameters you can use to configure Microsoft TCP/IP within the `[MSTCP]` section of your setup script. Many of these parameters accept a comma-separated list of values that looks like this:

```
DomainOrder=server1,server2
```

| Keyword | Description |
|---------|-------------|
| `DHCP` | Specifies whether TCP/IP is configured to use DHCP. Enabling DHCP effectively disables WINS. The default value is `1`. |
|  | 0    Don't enable DHCP. |
|  | 1    Enable DHCP. |
| `DNS` | Specifies whether DNS name resolution is enabled. The default value is `0`. |
|  | 0    Disable DNS. |
|  | 1    Enable DNS. |
| `DNSServers` | Specifies a comma-separated list of DNS server IP addresses. No default value exists for this parameter. |
| `Domain` | Specifies the domain of which the computer is a member. No default value exists for this parameter. |
| `DomainOrder` | Specifies a comma-separated list of DNS domains for resolving host names. No default value exists for this parameter. |
| `Gateways` | Specifies a comma-separated list of IP gateways in their order of precedence. No default value exists for this parameter. |

*Continued*

*Continued*

| Keyword | Description |
|---------|-------------|
| Hostname | Specifies the DNS host name for the computer. No default value exists for this parameter, but using **ComputerName** is typical. |
| IPAddress | Specifies the IP address of the computer. No default value exists for this parameter. |
| IPMask | Specifies the IP subnet mask for the computer, if DHCP is not enabled. No default value exists for this parameter. |
| LMHostPath | Specifies the path and filename of the LMHOST file to use. No default value exists for this parameter. |
| PrimaryWINS | Specifies the IP address of the primary WINS server. No default value exists for this parameter. |
| ScopeID | Specifies the ScopeID for the computer. No default value exists for this parameter. |
| SecondaryWINS | Specifies the secondary WINS server for the computer. No default value exists for this parameter. |
| WINS | Specifies whether WINS for NetBIOS name resolution is enabled. If DHCP is enabled, Setup ignores this parameter. The default value is **1**.<br><br>0   Disable WINS.<br><br>1   Enable WINS.<br><br>D   Enable WINS, getting parameters from DHCP. |

## [NWLink]

The following table describes settings for the IPX/SPX-compatible protocol that you can define within the [NWLink] section of your setup script. Setup uses these values only if you assign nwlink to protocols in the [Network] section.

| Keyword | Description |
|---------|-------------|
| Frame_Type | Specifies the default frame type for IPX. The default value is **4**.<br><br>0   802.3.<br><br>1   802.2. |

| Keyword | Description |
|---|---|
| | 2    Ethernet II |
| | 4    Auto. |
| | 5    Token ring. |
| | 6    Token ring SNAP. |
| NetBios | Specifies whether Setup installs NetBIOS support for IPX/SPX. The default value is 0. |
| | 0    Don't install NWNBLINK. |
| | 1    Install NWNBLINK. |

## [NWRedir]

The following table describes the parameters you can define in the [NWRedir] section of your setup script. These values configure the Client for NetWare Networks.

| Keyword | Description |
|---|---|
| FirstNetDrive | Specifies the first network drive that's available to attach to in a login script for Client for NetWare Networks. Assign a drive letter such as K to this value. The default value is F. |
| ProcessLoginScript | Specifies whether the Client for NetWare Networks parses the user's login script. The default value is 1. |
| | 0    Don't process the login script. |
| | 1    Process the login script. |
| PreferredServer | Specifies the preferred NetWare server. No default value exists for this parameter. |
| SearchMode | Specifies the NetWare search mode. The possible values range from 0 to 7, and the default value is 0. |

## [NWRedir4]

The following table describes the parameters you can use to configure the Service for NetWare Directory Services within the [NWRedir4] section of a custom setup script.

| Keyword | Description |
|---------|-------------|
| PreferredTree | Specifies the preferred NetWare Directory service tree. No default value exists for this parameter. |
| NameContext | Specifies the preferred context to which the user logs on. No default value exists for this parameter. |

## [NWServer]

The following table describes the parameters you can use to configure the File and Printer Sharing for NetWare Networks server within the [NWServer] section of a custom setup script.

| Keyword | Description |
|---------|-------------|
| BrowseMaster | Specifies whether the computer can be a browse master. The default value is 1. |
| | 0    Computer can't be a browse master. |
| | 1    Computer can be a browse master. |
| | 2    Computer is the preferred browse master. |
| Use_SAP | Specifies whether the computer uses Server Advertising Protocol browsing. Enabling this parameter allows the computer to be seen by any computer running the NetWare client, but the computer isn't visible in Network Neighborhood. The default value is 0. |
| | 0    Don't enable SAP browsing. |
| | 1    Enable SAP browsing. |

## [VRedir]

The following table describes the parameters you can use to configure the Client for Microsoft Networks server within the [VRedir] section of a custom setup script.

| Keyword | Description |
| --- | --- |
| LogonDomain | Specifies the domain to use to validate the user's credentials when he or she logs on to the computer. The default value is the value in **Workgroup**, which you set in the [Network] section. |
| ValidatedLogon | Specifies whether Windows 98 validates the user's logon credentials on the NT domain. The default value is 0. |
| | 0    Don't validate logon credentials. |
| | 1    Validate logon credentials. |

## [VServer]

The following table describes the parameters you can use to configure the File and Printer Sharing for Microsoft Networks server within the [VServer] section of a custom setup script.

| Keyword | Description |
| --- | --- |
| LMAnnounce | Specifies whether the computer can announce its presence to LAN Manager computers on the network. Enabling this option improves browsing performance, but increases traffic on the network. The default value is 1. |
| | 0    Don't announce on the network. |
| | 1    Announce on the network. |
| MaintainServerList | Specifies whether the computer can be a browse master. The default value is 2. |
| | 0    Computer can't be a browse master. |
| | 1    Computer is a browse master. |
| | 2    Computer can be a browse master if necessary. |

## [Printers]

You use this section of a custom setup script to install support for one or more printers. Each line in this section looks like the following, where *PrinterName* is an arbitrary name for the printer, *DriveModel* is one of the models defined in the appropriate INF files, and *Port* is the printer port or UNC path to a network printer queue:

```
PrinterName=DriveModel,Port
```

Listing 2-3 shows you an example.

**Listing 2-3** *Example [Printers] Section*
```
[Printers]
LaserJet 5=HP LaserJet 5,\\Server\Laser5
LaserJet III=HP LaserJet III,\\Server\Laser3
```

## [Strings]

The [Strings] section enables you to assign string values to keywords that Setup expands when it encounters them. Each line in this section looks like *name=value*, where *name* is the keyword and *value* is the value you want to assign to that keyword, enclosed in quotation marks. Anytime you enclose *name* in percent signs (%), Setup replaces the keyword with the value you assigned it, minus the quotation marks. The following table shows how Setup expands the values defined in Listing 2-4.

| Setup Script | Expanded |
| --- | --- |
| Name=%MyName% | Name=Jerry Honeycutt |
| Org=%IDG% | Org=IDG Books |

**Listing 2-4** *Example [Strings] Section*
```
[Strings]
MyName="Jerry Honeycutt"
IDG="IDG Books"
```

## [Install]

The [Install] section enables you to identify additional files that Setup copies to the user's computer when the user installs Windows 98 by using the setup script. The files specified in this section must be in the same physical location as the Windows 98 source files. Listing 2-5 shows you an example; the following table describes each section.

| Keyword | Description |
|---|---|
| [myfiles.Copy] | This section contains a list of the files to copy. The name of the section must be unique in the setup script, and you can define as many groups of files as you want by defining more than one section. The name of each section is arbitrary, but typically contains two parts separated by a period: a descriptive name and the keyword **Copy**. |
| [DestinationDirs] | This section identifies the destination for the files contained within a group. Each line in this section contains an item named after one of the file groups. You assign a destination to that name. In Listing 2-5, **myfiles.Copy** is assigned 25, which is a value that indicates the Windows folder. You can assign any path you like, or you can use one of the following values: |
| | 10    Machine folder |
| | 11    Windows System folder on target computer |
| | 25    Windows folder on target computer |
| [Install] | This section ties everything together by listing all the file groups you want to copy to the user's computer. Each line starts with the keyword **CopyFiles**, to which you assign the name of a section containing one or more files you want to copy. |

**Listing 2-5** *Example [Install] Section*

```
[Install]
CopyFiles=myfiles.Copy
```

```
[myfiles.Copy]
file1.ext
file2.ext

[DestinationDirs]
myfiles.Copy=25
```

# Enforcing Workgroup Names with Wrkgrp.ini

You use Wrkgrp.ini to specify a list of workgroups that users can join. Wrkgrp.ini prevents the uncontrolled number of workgroup names that's common when no controls are in place. If `Required` is `true`, the user must choose a value from Workgroup.ini; otherwise, the user can type a name other than that provided by Wrkgrp.ini. You can also use Wrkgrp.ini to associate preferred NetWare servers or NT domains with each workgroup.

You store Wrkgrp.ini in the same folder as the Windows 98 source files. If Wrkgrp.ini exists in the installation folder, Setup enables the user to choose from the Workgroups, NT domains, and preferred NetWare servers listed in it. Wrkgrp.ini contains two sections: `[Options]` and `[Workgroups]`. The following table describes the keywords you can use in the `[Workgroups]` section.

| Keyword | Description | |
|---------|-------------|---|
| ANSI | Specifies whether workgroup names are converted to ANSI from an OEM character set. The default value is `false`. | |
| | `true` | Convert character set from OEM to ANSI. |
| | `false` | Don't convert character set from OEM to ANSI. |
| Required | Specifies whether the user is limited to the choices provided in Wrkgrp.ini or can create his or her own workgroup names. | |
| | `true` | User is limited to choices provided by Wrkgrp.ini. |
| | `false` | User can create his or her own workgroup names. |

| Keyword | Description |
| --- | --- |
| `ForceMapping` | Specifies whether users can change the workgroup name, domain, or preferred server defined in Workgroup.ini. |
| | `true`    User can change workgroup name, and so on. |
| | `false`    User can't change workgroup name, and so on. |
| `Mapping` | Specifies a comma-separated list of network providers to which you can map network providers. Further, `Mapping` specifies the order in which mappings are in the `[Workgroups]` section. Workgroups map to the domain or preferred server by default. |
| `Default` | Specifies the default mapping for workgroups shown in the `[Workgroups]` section. Setup uses the default when no mapping is defined for the workgroup, allowing you to define a workgroup simply by listing its name. The value assigned to this keyword has the same format as mappings do in the `[Workgroups]` section. |

The `[Workgroups]` section defines a mapping for every workgroup available to the user. Each line in this section looks like *workgroup=mapping*, where *workgroup* is the name of the workgroup and *mapping* is an optional mapping. *Mapping* is a comma-separated list of network providers to which each workgroup name is mapped. Here's an example:

```
Development=DevelDomain,NWSERVER1
```

In this case, the `Development` workgroup is mapped to both the `DevelDomain` NT domain and the `NWSERVER1` preferred NetWare server. Note that you can map any number of network providers you require and can mix NT domains with NetWare servers.

# Adding Drivers to the Windows 98 Source Files

Does your installation meet these two requirements? First, have you copied the Windows 98 source files to the network so that you can automate the installation via setup scripts, or so that users can install Windows 98 from the network? Second, do you have additional device drivers that each user needs to install that aren't part of the normal Windows 98 source files?

If your installation meets these requirements, then the INF Installer, which is included on the Windows 98 CD-ROM in \Tools\Reskit\Infinst, can short-circuit one of the steps in your installation. This utility adds a device's INF and driver files to the Windows 98 source files so that they appear to be part of the normal source files. That way, the Setup program can install the device drivers during installation, relieving you or the user of later having to go back and install support for the device.

To use the INF Installer, launch it from the Windows 98 CD-ROM. Then, specify the path and filename of the INF file. The INF Installer retrieves the names of the driver files from the INF file. Also specify the path of the Windows 98 source files. Click Add, and the INF Installer copies the required files to the folder containing the source files and updates the existing INF and LOG files to match.

# Running Windows 98 Setup with a Script

You can start the Windows 98 Setup program with a custom setup script, regardless of where you store the source files or the setup script. That is, the setup script and the Windows 98 source files don't have to be physically located in the same drive or folder. You can publish a setup script on the network, for instance, that users can optionally use to install Windows 98 from a CD-ROM. You can distribute setup scripts to users on a floppy disk or in an e-mail message, too, which they can use when installing Windows 98 via source files stored in a shared network location. Here are some other common scenarios:

- **Installing fresh from a network location**. Give each user a boot disk that loads the network drives, logs on to the network, and starts the Windows 98 Setup program with the appropriate script.

- **Installing from the Windows 98 CD-ROM**. Make setup scripts available on the network that each user can use with the Windows 98 CD-ROM. For instance, you can create a different setup script for each department or some other groups of users.

- **Publishing a batch file that starts Setup**. Remove all ambiguity by making available a batch file that executes the appropriate command line for installing Windows 98 by using a setup script.

- **Pushing the installation by using a login script**. Store the Windows 98 source files and setup script in a central network location; then, automatically launch the Setup program from within the user's login script.

To start the Windows 98 Setup program with a custom setup script, follow these instructions:

- **Local computer**. If the Windows 98 source files are stored on the local computer, either on the CD-ROM or hard disk, use the following command line to start the Setup program with the setup script. *d* is the drive containing the Windows 98 source files and *path* is the path on that drive. *e* is the drive containing the setup script; replace *msbatch.inf* with the actual filename of the setup script.

```
d:\path\setup.exe e:\msbatch.inf
```

- **Network server**. If the Windows 98 source files are stored in a central location on the network, use the following command line to start the Setup program with the setup script. *server* is the name of the server that contains the source files and *path* is the share path on that server. *e* is the drive containing the setup script; replace *msbatch.inf* with the actual filename of the setup script.

```
\\server\path\setup.exe e:\msbatch.inf
```

# Automating Windows 98 Setup

Publishing the Windows 98 source files on the network eliminates the tedium involved in rolling out Windows 98 across the organization. You no longer have to fool around with the Windows 98 CD-ROM, but instead can install Windows 98 directly from the network. Combine network-based installation with custom setup scripts and you have an efficient means to roll out Windows 98 that eliminates user interaction, gives you a good amount of control over each user's workstation, and does so in far less time than manual installation. Whereas Microsoft is inconsistent in its recommendation of the number of workstations for which automated installation pays off, I recommend that you use it if installing Windows 98 on more than ten networked computers.

Windows 98 supports two types of automated installation: *push installation* and *pull installation*:

- **Push Installation**. You publish the source files and setup script on the network and force the user to install Windows 98 the next time he or she logs on to the network. You do this by invoking the Setup program with the script from within the user's login script. Alternatively, you can use a network management solution, such as Microsoft Systems Management Server, to launch the Windows 98 Setup program with the script.

- **Pull Installation**. You provide the user with a setup script and source files, and the user initiates the setup. The most common method for pull installation is to post the Windows 98 source files and setup script on the network, and e-mail the user a batch file that launches Setup with the script. You can also publish a link to the Setup program on an intranet or distribute a disk containing the batch file.

# Pushing the Setup Script with Login Scripts

The easiest way to push the Windows 98 installation is to invoke the Setup program from the user's login script. This method works with any protected-mode networking client and the following real-mode networking clients:

- Microsoft Workgroup Add-on for MS-DOS
- LAN Manager 2.*x* real-mode network client
- Novell NetWare real-mode network client (NETX and VLM)
- Windows for Workgroups real-mode and protected-mode clients

You can approach the login scripts in two ways. You can either change each user's login script so that it launches the Setup program or create a common Upgrade account to which each user logs in when he or she is ready to upgrade. Both have advantages and disadvantages.

- **Individual login scripts**. Changing every user's login script so that it launches the Setup program might not be practical in your organization. First, it might be a tiresome process that takes too much effort to complete. Second, you might not be able to prevent the login script from running the Setup program after Windows 98 is already installed. You can probably solve the setup-duplication problem by checking the MS-DOS version from within the login script, however, and not launching the Setup program if you detect the MS-DOS version is Windows 98.

- **A common Upgrade account**. You can create a common account to which all users log on when they're ready to upgrade to Windows 98. The setup script for the Upgrade account launches the Setup program with the script, installing Windows 98. After the user upgrades to Windows 98, the user has no reason to log in to this account again; thus, you limit the work to modifying the login script for a single account and you don't have to worry about the Setup program trying to start every time the user logs on to the network.

Changing every user's login script so that it launches the Setup program is not practical. First, it's a tiresome process, and second, you can't prevent the Windows 98 Setup program from launching again after it's already installed. Thus, you can create an Upgrade account on the network to which users log in when they're ready to upgrade their computers to Windows 98.

**Caution**

Pushing a Windows 98 installation by using a login script isn't advisable on large networks. The extra load brought on by hundreds or thousands of users simultaneously upgrading to Windows 98 can bring the entire network down. A better alternative is to use a network management product, such as Microsoft Systems Management Server, to manage the upgrade process, pushing the installation gradually through the organization while maintaining network integrity.

## Windows NT Networks

A login script for an NT network should have the following lines in it to launch the Setup program with the setup script:

```
net use drive \\servername\sourcefiles
drive:setup drive:msbatch.inf
```

*drive* is the drive letter to which you're mapping the source files. *\\servername\sourcefiles* is the UNC path that contains the Windows 98 source files, including the setup script. *msbatch.inf* is the filename of the setup script, which is usually Msbatch.inf.

To configure a Windows NT Server for automated installation, follow these steps:

**1.** Copy the Windows 98 source files from \Win98 on the CD-ROM to the installation point on the server.

2. Create a custom setup script. Name this script Msbatch.inf and copy it to the folder containing the Windows 98 source files.

3. Create a new user called Win98 (or something similar) by using User Manager for Domains, and then set a password for that user. Upgrade makes a good password; so does Win98. Select User Cannot Change Password and Password Never Expires. You might have to create this account for every domain to which a user is likely to log on.

4. Create the login script as described earlier in this section, copy it to \Winnt\System32\Repl\Export\Scripts, and assign it to the Win98 user.

5. Share the folder containing the Windows 98 source files and setup script so that the Win98 user has access to it.

## NetWare Networks

A login script for a NetWare network should have the following lines in it to launch the Setup program with the appropriate script:

```
attach server/sourcefiles:
map drive: server/sourcefiles:
drive:setup drive:msbatch.inf
```

*server/sourcefiles*: is the NetWare server and volume that contains the Windows 98 source files. *drive* is the drive letter to which you're mapping the source files. *msbatch.inf* is the filename of the setup script, which is usually Msbatch.inf.

To configure a NetWare server for automated installation, follow these steps:

1. Copy the Windows 98 source files from \Win98 on the CD-ROM to the installation point on the server.

2. Create a custom setup script. Name this script Msbatch.inf and copy it to the folder containing the Windows 98 source files.

3. Create a new user called Win98 or something similar and set a password for that user. Upgrade makes a good password.

Also select Allow User to Change Password to No and Force Periodic Password Changes to No. Assign this new account to the preferred server.

4. Create the login script and copy it to appropriate location on the server.

# Pulling the Setup Script with a Batch File

Pulling the installation can save stress on the network, especially if you provide the setup tools to only a handful of users at one time, waiting until they complete the installation to send the setup tools to additional users. Use this method only with experienced users whom you trust, however, because this gives the user a bit more control over the setup process.

To set up a pull installation for Windows 98, follow these steps:

1. Copy the Windows 98 source files from \Win98 on the CD-ROM to the installation point on the server. Share the installation point so that any user whom you want to upgrade can access the source files.

2. Create a custom setup script. Name this script Msbatch.inf and copy it to the folder containing the source files.

3. Create a batch file that launches the Setup program with the script, as described in "Running Windows 98 Setup with a Script" earlier in this chapter.

4. Use one of the following methods to allow each user to start the Setup program with the script:

   • E-mail the batch file to each user whom you want to upgrade.

   • Publish the batch file on an intranet Web page, making sure that only the users whom you want to upgrade have access to the source files.

   • Distribute to each user a floppy disk that contains the batch file.

# Chapter 3

# Debugging Installation and Startup

## Debugging Windows 98 Setup

You can avoid many problems with Setup if you take a few precautions before you start it:

- Scan the hard disk for viruses before starting Setup.
- Scan the hard disk for errors, using ScanDisk, before starting Setup.
- Make sure you have enough free disk space.
- Make sure you have enough free memory. Setup requires at least 432K to install Windows 98.
- Remove any device drivers that might cause problems with Setup. Strip the Config.sys and Autoexec.bat files down to the bare essentials. They should contain only the drivers required to start the computer and access the installation files.

- Make sure Setup has access to the installation files. If you're installing from a CD-ROM, ensure that the CD-ROM drivers are properly loaded. If you're installing from a network, make sure that the network drivers are properly loaded, that you can log onto the network, and that you can access the share containing the installation files.

Setuplog.txt and Detlog.txt contain information that might help you diagnose why Setup fails. If Detlog is choking on a particular device, for example, try removing the device and running Setup again. In most cases, the resolution involves using Safe Recovery. To use Safe Recovery, restart the Setup program. Setup then skips each step that was known to fail on the previous attempt. To restart Setup after it fails, recovering the previous attempt, follow these steps:

1. Click Exit to quit the Setup program. If that doesn't work, restart the computer by pressing Ctrl+Alt+Delete. If that doesn't work, power down the computer and turn it back on after waiting a few seconds.

2. Launch the Setup program again. When prompted, choose Safe Recovery, and click Continue. The Setup program skips the successful portions of the process and picks up where it left off.

3. If Setup fails again, repeat Steps 1 and 2 until it succeeds. The Setup program skips each failure every time you choose Safe Recovery. Thus, each additional failure is new. Stick with it, and you'll eventually make it through the entire process.

If Setup doesn't start at all, check the following:

- Make sure the Setup program can access the installation files on the CD-ROM, floppy disks, or shared network installation.

- Scan the computer for viruses that might prevent Setup from running.

- Make sure the computer has enough resources. Setup requires at least 432K of free conventional memory. If you don't have enough memory, remove device drivers from Config.sys and Autoexec.bat, using common sense regarding what's safe to remove.

- Check your memory configuration. Use Himem.sys and Emm386.exe to free conventional memory by adding the following lines to Config.sys, making sure you use the correct path to each driver.

```
device=path\himem.sys
device=path\emm386.exe noems
dos=high,umb
```

- Try copying the Windows 98 Setup files to your hard disk and removing all device drivers from Config.sys and Autoexec.bat.

If Setup fails before the first restart, check the following:

- Start Setup in Safe Recovery mode as described earlier in this section. Setup skips the step that caused it to fail on the previous attempt. Setup uses the information contained in Setuplog.txt to determine which step failed.

If Setup fails during hardware detection, check the following:

- Wait at least 10 to 15 minutes before giving up. Often, users misinterpret a long delay during detection for failure. A long delay is normal.

- Start Setup in Safe Recovery mode as described earlier in this section. Setup's hardware detection skips the device that caused the failure. Setup uses the information contained in Detcrash.log to determine which device caused the failure.

- Again, start Setup in Safe Recovery mode as described earlier in this section. This time, don't allow Setup to detect the hardware on the computer. To prevent hardware detection, choose the option that enables you to specify the device to detect in the Detect dialog box. Deselect each device.

If Setup fails because it found errors on the hard disk, check the following:

- Run ScanDisk on the hard disk to which you're installing Windows 98. You'll find ScanDisk.exe on the first Windows 98 Setup disk or in \Win98 on the CD-ROM.

- If you're unable to run ScanDisk before installing Windows 98, bypass this step by starting Setup with the /IS and /IQ command line options.

If Setup fails to install Windows 98 on a compressed drive, check the following:

- Free additional space on the host drive, or install Windows 98 on an uncompressed drive. You can free space by shrinking a Windows 3.1 temporary swap file, for instance, or by resizing it.

- If you're compressing the disk with SuperStor, you might need to decompress the disk before running the Windows 98 Setup program.

- If you're compressing the disk with XtraDrive, you must disable XtraDrive's write cache. See XtraDrive's documentation to learn how.

If Setup can't back up the Windows 95 system files while installing Windows 98, check the following:

- Windows 98 Setup can't make a backup copy of your system files if there isn't enough free disk space. Quit the Setup program, free up enough disk space to back up your system files, and restart Setup.

If Setup doesn't work with a custom setup script (Msbatch.inf), check the following:

- Double-check the contents of Msbatch.inf.

- Check Setuplog.txt to see whether the setup script worked properly.

- Verify that you can access the installation point on the server. Make sure that you can access the share and that your login script works correctly.

# Understanding Safe Detection

Windows 98 differentiates between Plug and Play and legacy devices, using Plug and Play detection for Plug and Play devices and an interactive query detection for legacy devices. The process it uses to detect hardware is called *safe detection*, which implies that Windows 98 can detect the hardware on a computer without causing the computer to fail. It does so by first looking for hints about the devices on the computer; then, if it finds hints, it employs the appropriate detection modules to get specific information about each device. Here are additional notes about safe detection:

- It detects resource conflicts early in the installation process, avoiding problems with IRQ, DMA, and I/O address contention.

- It avoids failures. Safe detection is a method of looking for hints in configuration files, ROM, and device drivers to determine whether a particular class of hardware is installed. If it finds hints of a particular class, it looks for specific information on specific ports; otherwise, it skips the entire class.

- It uses the information contained in Msdet.inf to determine which detection modules to load, referring to a particular INF file for each device class. This file also contains information about a class's resource usage and potential risk to the detection process.

- It examines each device= line to determine any resources that must be protected during detection. This prevents Windows 98 from detecting particular devices that are known to cause the process to fail. Setup prompts the user to confirm the classes it will skip during detection.

Windows 98 supports safe detection of network adapters, SCSI controllers, CD-ROM adapters, and sound cards. If it detects these devices, as described in the following list, Windows 98 goes on to load the appropriate detection module; otherwise, it skips the entire hardware class.

- **Network Adapters**. If Windows 98 finds Lsl.com or Ipx.com in memory, it queries them for the adapter's resource settings. Windows 98 also looks for adapter settings in Protocol.ini if it exists.

- **SCSI Controllers**. Windows 98 scans ROM for strings and Config.sys for device drivers that identify SCSI manufacturers.

- **Proprietary CD-ROM Adapters**. Windows 98 detects proprietary CD-ROM adapters by looking for their device drivers in Config.sys. It supports Mitsumi, Sony, and Panasonic adapters.

- **Sound Cards**. Windows 98 looks in Config.sys and System.ini for hints about sound cards installed on the computer.

## Reading the Log Files Created by Safe Recovery

Windows 98 Setup creates a handful of log files that you find in the root folder of the installation drive. These log files contain useful information about Setup if it fails before, during, or after hardware detection. Setup uses this information to continue the process safely as described here:

- If Setup fails prior to the detection process, it reads Setuplog.txt to determine the point at which it failed, as well as which parts of the process to repeat and which parts to skip.

- If Setup fails during the detection process, it reads Detcrash.log to determine which devices failed. It skips failed devices and verifies the devices it already detected. Detcrash.log exists only if detection failed.

The batch file shown in Listing 3-1 enables you to scan the log files automatically for errors. It searches each file for strings that are known to indicate problems and dumps the results in a file called Problems.txt.

**Listing 3-1** *Problems.bat*

```
echo "Setuplog.txt:" >Problems.txt
find /i /n "error" c:\Setuplog.txt >Problems.txt
find /i /n "failed" c:\Setuplog.txt >Problems.txt

echo "Bootlog.txt:" >Problems.txt
find /i /n "error" c:\Bootlog.txt >Problems.txt
find /i /n "failed" c:\Bootlog.txt >Problems.txt

echo "Detlog.txt:" >Problems.txt
find /i /n "error" c:\Detlog.txt >Problems.txt
find /i /n "failed" c:\Detlog.txt >Problems.txt
```

The following sections contain information about the log files that Windows 98 Setup creates during the installation process:

- Detlog.txt
- Netlog.txt
- Setuplog.txt

## Detlog.txt

Detlog.txt logs the results of the hardware detection process, including whether a particular device was found and any parameters for the device. Windows 98 creates a new Detlog.txt file each time you run hardware detection, renaming the previous version to Detlog.old. It creates a file called Detcrash.log only if detection fails during installation. Setup uses Detcrash.log during Safe Recovery to identify failed devices that it should skip. This is a binary file that contains essentially the same information as Detlog.txt.

The following list describes the entries you find in Detlog.txt. You can use these entries to determine the devices Setup detects, the configuration for each device, and any information about devices that failed detection.

- `AvoidMem=`*`memory`* specifies a region in upper memory to avoid.

- `Checking for:` *`device`* indicates that detection started looking for a particular device. If detection detects a device, you see a `Detected:` entry following `Checking for:`.

- `Custom Mode:` *`device`* describes a device that the user instructed Setup to skip.

- `DetectClass:` *`type`* indicates that safe detection found no hints. *`type`* indicates the device class:

  - `Skip Class Media` indicates sound cards.

  - `Skip Class Adapter` indicates proprietary CD-ROM adapters.

  - `Skip Class Net` indicates network adapters.

- `DetectClass Override:` *`type`* indicates whether the user chose to force Setup to detect a particular device class, even though it found no hints. *`type`* is the same as for `DetectClass`.

- **Detected:** *device_info* indicates that detection found a particular device. This entry is followed by information about the device, including its resource requirements.

- **Devices verified=**n specifies the number of devices verified based on information from the registry. If the value of *n* is 0, the registry is missing or contains no hardware information.

- **Parameters** *"parms"* indicates any switches specified on Setup's command line.

- **WinVer=**version provides the versions of MS-DOS and Windows in which the user launched Setup; the high word is MS-DOS and the low word is Windows.

If Setup fails during hardware detection, examine Detlog.txt for a likely cause by looking toward the end of the file. Setup records entries in the order they occur; thus, failures are likely to appear at the end of the file. Search also for the following strings when looking in Detlog.txt for failures:

- **error** indicates errors recorded during detection.

- **failed** indicates failures recorded during detection.

If you experience problems with hardware detection, make a note of each device installed on the computer. Then double-check the Add New Hardware Wizard to be sure each device is compatible with Windows 98. The Wizard lists any device that has been tested and shown to be compatible with the operating system.

## Netlog.txt

Netlog.txt describes the network components detected during the setup process. The following list describes the important entries in this log file.

- **ClassInstall** marks the beginning of network detection and indicates the device found during hardware detection.

- Examining class *type* indicates that detection is looking for a particular class:
  - Net indicates network adapters.
  - NetTrans indicates network protocols.
  - NetClient indicates network clients.
  - NetServices indicates network services.
- NdiCreate(*adapter*) indicates that setup created an object for the network adapter.
- NdiCreate(*client*) indicates that setup created an object for the network client.
- NdiCreate(*protocol*) indicates that setup created an object for the network protocol.
- Validating *protocol* indicates that setup added the protocol to the registry and bound it to the network adapter.
- Validating *client* indicates that setup added the client to the registry and bound it to the network adapter.

## Setuplog.txt

Setuplog.txt is an ASCII text file that you find in the root folder of the drive on which you installed Windows 98. This file logs the installation process, including information about each step and any errors. Windows 98 uses Setuplog.txt for Safe Recovery, but the file has other purposes as well:

- **Safe Recovery**. Setup uses Setuplog.txt to determine the step at which the installation process failed so it can skip that step if the user launches Setup again. The log file indicates when a step starts and finishes. If Setup sees that a step started but didn't finish, it skips that step on the next go-around.

- **Msbatch.inf.** Some of the information recorded in Setuplog.txt is the same as the information you'd put in a custom setup script. This includes the [OptionalComponents], [NameAndOrg], and [System] sections. When writing a script copy, paste these sections to Msbatch.inf; then, edit as required.

- **Troubleshooting.** If Setup fails altogether, examine Setuplog.txt to determine the reason. Look at the end of the file for a probable cause. Since Setup records entries in the order they occur, it's likely to log any failures at the end of the file. You can scan Setuplog.txt line by line looking for errors, or you can search the file for the following strings, which provide a good place to start your investigation:

  - detection indicates the status of hardware detection.

  - error indicates errors recorded during installation.

  - failed indicates failures recorded during installation.

# Configuring and Debugging the Startup Process

By default, Windows 98 boots directly to the graphical user interface (GUI) immediately after processing Autoexec.bat. You can start Windows 98 to the command prompt, or even to Safe mode, by using the boot menu. Restart the computer; then, press and hold the left Ctrl key until you see the boot menu. Alternatively, you can press F8 when you see the words Starting Windows 98. Windows 98 gives you just a few seconds to press F8, however, so act fast. If you want to increase the amount of time that Windows 98 gives you, change the BootDelay setting in Msdos.sys. Here's what you normally see on the boot menu:

1. Normal
2. Logged (\BOOTLOG.TXT)
3. Safe mode

4. `Step-by-step confirmation`

5. `Command prompt only`

6. `Safe mode command prompt only`

If Windows 98 is configured to use disk compression, you'll see an additional entry: `Safe mode without disk compression`. If you've configured Windows 98 to dual-boot with the previous version of MS-DOS, you'll also see `Previous version of MS-DOS`. Whereas Windows 95 had an option called `Safe mode with network support`, Windows 98 does not.

The following list shows the keys that you can use any time that you see `Starting Windows 98`, without having to display the boot menu first.

- **F8** displays the startup menu.

- **F4** starts the previous version of MS-DOS.

- **F5** starts Windows 98 in Safe mode.

- **Shift+F5** starts Windows 98 in Safe mode command prompt only.

- **Ctrl+F5** starts Windows 98 in Safe mode without disk compression.

- **Shift+F8** starts Windows 98 but confirms each step in the process.

# Configuring the Startup Process

Windows 98 enables you to configure the startup process by using Msdos.sys. This is a text file that looks much like an INI file with two sections: `[Paths]` and `[Options]`. Tables 3-1 and 3-2 describe the items allowed under each section. To change Msdos.sys, edit it with any text editor, such as Notepad.

**Table 3-1** *[Paths] Section of Msdos.sys*

| Setting | Description |
|---------|-------------|
| `HostWinBootDrv=` | Specifies the driver letter of the boot drive |
| `WinBootDir=` | Specifies the folder that contains the files required to start Windows 98 and is typically the folder in which you installed the operating system |
| `WinDir=` | Specifies the location of the Windows folder and should be the folder in which you installed Windows 98 |

**Table 3-2** *[Options] Section of Msdos.sys*

| Setting | Description |
|---------|-------------|
| `AutoScan=` | Specifies whether Windows 98 runs ScanDisk each time the computer starts. The default value is **1**. |
| | 0    Disable. |
| | 1    Prompt the user to run ScanDisk. |
| | 2    Start ScanDisk without prompting user. |
| `BootDelay=` | Specifies the amount of time that Windows 98 pauses while displaying **Starting Windows** for the user to press F8. The default is **2** seconds, and setting this value to **0** prevents any delay. |
| `BootFailSafe=` | Specifies whether Windows 98 starts Windows 98 in Safe mode. The default value is **0**, which starts Windows 98 normally. |
| | 0    Disable. |
| | 1    Start Windows 98 in Safe mode. |
| `BootGUI=` | Specifies whether to start the GUI. The default value is **1**, but setting this value to **0** starts the computer to the command prompt. |
| | 0    Start to the command prompt. |
| | 1    Start to the GUI. |

*Continued*

**Table 3-2** *Continued*

| Setting | Description |
|---|---|
| BootKeys= | Specifies whether the startup keys (F5, F8, and so forth) are available as Windows 98 starts. The default value is 1, and setting this value to 0 disables BootDelay. |
| | 0   Disable startup keys. |
| | 1   Enable startup keys and boot menu. |
| BootMenu= | Specifies whether to display the boot menu automatically. The default value is 0, which requires the user to press F8 to display the boot menu. |
| | 0   Don't display boot menu. |
| | 1   Automatically display boot menu at startup. |
| BootMenuDefault= | Specifies the default item on the boot menu. Set this value to the number that appears next to the menu item. |
| BootMenuDelay= | Specifies the amount of time, in seconds, that Windows 98 displays the boot menu before automatically selecting the default item. The default value is 30 seconds. |
| BootMulti= | Specifies whether the user can boot to the previous operating system from the boot menu or by pressing F4. This value must be 1 to dual-boot Windows 98 with another operating system. The default value is 0. |
| | 0   Disable dual-boot capabilities. |
| | 1   Enable dual-boot capabilities. |
| BootWarn= | Specifies whether the Safe mode startup warning is enabled. The default value is 1. |
| | 0   Disable Safe mode startup warning. |
| | 1   Enable Safe mode startup warning. |
| BootWin= | Specifies the default operating system. The default value is 1, which starts Windows 98 by default. Setting this value to 0 starts the previous operating system by default and requires Windows 98 to be configured with dual-boot capabilities. |
| | 0   Previous operating system is the default. |
| | 1   Windows 98 is the default operating system. |

| Setting | Description |
| --- | --- |
| DblSpace= | Specifies whether to load Dblspace.bin. The default is 1. |
| | 0    Do not load Dblspace.bin. |
| | 1    Load Dblspace.bin. |
| DoubleBuffer= | Specifies whether to load the double-buffering driver for SCSI controller. The default value is 0. |
| | 0    Do not load double-buffering driver. |
| | 1    Load double-buffering driver. |
| DrvSpace= | Specifies whether to load Drvspace.bin automatically. The default value is 1, whether or not compression is enabled. |
| | 0    Do not load Drvspace.bin. |
| | 1    Load Drvspace.bin. |
| LoadTop= | Specifies whether to load Command.com and Drvspace.bin at the top of conventional memory. The default value is 1, but set this value to 0 on a computer that connects to a Novell NetWare network. |
| | 0    Don't load at the top of conventional memory. |
| | 2    Load at the top of conventional memory. |
| Logo= | Specifies whether to display the animated logo as Windows 98 starts. The default value is 1, but setting this value to 0 avoids incompatibilities with a variety of memory managers and disables that annoying animation. |
| | 0    Disable the animated logo. |
| | 1    Enable the animated logo. |

Listing 3-2 shows an excerpt from a typical Msdos.sys file. For administrators, the most useful entry is BootKeys. Setting this item to 0 prevents users from being able to display the boot menu; thus, they can't start the computer to the command prompt. Other useful entries are BootDelay, which controls the amount of time that you have to press a boot key when you see Starting Windows 98, and BootMulti, which must be set to 1 if you want to dual-boot Windows 98 with a previous version of MS-DOS.

**Listing 3-2** *Example Msdos.sys*

```
;FORMAT
[Paths]
WinDir=C:\WINDOWS
WinBootDir=C:\WINDOWS
HostWinBootDrv=C

[Options]
BootDelay=10
BootMulti=1
BootGUI=1
DoubleBuffer=1
AutoScan=1
WinVer=4.10.1650
```

**Caution**

You might have noticed several odd-looking lines at the end of Msdos.sys. These lines are fillers that make sure Msdos.sys is greater than 1024 bytes. Some applications require Msdos.sys to be greater than this size, and reducing the size to less than 1024 bytes prevents those applications from working properly. Be careful that you don't delete these lines when changing Msdos.sys.

# Understanding Settings in Io.sys

Io.sys controls many of the settings that MS-DOS users control in Config.sys. The settings in the following list are controlled in Io.sys and don't require entries in Config.sys. You can't change them in Io.sys, but you can override them by adding a comparable entry to Config.sys.

- `buffers=` specifies the number of file buffers to create. The default value is 30, and changing this value is useful only if you have older programs that take advantage of buffers.

- `dos=high` loads MS-DOS into the High Memory Area (HMA). Io.sys uses `dos=high,umb` if you load Emm386.exe in Config.sys.

- `fcbs=` specifies the number of file control blocks that can be open simultaneously. `fcbs=` is useful only for older programs that require this setting. The default value is 4.

- `files=` specifies the number of buffers to create for file handles, which are used only by applications that use MS-DOS for file I/O. The default value is 60.

- `device=himem.sys` enables the High Memory Area.

- `device=ifshlp.sys` loads the Installable File System helper, enabling Windows 98 to make file system calls to the full file system. Without Ifshlp.sys, Windows 98 uses the minimum file system.

- `lastdrive=` sets the last drive letter available. This setting is available for MS-DOS applications that require it, but Windows 98 doesn't use it. The default value is z.

- `device=setver.exe` is loaded by Windows 98 for compatibility with older applications that are looking for a particular DOS version.

- `shell=command.com` loads the command processor. Windows 98 uses the `/p` switch by default, which makes the command processor process Autoexec.bat and then remain in memory.

- `stacks=` specifies the number and size of each stack frame. This value is used by MS-DOS applications, not Windows 98. The default value is 9,256.

Windows 98 moves the following settings from Autoexec.bat to Io.sys:

- `Net start` starts the network by loading the real-mode network components.

- `Set path` specifies the path for finding programs.

Listing 3-3 shows what the Windows 98 environment includes by default.

**Listing 3-3** *Default Windows 98 Environment*

```
tmp=c:\windows\temp
temp=c:\windows\temp
prompt=$p$g
path=c:\windows;c:\windows\command
compsec=c:\windows\command\command.com
```

# Troubleshooting Windows 98 Startup

Bootlog.txt, which you find in the root folder of the boot drive, contains a log of the startup process and is the most useful tool that you have for troubleshooting problems that occur when starting Windows 98. Windows 98 creates the log on two occasions:

- **When Windows 98 first starts**. The first time that you start Windows 98, it creates a log of the startup process and stores it in Bootlog.txt.

- **When you elect to create the log from the boot menu**. From the Windows 98 boot menu (which you can display by pressing F8 while Windows 98 displays `Starting Windows`), you can choose to log the startup process in Bootlog.txt.

The following table lists the entries that you should look for when troubleshooting startup problems. Each entry in the first column should be followed by the corresponding entry in the second column. If you see any entry for a device that says `Loading Device`, for example, you should see `LoadSuccess` following it. Otherwise, look to see whether that device has failed. You can also search Bootlog.txt for the words `error` and `fail`. These two words usually indicate a failure of some sort.

| Start | End |
|---|---|
| DEVICEINIT | DEVICEINITSUCCESS |
| Dynamic init device | Dynamic init success |
| Dynamic load device | Dynamic load success |
| Init | InitDone |
| Initing | Init Success |
| Loading Device | LoadSuccess |
| Loading Vxd | LoadSuccess |
| SYSCRITINIT | SYSCRITINITSUCCESS |

## Using the Emergency Startup Disk to Start the Computer

When Windows 98 won't start, the Emergency Startup Disk can provide access to your computer. Keep the disk updated by using the Add/Remove Programs Properties dialog box. Don't try to use a Windows 95 Emergency Startup Disk with Windows 98 — make sure that you create a new disk.

To create the Emergency Startup Disk, follow these steps:

1. Open the Add/Remove Programs Properties dialog box from the Control Panel, and click the Startup Disk tab.

2. Click Create Disk, and follow the instructions that you see on the screen.

To start the computer with the Emergency Startup Disk, follow these steps:

1. Put the Emergency Startup Disk in the boot floppy.

2. Restart the computer. If you've configured the BIOS not to start from the floppy, you'll have to reconfigure the BIOS

before starting the computer from a floppy. After the computer restarts, Windows 98 starts, and you see the boot menu.

3. Choose whether to enable the CD-ROM. The system starts to the command prompt.

Starting the computer with the Emergency Startup Disk provides access to the file system via MS-DOS, but it doesn't start the graphical user interface. Frequently, you can fix problems that prevent Windows 98 from starting properly at the command prompt, however. For instance, starting the computer with the Emergency Startup Disk enables you to remove device drivers that conflict with Windows 98 from Config.sys.

## Starting Windows 98 in Safe Mode for Troubleshooting

Safe mode loads only the mouse, keyboard, and VGA device drivers. It doesn't load any of the startup files, such as the Registry, Config.sys, and Autoexec.bat, nor does it load the [boot] or [386enh] sections of System.ini. Safe mode loads just enough of the operating system for you to be able to start and troubleshoot Windows. For instance, you'll want to start Windows 98 in Safe mode in the following circumstances:

- Windows 98 doesn't start at all; it stalls at the Start Windows message or the animated logo.
- The startup process takes an inordinately long time.
- The display adapter doesn't work properly.
- The computer crashes frequently.
- You get a series of unusual errors.

To start Windows 98 in Safe mode, follow these steps:

1. Restart the computer.

2. When you see Starting Windows, press F8 to display the boot menu. If you don't receive enough time to press F8, edit

Msdos.sys to change the delay time or to display the boot menu automatically.

**3.** Choose Safe mode from the menu.

Other Safe mode options on the boot menu include the following:

- **Step-by-Step Confirmation**. This option enables you to choose whether to process each command as Windows 98 starts. Press Y to process the command or N to skip the command. Here's what you typically see:
  - Load DoubleSpace driver?
  - Process the system Registry?
  - Create a startup log file (bootlog.txt)?
  - Process your startup device drivers (config.sys)?
  - Process your startup command file (autoexec.bat)?
  - Run win.com to start Windows 98?
  - Load all Windows drivers?

- **Safe Mode Command Prompt Only**. This option doesn't boot to the GUI, even in Safe mode. Use this option if Windows 98 won't start the GUI, even in Safe mode, or if you want to start to the command prompt so that you can use Win.com's command line options.

- **Safe Mode without Disk Compression**. This option starts the computer without disk compression. You won't have any access to compressed drives if you boot with this option, but it might be a last resort if Windows 98 stalls while accessing a compressed drive.

## Starting Windows 98 with Win.com Switches

Win.com supports the following switches, many of which are valuable when you find yourself troubleshooting problems starting Windows 98. To start Windows 98 with these switches, you first must start to the command prompt by choosing Command Prompt Only from the boot menu. Then, type `win.com`, followed by any of the switches shown in the following list, to start the Windows 98 GUI.

- `/d:f` disables 32-bit disk access.
- `/d:m` starts Windows 98 in Safe mode.
- `/d:s` prevents Windows 98 from using ROM addresses between F000:0000 and 1MB for breakpoints.
- `/d:v` handles interrupts from the hard disk controller.
- `/d:x` prevents Windows 98 from scanning adapter area for unused space.

# Part II

## Configuration

# Chapter 4

# Configuring Hardware

Device management doesn't get much easier than it is in Windows 98. With a combination of a Plug and Play computer, Plug and Play devices, and Windows 98, you almost never have to fuss around with the computer's hardware configuration. That is, you'll seldom have to shuffle around the resources assigned to each device or to figure out which device driver you should be using.

This chapter describes the versatile hardware support provided by Windows 98, including the buses and devices it supports and the technologies behind the scenes. This chapter also describes the fundamental tasks that you need to perform in Windows 98: installing and configuring devices, using hardware profiles, and controlling power management.

## Overview

Windows 98 groups devices and buses into classes. A *device class* is a category for related devices, such as keyboards, disk drives, and network adapters. A *bus class* is a category for buses, such as SCSI, IEEE 1394, and PCI. Windows 98 uses class installers to install drivers within a particular class. The information required for each of the following classes is contained in the Registry:

| | | |
|---|---|---|
| Adapter | Media | PC Card |
| Cdrom | Modem | Ports |
| Display | Monitor | Printer |
| FDC | MTD | SCSIAdapter |
| HDC | Net | System |
| HID | NetService | USBDevices |
| Keyboard | Nodriver | |

Windows 98 organizes devices in a hardware tree. The *hardware tree* represents the computer's current configuration and is stored in the Registry immediately under the Enum subkey of HKEY_LOCAL_MACHINE. The hardware tree is organized by bus type: ISA, PC Card, SCSI, and so forth. Each branch in the hardware tree is called a *device node*, and each device node contains a device ID, a list of required resources, a list of actual allocated resources, and an indication of whether the device is a bus. Windows 98 builds the hardware tree in memory each time the computer starts, and it updates the hardware tree any time the configuration changes (inserting a PC Card into the socket, for example).

You can work with the hardware tree in the Device Manager. Figure 4-1 shows the Device Manager, which represents the hardware tree using an outline control. The top level shows different device classes. Expand any device class to see the devices belonging to that class that are installed on the computer. To view a device's properties, select the device in the list, and then click Properties.

To open the Device Manager, do either of the following:

- Right-click My Computer, and choose Properties; then, click the Device Manager tab.

- Open the System Properties dialog box from the Control Panel, and then click the Device Manager tab.

Classes

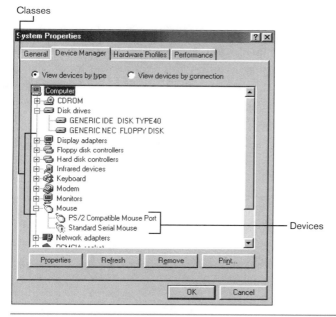

Figure 4-1 *The Device Manager*

# System Buses

A bus moves data among devices, memory, and the CPU. You connect one or more devices to a bus, and the devices use the bus to communicate with the rest of the computer; likewise, the computer uses the bus to communicate with the devices. The sections that follow describe the buses supported by Windows 98.

Buses transfer data at different speeds. Some buses are extremely slow, and others are extremely fast. For the USB and IEEE 1394 buses, Windows 98 supports two different transmission protocols, each of which transmits data at different rates. *Isochronous* transmission transfers data at a guaranteed fixed rate, which is usually quite high, to support multimedia and high-bandwidth devices. *Asynchronous* transmission does not guarantee a fixed rate and typically is slower. Asynchronous transmission can't occur on the bus while isochronous transmission is occurring.

## USB

The Universal Serial Bus (USB) is an external bus for Plug and Play support of keyboards, mice, disk drives, and so forth. The devices are external to the computer, avoiding the requirement that the user install an internal card or configure the device. Windows 98 automatically recognizes and configures USB devices and makes them immediately available after they're connected.

You can connect up to 127 USB devices to a single computer. This exciting innovation alleviates the x86 architecture's limitations imposed by its limited number of resources. Expect numerous USB devices that you can add to a computer without gobbling up another IRQ to appear on the market. Additionally, if you have an older computer that doesn't have USB support built in, you can add a USB adapter to the computer.

A USB bus has three types of components, each of which is described here:

- **Host**. The host is also called a *root*, *root tier*, or *root hub*. The host either is built into the computer's motherboard or is an adapter card. A host controls traffic on the bus and functions as a hub.

- **Hub**. Hubs provide a port to which you attach a device or another USB bus. A hub is responsible for detecting when devices are attached or removed from the bus. Some hubs draw power from the bus (*bus-powered*), whereas others draw power from an external source (*self-powered*). You can chain hubs together to support a larger number of devices.

- **Device**. You attach devices to the bus through a port, which is part of the hub. Examples of USB devices include keyboards, monitors, and mice. A device can also be a hub, enabling you to attach additional devices to the bus by plugging them into the device. For example, some USB monitors might have ports that enable you to plug a mouse and keyboard into them. Windows 98 supports a variety of USB devices, including the following:

- Audio devices
- Data gloves
- Digital PBXs
- Digital still cameras
- Digitizers
- ISDN terminal adapters
- Joysticks
- Keyboards
- Mice
- Modems
- Monitors
- Printers
- Scanners
- Speakers
- Telephones
- Video devices

USB supports two different transmission speeds. It uses 1.5 Mbps for low-bandwidth devices, such as mice and keyboards, and uses 12 Mbps for isochronous transmission.

## IEEE 1394

The IEEE 1394 bus, also known as *FireWire*, is designed for high-bandwidth devices, such as digital camcorders, cameras, and videodisc players. You can connect up to 63 devices to a single IEEE 1394 bus. By joining up to 1023 IEEE 1394 buses, you can connect up to 64,000 devices.

IEEE 1394 buses have four types of components:

- **Device**. Devices are attached to the bus. They usually have 3 ports but can have a maximum of 27. You can daisy chain up to 16 devices. Windows 98 dynamically assigns an address to each device on the bus.

- **Splitter**. A splitter provides additional IEEE 1394 ports.

- **Bridge**. A bridge isolates data traffic in a specific portion of the bus.

- **Repeater**. A repeater bridges the distance between two devices by retransmitting data.

IEEE 1394 provides the following three transmission speeds, asynchronous and isochronous, with faster transmission speeds in development:

S100: 98.304 Mbps

S200: 196.608 Mbps

S400: 393.216 Mbps

## PCI

Personal Computer Interconnect (PCI) is a high-performance bus used on Pentium and some other computers. PCI is built onto the computer's motherboard and provides a communication pathway between the CPU and memory through a bridge device that controls data transfer among the CPU, cache, and memory. The bridge also controls data transfer between each device on the bus and memory.

The maximum transfer rate for a PCI bus depends on the bus's clock rate:

```
clock_rate * bit_width_of_bus
```

## PC Card and CardBus

PC Card, formerly known as PCMCIA, supports multifunction cards, 3.3 Volt cards, and 32-bit PC Cards that are credit-card-sized adapters that you insert into a PC Card socket. PC Card sockets are typically found on portable computers, but you also can add a socket to any desktop computer. CardBus is a combination of PC Card 16 and PCI that gives PC Cards the 32-bit performance of the PCI bus.

## Other Buses

Windows 98 supports a variety of other buses, too, each of which is described here:

- **Industry Standard Architecture (ISA)**. ISA has been around for a while because it was designed for the IBM PC/AT. You can use Plug and Play ISA devices on existing computers, and legacy ISA adapters work well with the newer Plug and Play ISA cards.

- **Enhanced Industry Standard Architecture (EISA)**. EISA is an extension of ISA that is backward compatible with ISA.

- **Small Computer System Interface (SCSI)**. A SCSI bus enables you to chain up to 15 devices, each of which is assigned a unique device ID. With an internal SCSI host, you can chain devices externally and internally.

# Plug and Play

Plug and Play is an open standard that enables you to install new hardware with little user interaction. It supports devices on all the buses described in the previous sections. You insert a device and turn on the computer, and Windows 98 automatically recognizes and configures the device. The process that locates each device on the computer and allocates resources to it is called the *enumeration process:*

**1.** *Bus enumerators* detect each device on each bus.

2. *Resource arbitrators* allocate resources to each device and resolve conflicts between two devices that are requesting the same resource.

3. The Device Manager dynamically loads and configures the device driver for each device on the computer by using the information returned to it by the bus enumerators and resource arbitrators.

Even if you're using a legacy computer that doesn't support Plug and Play, you should use Plug and Play ISA devices in it. Windows 98 can still take advantage of the device's Plug and Play features, even though you don't have a Plug and Play BIOS. To take full advantage of Plug and Play technology, however, you should use a Plug and Play adapter with a Plug and Play BIOS and Plug and Play devices.

PC Cards are Plug and Play devices, and Windows 98 automatically enables support for PC Cards if you're installing one on a computer that has a PC Card socket. If you're not sure whether PC Card support is enabled, check the Device Manager for a PCMCIA Socket entry. If support is not enabled, open the PC Card icon from the Control Panel, or use the Add New Hardware Wizard to install it. Although Windows 98 can work with older PC Card drivers, you won't see the full benefit of PC Card technology if you're not using the latest protected-mode drivers supplied with the operating system. Windows 98 includes support for most PC Card devices, providing Plug and Play device drivers that support dynamic configuration. If Windows 98 doesn't provide a driver for a specific device, it probably provides a generic Plug and Play driver that works with it. Short of that, you must provide a driver from the manufacturer or use real-mode drivers.

**Caution**

If you're using a Plug and Play network adapter, make sure the PC Card socket and the network drivers are the same type. That is, both must be real-mode drivers, or both must be 32-bit protected-mode drivers. If one is real-mode and the other is protected-mode, Windows 98 might fail, or you might not be able to connect to the network.

You can get more information about the hardware that is compatible with Windows 98 by visiting Microsoft's Hardware Compatibility Labs on the Internet at `www.microsoft.com/isapi/hwtest.hcl.idc`.

# Win32 Driver Model

The Win32 Driver Model (WDM) is a device driver architecture that's used by Windows 98 and Windows 2000. One device driver works in both operating systems. WDM supports a variety of bus classes, including the following:

- **USB (Universal Serial Bus)**. USB provides a class driver and PCI enumerator. It supports USB hubs, UHCI and OHCI, and HID-compliant USB devices.

- **IEEE 1394**. Windows 98 provides an IEEE 1394 bus class driver and minidrivers for Texas Instruments and Adaptec host controllers.

The device classes supported by WDM include the following:

- **HID (Human Input Devices)**. The HID device class includes system devices, such as keyboards and mice, as well as gaming and other input devices.

- **DVD (Digital Video Disk)**. The device's manufacturer provides a driver for DVD.

- **Digital Audio**. Windows 98 provides minidrivers for WDM audio, USB audio, and IEEE 1394 audio. It provides a kernel-mode mixer and sample-rate converter.

- **Still Image**. Windows 98 provides WDM drivers for USB and SCSI still-image devices, such as digital cameras. It also supports imaging devices that are plugged into a serial or parallel port.

- **Video Capture**. Windows 98 provides minidrivers for USB and IEEE 1394 digital cameras.

# Installing Devices

When you install Windows 98, it collects an inventory of all the devices on the computer. It gets configuration data for many devices from the corresponding INF file in \Windows\Inf. It gets configuration data for most Plug and Play adapters straight from the device.

Windows 98 automatically detects and configures most Plug and Play devices. Other than plugging in the device and powering on the computer, you don't do anything at all. If Windows 98 fails to detect a Plug and Play device, however, you can use the Add New Hardware Wizard to start hardware detection. Regardless, you must always use the Add New Hardware Wizard to cause Windows 98 to detect legacy devices, and in cases where Windows 98 can't detect the device, you must manually specify some devices. After a device is installed, you can change its configuration by using the Device Manager or one of the alternative locations listed in the following table.

| To Configure This Device | Look in This Location |
| --- | --- |
| Display | Display Properties dialog box in the Control Panel |
| Modem | Modem Properties dialog box in the Control Panel |
| Mouse | Mouse Properties dialog box in the Control Panel |
| Multimedia | Multimedia Properties dialog box in the Control Panel |
| Network | Network Properties dialog box in the Control Panel |
| Printer | Printers folder in Windows Explorer |
| Unknown hardware | Add New Hardware Wizard in the Control Panel |

When Windows 98 installs a new device, it gets the device ID from the device. It uses that ID to locate an entry for the device in one of the Windows 98 INF files, which it finds in \Windows\Inf. It uses the information it finds in the INF file to create entries for the device in the Registry. In particular, it stores data in HKEY_LOCAL_MACHINE for the device and copies the device's driver files to the computer. The actual required Registry entries are described in the device's INF file, but you typically find `DevLoader` and `DriverDesc` values in the `System` key and `Driver` and `ConfigFlags` values in the `Enum` key.

# Installing a Plug and Play Device

To install a Plug and Play device, follow these steps:

1. Turn off the computer, if necessary, and insert the device. Some types of devices are *hot-pluggable*, which means that you can safely insert them while the computer is running. Examples of hot-pluggable devices include those designed for PC Card, USB, and IEEE 1394 buses. If you turned off the computer to install a device, turn on the computer.

2. When prompted, specify the location of the device-driver files. In many cases, Windows 98 automatically determines and installs the correct device driver, so you don't have to specify the files' location. In cases where Windows 98 doesn't come with a driver for the device, you have to specify the location of the device-driver files that are provided by the manufacturer. You can specify a location on a floppy disk, a CD-ROM, a Windows Update Web site, or some other path.

3. If the device is hot-pluggable, you can begin to use it immediately. Otherwise, restart the computer when Windows 98 prompts you.

# Installing a Legacy Device

To install a legacy device by using the Add New Hardware Wizard, follow these steps:

1. Turn off the computer, install the new device, and then turn the computer back on.

2. Open the Add New Hardware Wizard from the Control Panel; then, click Next to skip the introductory screens.

3. If appropriate, choose a device from the list of Plug and Play devices that Windows 98 finds on the computer. The devices in this list are detected on the computer but aren't yet installed. You don't see this list if Windows 98 doesn't detect any new devices. If you pick a device from this list, choose Yes, and then click Next. Windows 98 installs the device you selected, and you're finished. If you don't see the device in the list, choose No, and click Next.

4. If appropriate, choose a device from the list of devices that are unknown, not working properly, or disabled in the current hardware profiles. If you find in this list the device that you're installing, select it, and choose Yes. The Add New Hardware Wizard helps you troubleshoot the device. Otherwise, choose No, and click Next.

5. Specify whether you want Windows 98 to search for the device. If you choose Yes, Windows 98 probes the computer for new devices — a process that can take a long time, so be patient; otherwise, click No, and Windows 98 prompts you to specify the type of device, followed by the manufacturer and model.

6. Select the device class from the list provided, and click Next. Windows 98 displays a list of devices, organized by manufacturer, for that class.

7. Select the manufacturer from the list on the left side; then, select the device from the right-hand list. If you don't find your device in this list, Windows 98 doesn't include support for it. You can install a driver from the manufacturer by clicking Have Disk and following the instructions you see on the screen. To finish installing the device after you locate it, click Next, and follow the Add New Hardware Wizard's instructions.

# Using Real-Mode Drivers

You should almost always use 32-bit protected-mode drivers. Here's why:

- They enhance performance.
- They use memory more efficiently.
- They are dynamically loaded and configured.
- Their configuration data is stored in the Registry.

You can use 16-bit real-mode drivers with Windows 98, but use them only when absolutely necessary. You specify real-mode drivers in the Config.sys file, but Windows 98 unloads real-mode drivers that it can safely replace with a protected-mode driver. If you load a driver in Config.sys and Windows 98 determines that it can replace the real-mode driver with an equivalent protected-mode driver, Windows 98 unhooks the real-mode driver and dynamically starts the protected-mode driver. It does this only when it judges the driver safe to replace according to the following specifications:

- **Safe Drivers**. Safe drivers are real-mode drivers that Windows 98 determines it can safely replace with protected-mode drivers. Ios.ini in \Windows contains a list of safe drivers and TSR programs in the [SafeList] sections.

- **Unsafe Drivers**. Unsafe drivers are real-mode drivers that Windows 98 can't safely replace with a protected-mode driver. Any real-mode driver that uses data compression, encryption, mirroring, bad sector mapping, fault tolerance, or input/output controls defined by the vendor is considered unsafe.

To determine whether Windows 98 is using a real-mode driver, follow these steps:

1. Open the System Properties dialog box from the Control Panel, and click the Performance tab. The dialog box shown in Figure 4-2 appears.

2. Note whether any of the items lack "32-bit" beside them, which indicates that they're using a real-mode driver. In particular, look at the File System, Virtual Memory, Disk Compression, and PC Cards settings.

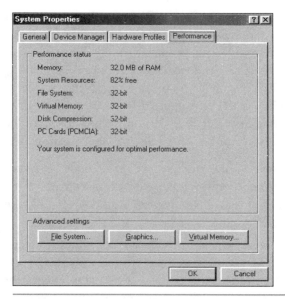

**Figure 4-2** *The Performance tab indicates whether a component is using real-mode or protected-mode drivers.*

If Windows 98 is stuck using a real-mode driver and you can't figure out why, take a look in Ios.log, which you find in \Windows. Windows 98 creates this log file when it can't replace a real-mode driver with a protected-mode driver. The top of the file indicates why the protected-mode driver wasn't used. If the file says something about Mbrint13.sys, consider that the problem might be a virus or some program that tampers with the master boot record.

# Using Windows 98 Extra Drivers

Windows 98 includes on the CD-ROM a variety of device drivers that aren't part of the normal installation. That is, you have to install these device drivers explicitly, either while you're installing the device or later by using the Device Manager's Driver tab for each device. The extra drivers you find on the CD-ROM include those for audio, display, DVD, input, modem, network, printers, power management, multifunction cards, disk, UPS, and Web TV.

Look in \Drivers on the Windows 98 CD-ROM to find a help file called Driver98.CHM (CHM is a compiled HTML help file). Open this file to view a list of all the device drivers available in Windows and in \Drivers. The drivers that are underlined as links are those that you find in \Drivers. Click the link to read the instructions for installing that driver.

# Configuring Devices

You use the Device Manager to change a device's configuration manually. The settings you can change in the Device Manager include the driver the device is using and the resources allocated to it. If you want to set preferences for a device, however, you should look in the Control Panel for the application corresponding to the device. Each device's property sheet typically has the following three tabs:

- **General**. This tab describes the device class, manufacturer, hardware version, and so on. The General tab also tells you whether the device is working properly and, if not, why. You use this tab to determine whether the device works in the current hardware profile, too.

- **Driver**. This tab provides information about the device's driver files, including the vendor, date, and so on. You can change drivers for the device by using this tab.

- **Resources**. This tab shows the resources allocated to the device. Resources include IRQs, I/O addresses, memory ranges, and DMA channels. You can choose to use the automatic settings, which means that Windows 98 is managing the device's resources, or you can use a specific configuration.

You can either let Windows 98 control the resources allocated to a device or set them manually yourself. When Windows 98 is controlling the device, it automatically assigns resources to the device and arbitrates conflicts between two devices trying to use the same resources. When you use fixed resources for the device, Windows 98 can't juggle resources to satisfy every device's needs and can't resolve conflicts. Note that Windows 98 always uses fixed resources for legacy devices, so the resources used by those devices aren't available for resource arbitration.

## Resolving Resource Conflicts

If you must change a device's resource allocation, thereby using fixed resources, use the Device Manager. When manually resolving conflicts, consider following these suggestions from Microsoft:

- Make sure to assign a free resource to the device. Windows 98 indicates whether a resource is already in use when you try to assign it to the device.

- Disable a conflicting Plug and Play device to free its resources. Assign those resources to the other device, and then reenable the Plug and Play device. Windows 98 allocates new resources to the Plug and Play device.

- Disable a legacy device, freeing its resources. You must physically remove the device and avoid loading the device drivers.

- Rearrange resources so that the resources required by a particular device are available. Some devices use a narrow range of resources. For instance, a network adapter might use only IRQs 7 through 11, and a sound card might be limited to IRQs 5 and 10. Assigning IRQ 5 to the sound card and IRQ 10 to the network adapter assures you that a conflict won't occur between the two devices.

# Allocating Fixed Resources to a Device

You can take either of two approaches when manually configuring the resources allocated to a device. You can use one of the basic configurations, which describes a known configuration for the device, or you can manually set each resource. To use a basic configuration, go to the Resources tab of the device's property sheet and choose one of the configurations from the drop-down list labeled Setting based on. To change a specific resource to a different value, select the resource in the Resources tab of the device's property sheet, and then click Change Setting. When you adjust the settings for a Plug and Play device, Windows 98 programs the device to use those settings. When you adjust the settings for a legacy device, you must change the jumpers and switches on the device so that its configuration matches the settings you specified in the Device Manager. To manually change resources allocated to a device, follow these steps:

1. Open the Device Manager, select the device in the list, and then click Properties to open the device's property sheet.

2. Click the Resources tab to see the dialog box. The list in the middle of the dialog box contains an entry for each resource allocated to the device. The first column indicates the types of resources, and the second column shows the value. The bottom of the dialog box describes conflicts with the resources assigned to other devices.

3. Deselect Use automatic settings, which means that Windows 98 no longer controls the resources assigned to the device.

4. Change each resource as needed. Select the resource in the list, and click Change Settings. Fill in the value for the resource, and click OK. Repeat this step for each resource you want to change. When editing a resource's value, Windows 98 indicates whether the current value conflicts with any other device's resources.

5. Close the device's property sheet and the System Properties dialog box. Restart the computer. If you changed settings on a legacy device, you must change the device's configuration by adjusting its jumpers to match.

A common method for installing legacy hardware is to use the Device Manager to locate available resources before installing or configuring the device. Install the device in the Device Manager, using the Resources tab to locate free resources that the device can use. Then, instead of restarting the computer, power it down. Configure the adapter card to match the settings you found in the Device Manager, and install the adapter in the computer. Power the computer back on. It should work on the first try.

# Removing a Device from the Computer

To remove a device from the computer, do one of the following:

- Delete the device from the hardware tree by selecting it in the Device Manager and pressing Delete. Although Windows 98 redetects Plug and Play devices, it won't redetect legacy devices until you run the Add New Hardware Wizard again.

- Disable the device in the current hardware profiles. (This process is described in the following section, "Supporting Different Hardware Sets with Hardware Profiles.")

- Physically remove the device from the computer, and delete the device from the hardware tree, as described in the first bulleted item. If you don't remove the device from the hardware tree, Windows 98 will indicate that the device isn't working properly.

## Changing a Device's Driver

To change a device's driver, follow these steps:

1. Open the Device Manager, and locate the device for which you want to use a different driver.

2. Click the Driver tab; then, click the Upgrade Driver button.

3. Follow the instructions you see on the screen to locate the driver files for the device.

## Printing the Computer's Device Configuration

You can print the computer's entire device configuration by using the Device Manager. If you're going to format a computer's drive and reinstall Windows 98, for example, consider printing the configuration so that you can properly configure it on the first try. Click Print in the Device Manager, and choose the report you want to print. You can choose to print a summary, the details of the selected device, or the details of all devices with a summary.

# Supporting Different Hardware Sets with Hardware Profiles

Hardware profiles determine the drivers that Windows 98 loads. Using multiple hardware profiles enables Windows 98 to support different configurations. For example, you might have two configurations for a portable computer: one to use when it's docked to a docking station and another to use when it's undocked. In the first case, the computer might be connected to the network, and in the second case, it isn't. Note that Windows 98 automatically creates hardware profiles for docked and undocked configurations.

Windows 98 prompts the user to choose a hardware profile only if it can't determine the correct profile to use. This might happen if two profiles are so similar that Windows 98 can't determine the correct one to use for the computer's current configuration. In rare cases, for example, Windows 98 might not be able to determine whether the computer is docked or undocked; thus, it prompts the user for the proper hardware profile to use.

## Creating a New Hardware Profile

To create a new hardware profile, follow these steps:

1. Open the System Properties dialog box, and click the Hardware Profiles tab.

2. Copy one of the existing hardware profiles by selecting it and clicking Copy. Specify a name for the new profile, and click OK.

## Enabling or Disabling a Device in the Hardware Profile

To specify whether a device is in the current hardware profile, follow these steps:

1. Open the Device Manager, and select the device you want to include in or exclude from the current hardware profile.

2. Click Properties to open the device's property sheet, and click the General tab.

3. If you want to remove the device from the current hardware profile, select the box labeled Disable in this hardware profile; otherwise, deselect it.

4. Restart the computer if requested.

# Controlling Power Management

Windows 98 supports two different kinds of power management:

- OnNow, as implemented via the Advanced Configuration and Power Interface (ACPI). This technology gives the operating system control over power management.

- Advanced Power Management, which is implemented in the BIOS.

The concept of power management schemes is new to Windows 98. Like color, mouse, and sound schemes, power schemes enable you to specify different configurations to use in different situations. By default, Windows 98 defines the following schemes:

- **Home/Office Desk**. This scheme is for desktop computers.

- **Portable/Laptop**. This scheme is for portable computers and quickly powers down the computer when it's not in use. It's designed to save battery power.

- **Always On**. This scheme makes sure the computer never enters a sleep state, but it does power down the monitor and hard disks after a while. This setting is intended for computers acting as personal servers.

Aside from using the predefined power schemes, you can adjust them to suit your needs better. You can also create your own power schemes. For instance, you might want to create a power scheme that never powers down the monitor if you're using a portable computer to give a presentation. To change an existing power scheme, follow these steps:

1. Open the Power Management Properties dialog box from the Control Panel, and click the Power Schemes tab. The list boxes on the left side apply when the computer is plugged into a wall outlet. The list boxes on the right side apply when the computer is running on batteries.

2. Change the timers that apply when the computer is plugged in and when it's running on batteries. If you choose Never, Windows 98 will not power down the computer.

3. Change the timers for the monitor and hard disks. The timers specify how much idle time elapses before Windows 98 powers down that device. Like the standby timers, you can specify timers that apply when the computer is plugged in and when it's running on batteries.

4. Click OK to save your changes.

To create a new power scheme, follow these steps:

1. Open the Power Management Properties dialog box from the Control Panel, and click the Power Schemes tab.

2. Click Save As, provide a name for the scheme, and click OK.

3. Change the power scheme as described in the previous instructions, and then click OK to save your changes.

## OnNow Power Management

OnNow power management enables the user to power down and power on the system quickly, avoiding the lengthy startup and shutdown times for which Windows is noted. With OnNow, the operating system controls the power management process. The Win32 Driver Model provides OnNow power management for USB and IEEE 1394 devices. Windows 98 also provides OnNow support for PCI and CardBus devices.

When the operating system is shut down, the computer actually keeps it in a low power state instead oturning it all the way off. This state is also known as a *sleep state*. OnNow has the capability to wake up to events, such as the phone ringing or the mouse moving. In addition, applications that are aware of OnNow power management participate in the power management process by adjusting their behavior when the computer is in a sleep state. When the user powers the computer back on, the operating system resumes, making the computer immediately available for use.

OnNow's instant-on features are more forward-looking than they are practical. According to Microsoft, each application and each device that the user installs has to be aware of OnNow power management for the whole system to work properly. Applications that aren't OnNow-aware can either keep the system from entering a sleep state or cause the system to crash when it wakes up. Upgrading to applications and devices that are aware of OnNow is expensive and not even possible in many cases. Even without these instant-on features, however, you still get the benefit of power schemes.

## Advanced Power Management

Windows 98 also supports the Advanced Power Management (APM) standard, which is controlled by the computer's BIOS. Unfortunately, each BIOS handles APM differently. Consult the document provided with the computer to determine how to configure APM.

APM works similarly to OnNow in that you can control the standby timers for the entire system as well as for specific components. APM also monitors the status of the battery and suspends the computer when battery power is low.

# Troubleshooting Devices

Windows 98 provides troubleshooters that you can use to diagnose most common hardware problems, including resource conflicts. To see the troubleshooters that are available, click the Contents tab in the Help window, then click Troubleshooting, and then click Windows 98 Troubleshooters. The Hardware Conflict troubleshooter helps you fix resource conflicts. Other troubleshooters for hardware include the following:

- Networking
- Modem
- DirectX
- Sound

- PC Card

Windows 98 provides several other troubleshooting tools that you can use to discover why a particular device is not working properly:

- **Device Manager**. Device Manager indicates whether a device is working properly and, if it isn't, provides some information about the reason. For instance, it might report that a resource conflict with another device exists.

- **Support Online**. Microsoft's Support Online (http://support.microsoft.com) is the ultimate collection of troubleshooting articles. These articles describe known problems with specific devices, as well as general approaches to fixing problems in Windows 98.

- **Windows Update**. Windows Update automatically logs on to the Internet and enables you to update the device drivers installed on the computer. Although Windows Update is a dream for administrators and power users, be careful about allowing users to run this support tool because you don't want everyone in the organization wandering around with different configurations.

The remainder of this section contains additional troubleshooting information that you won't get from the troubleshooters. Thus, use the troubleshooters first. If that fails to help, use the information in this section.

If the display works incorrectly or erratically, check the following:

- Most common problems are related to the video driver; look for an updated driver from the vendor or from Windows Update.

- Windows 98 might not properly detect the use of an improper resolution, color depth, or refresh rate. Try the lowest possible settings for each and see whether the display improves.

- Change the driver to the original driver provided by Windows 98. You can start the computer in Safe mode to verify that the problem is related to the driver. Safe mode uses the generic VGA driver.

If PC Card support is enabled but PC Cards do not work properly, check the following:

- Change the memory region used by the PC Card device. To do so, use the PC Card device's property sheet in the Device Manager, and set the memory region to a value higher than 10000.

- Change the interrupt used by the PC Card device in the Device Manager. Make sure that the new IRQ doesn't conflict with another device on the computer.

If SCSI devices don't work properly, check the following:

- Make sure that the ends, internal and external, of the SCSI bus are terminated. If you're not using any internal SCSI adapters, the bus should be terminated at the host adapter and on the last external device.

- Make sure the IDs are correct on each device.

- Make sure that you insert media into any removable media devices before installing the device in Windows 98. Windows 98 doesn't correctly detect removable media SCSI devices if they don't contain media.

- Use the Add New Hardware Wizard for Windows 98 to detect SCSI hosts when it doesn't detect them automatically.

- Note that Windows 98 displays SCSI tape drives and SCSI scanners as unknown devices in the Device Manager; so don't be alarmed if you don't see these devices listed by name.

- If you don't see a SCSI drive in My Computer, either a problem exists with the real-mode drivers in Config.sys, or the protected-mode drivers failed to load. Look in Ios.log for any error messages that tell you why.

- You might have to specify additional command line switches for the SCSI device in the Device Manager. Consult the manufacturer's documentation for more information.

If you're having difficulties with other types of devices, check the following:

- Windows 98 freezes when accessing the CD-ROM drive with real-mode drivers for Sound Blaster or Media Vision Pro Audio proprietary CD-ROM drives. Install protected-mode drivers.

- If the CD-ROM's performance worsens when using AutoPlay, turn off AutoPlay, and then turn it back on.

- If the computer's input devices fail to work, check the Device Manager for errors. In particular, look for I/O and IRQ resource conflicts.

- If the mouse or keyboard works erratically, check and update the mouse and keyboard drivers. Verify the port used for the mouse, too, and double-check that no resource conflicts exist. Make sure that you're not loading a real-mode mouse driver in Config.sys or Autoexec.bat.

If power management is not working correctly, particularly after suspending, do the following:

- Install and run the Power Management Troubleshooter. You find this program in \Tools\Mtsutil\Pmtshoot on the Windows 98 CD-ROM. After you install this program, it instructs you to suspend your computer. As the computer suspends, it records information about the state of various bits of the operating system and computer. When you restart the computer, you can view this information to determine what is causing power management to fail. Don't forget to uninstall the Power Management Troubleshooter when you're finished so that your computer runs correctly.

# Chapter 5

# Managing Disks and Files

## Understanding FAT32

A *file allocation table* (FAT) is a method for organizing the space on a disk. It indicates where on the disk each portion of a file is located by representing each file as a chain of numbers. Each number in the chain points to a specific cluster that contains a portion of the file. The original file system was 12-bit FAT, called FAT12, which supported 16MB logical drives. Microsoft introduced FAT16, which supports 2GB logical drives, with MS-DOS 3.0.

Microsoft introduced FAT32 with Windows 95 OSR2 and continues using it in Windows 98. FAT32 supports logical drives up to 2,047GB. The most notable improvement is that FAT32 uses 4K clusters for drives between 512MB and 8GB, resulting in a more efficient use of space. The file system also automatically detects when Windows 98 shuts down improperly, and runs ScanDisk before starting the graphical user interface (GUI). FAT32's only problem is that it's not compatible with FAT16. FAT32 uses four bytes to store cluster locations, and FAT16 uses only two bytes. The APIs that programs use to access the file system have changed, too. The result is that low-level programs written for FAT16 don't work on FAT32, and some operating systems support only FAT16, so dual-booting Windows 98 with them isn't possible with FAT32.

Note that Windows 98 provides updated versions of all the disk utilities that do support FAT32: Format, Fdisk, Defrag, and ScanDisk.

Cluster size is the most important determinant of how much data you can fit on a disk. The file system divides the disk into logical units, called *clusters*. A file is stored in one or more clusters, and a file's clusters don't necessarily have to be stored contiguously on the disk. In fact, the purpose of the file allocation table is to help the operating system locate all a file's clusters, regardless of their order on the disk. A smaller cluster size is better for efficiency. In the simplest example, imagine a 2K text file. If you store that file on a disk that uses 32K clusters, the disk is going to use 32K, no matter how small the file. Thus, the cluster size is the smallest amount of space a file can occupy, regardless of the file's actual size. Table 5-1 shows you the cluster size in FAT16 and FAT32 for different disk sizes. Consider also that few files are an exact multiple of the cluster size; a little bit is always left over that wastes an additional cluster. If every file on a disk containing 4,000 files used only half of its last 32K cluster, you'd be wasting about 64MB. 4K clusters in a similar situation waste a negligible amount of space.

**Table 5-1** *Cluster Sizes in FAT16 vs. FAT32*

| Size | FAT16 Cluster | FAT32 Cluster |
| --- | --- | --- |
| 260MB–511MB | 8K | NA |
| 512MB–1023MB | 16K | 4K |
| 1024MB–2GB | 32K | 4K |
| 2GB–8GB | NA | 4K |
| 8GB–16GB | NA | 8K |
| 16GB–32GB | NA | 16K |
| >32GB | NA | 32K |

The following are some additional notes about FAT32:

- FAT32 supports logical drives up to 2,047GB, whereas FAT16 supports logical drives only up to 2GB.

- FAT16 is compatible with a wider a range of operating systems than FAT32, including Windows NT 4.0 and OS/2.

- FAT16 is more efficient than FAT32 on drives smaller than 256MB, and FAT32 performs terribly in real-mode MS-DOS and in Safe mode.

- You can't use DriveSpace 3 to compress a FAT32 volume, but you can use it to compress a FAT16 volume.

- FAT32 uses space more efficiently than FAT16 by using smaller cluster sizes, resulting in a savings of up to 10 to 15 percent.

- FAT32 is more robust than FAT16. It can relocate the root folder, for example, and use a backup copy of the FAT; and the boot record contains backup copies of important data structures.

## Converting to FAT32

If you're putting Windows 98 on a newly formatted hard disk, let Fdisk create FAT32 partitions for you. If you're upgrading to Windows 98, you can use Drive Converter to convert a FAT16 disk to FAT32. Just remember that Windows 98 doesn't provide a utility to convert FAT32 to FAT16, so the conversion is permanent. Converting is worth doing, however, because you receive a performance bump and more available disk space.

Within Windows 98, you can use the protected-mode version of Drive Converter. You start it from the Start menu by choosing Programs ⇨ Accessories ⇨ System Tools ⇨ Drive Converter (FAT32). After you start Drive Converter, it scans the disk for incompatible applications. It finds a list of incompatible applications in the Registry at

HKEY_LOCAL_MACHINE\SYSTEM\CurrentControlSet\Control\ SessionManager\CheckBadApps400. Alternatively, you can run the real-mode version of Drive Converter in MS-DOS mode. The following code shows you the command line for the real-mode version of Drive Converter. The first two command line options are required; the rest are optional.

```
Cvt d: /cvt32 [/win] [1|2|4|8|16|32] [/nop] [/noscan]
[/min] [/nt5] [/hib] [/errlog file] [/help]
```

Here's a description of each option:

- *d:* specifies the letter of the drive to convert.
- /cvt32 prevents users from accidentally converting a drive. This parameter is required.
- /win enables Drive Converter to run in an MS-DOS VM rather than in MS-DOS mode.
- 1|2|4|8|16|32 specifies a cluster size. You should not use this option; just let Drive Converter calculate the optimal cluster size.
- /nop suppresses all warnings when the converter detects a problem.
- /noscan skips running ScanDisk before converting the disk. Don't skip this step, however, because finding any errors is important before starting the conversion process.
- /min suppresses the logic that prevents the converter from converting a drive if the disk is too small to convert.
- /nt5 converts a disk to FAT32 if a FAT32-enabled version of NT exists on the system and sets up the system to dual-boot Windows 98 and NT.
- /hib causes the converter to delete any hibernate files and proceed with the conversion. If the converter finds a hibernate file and this switch isn't used, the converter cancels the conversion.

- /errlog *file* writes a status code to an error log; *file* is the filename of the error log.
- /help displays Help for Drive Converter.

**Caution**

*Create an Emergency Startup Disk before converting to FAT32. A Windows 95 Startup Disk does not recognize FAT32 drives. Thus, use the Add/Remove Programs Properties dialog box to create an Emergency Startup Disk.*

# Testing Hibernate Features

FAT32 conversion causes problems with the hibernate features of some computers. Thus, Drive Converter takes the following actions if it finds such a feature on the computer:

- Converts the drive if the computer either has no APM/ACPI or has APM/ACPI with no hibernate file and no PC Card controller.

- Gives the user a warning if the computer either has APM/ACPI and a hibernate file or has APM/ACPI and a PC Card with no hibernate file. It checks for the following hibernate files in the root folder:
  - Amizvsus.pmf
  - Save2dsk.bin
  - PM_hiber.bin
  - Hibrn8.dat
  - Saveto.dsk
  - Toshiber.dat

You should test a computer's hibernate feature before you deploy Windows 98 throughout an organization, particularly if you're deploying onto portable computers. To test the hibernate feature with FAT32, convert a representative computer's disk to FAT32. Suspend and resume the computer to make sure it restarts correctly, and test the disk for errors by using ScanDisk to make sure the file system is still intact. You might also test a variety of other scenarios in which users are likely to find themselves. For instance, add the maximum amount of memory to a computer using FAT32 and test the hibernate feature. Test the computer's factory configuration by converting it to FAT32.

# Preparing a Disk

To prepare a computer to install Windows 98 on a newly formatted disk, you must first partition the disk by using Fdisk to create and activate a primary partition. Then, you use Format to lay down the file system on the disk. The following sections, "Partitioning" and "Formatting," describe both of these processes, respectively.

If the computer has multiple partitions, which might be the case if the drive is bigger than 2GB, you can combine them into one larger partition. Doing so is a four-step process:

1. Back up the computer.
2. Partition the disk with Fdisk, as described in "Partitioning."
3. Format the disk with Format, as described in "Formatting."
4. Restore the backup files.

## Partitioning

Fdisk, the utility you use to partition a disk, is on the Windows 98 Emergency Startup Disk and in \Windows\Command. You can also locate a copy on the Windows 98 CD-ROM. You start Fdisk from the command line by typing fdisk. When you start Fdisk, you see a prompt that asks whether you want to enable large disk support if the disk is larger than 512MB. Answer Yes to use FAT32, which supports partitions up to 2,047GB. Answer No to use FAT16, which supports partitions only up to 2GB. You should definitely consider enabling large disk support because many of the Windows 98 performance enhancements depend on FAT32.

If you're consolidating partitions, you must delete all the existing partitions and then create a new primary partition that uses all the available disk space. Choose Option 3 from the Fdisk menu to remove a partition; then, choose the type of partition you want to remove, and follow the instructions you see on the screen. Note that partitions must be removed in the following order:

1. Non-DOS partitions
2. Logical drives in an extended partition
3. Extended partitions
4. Primary partition

 **Caution**

Back up the computer *before* using Fdisk to remove a partition. Removing a partition irrevocably destroys the data on that partition.

After removing the partitions on a disk, create a primary partition for Windows 98. You can use all of the disk for the primary partition or leave space for an additional extended partition, which you can further subdivide into logical drives. To create a primary partition, follow these steps:

1. Choose Option 1 from the Fdisk menu. The Create DOS Partition or Logical DOS Drive screen is displayed.
2. Press 1 to create a primary DOS partition. The Create Primary DOS Partition screen is displayed.
3. Press Enter to use all the available disk space for the primary partition; or type **n**, press Enter, and then specify the amount of space you want to allocate to the primary partition. You can specify the space in megabytes or as a percentage by including the percent sign after the number.
4. Press Esc to return to the Fdisk menu.

# Formatting

Format lays down the file system on the disk. After partitioning a disk, you must format it before you can install Windows 98. You also must format any nonsystem disks before Windows 98 can read from or write to them.

If you're formatting a removable disk or a logical drive, you can use Windows Explorer. Right-click the drive, and choose Format to open the Format dialog box. You can always use Format on the MS-DOS command line, however. You find Format on the Emergency Startup Disk, on the Windows 98 CD-ROM, and in \Windows\Command. The following code shows you the command line for Format:

```
format d: [/v[:label]] [/q] [/f:size] [/b | /s] [/c]
format d: [/v[:label]] [/q] [/t:t /n:s] [/b | /s] [/c]
format d: [/v[:label]] [/q] [/1] [/4] [/b | /s] [/c]
format d: [/q] [/1] [/4] [/8] [/b | /s] [/c]
```

Here's a description of each option:

- /v[:label] specifies the disk's volume label.
- /q performs a quick format; the disk must already be formatted.
- /f:size specifies the size of a floppy disk: 160MB, 180MB, 320MB, 720MB, 1.2GB, 1.44GB, or 2.88GB.
- /b leaves space for the system files without copying them.
- /s copies the system files to the newly formatted disk.
- /t:t specifies the number of tracks on each side of the disk.
- /n:s specifies the number of sectors on each track.
- /1 formats a single side of a floppy disk.
- /4 formats a 5¼-inch or 360K floppy disk in a high-density drive.
- /8 formats the disk with eight sectors per track.
- /c tests clusters that are already marked as bad.

The following list describes the command lines that you use in various situations:

- To format a boot disk, use `format d: /s`.
- To format a data disk, use `format d:`.
- To erase a disk quickly, use `format d: /q`.

You can perform a quick format only on an already formatted disk. Quick format relies on information left by the previously performed full format and thus can erase the disk much more quickly. Full format lays down the entire file system, however, and takes much longer.

# Reserving Drive Letters for Removable Drives

Windows 98 enables you to control the drive letters it assigns to each removable media drive. On a CD-ROM drive, you reserve only one drive letter. For other types of removable media, you might reserve several drive letters, one for each potential partition on a single disk. If you reserve two drive letters for a drive, for example, and insert a disk that has four partitions, Windows 98 reports that some partitions aren't accessible, because you have to increase the drive letters reserved for the device. To reserve a drive letter for a removable drive, follow these steps:

1. Open the System Properties dialog box from the Control Panel, and click the Device Manager tab.

2. Select from the list the item that represents the removable drive, click Properties to display its property sheet, and then click the Settings tab.

3. Select a start drive letter and an end drive letter in the Reserved drive letters area at the bottom of the dialog box. Be sure to allocate enough drive letters to cover each partition on any removable media that you might insert in the drive.

4. Close the device's property sheet and the System Properties dialog box to save your changes.

# Configuring the Recycle Bin

Unless you permanently delete a file by holding the Shift key as you delete it, Windows 98 stores files that you delete in the Recycle Bin. This is a special folder on the disk that caches deleted files on a first in, first out basis. Because deleted files are stored in the Recycle Bin, they still occupy disk space. You can determine how much disk space Windows 98 allocates to the Recycle Bin, however. To configure the Recycle Bin, follow these steps:

1. On the desktop, right-click the Recycle Bin, and choose Properties. The Recycle Bin Properties dialog box is displayed.

2. If you want to specify settings for each individual drive, select Configure drives independently; otherwise, select Use one setting for all drives. The following list describes both options:

   - **Configure drives independently**. Click each drive's tab, and specify the amount of space to allocate to its Recycle Bin. Alternatively, if you don't want to store deleted files in this drive's Recycle Bin, select Do not move files to the Recycle Bin.

   - **Use one setting for all drives**. Specify the amount of space to allocate to the Recycle Bin. You can select Do not move files to the Recycle Bin if you don't want to store any deleted files in the Recycle Bin.

3. Close the Recycle Bin Properties dialog box to save your changes.

You can empty the Recycle Bin any time, freeing additional disk space, by right-clicking the Recycle Bin icon and choosing Empty

Recycle Bin. You can also delete a file without moving it to the Recycle Bin by holding down Shift while you delete the file.

# Maintaining Disks

Having a regular maintenance routine keeps each disk on the computer healthy, virtually eliminating the chances of your losing important data. Here's a suggested routine:

- **Backup**. Back up the computer at least once a week. If the data changes frequently, do an incremental backup daily.

- **ScanDisk**. Run ScanDisk weekly to check for and repair errors.

- **Disk Defragmenter**. Occasionally run Disk Defragmenter to optimize the file system.

- **Disk Cleanup**. Run Disk Cleanup on a regular basis to remove unwanted files from the computer.

You can access the disk tools more quickly via each disk's property sheet rather than starting the disk tools from the Start menu. Right-click any drive in Windows Explorer, choose Properties, and then click the Tools tab. The Windows 98 Properties dialog box for the drive you selected is displayed. Click Check Now to run ScanDisk on that drive; click Backup Now to back up the contents of that drive; or click Defragment Now to optimize the drive.

Following this routine manually is a bit much to ask and almost never happens. You should schedule each of the above items as jobs in Task Scheduler. Task Scheduler automatically launches Microsoft Backup, ScanDisk, Disk Defragmenter, and Disk Cleanup and records the results. You can set up many of the jobs in the routine automatically by running the Windows Tune-Up Wizard. Choose Start ➪ Programs ➪ Accessories ➪ System Tools ➪ Windows Tune-Up to launch the Windows Tune-Up Wizard. You can use Tune-Up Wizard two ways: The first dialog box gives you the choice of either using the most common tune-up settings or customizing each setting. If you choose to use the most common tune-up settings, the Tune-Up Wizard asks you whether you want to schedule the tasks at Nights, Midnight to 3:00 AM; Days, Noon to 3:00 PM; or Evenings, 8:00 PM to 11:00 PM. If you choose to customize the tune-up settings, you have complete control over which utilities Tune-Up Wizard schedules and the time for which it schedules them. To create customized settings for the Windows Tune-Up Wizard, follow these steps:

1. Start the Windows Tune-Up Wizard.

2. Select Custom – Select each tune-up setting myself, and then click Next.

3. Choose a schedule. You can pick between Nights, Days, Evenings, or Custom. Even if you pick one of the suggested schedules, you can still customize it; therefore, you should pick one of the predefined schedules and then fine-tune it later. Click Next.

4. Select the programs that you want to keep in your StartUp folder. By default, Windows Tune-Up Wizard selects all the programs. If you want to remove a program from the StartUp folder, deselect it. Click Next.

5. Select Yes, speed up my programs regularly, if you want to schedule Disk Defragmenter. Then, click Reschedule to change the schedule and Settings to change Disk Defragmenter's settings. If you don't want to schedule Disk Defragmenter, select No, do not speed up my programs. Click Next.

6. Select Yes, scan my hard disk for errors regularly, if you want to schedule ScanDisk. Then, click Reschedule to change the schedule and Settings to change ScanDisk's settings. If you don't want to schedule ScanDisk, select No, do not scan my hard disk for errors. Click Next.

7. Select Yes, delete unnecessary files regularly, if you want to schedule Disk Cleanup. Then, click Reschedule to change the schedule and Settings to change Disk Cleanup's settings. If you don't want to schedule Disk Cleanup, select No, do not delete unnecessary files. Click Next.

8. If you want to run each scheduled utility immediately, select When I click Finish, perform each scheduled tune-up for the first time.

9. Click Finish to close the Windows Tune-Up Wizard.

After scheduling tasks such as ScanDisk and Disk Defragmenter via the Windows Tune-Up Wizard, you can adjust each task's settings manually to better suit the user's needs. Other than in very specialized situations, the tasks scheduled by the Wizard are the only ones required by most users.

## Scanning a Disk for Errors

Windows 98 provides ScanDisk for detecting and fixing disk errors. You find two versions of it: a graphical version to run in Windows 98 and a text version to run in MS-DOS. You start the graphical version from the Start menu by choosing Programs ⇨ Accessories ⇨ System Tools ⇨ ScanDisk. You find the MS-DOS version in \Windows\ Command or on the Emergency Repair Disk.

ScanDisk can detect and repair errors in the following areas:

- Long filenames
- File allocation table
- Folder structure
- File system structure
- Physical disk surface
- DriveSpace 3 or DoubleSpace volume headers, volume file structure, compression structure, and volume signature

To scan a disk for errors by using ScanDisk, follow these steps:

1. Launch ScanDisk from the Start menu.

2. From the list of drives, select the drive you want to scan for errors.

3. Select the type of test you want to run. Standard checks the files and folders for errors. Thorough checks the files and folders for errors and scans the disk for physical errors. If you choose Thorough, click Options to specify which areas to test.

4. If you want ScanDisk to repair errors without prompting you first, select Automatically fix errors.

5. Click Start to begin scanning the disk for errors.

## Backing Up a Disk's Contents

The backup utility that comes with Windows 98, called Microsoft Backup, is greatly improved over the backup utility from Windows 95. It's similar to most other backup utilities that you've used, particularly Backup Exec, and has corrected the issues with incremental and differential backups. It supports backups to local, removable, and network drives on parallel, IDE/ATAPI, and SCSI buses.

You start Microsoft Backup by choosing Programs ⇨ Accessories ⇨ System Tools ⇨ Backup from the Start menu. Alternatively, click Backup on the Tools tab of the disk's Properties dialog box. The first time you start Microsoft Backup, it asks you to configure the backup hardware on the computer. Follow the instructions you see on the screen to start the Add New Hardware Wizard. Thereafter, you can use the Backup and Restore Wizards to back up and restore the computer. You can also create your own backup job by choosing Job ⇨ New. Then, choose the folders and files you want to back up, and click Start to begin.

Microsoft Backup supports three kinds of backups:

- **Full system backup** backs up all the files on the computer.

- **Differential backup** backs up all the files that have changed since the last full system backup. This type of backup takes longer, but the restoration process is faster than with incremental backups because you have to restore only the last full system backup and the latest differential backup. The latest differential backup contains all the files that have changed since the last full system backup.

- **Incremental backup** backs up all the files that have changed since the last full system backup, differential backup, or incremental backup. This type of backup is quick, but its restoration process takes longer than a differential backup's. You have to restore the original full system backup and each individual incremental backup since the full system backup. If you've performed 20 incremental backups since the last full system backup, you have to restore all 20 to restore the system.

## Optimizing the File System

In an ideal world, Windows 98 would store all a file's clusters contiguously on the disk. Over time, however, a file actually becomes fragmented because Windows 98 can't always find enough space to store all a file's clusters contiguously; thus, Windows 98 scatters the file's clusters all over the disk. Such fragmentation hurts the system's performance because reading a contiguous group of clusters is much faster than reading scattered clusters. To improve the system's performance, you use a defragmenter, such as the one that comes with Windows 98, to consolidate each file's clusters on the disk.

Disk Defragmenter is improved in Windows 98 to make programs start a lot faster. When the user starts an application, Windows 98 records the order in which the file system accesses clusters used by the application during startup. This includes clusters occupied by the application's EXE and DLL files as well as its data files. Windows 98 uses Task Monitor to monitor each program when it starts and to record its disk access pattern as it starts. Task Monitor records that information in log files that it stores in

\Windows\Applog. The format for the name of each log file is *appname*.lg*d*, where *appname* is the name of the application and *d* is the drive letter from which it starts. For example, Notepad.lgc is a log file for Notepad that starts on drive C. Disk Defragmenter uses that information to optimize the disk so that each application loads faster. When Disk Defragmenter starts, it uses Cvtaplog.exe to build a file called Applog.dt*d* (where *d* is a drive letter) for each drive on the system. Disk Defragmenter uses the information in Applog.dt*d* to optimize cluster placement so that applications start faster.

To optimize a disk with Disk Defragmenter, follow these steps:

1. Start Disk Defragmenter from the Start menu.
2. Choose a disk from the Select Drive dialog box, and then click OK. Disk Defragmenter begins working.

You should shut down any other programs and avoid using the computer while running Disk Defragmenter. If this utility detects any changes to the disk while it's running, such as saving a value to the Registry or closing a document, it starts over from the beginning.

# Removing Unnecessary Files

Some of the most frequent problems arise from a full disk and temporary files. Disk Cleanup helps maintain the user's computer by removing temporary Internet files, downloaded program files such as ActiveX controls, and other miscellaneous temporary files found in C:\Windows\Temp. Disk Cleanup also empties the Recycle Bin. The amount of disk space that Disk Cleanup can recover varies, but is usually dramatic.

To start Disk Cleanup, choose Programs ⇨ Accessories ⇨ System Tools ⇨ Disk Cleanup from the Start menu. Alternatively, right-click a drive's icon in Windows Explorer, and then click Disk Cleanup on the General tab of the drive's property sheet. Windows 98 also has a feature that automatically notifies a user when the amount of free disk space falls below a preset threshold and then prompts the user to run Disk Cleanup. Disk Cleanup's window has two tabs. The first tab, Disk Cleanup, enables you to remove temporary files, remove downloaded program files, and empty the Recycle Bin. The second tab, More Options, enables you to save disk space in other ways. For example, you can remove the Windows 98 Setup components, remove installed programs by launching the Add/Remove Programs Properties dialog box, or convert your drive to FAT32 by launching the Drive Converter.

To free disk space with Disk Cleanup, follow these steps:

1. Start Disk Cleanup. Disk Cleanup displays a status window while it collects information about the temporary files on your disk.

2. Select the types of files you want to remove by clicking the check box next to each description until you see a check mark.

3. Click OK, and then confirm that you want to remove the files. Disk Cleanup displays a status window while it removes the files from your disk.

Disk Cleanup pops up on its own if the user is running low on disk space. This occurs only when Windows 98 is trying to allocate disk space for a new file or to extend a file and it detects that disk space has fallen below a threshold of 25MB to 65MB. As a result, Windows 98 displays a low disk space notification, which prompts the user to run Disk Cleanup.

# Compressing the Computer's Files

A compressed drive is not a real disk; it's a compressed volume file (CVF). A CVF might contain 500MB of data but occupy only 300MB of actual disk space. Windows 98 stores CVF files in the root folder of the host drive in files called something like Drvspace.*nnn* or Dblspace.*nnn*, where *nnn* is a sequence number starting with 000. A host drive can contain more than one CVF file, which is why sequence numbers are used. Software drivers make these CVF files act and work like real disks as far as other applications are concerned. The software drivers compress data as it's written to the CVF and uncompress data as it's read.

*DriveSpace 3* is the technology in Windows 98 that implements compression. It supports compression on any removable media and on fixed disks, almost doubling the amount of data you can store on the disk. The Windows 98 version of DriveSpace 3 recognizes FAT32 volumes but does not compress their contents; thus, you must use FAT16 if you want to use compressed disks.

You use a compressed disk in the same way you use any other disk on the computer. You can view its contents in Windows Explorer, for example, or scan it for errors by using ScanDisk. Note that after compressing a disk, you end up with the following two drives:

- **Host drive**. Windows 98 creates a host drive that contains the CVF and any remaining free disk space. You can use the free space on the host drive to store files that must remain uncompressed, such as a Config.sys file that's required to start the computer. If you compress the boot drive, for example, you can store the system files on the host drive so that the system can start.

- **Compressed drive**. The compressed drive represents the contents of the CVF. The files in the CVF are compressed, and you can't access them unless the compression drivers are running. For example, if you start Safe mode without Compression, for example, you can't access the files in a CVF.

## Enabling Disk Compression

Windows 98 doesn't install disk compression by default. You have to choose it when installing Windows 98 or add it later by using the Add/Remove Programs Properties dialog box to add the Disk Compression tools component. After installing disk compression,

Windows 98 adds the Compression Agent and DriveSpace 3 short-cuts to the Start menu.

## Creating a Compressed Drive

Windows 98 makes the compression tools easy to access from each drive's property sheet. Right-click an uncompressed drive in Windows Explorer, choose Properties, and then click the Compression tab to display the dialog box shown in Figure 5-1. The top portion of the resulting dialog box shows how much space you gain by compressing the entire disk, thus hiding the host drive. The bottom portion of the dialog box shows how much space you gain by compressing only the unused space on the disk, leaving the host drive available for use.

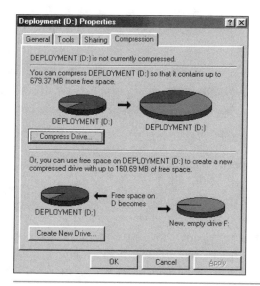

**Figure 5-1**  *This dialog box projects how much space you gain by compressing the disk or creating a new compressed disk from unused space.*

To compress a disk with DriveSpace 3, follow these steps:

1. Right-click a drive in Windows Explorer, choose Properties, and click the Compression tab. If you don't see the Compression tab, you have to install DriveSpace 3 from the Add/Remove Programs Properties dialog box. Note that you won't see the Compression tab if the disk is formatted using FAT32.

2. Click Compress Drive to compress the entire disk and hide the host drive; or click Create New Drive to create a compressed disk from the unused space on the disk, leaving the host drive available for use.

3. Follow the instructions on-screen. DriveSpace 3 scans the disk for errors and prompts you to back up the system. The entire process can take from several minutes to several hours, particularly if you're compressing an existing disk with a lot of files.

After compressing a disk, you'll notice two new files in the root folder of the boot drive: Drvspace.bin and Dblspace.bin. You'll also notice that Windows 98 adds the following line to the Config.sys file:

```
DEVICEHIGH=C:\WINDOWS\COMMAND\DRVSPACE.SYS /MOVE
```

A compressed drive's property sheet is different from an uncompressed drive's property sheet. Right-click a compressed drive in Windows Explorer, choose Properties, and click Compression. This dialog box shows you how much space you've saved and attributes the savings to each type of compression that DriveSpace 3 supports. You can start Compression Agent by clicking Run Agent or start DriveSpace 3 by clicking Advanced. Compression Agent recompresses the files on the compressed drive, while DriveSpace 3 enables you to fine-tune the compression settings.

You can store the Windows 98 system files on a compressed volume. There is a performance penalty, though. In particular, the Windows 98 swap file can reside on a compressed disk if you're using the protected-mode driver to control it (Drvspace.vxd). If you're using the real-mode drivers to control the swap file, however, you should move the swap file to an uncompressed drive or to the compressed disk's host drive.

## Using Compression Agent

Compression Agent enables you to fine-tune how Windows 98 compresses files. You can specify the type of compression to use (UltraPack, HiPack, or Standard) as well as which files, folders, and file types Windows 98 will compress. You can start Compression Agent from the Start menu by choosing Programs ➪ Accessories ➪ System Tools ➪ Compression Agent. Alternatively, you can right-click a compressed disk, choose Properties, click the Compression tab, and click Run Agent. The best way to launch Compression Agent is via the Task Scheduler, however, which runs Compression Agent on a regular basis to recompress files, yielding a better compression ratio.

Compression Agent enables you to set policies that determine which type of compression it uses. You can set these policies for a particular file, a group of files, and folders. These policies include never compressing, always compressing with UltraPack, or always compressing with HiPack. Here's a description of the compression levels that DriveSpace 3 supports:

- **Standard** is a faster compression with a lower compression ratio.

- **HiPack** uses the same encoding techniques as standard compression but gets a better compression ratio, all things being equal.

- **UltraPack** uses an encoding technique that provides the best possible compression ratio but is much slower than standard or HiPack compression. The only way to compress files with UltraPack is to run Compression Agent, which stores infrequently used files in this format.

To set policies for Compression Agent, follow these steps:

1. Open Compression Agent, and click Settings. The Compression Agent Settings dialog box is displayed.

2. Select the files on which you want to use UltraPack. You can choose between the following settings:

   - **Do not UltraPack any files** doesn't use UltraPack with any files. Use this setting if you're more concerned with performance than disk space.

   - **UltraPack all files** uses UltraPack with all files. Use this setting if you're more concerned with disk space than performance.

   - **UltraPack only file not used...** uses UltraPack with all files that are older than the given number of days. Compression Agent uses the date last modified to determine how old the file is.

3. Select whether you want Compression Agent to use HiPack with the remaining files. Select Yes to use HiPack; otherwise, select No.

4. Click Exceptions to specify any exceptions to the policies you selected in Steps 2 and 3. For all files, folders, or file types, you can specify a specific compression method to use, including no compression.

5. Click Start, and Compression Agent recompresses the files in the compressed disk by using the policies you defined.

## Adjusting Compression Settings

DriveSpace 3 estimates the amount of free space on a compressed drive, based on the estimated compression ratio. You can manually set an estimated compression ratio or, better yet, use the compression ratio of the files already in the compressed disk. For example, if the files in the compressed disk are half of their uncompressed size, the compression ratio is 2 to 1. When calculating the free space available on the compressed drive, DriveSpace 3 multiplies the actual free space by the compression ratio. For example, if 100MB are free on the host drive and the CVF has an estimated compression of 3 to 1, DriveSpace 3 estimates that approximately 300MB are free in the CVF. To manually change the estimated compression ratio, follow these steps:

1. Launch DriveSpace 3 from the Start menu or from the Compression tab of the compressed disk's property sheet. The DriveSpace 3 window is displayed.

2. Select the drive in the list, and then choose Advanced ⇨ Change Ratio from the main menu to display the Compression Ratio dialog box.

3. Adjust the slider to the left to decrease the compression ratio or to the right to increase the compression ratio.

4. Close the Compression Ratio dialog box to save your changes.

Aside from adjusting the compression ratio, DriveSpace 3 enables you to change the amount of space allocated to the CVF on the host drive. You can give more space to the CVF, which makes the compressed drive bigger and the host drive smaller, and vice versa. To adjust the amount of space allocated to the compressed drive, follow these steps:

1. Start DriveSpace 3 from the Start menu or from the Compression tab of the compressed disk's property sheet.

2. Select the drive, and then choose Drive ⇨ Adjust Free Space from the main menu to display the Adjust Free Space dialog box.

3. Move the slider left to provide more free space on the host drive and less space on the compressed drive, or move the slider right to provide less space on the host drive and more space on the compressed drive.

4. Close the Adjust Free Space dialog box to see your changes.

Compression Agent's default settings are appropriate for most computers. These settings specify that the Compression Agent doesn't compress files as you save them but instead compresses them later when you're not using the computer. It also compresses infrequently used files with UltraPack and compresses all other files with HiPack. Here are some suggestions for configuring Compression Agent:

- **To get more space**. If you want to free the maximum amount of disk space possible, however, you should adjust these settings. Use UltraPack for most (if not all) files and compress files as you save them. If you're not using a Pentium computer, use HiPack instead of UltraPack because UltraPack is much slower than HiPack.

- **To get better performance**. If you want to gain some of the benefits from compression without sacrificing too much performance (or if the computer is a dog), don't compress files as you save them, and use the standard compression format. You can schedule Compression Agent so that it compresses files later when you're not using the computer. Also, prevent Compression Agent from compressing files that you use frequently, such as EXE and DLL files.

# Understanding Long Filenames

Windows 98 supports filenames with up to 255 characters, including spaces and other special characters. The old MS-DOS filenames are limited to eight characters. Windows 98 supports long filenames through a bit of a kludge, however, which involves generating aliases for long filenames. Here are the rules that Windows 98 uses to create an alias for a long filename:

- It takes the first 8.3 filename characters of the long filename. That is, Windows 98 skips any character that's not valid in an 8.3 filename, such as spaces.

- It takes the first six characters of the long filename that are valid in the 8.3 file-naming scheme.

- It appends ~*n* to the end of the filename, where *n* is a number starting from 1 that makes the filename unique in that folder.

- It uses the first three characters after the last period as the file extension. Thus, if the long filename contains two periods, the first three characters after the second period become the file's extension.

A file called `This is a long filename.document` becomes `Thisis~1.doc`. If a file called `Thisis~1.doc` already exists in the folder, Windows 98 uses `Thisis~2.doc`, instead.

Filenames can contain any of the following characters:

- Letters and numbers
- Spaces
- ASCII characters greater than 127
- ~ ! @ # $ % ^ & ( ) _ - ' + , ; = [ ]

Some programs, particularly older 16-bit programs, don't support long filenames. You can fool these programs by using the long filename's alias, though. For example, if you want to install a 16-bit Windows program in C:\Program files\MyProg, specify the path as C:\Progra~1\MyProg, instead. The application will use the 8.3 filename for the folder, but you'll still see it as a long filename. If you're not sure of the alias for a given folder, look at the folder's property sheet.

Even though Windows 98 and its applications support long filenames, some applications don't handle long filenames containing spaces very well. If you try to open a file called `This is a file.doc`, for example, you might see an error message that says `Can't find This`. The application didn't see the rest of the filename because of the first space. To fix this problem, enclose the entire filename in quotation marks when using it on a command line.

# Long Filenames on a Network

Windows 98 supports long filenames on the following network file systems:

- NTFS on Windows NT version 4.0 or greater
- FAT16 on Windows NT version 3.5 or greater
- NetWare volumes
- HPFS on OS/2
- UDF file system
- CDFS file system for CD-ROMs

In some cases, the network server must be properly configured to support long filenames with Windows 98. Before Windows 98 can copy long filenames to a NetWare server, you need to modify the Windows 98 Registry and add name-space support on the NetWare server. To modify the Registry to support long filenames, follow these steps:

1. Start the Registry Editor.

2. Open the key following:

   ```
   Hkey_Local_Machine\System\-CurrentControlSet\
   Services\VxD\Nwredir
   ```

3. Create a new binary value by choosing Edit ➪ New ➪ Binary Value, and name the value LFNSupport. Set its value to 0x10.

4. Close the Registry Editor, and restart the computer.

To add name-space support to a NetWare 3.1*x* server, follow these steps:

1. At the NetWare command prompt, type load os2, and press Enter. You should see the OS2 module load.

2. Adding a name space requires free disk space. Make sure at least 10 percent of the total amount of disk space is still available before proceeding! At the NetWare prompt, type

   ```
   add name space OS2 to volume xxx
   ```

where *xxx* is the name of the volume to which you are installing the name space. Add the name space to each volume that needs to support long filenames.

3. Load the NetWare editor and modify the Startup.cfg file, usually located on your boot drive C. At the NetWare command prompt, type `load edit`, and press Enter. When you are prompted for the filename, enter `c:\startup.cfg`.

4. At the top of the Startup.cfg file, type

   ```
   load c:\dir\os2.nam
   ```

   where *dir* is the directory in which you have your NetWare server startup files. The next time that you reboot the NetWare server, make sure that OS2.nam resides in that directory on the boot partition of your server.

NetWare 4.1*x* no longer uses the OS2 name space. It supports the LONG name space. To install long filename support in NetWare versions 4.1*x* and greater, simply follow the preceding instructions and replace OS2 with LONG.

## Administering Long Filenames on a Network

Some programs don't work well with long filenames. For those programs, use Lfnbk to remove filenames before using the program, and then use the same utility to restore long filenames after using the program. For example, if you must use a backup utility that doesn't support long filenames, remove long filenames with Lfnbk, back up the computer, and then restore long filenames after you're finished. Lfnbk.exe is on the Windows 98 CD-ROM in \TOOLS\reskit\file\lfnback. Copy this file to the computer to use it. You can also distribute this file as part of a setup script.

The following line shows you the command line for Lfnbk:

```
Lfnbk [/v] [/b | /r | /pe] [/nt] [/force] [/p] [d:]
```

Here's a description of each option:

- `d` specifies the drive letter.
- `/v` specifies to output information to the screen (verbose).
- `/b` backs up and removes long filenames from the disk.
- `/r` restores backed-up filenames to the disk.
- `/pe` extracts errors from the backup file.
- `/nt` prevents restoration of backup dates and times.
- `/force` forces Lfnbk to run, ignoring all warnings.
- `/p` lists long filenames without converting them to 8.3 aliases.

**Caution**

Don't change the computer's directory structure between the time you remove long filenames and the time you restore them. Changing the directory structure by adding, removing, or renaming a folder makes restoring the long filenames impossible.

Other considerations for long filenames include the following:

- You can view the long filenames associated with each 8.3 filename by typing `dir` and pressing Enter at an MS-DOS command prompt.
- MS-DOS applications running in MS-DOS mode cannot see long filenames because only the real-mode file system is running.
- Surround long filenames in quotation marks when specifying long filenames on the MS-DOS command line. This applies only to MS-DOS running in VM.
- Limit the size of long filenames. Even though you can create a long filename that's up to 255 characters, the entire path is limited to 260 characters.

- Consider publishing a set of filename conventions if your organization has a lot of users. This set of conventions should ensure that users are using long filenames that generate expected 8.3 filenames so that files can easily be found if long filenames are lost. For example, you can specify that long filenames should contain the most identifying information in the first six characters of the filename.

# Troubleshooting the File System

When troubleshooting FAT32, keep the following points in mind:

- You can't share a FAT32 disk with another operating system that doesn't support it.

- Windows NT 4.0 doesn't support FAT32, but Windows NT 2000 will.

- DriveSpace 3 does not support FAT32.

- Chkdsk does not work on FAT32 drives; use ScanDisk instead.

- Windows 98 has limited support for file control blocks on FAT32.

- Programs that aren't aware of FAT32 might not work well with files larger than 2GB. Some programs don't properly report the amount of free space on drives larger than 2GB.

- Interlink does not work on a FAT32 drive.

You can use the Troubleshooting tab in the File System Properties dialog box to test different settings if you're having trouble with the file system. To test settings by using the Troubleshooting tab, follow these steps:

1. Open the System Properties dialog box from the Control Panel, and click the Performance tab.

2. Click the File System button, and then click the Troubleshooting tab. Enable the settings you want to test by clicking their check boxes, and then click OK.

3. If the problem doesn't go away, repeat Steps 1 and 2 with a different setting.

If the file system performs poorly, do the following:

- Adjust the file system's cache using the File System Properties dialog box, which you open by clicking File System on the Performance tab of the System Properties dialog box.

- Prevent the floppy disk device driver from using first in, first out. See ForceFIFO=0 in `HKEY_LOCAL_MACHINE\System\ CurrentControlSet\Services\Class\FDC\0000`.

If you're having problems with large hard drives, consider the following:

- Windows 98 networking clients do not report network drives that are larger than 2GB to maintain compatibility with MS-DOS applications that assume a 2GB drive limit.

- If you can create only an 8GB partition on a drive that's larger than 8GB, your problem might be caused by a drive controller that doesn't support the full set of interrupt 13 extensions. If Windows 98 doesn't detect the presence of these extensions, it uses a limit of 7.9GB.

If you can't use some older file utilities, do the following:

- Consider using utilities designed for Windows 98, which support long filenames and FAT32. Otherwise, try removing long filenames, as described earlier in this chapter, before using the utility.

- If you're using Disk Manager, upgrade to version 7.04 or greater.

- Some disk compression programs, such as Stacker, don't deal well with long filenames. Consider using DriveSpace 3 instead.

If you encounter problems using Microsoft Backup, consider the following:

- If Microsoft Backup doesn't detect your tape drive, consider that Microsoft Backup might not support your drive. Note also that the Add New Hardware Wizard does not detect tape drives. Don't be alarmed if you don't see your tape drive in the Device Manager; you must allow Microsoft Backup to detect it.

- If backing up to a tape drive is slower than 1.5MB per minute, you might have a conflict between the tape drive and video adapter. Work around this problem by starting the tape backup and opening a full-screen MS-DOS window until the backup finishes.

- Microsoft Backup works with QIC 40, 80, and 3010 drives connected to the primary floppy disk controller from Colorado Memory Systems, Conner, Iomega, and Wangtek. It also supports Colorado Memory Systems drives connected to the parallel port. Microsoft Backup does not support drives connected to the secondary floppy controller or any of the following drives:

  - Archive drives
  - Irwin AccuTrak tapes
  - Irwin drives
  - Mountain drives
  - QIC Wide tapes
  - QI 3020 drives
  - SCSI tape drives
  - Travan drives
  - Summit drives

# Chapter 6

# Configuring the Desktop

## Configuring Windows Explorer

Windows Explorer contains various settings that the user can change to affect how it looks and works. The user can control whether Windows Explorer displays hidden and system files, for instance, or whether it allows all-uppercase filenames. The majority of the options are check boxes, which make it possible for you to enable or disable an option. Hidden files is a group of option buttons, however, that enable you to choose between three different methods for displaying files in Windows Explorer. To configure Windows Explorer's options, follow these steps:

1. Choose View ⇨ Folder Options from the main menu and click the View tab.

2. Change each option that you want to change and then close the Folder Options dialog box to save your changes. The following list shows the available options, which are self-explanatory:

    - Remember each folder's view settings
    - Display the full path in the title bar
    - Hide file extensions for known file types
    - Show Map Network Drive button in toolbar

- Show file attributes in Detail view
- Show pop-up description for folder and desktop items
- Allow all-uppercase filenames
- Hidden files
- Hide icons when desktop is viewed as Web page
- Smooth edges of screen fonts
- Show window contents while dragging

The Advanced tab in the Internet Explorer Internet Properties dialog box looks very similar to the View tab in the Windows Explorer Folder Options dialog box, but it contains vastly different options. You can access the Internet Properties dialog box only from within Internet Explorer, by choosing View ⇨ Internet Options from the main menu, or by opening it from the Control Panel.

# Customizing How Folders Work

Part of the new Windows 98 Internet integration is making folders look and act like Web pages. This goes all the way down to making each filename look like a link and enabling the user to preview files in the left side of the folder. The Folder Options dialog box gives the user three options for controlling this feature:

- **Web Style** enables all Web-related features for Windows Explorer.

- **Classic Style** tells Windows Explorer to behave as it did in Windows 95.

- **Custom** enables the user to pick and choose the Web-related features.

To configure the Windows Explorer Web-related features, follow these steps:

**1.** Choose View ⇨ Folder Options from Windows Explorer's main menu and click the General tab.

2. Choose between Web style, Classic style, or Custom style. If you choose Custom, click the Settings button to see the Custom Settings dialog box. Select the options you want to enable, as described in the following list:

   - **Active Desktop**. Choose to use either the new Active Desktop or the Windows classic desktop. Click Customize to further configure the Active Desktop.

   - **Browse folders as follows**. Choose whether to open folders in the existing Explorer window or in a new window when browsing in a folder.

   - **View Web content in folders**. Choose whether to view all folders that have HTML content as Web pages or to view folders as Web pages only if you choose View ⇨ as Web Page from the Windows Explorer main menu.

   - **Click items as follows**. Choose the single-click or double-click interface. If you choose the single-click interface, you can also choose between underlining all folder names and filenames in the folder or underlining a folder name or filename only when you point at it.

3. Close the Custom Settings and Folder Options dialog boxes to save your changes.

## Displaying a Folder as a Web Page

Viewing a folder as a Web page is different from the classic style in that each folder contains a background image and additional text along the left side of the folder. To view a folder as a Web page, choose View ⇨ as Web Page from the main menu. The following list describes what you see in a variety of different types of folders:

   - **\Control Panel**. The folder contains a brief description of the selected Control Panel application on the left side, along with links to Microsoft's home page and technical support.

- **\Windows**. The folder initially contains a warning about tampering with the contents of this folder. Click the Show Files link, and Windows Explorer opens the contents of the folder, which looks like any other folder when viewed as a Web page.

- **\Dial-Up Networking**. The left side of the folder contains an overview of the selected connection, which includes the name, phone number, and modem.

- **\Normal Folders**. The left side of the folder contains the full filename and file type of the selected file, as well as the file's modification date and a preview, if one is available. Most image and HTML files can be previewed in Windows Explorer.

Aside from previewing a file on the left side of a folder, the user can also display a thumbnail of each file in place of its icon. This is particularly useful when one is viewing a folder that contains many images or HTML files. To display thumbnails, right-click the folder and choose Properties; then, select Enable thumbnail view, and close the folder's Properties dialog box. After enabling the thumbnail view, you switch to it by choosing View ⇨ as Web Page from the Windows Explorer main menu. You see this menu option only in folders for which you've enabled thumbnail views. Windows Explorer stores thumbnails in a Thumbs.db file that you find in each folder for which you've enabled thumbnail views.

For most users, the default HTML file that Windows Explorer uses to display a folder as a Web page is good enough. You can further customize it, however, by including additional text or changing the background image. You might want to include your corporate logo in the background of each folder, for instance, or provide a link to the company's technical support pages on the intranet. When you customize a folder, Windows Explorer creates a hidden file called Folder.htt in the folder. This file contains HTML content that

Windows Explorer uses to display the folder. To further customize how Windows Explorer displays a folder, follow these steps:

1. Choose View ⇨ Customize this Folder, from the Windows Explorer main menu. You see the Customize this Folder dialog box.

2. Choose one of the following options and click Next:

    - **Create or edit an HTML document**. Click Next, and Windows Explorer creates a file called Folder.htt in the folder and opens it in Notepad. Make your changes and save them to the given filename.

    - **Choose a background picture**. Windows Explorer presents a list of images from which you can choose. The images it displays are all in \Windows. Alternatively, click Browse to locate any image on the computer's hard disk. Click Next when finished.

    - **Remove customization**. Click Next, and Windows Explorer removes Folder.htt from the folder, restoring the folder to its original state before customization.

3. Close the Customize this Folder dialog box.

## Adding Actions to the Shortcut Menu

Users can right-click most objects in Windows Explorer to display a shortcut menu. This menu contains a list of actions that the user can perform on that particular type of object. For instance, right-click a Microsoft Word document and you can choose to Open, Print, or Delete it. Actions that you see at the top of a shortcut menu are specific to that particular file type. Actions that you see below the first line apply to almost all objects.

You can customize the top part of a file type's shortcut menu by adding actions to it. In reality, these actions are nothing more than file associations for each type that are stored in the Registry. DOC files are normally associated with WordPad, but if you install

Microsoft Word, Word associates DOC files with itself. However, you might want the option of choosing which program opens a file. Add WordPad to the DOC file's context menu, and you can choose Open to open the file in Microsoft Word, or choose Open in WordPad to open the document in WordPad. To add actions to a file type's context menu, follow these steps:

1. Open the Registry Editor. If you're editing a remote computer's Registry, connect to that computer by choosing Registry ⇨ Connect Network Registry from the main menu.

2. Under HKEY_CLASSES_ROOT, locate the file type to which you want to add an action. The easiest way to find the file type is to find the file extension first; then, note the default value entry, which contains the name of the file type associated with that extension.

3. Open the shell subkey under the file type.

4. Create a subkey under shell for the new action. Give this subkey a brief name that describes the action, such as "open in wordpad." Change the new subkey's default value entry so that it reflects the text you want to display on the context menu. Precede the option's hotkey with an ampersand (&), and Windows Explorer underlines it in the menu.

5. Create a subkey under the new action called command. Then, set this new subkey's default value entry to the command line that performs the action. For instance, to open the object in WordPad, the command line would be WordPad.exe "%1". Note that the quotes are required for some applications to correctly parse a command line that contains a long filename containing spaces. The extent of your changes should look like this:

```
HKEY_CLASSES_ROOT
    Filetype
```

```
Shell
    name
        (default) = menu text
        command
            (default) = command line
```

**6.** Your changes are immediate; close the Registry Editor.

Alternatively, you can add actions to a file type's shortcut menu by using the File Types tab of Windows Explorer's Folder Options dialog box by following these steps:

**1.** Choose View ⇨ Folder Options and click the File Types tab.

**2.** Select from the Registered file types the file type you want to edit. You can click New Type to create a new association between a particular file extension and program. After selecting or creating the file type, click Edit to display the Edit File Type dialog box.

**3.** Click New to add a new command to the file type's shortcut menu. Windows Explorer displays the New Action dialog box.

**4.** In the New Action dialog box, type the name of the command as you want to see it on the shortcut menu. You can prefix any letter with an ampersand to indicate it is a hotkey. In Application used to perform action, type the command line to execute when the user chooses this command. Alternatively, click Browse to locate the program you want to run.

**5.** Close the New Action, Edit File Type, and Folder Options dialog boxes to save your changes.

# Configuring the Active Desktop

The Active Desktop is another new feature that integrates Internet technology with Windows 98. It enables the user to view desktop content, such as icons and shortcuts, alongside Web-related content, which includes any HTML file or Active Desktop component. You can think of the Active Desktop as having two separate layers:

- **Icon layer.** The icon layer contains the local desktop content. This includes all the shortcuts and files that you find in \Windows\Desktop or, if user profiles are enabled, in \Windows\Profiles\\*User*\Desktop.

- **HTML layer.** The HTML layer contains all the Web-related content. This includes any Active Desktop components that you subscribe to on the Internet and, potentially, an HTML document used as wallpaper. You can include any HTML file on the desktop and then move and resize it as you see fit.

Users enable the Active Desktop by right-clicking any free space on the desktop and choosing Active Desktop ⇨ View as Web Page. Along the left side, they see the normal desktop icons, which are stored in \Windows\Desktop. Just to the right of the icons, they see a custom HTML file that's stored on the local computer, and on the bottom right they see the channel bar, which is an Active Desktop component. The background is HTML wallpaper, too, as opposed to a background image.

Microsoft makes a variety of Active Desktop components available for Windows 98. Many of these contain very little information and are more useful to keep you updated on, or provide links to, a larger Web site. You find the following components, among others, at http://www.microsoft.com/ie/ie40/-gallery.

- Stock ticker
- Internet search utility
- Weather map
- Sports ticker
- News ticker

# Creating an HTML Wallpaper

Users can create their own desktop wallpaper from any HTML file. The best reason to create wallpaper is if you want every desktop in the organization to have a similar look — perhaps a corporate logo. Regardless of how you create the HTML file, whether you use FrontPage Express or another product, keep the following notes in mind:

- **Keep the background color neutral.** The user can't override the background color of HTML wallpaper without either editing the HTML file or disabling the wallpaper.

- **Don't clutter the HTML wallpaper.** Keep the wallpaper simple. A few well-placed images that leave users plenty of space to organize their desktop icons will do the trick. Consider limiting any images to one corner of the desktop.

- **Use ALIGN and VALIGN attributes.** Use these attributes to align content at the top, bottom, left, or right of the desktop, so that Windows Explorer properly draws the background in all situations.

- **Check the wallpaper at various resolutions.** Unless you know for sure that all users in the organization use the same display resolution, test the wallpaper at all available resolutions to make sure that Windows Explorer draws it the way you intend.

To use an HTML file as the desktop's background wallpaper, follow these steps:

1. Open the Display Properties dialog box from the \Control Panel and click the Background tab.

2. Click Browse to locate the HTML file on the computer or network.

3. Close the Display Properties dialog box to save your changes.

Users will find that HTML wallpaper looks better if you set the desktop color so that it's the same as the background color used in the HTML file. That way, the background used behind each icon on the desktop blends in with the background of the HTML file.

## Adding Components to the Desktop

Active Desktop components are essentially HTML files, but they have a few interesting characteristics. Most components include objects, whether ActiveX or Java. Most components also are such that you subscribe to them, and Internet Explorer automatically downloads updated content to the desktop on a publisher-determined schedule. Examples of Active Desktop components include sports, news, stock tickers, maps, and other components that keep you updated with the latest content on a larger Web site. Windows 98 draws each Active Desktop component on the desktop in what's essentially a floating frame. You can move around each component, resize it, or close it. When you hover the mouse over a component, Windows 98 draws a border around it and puts a small title bar at the top. To work with an Active Desktop component's window, do the following:

- To move a component, hover the mouse over it until the title bar appears; then, drag the title bar to the component's new location.

- To resize a component, hover the mouse over it until the border appears; then, drag any side of the border to resize the window.

- To close a component, hover the mouse over it until the title bar appears; then, click the Close button.

- To redraw the component, right-click anywhere within it and choose Refresh from the context menu.

- To redownload the component from the Internet, right-click anywhere within it and choose Update Now.

Web pages from which you can subscribe to a component contain a button labeled something like Subscribe or Add Active Desktop Component. Clicking the button downloads the component's CDF file to the computer and adds a subscription to the \Subscriptions folder in \Windows. Regular subscriptions also provide Active Desktop components that you don't have to subscribe to separately; they're just part of the package. To add an Active Desktop component to the Windows 98 desktop, follow these steps:

1. Open the Display Properties dialog box from the Control Panel and click the Web tab.

2. Make sure that you enable View my Active Desktop as a Web page.

3. Click New to see a window that offers you a visit to the Active Desktop gallery. Click Yes if you want to see the components that Microsoft offers. Otherwise, click No and you see the New Active Desktop Item dialog box.

4. Type the URL of the component in the space provided. Optionally, Browse to locate an HTML file on the local computer.

5. Close the New Active Desktop Item dialog box to save your changes. This returns you to the Display Properties dialog box with the new component enabled.

You can add any HTML file to the desktop, including one that you create yourself and store on the local computer. You can add an HTML file that contains links to your favorite Web sites, for example, or an HTML file that submits the contents of a form to your favorite search engine. When building an HTML file for inclusion on the desktop, the most important thing to remember is to keep the content small so that it fits into a reasonable amount of space.

## Working with Desktop Shortcuts

Shortcuts work no differently in Windows 98 from the way they did in Windows 95. They provide links, which you can store anywhere on the disk, that open files in other locations. This section describes some of the ways you can create shortcuts. To create a shortcut, do any of the following:

- Drag an object with the right mouse button.
- Right-click in any folder and choose New ➪ Shortcut.
- Right-click an object and choose Send To ➪ Desktop as Shortcut.

Quickly locate a file to which you want to create a shortcut by using Find. Choose Find ➪ Files or Folders from the Start menu, type the name of the file, and then press Enter. After Find shows the file in the list, select the file and choose File ➪ Create Shortcut from the main menu.

# Customizing the Taskbar

The Windows 98 taskbar is greatly enhanced over the Windows 95 taskbar. The taskbar now has toolbars that enable you to launch documents and programs quickly, and the Start menu is improved. The following sections, "Toolbars" and "Start Menu," describe these new features. Users configure the taskbar by right-clicking on any unused part of the taskbar to open the Taskbar Properties dialog box. They can then choose from any of the following options:

- Always on top
- Auto hide
- Show small icons in Start menu
- Show clock

# Toolbars

Toolbars provide a quick way to open a document or application, just as toolbars in applications like WordPad provide quick access to commonly used features. Windows 98 creates a default toolbar called Quick Launch. This toolbar starts Internet Explorer and Outlook Express, among other programs. Right-click any open area on the taskbar and choose Toolbar; then, you can choose from any of the other available toolbars to add to the taskbar, as listed here:

- **Address**. This is the address toolbar from Internet Explorer. It provides a quick means to opening a Web site from the taskbar.

- **Links**. This is the links toolbar from Internet Explorer. The shortcuts in this toolbar come from \Windows\Favorites\Links.

- **Desktop**. This toolbar displays the contents of the desktop. It displays whatever shortcuts it finds in \Windows\Desktop.

Users can create new toolbars that contain shortcuts to any files on the disk. Toolbars display the contents of a folder, much as the Start menu displays the contents of \Windows\Start Menu. Note that users can create toolbars for any folder, including the \Control Panel, \Dial-Up Networking, or \My Computer folders. After they create a toolbar and specify a folder for it, they can add shortcuts to the toolbar by dragging shortcuts onto it, or they can drag shortcuts into the folder associated with the toolbar. To add a toolbar to the taskbar, follow these steps:

1. Right-click in any open area on the taskbar. Choose Toolbars ➪ New Toolbar. You see the New Toolbar dialog box.

2. Select a folder on the hard disk. The folder must already exist prior to your selecting it in the New Toolbar dialog box; you can't create the folder on the fly.

3. Close the New Toolbar dialog box to see the new toolbar.

To add a shortcut to a toolbar, do either of the following:

- Drag-and-drop a shortcut onto the toolbar.
- Drag-and-drop a shortcut into the toolbar's folder.

You can dock and undock toolbars by dragging them on and off the taskbar. This works just like dockable toolbars in applications such as Office.

## Start Menu

The Start menu contains several new submenus that did not exist in Windows 95:

- **Favorites**. This is the same menu you find in Internet Explorer and contains links to the user's favorite Web sites.
- **Documents**. This submenu contains a new persistent link to the \My Documents folder.
- **Settings**. This submenu now contains items for the Active Desktop, Folder Options, and Windows Update, in addition to those for the Taskbar, Control Panel, and Printers.
- **Find**. This submenu contains new items called On the Internet, which opens Internet Explorer's search site, and People, which opens Outlook Express' address book.

The most important new feature in the Start menu is that you can organize it in-place. You can certainly open the \Windows\Start menu in Windows Explorer and move the shortcuts around, as in Windows 95. Alternatively, you can move shortcuts around on the menu itself, which enables you to see changes as you make them. The Start menu even enables you to specify the exact placement of each shortcut on the menu, rather than sorting each menu alphabetically. You have this control only in the Programs and Favorites submenus, by the way, but not in any of the other submenus such as Settings.

Here are some common tasks that users can perform on the Start menu:

- To reposition an item or folder on a submenu, drag-and-drop it to its new location.

- To move an item or folder to a different subfolder, drag-and-drop it to its new folder. As you're dragging the file, Windows 98 opens any submenu to which you point, enabling you to drop the file on that submenu.

- To remove an item or folder from the Start menu, right-click the item and choose Remove. Confirm the operation.

- To change an item's properties, right-click it and choose Properties.

 **Tip**

You can quickly reset the sort order for the Start menu so that it's alphabetical, including the \Programs and \Favorites folders, by removing `HKEY_CURRENT_USER\Software\ Microsoft\Windows\CurrentVersion\Explorer\ MenuOrder` from the Registry.

# Using the Control Panel

The following table lists the icons available in the \Control Panel and the name of the property sheet that each icon opens. Each of the sections that follow describes the applications that are most useful for configuring how Windows 98 looks and feels. You see a more detailed description of each application when you view the \Control Panel as a Web page and highlight it. You can open the \Control Panel in Windows Explorer, in \My Computer, or from the Settings submenu on the Start menu.

| Clicking This Icon | Opens This Property Sheet |
|---|---|
| Add New Hardware | Add New Hardware Wizard |
| Add/Remove Programs | Add/Remove Programs Properties |
| Date/Time | Date/Time Properties |
| Display | Display Properties |
| Fonts | \Fonts folder in Explorer |
| Game Controllers | Game Controllers |
| Infrared | Infrared Monitor |
| Internet | Internet Properties |
| Keyboard | Keyboard Properties |
| Mail | Internet Accounts |
| Modems | Modems Properties |
| Mouse | Mouse Properties |
| Multimedia | Multimedia Properties |
| Network | Network |
| Passwords | Passwords Properties |
| PC Card (PCMCIA) | PC Card (PCMCIA) Properties |
| Power Management | Power Management Properties |
| Printers | Printers folder in Explorer |
| Regional Settings | Regional Settings Properties |
| Sounds | Sounds Properties |
| System | System Properties |
| Telephony | Telephony Properties |
| Users | Enable Multi-user Settings |

# Display

The Display Properties dialog box enables you to configure how Windows 98 looks. You can configure a screen saver, for example, or change the color and fonts used in each window. The following list describes the contents of each tab of the Display Properties dialog box:

- **Background**. Specify a picture or HTML file to use as the background for the desktop.

- **Screen Saver**. Select and configure the screen savers that Windows 98 provides.

- **Appearance**. Change the appearance of Window 98. You can change the color and size of each window component and the fonts used in various places. Alternatively, choose one of the predefined color-coordinated themes.

- **Effects**. Choose the special effects that you want to use in Windows 98. The most useful effects are Smooth edges of screen fonts, which makes the screen easier to read, and Show window contents while dragging, which enables you to drag-and-drop the entire window rather than just an outline of it.

- **Web**. Configure the Active Desktop.

- **Settings**. Change the display settings, including the color depth and resolution. You can also change monitor and display adapter settings. Note that you don't have to restart the computer to change color depth and resolution.

# Keyboard

The Keyboard Properties dialog box enables you to control how the keyboard feels in Windows 98. You can change *repeat delay*, which is the amount of time you must press a key before Windows 98 starts repeating it, and the *repeat rate*, which is how fast Windows 98 repeats a key. You can also change how fast the cursor blinks — a useful customization if you have trouble finding the text cursor on the screen.

# Mouse

The Mouse Properties dialog box provides the ability to change how the mouse behaves in Windows 98. Note that some vendors provide additional icons in addition to the Mouse icon in the \Control Panel. The following list describes each tab on this dialog box. Note that this dialog box might be a bit different for different types of mice.

- **Buttons**. Choose between using the mouse left- or right-handed. You can also specify the double-click speed, which is the amount of time that must pass between two mouse clicks before Windows 98 considers both clicks to be a double-click.

- **Pointers**. Pick one of the predefined pointer themes or click Browse to use a specific mouse pointer in a specific case. Windows 98 defines mouse pointers for each of the following cases:

    - Normal Select
    - Help Select
    - Working in Background
    - Busy
    - Precision Select
    - Text Select
    - Handwriting
    - Unavailable
    - Vertical Resize
    - Horizontal Resize
    - Diagonal Resize 1
    - Diagonal Resize 2
    - Move
    - Alternate Select
    - Link Select

- **Motion**. Enable features that make the mouse pointer easier to follow; this option is especially useful on portable computers. These options include Pointer speed, which specifies how fast the mouse pointer moves in relation to the movement of the mouse, and Pointer trail, which leaves an animated trail behind the mouse, much like exhaust trails left behind a jet.

## Sounds

The Sounds Properties dialog box enables you to associate sounds with different events in different applications. You can associate a sound with the Minimize event, for example, which causes that sound to play when you minimize a window.

Sounds are associated with applications. When you install an application, it registers the sound events it supports in the Registry. The Sounds Properties dialog box displays each registered application and the sound events it supports. You can then associate any sound file on the computer with the event of any registered application. Instead of specifying sounds for each individual event, you can select one of the predefined themes that come with Windows 98.

## Desktop Themes

Originally part of Microsoft Plus! (an optional Windows 95 add-on), Desktop Themes helps you personalize your computer with minimum effort. You choose a coordinated theme that contains colors, sounds, mouse pointers, and other elements; then, Windows 98 changes the appropriate settings in the Display Properties, Sounds Properties, and Mouse Properties dialog boxes. The following are included in each theme:

- Colors
- Desktop wallpaper
- Font and window sizes
- Font names and styles

- Icons
- Mouse pointers
- Screen savers
- Sound events

Desktop Themes is an optional component that you can add either when you install Windows 98 or later by using the Add/Remove Programs Properties dialog box. Change themes by using the Desktop Themes dialog box, which you open from the \Control Panel. This dialog box enables you to select a theme, preview each portion of a theme, and even create your own custom themes. Administrators might want to create a corporate theme using Desktop Themes and distribute it to each workstation on the network by using policies.

# Customizing Windows 98 with Tweak UI

Windows 98 comes with a utility called Tweak UI that enables the user to customize the Windows 98 user interface. You find it on the Windows 98 CD-ROM in the Resource Kit sampler; it's in \Tools\Reskit\PowerToy. To install it, right-click Tweakui.inf and choose Install. Open TweakUI from the \Control Panel. The following list describes each tab on this dialog box:

- **Mouse**. Customize how the mouse works. For example, you can configure the mouse to automatically bring windows to the front as you point at them.

- **General**. Configure any special effects, as well as the location of any special folders and the search tool used by Internet Explorer.

- **Explorer**. Customize Windows Explorer. You can specify whether shortcuts have an overlay, for instance, or whether Windows Explorer saves its settings when you close it.

- **IE4**. Customize various Internet Explorer settings.

- **Desktop**. Choose the icons that you want to display on the desktop. This tab also enables you to create shortcuts to various system folders, which you can put anywhere on the computer.

- **My Computer**. Choose the drives that appear in \My Computer.

- **Control Panel**. Choose the applications that appear in \Control Panel.

- **Network**. Configure Windows 98 to log the user on to the network automatically, without the user first having to specify a name or password.

- **New**. Specify which file types appear when you right-click a folder and choose New. You can simply hide a file type or remove it altogether.

- **Add/Remove**. Add applications to or remove them from the list of programs that you can uninstall. This is useful if you manually removed a program from the computer but its entry still appears in the Add/Remove Programs Properties dialog box.

- **Boot**. Configure boot options for the computer.

- **Repair**. Repair various components in Windows 98. For instance, you can rebuild the icon cache or look for errors in the file associations stored in the Registry.

- **Paranoia**. Clear various history lists, including the Document, Find in Files, Last User at logon history lists. You can also choose whether data and audio CDs start playing immediately after inserting them.

# Administering the Interface

As an administrator, you might have requirements for managing the configuration of each user's workstation, including the look and feel. You use the System Policy Editor to create policy files (POL) that

Windows 98 automatically downloads to the users' computers each time they log on to the network, thereby increasing the amount of control you have over their computers. The possibilities for administering the user's desktop include the following:

- **User profiles**. User profiles enable each user to maintain his or her own settings, even if more than one user shares the same computer.

- **Mandatory user profiles**. Mandatory user profiles assure that each user starts the session with the same settings every time he or she logs on to the computer. This is a bit draconian, however, because every setting is specified by the administrator, leaving the user with no way to customize or personalize the computer.

- **System policies**. System policies enable you to choose certain settings that you might want to force each user to use. You can specify policies for an individual, a group of users, or a group of computers.

- **Custom setup scripts**. Custom setup scripts are your best opportunity to start each user with a similar configuration. You can choose the options that Windows 98 installs, set an initial configuration, and configure each workstation for remote administration so that you can use profiles and system policies.

Windows 98 defines a plethora of policies that you can use to control the user interface. The policy files called Common.adm and Windows.adm contain few useful settings for the interface, but you can find extremely useful settings in a policy file called Shellm.adm. Make sure that you don't have a policy file open, and then choose Options ⇨ Policy Template from the main menu; then, click Add to add Shellm.adm to your list of templates. Setup installs this file in \Windows\Inf, so you might have to explicitly type the path if the system files are hidden. The following list describes the user-specific policy categories available in this policy file. Take special note of the

Start Menu policies, which contain settings most commonly requested by administrators:

- **Desktop** contains policies that enable you to prevent users from changing the Active Desktop. You can prevent users from changing the desktop wallpaper, for example, or prevent them from adding components to the Active Desktop. Take particular note of the following subcategories:

  - **Desktop Restrictions** contains policies that allow you to disable the Active Desktop, prevent changes to the Active Desktop, and hide the Internet Explorer icon.

  - **Active Desktop Items** enables you to prevent the user from adding, deleting, editing, or closing any Active Desktop items.

  - **Desktop Wallpaper Settings** contains policies that disable HTML wallpaper or prevent the user from changing the wallpaper.

  - **Desktop Toolbars Settings** enables you to disable toolbars altogether or prevent the user from resizing toolbars.

- **Start Menu** enables you to remove individual items from a user's Start menu, including Programs, Favorites, Find, Run, and Logoff. You can also disable the document and Run history lists.

- **Shell** contains policies that control how the Explorer shell works. Try disabling the use of context menus in the shell, which is another request heard from administrators who need to lock down a workstation. You can also disable the new Windows 98 user interface and revert to the classic Windows 95 user interface.

# Chapter 7

# Connecting to the Internet

## Creating an Internet Connection

Of the many ways you can connect to the Internet, the following four are built into the Windows 98 operating system:

- Use the Internet Connection Wizard to configure Windows 98 and each client to connect to the Internet automatically.

- Join one of the online service providers that Windows 98 includes in C:\Program Files\Online Services. You can choose between America Online, AT&T WorldNet, CompuServe, the Microsoft Network, and Prodigy.

- Install Dial-Up Network and TCP/IP; then, configure your own Dial-Up Networking connection to your Internet service provider.

- Connect to the Internet via your local area network, which probably means you must configure the computer for a proxy server.

Before configuring Windows 98 to connect to the Internet, you must have a connection available. Internet service providers (ISPs) are a dime a dozen and are easy to find in any metropolitan area.

Alternatively, your telephone company probably offers Internet connectivity. If all else fails, however, you can use the online services that come with Windows 98, or you can use the Internet Connection Wizard to set up an account with one of the many national service providers. The national providers provide service to more areas than smaller service providers, but the smaller providers generally have better service and lower prices. To set up an online service provider in Windows 98, follow these steps:

1. Determine which service provider you want to use: America Online, AT&T WorldNet, CompuServe, the Microsoft Network, or Prodigy.

2. Choose Programs ⇨ Online Services from the Start menu, and pick the online service you chose in the previous step.

3. Follow the instructions that you see on the screen to set up an account with the chosen provider and install its software on your computer.

After installing an online service provider on your computer, you can save a small bit of disk space by removing the online services files from your computer. To do so, remove the Online Services component on the Windows Setup tab of the Add/Remove Programs Properties dialog box.

## Connecting with Dial-Up Networking

To use Dial-Up Networking to connect to an ISP, you must do the following:

1. Obtain a connection to the Internet. (See preceding section for details.)

2. Install TCP/IP and Dial-Up Networking on your computer.

3. Install a modem that's compatible with your ISP.

4. Create and configure a Dial-Up Networking connection that dials the ISP and logs on to its network.

To install TCP/IP, follow these steps:

1. Open the Network dialog box from the Control Panel.

2. Click Add, choose Protocols from the list, and click Add again.

3. Choose Microsoft from the list of manufacturers and TCP/IP from the list of protocols.

4. Click OK to close the Select Network Protocol dialog box, and close the Network dialog box to copy the required files to your computer.

5. Restart the computer.

You install Dial-Up Networking via the Windows Setup tab in the Add/Remove Programs Properties dialog box. After the Setup program copies the required files to your computer, you'll have to restart the computer.

After installing the required software, TCP/IP, and Dial-Up Networking, you must configure your computer to connect to the ISP. The instructions you see in this section work for most service providers, but if your ISP has special requirements, consult with it to find out how best to configure your connection.

To create a new Dial-Up Networking connection, follow these steps:

1. Open the Dial-Up Networking folder from My Computer or within Windows Explorer.

2. Double-click the Make New Connection icon. The Make New Connection Wizard appears. If no connections are present in the folder, the wizard appears automatically.

3. Type a name for your connection, and choose the modem that you want to use with it. Click Next to specify the service provider's phone number.

4. Type the area code and phone number of your ISP in the spaces provided, and optionally, choose the country where the service provider is located. Click Next to continue.

5. Click Finish to save your connection in the Dial-Up Networking folder.

To configure your Dial-Up Networking connection for your service provider, follow these steps:

1. Open the connection's property sheet from the Dial-Up Networking folder by right-clicking it and choosing Properties. Click the Server Types tab.

2. Deselect Log on to network so that Windows 98 does not try to log on to your service provider as though it were an NT or NetWare network. Make sure also that TCP/IP is the only protocol selected at the bottom of the dialog box. The Server Types tab should look the same as the one shown in Figure 7-1.

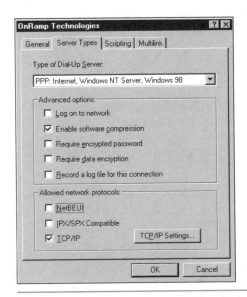

**Figure 7-1** *Make sure this dialog box looks the same in your connection.*

3. Click the TCP/IP Settings button to open the TCP/IP Settings dialog box. If your Internet service provider does not dynamically assign a DNS server, which is usually the case, select Specify Name Server Address, and fill in the DNS server's IP addresses in the spaces provided. Then, if your ISP provides you a static IP address, which is usually not the case, select Specify An IP Address, and type your IP in the space provided. Click OK to save your changes.

4. Close the Dial-Up Networking connection's property sheet to save your changes.

Some ISPs don't support PAP or CHAP, which are password authorization protocols that Dial-Up Networking can use to log you on to the ISP automatically. In addition, Windows 98 can't automatically log you on to the ISP if you're using a Serial Line Internet Protocol (SLIP) connection, an older connection protocol that's not used much. If you find yourself in either of these situations, you can use a script to connect to the ISP automatically. Open the Dial-Up Networking connection's property sheet, and click the Scripting tab, which is where you specify the location of a script to use for connecting to the ISP. Click Browse, and four scripts are displayed in the Open dialog box. In almost every case, one of the following scripts automatically logs you on to your ISP:

- **Cis.scp** logs on to CompuServe.

- **Pppmenu.scp** logs on to ISPs that use a Point-to-Point Protocol (PPP) menu to gain access to the ISP.

- **Slip.scp** logs on to ISPs that use the SLIP connection protocol instead of PPP.

- **Slipmenu.scp** logs on to ISPs that use the SLIP connection protocol as well as the SLIP menu, which is similar to a PPP menu.

Manually configuring your computer to connect to an ISP is probably a bit more work than you need to take on. The Internet Connection Wizard, which Windows 98 provides with Internet Explorer 4.0, automatically configures your computer to connect to the Internet after asking a few simple questions. The following instructions help you use the Internet Connection Wizard to connect to the Internet:

1. Choose Programs ⇨ Internet Explorer ⇨ Connection Wizard from the Start menu. You see the Internet Connection Wizard's first dialog box, which presents you with the following options:

   • I want to sign up and configure my computer for a new Internet account. (If you select this option, make sure that your telephone line is connected to your modem.)

   • I have an existing Internet account through my phone line or a local area network (LAN). Help me set up my computer to connect to this Internet account.

   • My computer is already set up for the Internet. Do not show this wizard again.

2. Choose one of the options described in the previous step, and then follow the instructions that you see on the screen. The steps that the Internet Connection Wizard walks you through depend on how you answer its questions, but you see many of the following steps in various orders:

   • **Setting Up Your Computer for the First Time**. This step installs the software required to connect to the Internet, including Dial-Up Networking and TCP/IP. It also checks your modem and dialing properties to make sure they're correct.

- **Signing Up for an Internet Account**. The Internet Connection Wizard starts Internet Explorer to display a list of ISPs from which you can choose. It uses Microsoft's referral service to obtain this list, so you must connect your computer's modem to a phone line if you chose the first option in Step 1.

- **Setting Up Your Internet Software**. The Internet Connection Wizard installs the software required to connect to the ISP you chose. After this step, you'll be able to browse the Internet by using either Internet Explorer or Exchange e-mail with Outlook Express Mail and News.

## Connecting via the Network

Microsoft Proxy is one of the most popular commercial proxy servers for Windows NT networks because it integrates fully with Internet Information Server. Other proxy servers, such as the one sold by Netscape, work equally well. You can even find a handful of lightweight shareware proxy servers at shareware sites such as http://www.hotfiles.com. Regardless of the vendor that provides your proxy server, the servers all work about the same. Each user must install client software on his or her computer that knows how to send Winsock requests to the proxy server. That means that the proxy server client must replace the Winsock libraries on the user's computer. Installing the client for Microsoft Proxy is straightforward: run the setup program you find in the \Mspclnt share on the NT server. The setup program automatically installs the client, replaces the Winsock libraries, and configures your browser to use the proxy.

Most Winsock applications work flawlessly with the proxy server, requiring no changes to their configuration, because the Winsock applications unknowingly use Winsock libraries that are designed to route requests to the proxy server rather than via the normal channels. You sometimes must configure your Web browser to take advantage of the cache on the proxy server, however. In Internet Explorer, you do that on the Connections tab of the

Internet Options dialog box. To configure Internet Explorer for a proxy server, follow these steps:

1. Choose View ⇨ Internet Options from Internet Explorer's main menu, and click the Connection tab.

2. Select Connect to the Internet using a local area network.

3. Select Access the Internet using a proxy server, and configure your proxy server appropriately. That is, type the address of the proxy server in Address and its port number in Port. If you must configure a different proxy or port for individual protocols, click Advanced.

4. Click OK to close the Internet Options dialog box.

If you have a direct network connection to the Internet and that connection isn't provided by a proxy server, you must specify the address of the DNS server that translates host names into IP addresses. You do that on the DNS Configuration tab of the TCP/IP Properties dialog box, which you open from the Network dialog box in the Control Panel. You might also have to configure a gateway for your connection on the Gateway tab of the TCP/IP Properties dialog box. If in doubt, consult with your ISP to check the TCP/IP settings you should use.

To configure DNS for a direct LAN connection to the Internet, follow these steps:

1. Open the Network dialog box from the Control Panel.

2. Select TCP/IP from the list of networking components, click Properties, and click the DNS Configuration tab of the TCP/IP Properties dialog box.

3. Select Enable DNS, and type your host and domain names in the spaces provided.

4. In DNS Server Search Order, type the IP address of your DNS server, and click Add.

5. Close the TCP/IP Properties and Network dialog boxes to save your changes, and restart the computer when prompted.

To configure a gateway for your LAN connection to the Internet, follow these steps:

1. Open the Network dialog box from the Control Panel.

2. Select TCP/IP from the list of networking components, click Properties, and click the Gateway tab of the TCP/IP Properties dialog box.

3. In New Gateway, type the gateway required for your Internet connection, and then click Add.

4. Close the TCP/IP Properties and Network dialog boxes to save your changes, and restart the computer when prompted.

You can use the Internet Explorer Administration Kit Profile Manager to configure each user's Internet connection automatically. Use the Kit to create a custom configuration that includes the connection, and then distribute that connection to each user. The users don't even have to know that they're using a proxy server because the configuration you create takes care of these details for them.

# Securing Internet Explorer 4.0

If you see a padlock on the right side of the status bar, you know that you are on a site that has security. You can also assume that the site is secure if the URL begins with the protocol https. If you want to know just what type of security the site is using, right-click in a clear area of the page that you are viewing, and choose Properties ⇨ Security tab.

If you look at the \Windows\Temporary Internet Files folder, you'll notice the random names for the four subfolders. This is a security feature. Theoretically, someone can embed a destructive program in a Web page and then run it from the cache, but he or she must have the exact path name. This is not as easy to determine with four random subfolder names.

# Cookies

Internet Explorer stores cookies in \Windows\Cookies. The cookie filenames usually consist of your host name followed by an @ symbol and then the name of the Web site. The files have a .txt extension and are readable, but they don't make much sense.

If you have Internet Explorer set to warn you about incoming cookies, you'll get a cookie alert message. You can choose whether to accept the cookie. If you want to accept all cookies, you can turn off this warning mechanism by choosing View ➪ Internet Options and clicking the Advanced tab. Under Cookies, mark Always Accept Cookies. If you don't want any cookies on your computer, mark Disable All Cookie Use.

# Security Zones

Microsoft's security model divides Internet sites into four different types, or *zones*:

- **Local Intranet Zone** comprises Web sites within your own company.
- **Trusted Sites Zone** comprises sites that you expect won't contain a computer virus or harmful code.
- **Restricted Sites Zone** comprises sites that *do* contain the potential risk of viruses and antisocial behaviors.
- **Internet Zone** comprises everything else.

The Security tab on Internet Explorer's Internet Options dialog box enables you to set a different level of security for each zone: High, Medium, Low, or Custom. You need to add the Web sites by name in the first three zones for this security system to work. To fully customize each zone, select the zone in the Zone drop-down list, click the Custom option button, and then click the Settings button to display the Security Settings dialog box. Table 7-1 shows the choices you're making when you adopt a High, Medium, or Low security setting.

**Table 7-1** *Internet Explorer's Security Settings*

| Description of Event | High | Medium | Low |
| --- | --- | --- | --- |
| Script ActiveX controls marked safe for scripting | Enable | Enable | Enable |
| Run ActiveX controls and plug-ins | Disable | Enable | Enable |
| Download signed ActiveX controls | Disable | Prompt | Enable |
| Download unsigned ActiveX controls | Disable | Disable | Prompt |
| Initialize and script ActiveX controls not marked as safe | Disable | Disable | Prompt |
| Java permissions (security level) | High | High | Low |
| Active scripting | Enable | Enable | Enable |
| Scripting of Java applets | Disable | Enable | Enable |
| File downloads | Disable | Enable | Enable |
| Font downloads | Prompt | Enable | Enable |
| User Authentication / Logon | Prompt | Automatic | Automatic |
| Submit nonencrypted form data | Prompt | Prompt | Enable |
| Launching applications and files in an IFRAME | Disable | Prompt | Enable |
| Installation of desktop items | Disable | Prompt | Enable |
| Drag-and-drop or copy and paste files | Prompt | Enable | Enable |
| Software channel permissions | High | Medium | Low |

In addition to the security settings in the Security tab of the Internet Options dialog box, other setting are located in the Advanced tab of the same dialog box. Scroll down to the Security heading to display the choices:

- PCT and SSL refer to *Private Communications Technology* and *Secure Sockets Layer*, respectively. These are two encryption standards that let you enter sensitive information, such as credit card numbers, in Web page forms. Few reasons exist to turn off these settings, unless you want to send out your credit card number as plain text.

- Do Not Save Encrypted Pages to Disk turns off some of the Windows 98 caching. Doing so could hurt your Internet browsing performance.

- I recommend clearing the box labeled Warn If Changing Between Secure and Not Secure Mode, unless you've turned off PCT or SSL for some reason. I also suggest that you keep Check for Certificate Revocation turned off and keep Warn About Invalid Site Certificates turned on.

# Configuring the Cache and History

To make sure that you have the latest information from a site, you can force Internet Explorer to retrieve a new copy of a Web page instead of using a copy from the cache. Just choose View ⇨ Refresh or press the F5 key. Here are additional ways in which you can manage the cache and history folders:

- You can designate one of three times for Internet Explorer to refresh a Web page: every time you view it, each time you start Internet Explorer, or not until you press F5. To do this, choose View ⇨ Internet Options in an Internet Explorer window, and click the General tab; then, click the Settings button, and choose from the options at the top of the Settings dialog box.

- You can also set the size of the Internet cache folder (\Windows\Temporary Internet Files) in the Settings dialog box. Slide the slider, located under Amount of Disk Space to Use, to a percentage of the hard disk that you are willing to use for caching these Internet files.

- Click the View Files button in the Settings dialog box to view the contents of Internet Explorer's cache. If you order the files by Internet address, all the files from the same site show up next to each other.

## Cache Folder

If some of the files in your Internet cache are corrupt, this can lead to Internet Explorer crashes and various error messages. These include errors indicating cross-linked files and Kernel32.dll errors. If the errors are not so bad that you can't start Internet Explorer, click the Internet Explorer icon, choose Views ⇨ Internet Options, and then click the Delete Files button in the General tab. You should also click the Clear History button. To delete files from the Internet cache when you can't start Internet Explorer, follow these steps:

1. Choose Start ⇨ Shut Down ⇨ Restart in MS-DOS Mode ⇨ OK.

2. At the DOS prompt, type `Attrib -s c:\Windows\Tempor~1`, and press Enter.

3. At the DOS prompt, type `Deltree \Windows\Tempor~1`, and press Enter.

4. Type `exit`, and press Enter.

You can tell Internet Explorer to store its cached files in a different folder, which might be a good idea if you have limited space on the drive that contains the \Windows folder. To specify a different folder for your cached Web pages, right-click the Internet Explorer icon on your desktop, choose Properties ⇨ General tab, click the Settings button, and then click the Move Folder button. In the Browse for Folder dialog box, highlight the desired folder, and click OK. You have to restart Windows for the change to take effect. Note that when you specify a new cache folder, Internet Explorer deletes all the cached files from the original folder.

## History Folder

If you get error messages stating that not enough memory exists when you try to view the History folder, you might have too many entries for Internet Explorer to handle correctly. If clicking your Clear History button (View ⇨ Internet Options ⇨ General ⇨ Clear History) doesn't get rid of these error messages, take the following steps:

1. Choose Start ⇨ Shut Down ⇨ Restart in MS-DOS Mode ⇨ OK.

2. At the DOS prompt, type `Attrib -s c:\Windows\Tempor~1`, and press Enter.

3. Type `Deltree \Windows\Tempor~1`, and press Enter.

4. Type `Attrib -s c:\Windows\History`, and press Enter.

5. Type `Deltree \Windows\History`, and press Enter.

6. Type `exit`, and press Enter.

After you run Regsvr32, you might discover that the Desktop.ini file in your History folder has been deleted. As a precaution, you might want to put a copy of it in your personal My System folder before you run Regsvr32. To create a copy of the Desktop.ini file that's stored in the History folder, use Notepad to create a text file with the following contents:

```
[.ShellClassInfo]
UICLSID={FF393560-C2A7-11CF-BFF4-444553540000}
CLSID={FF393560-C2A7-11CF-BFF4-444553540000}
```

Save this file as History\Desktop.ini. When and if you need to put it back in your History folder, copy it there, rename it as Desktop.ini, and set its attribute to hidden.

# Using the IEAK Profile Manager

The *Windows 98 Resource Kit*, published by Microsoft, automatically installs the Internet Explorer Administration Kit (IEAK) Profile Manager. This administrative tool enables you to customize Internet Explorer's configuration to a great degree. Like the System Policy Editor, the IEAK Profile Manager enables you to create custom configurations for groups, individual users, or the default user. You can then package Internet Explorer together with these configuration files for distribution throughout the organization, or you can put the configuration files on the network and point each user's browser to them.

You access the IEAK Profile Manager from the Microsoft Management Console; the program is called Profmgr.exe, and it's located in the Deployment Tools folder. If you don't find it there, run it from Netadmin\Profmgr on the CD-ROM. The Profile Manager's window is divided into two panes. The left pane shows an outline containing a variety of objects, and the right pane shows options for each object. Select an object in the left pane, and set options for it in the right pane. Then, save the profile by choosing File ⇨ Save from the main menu. As a result, the Profile Manager creates an INS file and one or more CAB files that contain an assortment of other configuration files.

You have a few different choices for deploying your custom configuration to the organization:

- Package Internet Explorer's source files along with your custom configuration files, and distribute those files for installation.

- Post the INS and other CAB files to the server, and configure Internet Explorer to use those settings on the Connection tab of the Internet Options dialog box.

- Distribute the custom configuration via Internet Explorer's open software distribution (OSD) technology, which makes online software distribution via the intranet possible.

The *Microsoft Internet Explorer Resource Kit*, published by Microsoft, contains much more information about using the IEAK Profile Manager. The *Windows 98 Resource Kit* contains a few pages of information, but not enough to help you use the Administration Kit for serious deployment in your organization.

# Troubleshooting Internet Explorer

If you have URLs in your History folder whose names are longer than 256 characters, Disk Defragmenter might hang. ScanDisk won't find any problems. You can get around this problem by deleting the History folder.

If you have enabled the Content Advisor rating system, you may find that Internet Explorer takes its own sweet time downloading Web sites. Check to see whether you can speed up your browsing by disabling ratings. In Internet Explorer, choose View ⇨ Internet Options ⇨ Content tab, and then click the Disable button.

Numerous problems with the Windows 98 interface can be traced to a corrupt password file. If this happens, you may get this error message: `MPREXE caused an invalid page fault in module Kernel32.dll`. If you get this message, delete or rename the files in the \Windows folder that have the extension PWL.

If you are trying to view your own start page and you get an error message stating that Internet Explorer can't find the site, you may have an old, missing, or corrupt Url.dll file. One potential source of the problem is that if you uninstalled earlier beta versions of Netscape Navigator, they didn't restore the original Url.dll file. To fix Url.dll, follow these steps:

1. If you can find the Url.dll file in the Windows\System folder, remove or rename it.

2. At a DOS prompt, type `copy C:\Windows\Sysbckup\Url.dll C:\Windows\System`, and then press Enter.

3. Choose Start ⇨ Shut Down ⇨ Restart ⇨ OK.

You can set Internet Explorer to open in its own memory space each time it is invoked. It takes a bit longer to start (because it has to read the executable code again instead of using the code that is already in memory) and uses a little more memory. You set Internet Explorer to use a new process by choosing View ⇨ Internet Options ⇨ Advanced tab and marking the check box labeled Browse in a New Process.

# Publishing a Peer Web

If the Personal Web Server (PWS) is not already installed, install it using the Add/Remove Programs icon in the Control panel.

Administration is performed from the Personal Web Manager, which you can start either by double-clicking the Personal Web Server icon in the taskbar or by choosing Start ⇨ Internet Explorer ⇨ Personal Web Server ⇨ Personal Web Manager. The following five windows are associated with the Personal Web Manager:

- **Main window.** This window displays the domain name that is used to access PWS. You can view and modify the home directory (physical directory) that is used as the home directory for the Web server. The Main window also includes a button to stop and start the Web server, and a set of monitoring statistics.

- **Publish window.** This window contains a wizard that publishes files to the Web server's WebPub directory (\InetPub\WebPub). These files are automatically included on the home page that is created through the Web Site window

- **Web Site window.** This window contains a wizard for creating or changing a personal home page. The home page can include a guest book in which people leave you messages. This window also provides access to the guest book messages that people have left.

- **Tour window.** This window contains a quick overview of the features of Personal Web Server.

- **Advanced window.** This is the primary configuration window for PWS. The parameters available from this window are the following:

    - *Virtual Directories* enables maintenance of the mappings between virtual and physical directories. The virtual directory structure for the Web site is displayed in an Explorer-style tree.

    - *Default Document* provides control over whether the browser looks for default documents when no document name is specified and, if so, what the name of the default document should be.

- *Allow Directory Browsing* determines whether a directory content list is displayed if no default document is present.

- *Save Web Site Activity Log*, if checked, enables logging of site visitors and what they access.

To define your \Web98 directory as a virtual directory, follow these steps:

1. From the Main page in Personal Web Manager, note the http name assigned to your server's home page. You need the http name to reference anything on your Web server. This name is equivalent to an Internet domain name, such as `www.idg books.com`.

2. From the Advanced tab in Personal Web Manager, highlight the existing virtual directory that will contain the new virtual directory. For this example, highlight the Home directory. Click the Add button.

3. In the Directory property field, enter the physical directory path (c:\Web98, for example). In the Alias field, enter the name you want to use to refer to this directory through the Web server (Web98, for example). Click OK.

4. Verify that the new virtual directory exists in the list. Call up the browser and access your new directory by requesting `http://home page/Web98`. If your new directory contains a default document, it should be displayed. If not, you should get a directory listing of the Web98 contents, assuming you have checked Allow Directory Browsing on the Advanced tab.

# Installing the FrontPage Server Extensions

Before publishing HTML documents to PWS, you must make sure that you've installed the FrontPage Server Extensions:

1. Click the Upgrade button to ensure that your Server Extensions are up to date and not left over from some old FrontPage beta you downloaded and installed some time ago.

2. Click the Check and Fix button. This checks your Personal Web Server installation and makes sure that all required files and directory authorizations are accounted for. This option corrects any problems it finds, such as missing or corrupt files.

3. After your FrontPage Extensions have been verified, you are ready to begin saving Web pages with Web Publishing Wizard and accessing them through your Personal Web Server. Before you leave the FrontPage Server Administrator, take a look at the Help facility. Help contains a good list of "how to" instructions, including how to change the name of your server's root directory.

## Saving Web Pages with Web Publishing Wizard

Choose either File ➪ Save or File ➪ Save As in FrontPage Express to invoke the Web Publishing Wizard automatically. You can use the following process to save any Web page to your http://*servername*/Web98 directory. To save a Web page with Web Publishing Wizard, follow these steps:

1. Open the HTML file. Choose File ➪ Save As.

2. Enter a title and the URL where you want your page to be saved (for example, http://*servername*/Web98/website.htm). Click OK.

3. If your page contains a graphic, you are first asked where to save the graphic. By default, Web Publishing Wizard suggests the same Web server directory that contains your Web page. You may, however, change the location to a different directory (for example, http://*servername*/Web98/images/sampgif.gif). The good news is that wherever you place the graphic, Web

Publishing Wizard adjusts the link on the page to point to the proper place. Specify the desired image location, and click Yes.

4. After the save process completes, return to the browser and request the URL location where you saved your Web page. After the Web page appears, choose View ⇨ Source from the browser, and review the code that was generated by FrontPage Express and published by Web Publishing Wizard.

# Chapter 8

# Working with Applications

## Installing Applications

You use different steps to install Windows 98, Windows 3.1, and MS-DOS applications. Vendors design Windows 98 applications so that you can easily install and remove them by using the Add/Remove Programs Properties dialog box. These applications log information in the Registry, such as the path to the uninstall program, so that you can automatically remove them. When you install a Windows 98 application by using Add/Remove Programs, Add/Remove Programs searches the CD-ROM and floppy drives for Setup.exe or Install.exe. If it finds either file, it launches the program to start the installation. You can start the installation program in Windows Explorer, incidentally, and still get the benefit of automatically removing the application by using Add/Remove Programs.

To install a Windows 98 application by using the Add/Remove Programs, follow these steps:

1. Insert your CD-ROM or floppy disk in the appropriate drive. If you insert a CD-ROM and the setup program automatically starts, the CD-ROM supports *autorun*; if so, follow the setup instructions you see on-screen.

2. Open the Add/Remove Programs Properties dialog box from the Control Panel.

3. Click Install to see the Install Program from Floppy Disk or CD-ROM dialog box.

4. Click Next to move to the Run Installation Program dialog box. In Command line for installation program, you see the setup program that Add/Remove Programs found. If this program is incorrect, click Browse to locate the setup program elsewhere on the computer.

5. Click Finish, and Add/Remove Programs launches the setup program.

You can launch a Windows 3.1 or MS-DOS application's installation program automatically by using Add/Remove Programs, but only if the program is called Setup.exe or Install.exe and is located in the root folder of the installation disk. Windows 3.1 and MS-DOS applications don't store uninstall information in the Registry, so you won't be able to remove them automatically. If the installation program is called something other than Setup.exe or Install.exe, you must start it by using Windows Explorer or by changing the command line in the Add/Remove Programs dialog box. If you upgrade Windows 3.1 to Windows 98, Windows 98 automatically moves information regarding your applications to the Registry and creates shortcuts for them on the Start menu. If you install Windows 98 in a different folder, though, you have to reinstall your Windows 3.1 applications in Windows 98.

To install an application that doesn't have an installation program, follow these steps:

1. Create a folder under C:\Program Files for the application. You can use a long filename for the folder, even if you're installing a Windows 3.1 or MS-DOS application.

2. Copy all the application's files to the new folder. If the files are compressed, uncompress them. If it's a ZIP file, for instance, you can use WinZip to decompress it.

3.  Create a shortcut on the Start menu for the application's EXE file. Then, on the Start menu, right-click the application's shortcut, choose Properties, and make sure the command line and working directories use 8.3 filenames. The 8.3 filename for C:\Program Files is C:\Progra~1, for example. Here's where to find the path for Windows 3.1 and MS-DOS applications:

    - **Windows 3.1 applications**. Click the Shortcut tab. Check the paths in Target and Start in.

    - **MS-DOS applications**. Click the Program tab. Check the paths in Cmd line and Working.

### Caution

Make backup copies of Config.sys and Autoexec.bat before installing a Windows 3.1 application in Windows 98. After installing the application, make sure the installation program didn't add unnecessary lines to either file. Some Windows 3.1 installation programs add Share.exe to your Autoexec.bat file, for example, which is not required in Windows 98.

# Adding Components to and Removing Them from Windows 98 Applications

To add or remove components for an installed application, follow these steps:

1.  Open the Add/Remove Programs Properties dialog box from the Control Panel.

2.  From the list of applications, select the application you want to modify.

3.  Click Add/Remove. To add to or remove components from the application, follow the instructions you see in the setup program.

4.  Close the Add/Remove Programs Properties dialog box.

Some setup programs don't enable you to add or remove components after the application is installed. If you want to change such an application's setup, you must completely reinstall the application.

# Installing Applications in a Dual-Boot Configuration

If you created a dual-boot configuration by installing Windows 98 in a separate folder from Windows NT or Windows 3.1, you must reinstall your already-installed applications to use them in Windows 98. You can't just copy shortcuts from Windows NT to Windows 98, because the application's configuration data is stored in the Windows NT Registry, not the Windows 98 Registry. Sometimes, an application installs support files in the Windows NT folder, too, that it won't find in the Windows 98 folder.

When you reinstall an application in Windows 98, make sure you install the application in the exact same folder in which it's already installed. That way, you won't waste disk space by having two different copies of the application's binary files. Even though you install an application in the exact same folder, you'll have two different configurations for the application. Settings that you make while running the application in Windows NT won't be reflected in Windows 98, and vice versa. Note also that you should be careful when removing the application from one operating system or the other. Make sure the setup program doesn't remove shared files that are stored within the Program Files folder, since these files are still required to use the application in the other operating system. Removing shared files from the system folder is OK, however, since these files are duplicated in the other operating system's system folder.

# Sharing Applications on the Network

You can also copy an application's setup files to a network drive and allow users to install the application from the server. Make sure that you have enough licenses to cover each user that installs the application, though. To copy applications to a network drive, follow these steps:

1. Create a share for the application's source files on the network.

2. Set the share's permission so that only those who have a license to install the application have access to the share.

3. Copy the application's source files to the share. Duplicate the folder structure of the application's source media.

To make installing an application from the network even easier, you can add a Network Install tab to the Add/Remove Programs Properties dialog box, which shows users a list of the applications available to be installed from the network. To create a Network Install tab in Add/Remove Programs, follow these steps:

1. Create a text file called Apps.ini that contains a list of applications that are available on the network and place it on the server. Each line in Apps.ini looks like the following:

   `ApplicationName = UNC Path`

   `ApplicationName` is the name of the application as you want users to see it on the Network Install tab, and `UNC Path` is the network path to the application's source files. If the application's setup program can't handle UNC paths, put an asterisk (*) before the UNC path.

2. In the Registry, add the string value entry `appinstallpath` to `HKLM\Software\Microsoft\Windows\Current Version`. Change its value to the UNC path of the Apps.ini file that you created in Step 1, including the actual filename.

You can install many applications *on* a network. This works as long as the setup program copies all the application's files to the install folder and the application doesn't rely on the Registry to contain certain configuration data before it executes for the first time. You install the application on a network server and then create a shortcut to the application on the user's desktop.

# Running Applications in Windows 98

Windows 98 provides many ways to start an application:

- Open the application's shortcut from the Start menu.
- Open a shortcut that you create on the desktop.
- Open the application's EXE file in Windows Explorer.
- Click an application's shortcut on the Quick Launch toolbar.
- From the Start menu, choose Run, type the application's path, and then press Enter. Alternatively, you can drag an EXE file to the Run dialog box, provide additional command line parameters, and then press Enter.
- Open a document in Windows Explorer or from the Start menu's Run dialog box. Windows 98 launches the document in the program that's associated with the document.
- Launch an application from the command prompt. Type the application's name and press Enter. Optionally, if you want more control over how the program starts, launch the application by using the Start command. The following shows you the command line for start:

  `start [options] [program|document] [arguments]`

  *options* can be any of the following:

  - `/m` runs the program minimized.
  - `/max` runs the program maximized.
  - `/r` runs the program restored.
  - `/w` prevents the program from returning until the other program exits.

# Launching Applications When Windows 98 Starts

You can cause Windows 98 to launch particular programs each time it starts, making those applications available at the beginning of the session. For example, you might launch your e-mail client each time Windows 98 starts so that it's immediately available.

Some programs automatically put a shortcut in the StartUp folder. These programs are usually utilities that you want available during your entire session, and you usually find their icons in the system tray in the bottom-right corner of the taskbar. To launch an application from the StartUp folder, follow these steps:

1.  Create a shortcut for the application in the StartUp folder, which you find in C:\Windows\Start Menu\StartUp on a single-user machine or in C:\Windows\*Username*\Start Menu\StartUp on a profile-enabled machine.

2.  Optionally, change the shortcut so that the application starts in a minimized or maximized window, depending on your preference. Right-click the shortcut's icon and then choose Properties. (You can also set other properties, such as the working directory that the application will use.) Select your choices and then click OK to save your change.

3.  Restart your machine to test the new shortcut.

To launch an application from the Run registry key, follow these steps:

1.  Open `HKCU\Software\Microsoft\Windows\CurrentVersion\Run` in the Registry Editor. You might have to create this key.

2.  Add a string value entry for each program that you want to run when Windows 98 starts. The name of the value entry is arbitrary and the value is a valid command line, including command line arguments.

**3.** Close the Registry Editor and restart your machine to test your changes.

> **Tip**
>
> If a program launches each time you start Windows 98, but you can't find it in your StartUp folder or the Run Registry key, look in C:\Windows\All Users\Start Menu\StartUp. The desktop and Start menu in C:\Windows\All Users applies to all users who log on to the computer. Note that some applications still start automatically by adding entries to the load= line in Win.ini.

## Running Applications in a Multiuser Environment

I haven't yet found an application that doesn't run in a multiuser (user profiles enabled) environment. That is, even though you installed the application from one user account, the application works for other users who log on to the computer. Keep the following considerations in mind, however, when you intend multiple users to use an application:

- Windows 98 applications store settings in the Registry. Machine-specific settings go in HKLM, and user-specific settings go in HKCLU. If the application depends on finding certain values in HKCLU each time it starts, and it won't re-create those settings if they're missing, you can't use the program with multiple users unless you duplicate the settings in each user's User.dat file by using the Registry Editor.

- Some applications, such as Outlook Express, store application data files in the user's profile folder. Look in \Application Data. If the application doesn't re-create this data for each new user who uses the application, you must duplicate the data, to use the application with multiple users.

- Many applications store application data outside the user's profile. For example, Post-it Software Notes from 3M stores the user's data in the same folder as the application's binary files; thus, every user who tries to use this application shares the same data. Check HKCU in the Registry for a value entry that's read by the application and that enables you to point the application to a different path for each user.

## Associating a File Type with an Application

To associate a file type with an application, follow these steps:

1. Select a document of the type you want to associate with an application.

2. Hold the Shift key while you right-click the document and then choose Open With. If you've enabled the Windows 98 single-click feature, you must select the file, by holding the mouse pointer over it before right-clicking it.

3. In the Open With dialog box, select the application that you want to associate with the document type from the box labeled Choose the program you want to use. Alternatively, click Other to browse your hard drive for other programs.

4. Select Always use this program to open this type of file and then click OK. Windows 98 associates the file type with the application and launches the document you selected in the application.

**Tip**

You can work with Windows 98 file associations directly. Choose View ⇨ Folder Options from Windows Explorer's main menu. Click New Type to add a new file association. Otherwise, select a file association from Registered file types and then click Edit to change it.

# Handling Failed or Unresponsive Applications

If an application fails or stops responding, you can kill the application's task without quitting Windows 98 or other applications. To see a list of running applications, press Ctrl+Alt+Delete. If you see Not responding next to an application's name, the application has probably failed.

To close a failed application, follow these steps:

1. Press Ctrl+Alt+Delete. You see the Close Program dialog box, which displays Not responding next to the name of each application that has failed.

2. Select a failed application and click End Task. Windows 98 confirms that you want to close the failed application; click End Task to do so. You will likely lose any unsaved data.

Some applications have more than one process. For example, Microsoft Outlook starts Mapisp32.exe in addition to Outlook.exe. If you close either task because it's not responding, the remaining process might continue running. If so, either it runs indefinitely, until you close it, or it eventually stops responding. You won't be able to restart the application, either, until you close the remaining process.

Dr. Watson was around in Windows 3.1 and has been reintroduced in Windows 98 as Dr. Watson 32. This handy utility collects important information about an application when it crashes. Dr. Watson creates a log file, which the user gives to a support person to help diagnose and fix the problem, that contains the following information:

- The name of the component that crashed
- The computer's characteristics, such as the CPU, memory, and so forth
- A list of all the processes running on the computer
- A list of the applications that run when Windows 98 starts

- A list of all the drivers installed on the computer

- A list of all the DLLs in use at the time of the crash

- Details about the crash itself, such as the contents of the CPU's registers

To log information when a program crashes with Dr. Watson 32, follow these steps:

1. Create a shortcut to C:\Windows\Drwatson.exe to your StartUp folder, so that Dr. Watson starts each time you boot your computer.

2. If a program crashes, Dr. Watson generates a log and displays a dialog box that uses the application's command line as a title. Dr. Watson stores each log file in C:\Windows\ Drwatson, with the WLG file extension.

3. Click Details on the Crash dialog box to open the log in Dr. Watson. The standard view, which is the default for Dr. Watson, doesn't provide you with much information; choose View ⇨ Advanced View to see the log displayed.

4. Close Dr. Watson. Then, close the first dialog box to remove the offending program from memory.

**Tip**

You can generate a log file any time by using Dr. Watson. Right-click Dr. Watson's icon in the system tray and choose Dr. Watson. Dr. Watson generates a log that reflects your current environment. Save the information to disk by choosing File ⇨ Save As from the main menu.

If you have any doubt about the compatibility of a particular program with Windows 98, see the compatibility list in C:\Windows\Programs.txt. If you're trying to run a Windows 3.1 application that you believe is incompatible with Windows 98, try using the Mkcompat utility, which you find in the Windows folder. You use this program to change certain characteristics of a program so that it might work in Windows 98.

# Running MS-DOS Applications

Usually, you don't need to do anything special to run an MS-DOS application in Windows 98. Occasionally, however, you might need to tweak an application's settings for it to run properly. Windows 98 doesn't provide a *Program Information File* (PIF) editor, as does Windows 3.1, but you can still configure each MS-DOS application individually. Right-click an application's EXE file and choose Properties to create settings in a PIF file. Windows 98 stores the PIF file in the same folder as the EXE file.

Windows 98 looks for an EXE file's PIF file in several locations, in the following order:

1. The same folder as the EXE file

2. C:\Windows\Pif

3. The path specified in the PATH environment variable

4. C:\Windows\INF\Apps.inf

5. C:\Windows\_Default.pif

Apps.inf contains a section called [PIF98] that contains an entry for each MS-DOS application known to Windows 98. Each entry describes the application's title, its icon, and its working folder. Each entry also contains a reference to another section within Apps.inf that describes the application's working requirements, such as the amount of memory the application requires.

_Default.pif is the default PIF file for MS-DOS applications. Windows 98 uses _Default.pif when it can find no other PIF information for the application. If you don't have a _Default.pif file, you can create one from a copy of Dosprmpt.pif.

To change the properties for an MS-DOS application, follow these steps:

1. Right-click the application's PIF or EXE file and choose Properties, which displays the properties for the program.

2. On each tab, make the changes you want, as described in the upcoming sections: "General," "Program," "Font," "Memory," "Screen," and "Misc."

3. Click OK to save your changes.

## General

You use the General tab to view information about the type, location, size, and modification dates for the application. You can also change the EXE file's attributes.

## Program

The Program tab of the application's General Properties dialog box describes how to run the program. Here's a description of each option on this tab:

- **Screen name**. Type the application's name as it appears in the title bar.

- **Cmd line**. Type the command line, including drive, path, filename, and arguments required to run the application.

- **Working**. Type the working directory for the application.

- **Batch file**. Type the path and filename of a batch file to run before launching the application. Use this to create a customized environment.

- **Shortcut key**. Create a keyboard shortcut to quickly launch the application. Put the cursor in this field and press the key combination you want to use. Press Backspace to remove the shortcut key.

- **Run**. Select the window style in which to launch the program: Normal window, Minimized, or Maximized.

- **Close on exit**. Select this option to close the window automatically after the application stops.

# Font

You use the Font tab to change how text in the MS-DOS window looks. Select from the Available types area of the Font tab the types of fonts you want to have available; then, select a size from the Font size area.

# Memory

The Memory tab enables you to configure how much of each memory type is available to the application:

- **Conventional memory**. The first 640K of memory in your computer.

- **Expanded (EMS) memory**. Installed by an expanded memory card or emulated by an expanded memory manager.

- **Extended (XMS) memory**. An extension of the computer's original 1MB address space. Extended memory always starts at the end of the upper memory area: 1,024K.

- **MS-DOS protected-mode (DPMI) memory**. Windows 98 provides DPMI memory as expanded memory for those applications that require it. If you load EMM386.EXE in Config.sys with the `noems` argument, Windows 98 can't provide DPMI memory. Use the `ram` argument, instead, or use the `x=mmmm-nnnn` statement to allocate space in the upper memory area for an EMS page frame.

# Screen

The screen properties for an MS-DOS application describe how Windows 98 displays the application. The following list describes each option on this tab:

- **Full-screen**. Select to open the application full-screen.

- **Window**. Select to open the application in a window.

- **Initial size**. Select the number of lines you want to show in the window.

- **Display toolbar**. Select to display a toolbar on the application's window.

- **Restore settings on startup**. Select to restore the original windows settings each time you start the application.

- **Fast ROM emulation**. Select to emulate video functions in read-only memory. This makes text output faster and makes some MS-DOS applications work better when they don't display text correctly.

- **Dynamic memory allocation**. Select to make more memory available to other applications when the MS-DOS application is using a video mode that requires less memory.

## Misc.

The misc. properties enable you to configure (in addition to other options) how the MS-DOS application multitasks. The following list describes each option on this tab:

- **Allow screen saver**. Select to enable the screen saver to start while this program is active.

- **QuickEdit**. Select if you want to use the mouse to highlight text without first having to click Mark on the toolbar.

- **Exclusive mode**. Select if you want to use the mouse exclusively with the program; you won't be able to use the mouse in Windows while the program is running.

- **Always suspend**. Select if you want Windows 98 to suspend the program when it's in the background.

- **Warn if still active**. Select if you want Windows 98 to give you a warning message if you try to close the application's window while it's still running.

- **Idle sensitivity**. Adjust the amount of time that Windows 98 allows the program to remain idle before Windows 98 reduces its CPU resources. Drag the slider left to allow the program to remain idle longer; drag it right to allow the program less time to remain idle.

- **Fast pasting**. Select to use a faster method for pasting data into the application. If you have difficulty pasting into an application, clear this check box.

- **Windows shortcut keys**. Select the shortcut keys you want to reserve for Windows 98 use, instead of for use by the application. Deselect a particular key combination if an MS-DOS application requires it, ensuring that Windows 98 ignores that combination while the application is running.

# Launching MS-DOS Applications in MS-DOS Mode

You can run most MS-DOS applications in Windows 98, whether full-screen or in a window. Some applications expect complete control of the computer, however, and for those misbehaved programs, Windows 98 provides MS-DOS mode, for which it does the following:

- Closes all open processes

- Loads a real-mode copy of MS-DOS

- Removes itself from memory, with the exception of a small stub

- Provides the application with complete control of the machine

Windows 98 might automatically detect that an MS-DOS application requires MS-DOS mode to run. If so, Windows 98 warns you that it's going to shut down to MS-DOS mode, to run the application. You have the option of not running the application, however, to remain in Windows 98. In other cases, you might have to configure an MS-DOS application specifically to run in MS-

DOS mode. Resort to this option only if the application doesn't seem to run well in Windows 98. To run an MS-DOS application in MS-DOS mode, follow these steps:

1.  Right-click the application's EXE or PIF file and choose Properties.

2.  Click Advanced on the application's Program tab to see the Advanced Program Settings dialog box.

3.  Select MS-DOS mode.

4.  Close the Advanced Program Settings dialog box. Launch the program to test your new settings. You return to Windows 98 when you quit the MS-DOS application.

To create a custom configuration for an MS-DOS application, follow these steps:

1.  Open the application's Advanced Program Settings dialog box.

2.  Select Specify a new MS-DOS configuration. Windows 98 enables the CONFIG.SYS for MS_DOS mode and AUTOEXEC.BAT for MS-DOS mode text boxes.

3.  Create a custom configuration for the application. Type the Config.sys to use for the application in CONFIG.SYS for MS-DOS mode. Type the Autoexec.bat to use for the application in AUTOEXEC.BAT for MS-DOS mode.

4.  Close the Advanced Program Settings dialog box to save your changes.

 **Tip**

You can shut down Windows 98 to MS-DOS mode without launching an MS-DOS application. Choose Shut Down from the Start menu, and then choose Restart in MS-DOS mode from the Shut Down Windows dialog box. If you want to execute a program each time you shut down to MS-DOS mode, add it to Dosstart.bat, which you find in C:\Windows. You want to add Mscdex.exe to Dosstart.bat, for example, so that your CD-ROM drive is available in MS-DOS mode.

# Organizing Applications on the Start Menu

To add a shortcut to the Start menu by using drag-and-drop, follow these steps:

1. In Windows Explorer, locate the EXE file for which you want to add a shortcut to the Start menu.

2. Drag the EXE file from Windows Explorer and drop it on the Start button. Windows 98 adds the shortcut to the top of the Start menu, but you can move it to a different folder.

To add a shortcut to the Start menu by using the Create Shortcut Wizard, follow these steps:

1. Choose Settings ➪ Taskbar & Start Menu from the Start menu to see the Taskbar Properties dialog box.

2. Start the Create Shortcut Wizard. To do so, click the Start menu Programs tab and click Add.

3. Type the path and filename of the program you want to launch with the shortcut. Optionally, click Browse to locate the file on your hard drive.

4. Click Next and then select the folder in which you want to store the shortcut. The wizard shows you all the program folders available on the Start menu. To create a new folder, select a folder from the list; then, click New Folder to create a folder underneath the one you selected.

5. Click Next and then type a name for the shortcut. This is the name as it appears in the Start menu, and is also the root filename given to the shortcut on the hard drive.

6. Click Finish to close the Create Shortcut Wizard.

# Organizing Shortcuts by Using Windows Explorer

The shortcuts you see under Programs on the Start menu are in C:\Windows\Start Menu\Programs. On a multiple-user machine, the shortcuts are stored in C:\Windows\Profiles\*Username*\Start Menu, where *Username* is the name of the current user.

If you're making sweeping changes to your Start menu, your best bet is to start off by organizing your Start menu in Windows Explorer. To open the Start menu in Explorer, right-click the Start button and choose Explore. In the Start menu, you can create new folders, remove folders and shortcuts, and drag shortcuts from one folder to another. The Start menu should recognize your changes immediately; if it doesn't, log off of the computer and log back on.

# Organizing Shortcuts by Using Drag-and-Drop

To sort the shortcuts on the Start menu, follow these steps:

1. On the Start menu, open the program menu you want to sort.

2. Drag each shortcut and folder to its new location on the menu. As you're dragging the item, Windows 98 highlights the item's original position and indicates its new position with a horizontal line.

To move an item from one folder to another, follow these steps:

1. Open the program folder containing the shortcut or folder you want to move.

2. Drag the shortcut to its new location. Start dragging the shortcut. As you hold down the left mouse button, point at the program folder to which you want to move the item. After the item's new location opens, place the shortcut on the menu as if you were sorting the menu.

# Removing Applications

Windows 98 programs are easy to remove; you use the Add/Remove Programs Properties dialog box. Applications built for Windows 98 store uninstall information in the Registry so that you can accurately remove them from your computer. These applications know which program files and Registry entries are safe to remove. They're even smart enough to leave shared files alone, because Windows 98 keeps track of how many programs are using a shared file, and as long as the file is in use by more than one program, the uninstaller won't remove it. To remove a program automatically by using Add/Remove Programs, follow these steps:

1. Open the Add/Remove Programs Properties dialog box from the Control Panel.

2. Start the application's uninstaller by selecting the application that you want to remove from the list of installed applications; then, click Add/Remove.

3. Follow the instructions you see on the screen. Some applications give you the choice to either completely remove the program or just add and remove components. If your goal is to completely remove the program, make sure you do so — deselecting all the application's components in the setup program's add/remove mode won't always remove the application's support files.

Unless a Windows 3.1 application provides an uninstall program, which isn't common, removing them is more complicated. If you just remove the application's install folder, you leave many other files behind in the Windows folder. If you try cleaning out the Windows folder, you run the risk of removing files that other applications require. My suggestion is that you read the application's documentation carefully to see whether it provides any uninstall instructions. Other than that, you might try one of the third-party tools available for removing applications.

**Caution**

Manually removing an application can render your system useless if you accidentally delete a shared file that Windows 98 relies on. Exhaust every alternative and back up your computer before resorting to this process.

To manually remove a program by using the Registry Editor and Windows Explorer, follow these steps:

1. **Program files**. Remove the application's files from C:\Program Files. Usually, this is a safe operation, because no other program should be sharing them.

2. **Orphaned DLLs**. Move any orphaned DLLs and other support files from C:\Windows into a backup folder. If your computer doesn't work properly after restarting, you can restore enough of the support files to get your computer working again. If your computer does work properly after a time, go ahead and remove the files from the backup folder. Here are a few tips for deciding whether a DLL belongs to the application that you're removing:

   • Check the company and product name on the Version tab of the DLL's properties. If the same vendor and product appear in the DLL, move it to the backup folder.

   • Search for references to the DLL on your hard drive. Choose Find ⇨ Files and Folders from the Start menu. Type **\*.dll; \*.exe** in Named and then type the name of the DLL, without a path or file extension, in Containing text. If Windows 98 doesn't find any additional files referencing the DLL, move it to the backup folder.

3. **System files**. Remove references to the application from your system files. Back them up first. Check System.ini, Win.ini, Autoexec.bat, and Config.sys for any references to the application's path; remove them.

4. **The Registry**. Remove references to the application from the Registry. Here are some tips for locating Registry entries belonging to the application:

- Look for any file associations that obviously belong to the application. You can search the Registry for the application's EXE filename to find them.

- Search the Registry for the program's path. If the program is installed in C:\Program Files\\*Program*\\*ProgramName*, search for both C:\Program Files\\*Program* and C:\Program Files\\*Program*\\*ProgramName*.

- Search the Registry for the program's and vendor's names. Search for partial-name matches. If you're removing a program called "Don't Tread on Me for Windows 98," search for "Tread" in addition to the application's full name. Also search for common acronyms used for the application.

- Look in `HKLM\Software` and `HKCU\Software` for any sub-keys belonging to the application. These subkeys should have a name that contains some form of the company's name.

5. **Start Menu**. Remove the application's shortcuts from the Start menu.

# Tracking Installation Changes

The best insurance you have against an errant application's setup program is to take a "snapshot" of your computer before installing the application. That way, if something goes awry, you have a better chance of diagnosing the problem, and possibly even fixing it.

To save a snapshot of your computer before installing an application, follow these steps:

1. Save a complete folder listing in a text file. Redirect the `dir` command to a text file; make sure that you use the `/s` argument to include subdirectories in the listing, like this:

   `dir/s >snapshot.txt`

2. Save the Registry to a REG file by exporting its entire contents. Select My Computer in the Registry Editor and then choose Registry ⇨ Export Registry File from the main menu. Provide a filename in File name and then click Save.

3. Stash both files in a safe place. You can repeat this procedure to create another snapshot; then, you can compare both snapshots, as described in the next set of instructions.

To discover what changes a setup program made to your computer, follow these steps:

1. Create a new snapshot of your computer. Make sure you don't overwrite the files from the previous snapshot, though.

2. Compare the two snapshots. You can use a text-comparison utility, some of which are available online as shareware. Optionally, you can use Microsoft Word to compare both snapshots.

3. Make note of any changes made in the directory listing and in the REG file.

**Tip**

ConfigSafe 95, published by Imagine LAN, Inc., is a must-have utility for those folks who are concerned about their configuration. It periodically takes snapshots of your computer's Registry, folder structure, and files. Then, you can use ConfigSafe 95 to compare your configuration to any of the snapshots, or even revert to a previously saved configuration. ConfigSafe 95 also comes with an MS-DOS utility that you can use to fix your computer when you can't start Windows 98. You learn more about ConfigSafe 95 at Imagine LAN's Web site: `http://www.imagine-lan.com`.

# Locating Application Settings

Applications with the "Designed for Windows" logo store their settings in the Registry. In fact, the only applications that still use INI files for settings are older Windows 3.1 programs and programs from some vendors that just refuse to cooperate. In most Windows 98 applications, you change settings by choosing Tools ➪ Options from the main menu. Applications persistently store these settings and other information in the Registry.

Because the organization of the Registry is somewhat standardized, most applications store their settings in exactly the same manner:

- User-specific settings go in HKEY_CURRENT_USER.
- Machine-specific settings go in HKEY_LOCAL_MACHINE.

Many applications store settings under both HKLM and HKCU. The settings an application stores in HKLM apply to every user that logs on to the computer, whereas the settings in HKCU apply only to the current user. Some applications store default user-specific settings in HKLM, too, and then copy those settings to HKCU when a new user logs on to the computer for the first time.

The organization of an application's settings, other than the preceding two Registry keys, is almost identical: \Software\Company\Product\Version, where Company is the name of the vendor, Product is the name of the application, and Version is the version number of the application. Note that some vendors don't actually use a version number for Version; they use the subkey CurrentVersion to represent the most current version, instead. The following line shows you an example for Microsoft Office:

```
\HKEY_CURRENT_USER\SOFTWARE\Microsoft\Office\8.0
```

## File Associations in the Registry

The largest part of the Windows 98 Registry is HKEY_CLASSES_ROOT, which contains all the file associations. If you open the Registry Editor and examine HKCR's subkeys, you'll notice two types that make up a file association:

- *.ext.* You see one entry for each file extension that has an association in the Registry. For instance, you see an entry for BAT files called \.bat.

- *filetype.* Each entry that does not begin with a period is mostly likely a file type, which associates one or more actions with a file extension.

The easiest way to put everything together is to look at what happens when you open a file in Windows Explorer:

1. The user right-clicks a DOC file and chooses Open.

2. Windows 98 locates the .doc subkey in HKEY_CLASSES_ROOT and retrieves its default value entry. By default, it finds Wordpad.Document.1.

3. Windows 98 looks up the Wordpad.Document.1 subkey or whatever value it found in the previous step under HKEY_CASSES_ROOT. This is the file type.

4. Within the file type, Windows 98 looks for a subkey in the form shell\\*verb*\\command, where *verb* represents the action the user chose from the right-click menu.

5. Windows 98 retrieves the default value entry for the subkey that it finds in Step 4 and then executes that as a command.

You almost never have a good reason to change a file association in the Registry. Windows Explorer handles file associations via the File Types tab of the Options dialog box. You can also associate a particular file with a different application by holding the Shift key down while you right-click the file; then, choose Open With, select the program in which to open the file, and choose Always use this program to open this type of file.

## Application Files on the Disk

Microsoft has made conventions that define where an application should puts its files on the disk. Gone are the days when an application can spray DLLs and INI files all over the Windows folder. If you understand the following conventions, you'll be able to locate program files on the disk easier:

- Applications are installed in \Program Files. The application's setup program creates a folder in \Program Files that's named after the company or product.

- Applications do not store private files anywhere in \Windows.

- Applications can store shared libraries in \Windows\System.

- Applications should store user-specific data in the user's profile path under \Application Data.

**Tip**

Windows 3.1, MS-DOS, and some badly behaved Windows 98 programs do not support long filenames and can't be installed in \Program Files. You can fool these programs by installing them in \Progra~1, however, which is the 8.3 equivalent of the long filename.

# Troubleshooting Applications in Windows 98

If you can't install an application to your hard drive,

1. Make sure you've disabled your virus scanner before trying to install the application. If a virus scanner is running while you try to install an application, according to Microsoft, Windows 98 might stop responding and you might see any of the following error messages:

    - Unexpected DOS Error 5

- Setup Initialization Error
- Divide Overflow
- Sharing Violation
- Insufficient Memory or Disk Space
- Error Reading from Drive A
- Cannot Detect setup.exe on Drive A
- Unexpected exit, please report this to Microsoft Product Support
- Setup Error 797

**2.** Make sure that you have enough free disk space to install the application. Check the product's packaging or documentation to see how much disk space the installation requires.

**3.** Make sure you have enough free memory to install the application. Check the product's packaging or documentation.

**4.** Close any other running applications. Press Ctrl+Alt+Delete to see a list of running applications.

**5.** Check the health of your hard drive. Run both ScanDisk and Disk Defragmenter.

**6.** Make sure the setup disks aren't damaged. Open the setup disks in Windows Explorer; can you read them? Copy the setup files to your hard drive. You might also try installing the application on a different computer; if you can't do so, the setup disks are possibly damaged.

**7.** Use the System File Checker to make sure your Windows 98 system files are correct.

If you can't run an application in Windows 98,

**1.** Change video modes. Can you run the application with the standard VGA driver? If so, you might need to get an updated video driver from the manufacturer.

2. Check the memory required by the program against the amount available on the computer when you try to launch the application. See the product's packaging or documentation.

3. Check the free disk space required by the program against the amount of disk space available when you try to launch the application. See the product's packaging or documentation.

4. Try launching the application with no other applications running. Press Ctrl+Alt+Delete to see a list of running applications.

5. Check your temporary folder. The TEMP environment variable contains the path of your temporary folder. If the folder indicated by TEMP is not present, create it.

6. Start Windows 98 without loading any programs from the StartUp folder. To do so, press and hold down the Shift key while the operating system boots. Don't release the Shift key until the operating system has finished starting. You can also prevent applications from starting by emptying the Run keys from the Registry: HKCU\Software\Microsoft\Windows\CurrentVersion\Run.

# General Protection Faults

Windows 98 is not as stable as Windows NT; thus, you do see the occasional general protection fault (also called the "blue screen of death"). If you understand how GPFs occur, you often can fix the problem before it worsens. The most typical cause of a GPF is an application trying to access a memory region that doesn't belong to it. That is, the application is trying to step on someone else's memory. As a result, Windows 98 stops the program before it can do any damage to the system, which brings the system to its knees.

The following are explanations for GPFs that occur in different circumstances:

- **MS-DOS programs**. Each MS-DOS program runs in its own VM. Thus, GPFs in MS-DOS programs do not affect any other program. You still see a blue screen telling you the program failed, however, which terminates the program after you click OK.

- **16-bit Windows programs**. All the 16-bit Windows programs that run in Windows 98 share the same address space; thus, all other 16-bit Windows programs stop until you clear the blue screen. After you close it, the other 16-bit Windows programs might continue running, as long as the error wasn't severe enough to crash those, too.

- **32-bit Windows programs**. GPFs in 32-bit Windows programs affect only the program that caused it. 32-bit Windows programs have private address spaces and can't trample another application's data.

- **Device drivers**. GPFs caused by device drivers are serious. If a device driver causes a GPF, restart your computer shortly after. Then, investigate the reason for the GPF and look for information on Microsoft Support Online that might explain it.

## Resources Used by Applications

Windows 98 provides a utility called Resource Meter that you can use to see how much memory is available on the computer. Resource Meter is not installed by default, but you can install it by using the Windows Setup tab of the Add Remove Programs Properties dialog box. Afterward, you start Resource Meter by choosing Start ⇨ Programs ⇨ Accessories ⇨ System Tools ⇨ Resource Meter. The first time you start

Resource Meter, it displays a warning that tells you it's going to use memory just like any other program; select Don't display this message again and click OK. Resource Meter loads into the system tray, which is the area on the taskbar that contains the clock. Double-click Resource Meter's icon to display its window.

## Versioning Problems with Older Applications

Some programs, particularly MS-DOS programs, have an annoying habit of not running if they're designed for a DOS version other than 7.0. The authors of programs written for MS-DOS version 5.0 never thought they'd see the day that version 7.0 would be around. However, you can trick such a program into running by using the version table, which Windows 98 loads by default.

Setver is a utility that maintains a list of applications and version numbers. When a particular application requests the version number for MS-DOS, Setver looks up the application and returns its corresponding value — as long as an entry for it exists in the database. The following list describes Setver's command line, and the instructions that you see in this section show you how to use it to add an application and version number to the database:

```
Setver.exe [path] filename v.vv
Setver.exe filename /delete /quiet
```

- [path] specifies the drive and path of Setver.exe.
- filename specifies the name of the MS-DOS EXE file.
- v.vv specifies the major and minor version to report to the application.
- /DELETE deletes the entry for the given application.
- /QUIET deletes the entry without displaying a message.

To add an application to the version table, follow these steps:

1. Determine the EXE filename of the application and the MS-DOS version number that it's expecting.

2. At the command prompt, type the following command and press Enter:

```
setver filename.exe v.vv
```

Other applications check the version of Windows that's running on the computer and refuse to run if the version isn't exactly 3.10. You fix such an application by adding it to the [Compatibility] section of Win.ini. The item name is the compiled module name, which you can find by right-clicking the program's EXE file; then, choose Quick View and look for an entry called Module Name. Then, add the following line to the [Compatibility] section of Win.ini:

```
module_name=0x00200000
```

# Applications That Replace System DLLs

A surprising number of applications misbehave by replacing system DLLs with versions of their own. One example is Netscape Communicator, which overwrites Msvcrt40.dll with its own supposedly optimized version. The problem with this behavior is that it can prevent other applications from working properly. Some applications don't replace system files just to be smart; they do it because the programmer didn't write the code that is necessary to make sure that a newer file isn't replaced. Regardless, Windows 98 provides better means by which you can control the versioning of its system files:

- **Version Checking**. Each time an application replaces a system file, Windows 98 backs up the original file. If you're not pleased with the application's behavior, you can use the Version Conflict Manager to restore the original. To start Version Conflict Manager, choose Version Conflict Manager from the Tools menu of System Information. System Information is on the Start menu under Tools.

■ **System File Checker**. The System File Checker keeps a log of all the system files installed on the computer. You use this utility to check the integrity and version number of each system file on the computer.

To verify the system files by using System File Checker, follow these steps:

1. Start System File Checker.

2. Click Start, and the System File Checker checks each system file, showing its progress in the bottom portion of the window. This process can take several minutes; be patient. If System File Checker finds a corrupt file, it displays the File Corrupted dialog box. Choose one of the options described next and follow the instructions that you see on-screen:

   • **Update verification information**. If you know the file has been updated and is OK, choose this option to update the System File Checker's verification data file.

   • **Restore file**. Select to restore the file from the original installation disks. Windows 98 prompts you for the location of the original file.

   • **Ignore**. If you're not sure what to do, select this option to ignore the warning temporarily. System File Checker prompts you again the next time.

3. When it's finished, you see the Finished dialog box. Click OK to close it, or click Details to see more information about the files System File Checker scanned.

4. Close System File Checker.

# Chapter 9

# Managing Printers and Fonts

## Installing a Printer

Windows 98 provides several different ways to install printer drivers:

- **Add Printer Wizard**. Start the Add Printer Wizard from the Printers folder.

- **Plug and Play**. Plug a Plug and Play printer into your computer, and Windows 98 automatically installs the appropriate driver files after you restart the computer.

- **Point-and-Print**. When you open a network printer queue that is configured with Point-and-Print information, Windows 98 automatically installs support for it.

- **Setup scripts**. You can automatically install printer support by using a custom setup script. You use the `[Printers]` section of a custom setup script to install support for one or more printers. Each line in this section looks like the following, where `PrinterName` is an arbitrary name for the printer, `DriveModel` is one of the models defined in the appropriate INF files, and `Port` is the printer port or UNC path to a network printer queue: `PrinterName=DriveModel,Port`.

The following list shows you an example:

```
[Printers]
LaserJet 5=HP LaserJet 5,\\Server\Laser5
LaserJet III=HP LaserJet III,\\Server\Laser3
```

When you upgrade to Windows 98, the Setup program automatically installs drivers for any printers it finds in the previous configuration. When you install a fresh copy of Windows 98, or if the previous configuration didn't include a printer, the Setup program automatically starts the Add Printer Wizard.

## Local Printers

You use the Add Printer Wizard to install support for your printer. You find the Add Printer Wizard in the Printers folder, which you can open by choosing Settings ⇨ Printers from the Start menu; you also can open it from the Control Panel, My Computer folder, or Windows Explorer. To install a local printer by using the Add Printer Wizard, follow these steps:

1. Start the Add Printer Wizard and click Next to skip the first screen.

2. Select Local printer and click Next.

3. Choose your printer. Select the manufacturer from the first list and then choose the exact printer model from the second list. In cases where you don't find the exact printer model, choose the closest model possible and it'll probably work OK. Click Next to continue.

4. Choose the port to which the printer is connected. You see an entry in the list for each parallel and serial port on your computer, as well as for FILE:. Optionally, click Configure Port to determine whether you want to spool MS-DOS print jobs or you want Windows 98 to check the status of the port before printing to it. Click Next to continue.

5. In the space provided, type a friendly name for the printer. This is the name you'll see in the Printers folder.

6. If you want to print a test page, choose Yes; then, click Finish and Windows 98 copies the printer drivers from your CD-ROM or the network installation path to your computer.

To change the printer's settings, follow these steps:

1. Open the Printers folder; then, right-click the printer and choose Properties.

2. Change the printer's settings and then close the printer's Properties dialog box to save your changes. The dialog box you see in this step is potentially different for each printer you install.

# Network Printers

The printing architecture fits seamlessly into the Windows 98 networking architecture. It has three primary components:

- **Win32 and Win16 print APIs**. The print APIs provide an interface to open, write, and close print jobs. They work with both local and remote print queues, providing additional support for queue management.

- **Print router**. The print router is part of Spoolss.dll. It routes print requests to the appropriate Print Provider Interface (PPI) drivers. Local requests go to the local PPI. Remote requests go to the appropriate remote PPI.

- **Print Provider Interface (PPI)**. The PPI is modular, so it plugs neatly into Windows 98 networking components. The local PPI supports local printing, sending requests to local ports and queues. Network PPIs support network printing, sending requests to the appropriate network redirector. You learn about the PPI for Microsoft Networks in "Windows NT Print Servers" and the PPI for Novell Networks in

"NetWare Print Servers," both later in this chapter. One additional PPI, WinNet16PPI, provides compatibility with Windows 3.1 applications.

### Caution

Failures in the print router go unnoticed. If the print router fails, for example, you never receive an error message – the print job just disappears.

Point-and-Print enables you to store printer information on the print server. Users can install support for the printer without hassling with the Add Printer Wizard. Windows 98 then automatically copies the printer information from the print server. The type of information that Windows 98 copies depends on the type of print server, which can include the printer driver files, the name of the print server, printer model information, and printer settings. If the print server doesn't provide the driver files, Windows 98 uses the printer model information to determine which drivers to install. To install a network printer by using Point-and-Print, do any of the following:

- Right-click the printer in Network Neighborhood and choose Install.

- Open the print queue in Network Neighborhood, and Windows 98 prompts you to install the printer driver files.

- Point the Add Printer Wizard to the network printer queue by choosing Network printer, as described in the following steps:

1. Start the Add Printer Wizard and click Next to skip the first screen.

2. Select Network printer and click Next.

3. Type the UNC path to the printer in Network path or queue name, or click Browse to locate the printer.

   **4.** Click Next and follow the instructions you see on the screen.

- Drag the Printer icon from Network Neighborhood to the desktop.

- Type the path of the print queue in the Run dialog box.

- Drag-and-drop a document onto the printer in Network Neighborhood; Windows 98 prompts you to install the printer driver files.

## Windows 98 Print Servers

Windows 98 does return Point-and-Print information, such as printer driver files and printer settings. Users can connect to a remote printer on a Windows 98 print server simply by opening the print queue.

To share a printer in Windows 98, you must be running a 32-bit, protected-mode networking client, and the file and printer sharing services must be installed. You can share the printer with either share-level or user-level security. When you share a printer in Windows 98, it creates a special hidden share called PRINTER$ that shares information about the printer, such as the driver files and printer configuration.

## Windows NT Print Servers

When connecting to a printer on a Microsoft Network, Windows 98 uses the PPI for Microsoft Networks. The PPI for Microsoft Networks is implemented in Mspp32.dll and works with Msnet32.dll, Ifsmgr.vxd, and Ifshlp.sys to route print requests. The print router sends requests to the Mspp32/Msnet32 layer, which forwards requests to manage the print queue directly to the redirector. This layer sends print jobs to Ifsmgr.vxd, which handles the print request as a normal file I/O and then forwards the request through the redirector.

Windows 98 provides an RPC print provider that gives you complete information about print jobs on a Windows NT print server. It contains all the code necessary for a Windows 98 client to administer Windows NT print queues. You install the RPC print provider from \Tools\Reskit\Netadmin\Rpcpp on the Windows 98 CD-ROM. Read the INF file that you find in this folder for more instructions.

The WinNet16 print provider provides backward-compatibility with Windows 3.1 applications and for when the computer is using a real-mode networking client. WinNet16 essentially is the same as the PPI for Microsoft Networks, except that WinNet16 adds an additional layer to thunk 32-bit requests to 16-bit requests in the WinNet16.drv layer, which passes the request to the real-mode networking client via 3pnet16.386.

Windows 98 can't use the Point-and-Print information returned by a Windows NT print server, other than the printer model information, which it uses to look up printer information in the Msprint.inf, Msprint2.inf, Msprint3.inf, Msprint4.inf, and Prtupd.inf INF files. If Windows 98 finds a matching printer model, it installs the appropriate driver files from either the Windows 98 CD-ROM or the network installation folder. If it doesn't find matching printer information in the INF files, it prompts the user for the driver by using the Add Printer Wizard. Windows 98 also can't retrieve printer settings from a Windows NT print server, so the user must configure the printer settings manually.

## NetWare Print Servers

The PPI for NetWare Networks is almost identical to the PPI for Microsoft Networks. It uses Nwpp32.dll instead of Mspp32.dll and Nwnet32.dll instead of Msnet32.dll. The redirector is Nwredir.vxd. With a real-mode networking client (NETX or VLM), the redirector is a bit different, passing requests from Nw16.dll to Vnetware.386 to the real-mode client.

Windows 98 does retrieve Point-and-Print information from a NetWare print server. NetWare stores Point-and-Print information in the bindery or the Novell Directory Services (NDS) directory tree. You must have supervisor privileges both on the server and for the Root object on the NDS tree when implementing Point-and-Print for the first time. When the user accesses a NetWare print server, Windows 98 automatically copies and installs the appropriate drivers to the computer. It doesn't retrieve printer settings from the print server, however, so the user must adjust them manually. To configure the Point-and-Print information on a NetWare server, follow these steps:

1. Open the print queue on the NetWare print server.

2. Choose File ⇨ Point And Print Setup from the main menu.

3. Choose Set Driver Path, and type the UNC path of the printer driver files: \\*server*\*path*.

4. Choose Set Printer Model and select the manufacturer; then, select the printer model.

5. Click OK to save your changes.

# Printing a Document

To print a document, do any of the following:

- Choose File ⇨ Print from the application's main menu or click the Print button in the application's toolbar.

- Right-click the document in Windows Explorer and choose Print.

- Add a shortcut for the printer to the Send To folder; then, right-click the document in Windows Explorer and choose Send To followed by the printer.

- Drag the document from Windows Explorer and drop it on the printer's icon. You can drop a document on the printer's icon in the Printers folder, in Network Neighborhood, or on your desktop.

Although most 32-bit applications can use UNC printer names that look like \\*server*\\*printer*, most 16-bit applications can't. If you must have a redirected port to which you can print from such an application, use the command net use lpt1: \\*server*\\*printer* or capture the port in the Printers folder. To capture a port, select the printer and choose File ➪ Capture Printer Port from the Printers folder's main menu.

When you print a document by dragging its icon to the printer's icon or by right-clicking the document and choosing Print, Windows 98 opens the document in the application and commands the application to print it. You must have an application installed on your computer that can open that particular document. Inso's Quick View, which you see mentioned from time to time in this book, enables you to view most popular data files without actually owning the application. It also enables you to print any document that it can view, including most word processing, spreadsheet, and graphics files, without owning the application. And Quick View tends to print much faster, too. You can download an evaluation copy of Inso's Quick View from its Web site at http://www.inso.com.

## Working with the Print Queue

You can remotely manage the print queue from Windows 98. You can manage the print queue on a Windows NT print server from a Windows 98 workstation, for example, as long as you have administrative privileges for the printer. Here are the things that managing a print queue consists of:

- View the print queue
- Pause the entire print queue or individual jobs
- Resume the entire print queue or individual jobs
- Delete one or more jobs from the print queue

To manage a print queue from Windows 98, follow these steps:

1.  Open the printer from the Printers folder or, if you put a shortcut to the printer on your desktop, from your desktop.

2.  Perform any of the tasks described in the following list:

    - To pause the print queue, choose Printer ⇨ Pause Printing.

    - To remove all print jobs, choose Printer ⇨ Purge Print Documents.

    - To pause all documents, select the documents you want to pause; then, choose Document ⇨ Pause Printing.

    - To remove documents, select the documents you want to remove; then, choose Document ⇨ Cancel Printing.

3.  Close the print queue window.

# Printing When the Printer Is Not Available

Users can output to a print queue even if the printer is offline. Windows 98 stores the print job on the user's computer, deferring the job until the printer is online. This feature is great for mobile users, for example, enabling them to print while not connected to the network; then, Windows 98 outputs the job to the printer when they return to the office.

Windows 98 dims the printer's icon when the printer is offline.

Deferred printing works only with remote printers. That is, if the print server is down or the user undocks the portable computer, the user can batch up jobs to be printed when the printer is available. However, deferred printing doesn't work if the user unplugs a local printer from the computer.

To force a printer to work offline, follow these steps:

1. Open the Printers folder.

2. Right-click the printer's icon and then choose Use Printer Offline. Windows 98 dims the printer's icon, and you see a check mark next to Use Printer Offline the next time that you right-click the icon. This just causes Windows 98 to defer your print jobs; it doesn't affect the network printer in any way.

3. When you're ready to unspool your print jobs to the queue, right-click the printer's icon again and choose Use Printer Offline. Windows 98 undims the printer's icon and starts outputting the jobs to the print server.

Deferred printing is a great way to protect sensitive information, especially if the print room's on the opposite side of the building and you're printing sensitive documents, such as salaries. Put the printer offline, as you learned in this section, print all your jobs, and then put the printer back online. All your print jobs print at one time, instead of being scattered throughout the day. That means one trip to the print room to collect all of your print jobs, and, if you run fast enough, you can get there before anyone else sees your documents.

## Printing from MS-DOS Applications

MS-DOS applications print directly to the 32-bit Windows print spooler. The print spooler intercepts data intended for the printer port and puts it in the print queue. While MS-DOS applications can't possibly use EMF files, the print spooler does still return control to the application quicker than if the application was working directly with the printer, thus improving overall performance. Intercepting the application's printer output poses no problems with device contention, either, because this process is managed by the print spooler's virtual device driver.

# Troubleshooting Printing Problems

The very first thing that you should do if your printer is not work-ing properly is to open Printers.txt from \Windows. This document describes various problems related to the following specific printers, one of which might be yours:

- Canon Color Bubble-Jet

- Fargo Primera and Primera Pro

- Hewlett-Packard DeskJet: 600, 600c, and 850c

- Hewlett-Packard LaserJet: 4, 4Si, 4L, 4P, 4 Plus, 4v, 5P, and Color

- Hewlett-Packard PostScript 4M through 5MP

- LexMark

- QMS JetScript

- LaserMaster Printers

- NEC SilentWriter Superscript 610

- Panasonic KX-P 6100, KX-P 6300, KX-P 6500

Windows 98 troubleshooting wizards include a Print Troubleshooter Wizard that walks the user step by step through diagnosing common printer ailments. To use the Print Troubleshooter Wizard, open Troubleshooting ⇨ Windows 98 Troubleshooters ⇨ Print from the content tree in Help.

If you're still stuck, try the following general troubleshooting steps, which can diagnose and fix most printer problems:

1. Check the printer cables and make sure the printer is powered up.

2. Make sure the printer has paper, doesn't have a paper jam, and isn't reporting any other problems such as low toner. If the printer reports low toner, you can usually get a bit more life out of the toner cartridge by removing it, gently shaking it from side to side, and then replacing it.

3. Clear the printer's buffer. Power down the printer, wait a few minutes, and turn the printer back on.

4. Check that the printer configuration shown in Windows 98 matches the printer's actual configuration.

5. Try another print driver or use a generic driver, such as Generic/Text Only. If you're able to print, check the printer driver and reinstall it, if necessary. In many cases, reinstalling a printer driver can fix problems with a corrupt configuration.

6. Check the amount of free disk space on your computer. Each spool file requires a lot of disk space. Use Disk Cleanup to remove unnecessary files from your computer's disk.

7. Try other documents in the same application. If the document prints, you might have problems with that single document. For example, the document might be too complex for the printer or it might use a font that the printer has trouble with.

8. Try another application. If the document prints, consider that the first application isn't working properly and report the problem to the vendor.

   Print directly to the printer port. You can either disable print spooling or print to a file and copy the file to the port.

To disable print spooling, follow these steps:

1. Right-click the printer, choose Properties, and then click the Details tab.

2. Click Spool Settings to display the Spool Settings dialog box.

3. Choose Print directly to the printer.

4. Close the Spool Settings and the printer's Properties dialog boxes.

To copy a print file directly to a printer port, follow these steps:

1. Print the document to a file. If the application uses the common Print dialog box, choose Print to file and then click OK. Windows 98 prompts you for a filename.

2. Copy the file to the printer port by using the following MS-DOS command:

```
copy /b filename lpt1:
```

/b indicates that you're copying a binary file, *filename* is the name of the print file, and lpt1: is the printer port.

# Diagnosing Specific Printer Problems

If nothing prints, follow these steps:

1. Check the amount of disk space available on your computer. If enough room isn't available for the spool file, Windows 98 can't print your job. Thus, try cleaning several megabytes of unused files off of the disk and retry the print job.

2. Disable spooling as described in the following steps:

   a. Right-click the printer, choose Properties, and then click the Details tab.

   b. Click Spool Settings to display the Spool Settings dialog box.

   c. Choose Print directly to the printer.

   d. Close the Spool Settings and the printer's Properties dialog boxes.

3. Clear any stuck spool files by removing every file you find in \Windows\Spool\Printers. Also remove any temporary files from \Windows\Temp that look like Emf*.tmp. Last, restart your computer so that Windows 98 cleans up its act.

If graphics print incorrectly, follow these steps:

1. Disable spooling, as described earlier in this section.

2. Use a PostScript driver, if supported by the printer. If this works, the problem is in the Windows 98 universal driver: Unidrv.dll. Try replacing Unidrv.dll. If that fails, consult the manufacturer for updated drivers that will work with the printer.

3. Try printing a similar document or a document with the same images from another application. If this works, the problem is likely with the application or with the GDI. Consult the vendor for updates that fix the problem.

4. Print smaller and fewer jobs to see whether the spooler is getting confused by big jobs or by handling too many jobs at one time.

5. Copy an encapsulated PostScript file directly to the printer.

6. Change from vector- to raster-graphics mode if you are using a PostScript printer. This option uses less virtual memory on the printer. If this works, adjust the printer's virtual memory settings.

If the printer outputs only a portion of the page, follow these steps:

1. Check the printer's memory or print at lower printer resolutions.

2. Check and adjust the printable region of the printer. Windows 98 clips the output so that it fits within the printer's printable region.

3. If you are missing portions of text, double-check that the font is valid. To do so, try using the same font in a different document, or a different font in the same document. If it doesn't render properly, use a different font.

4.  Simplify the document. Remove graphics, excessive fonts, and so forth. In order to output the original document, consider upgrading the printer's memory.

5.  Choose Print TrueType as graphics, located on the Fonts tab of the printer's Properties dialog box.

If documents are slow to print, follow these steps:

1.  Defragment the computer's disk.

2.  Check the amount of free space on the disk. Limited free space severely affects the performance of the print spooler.

3.  Make sure the computer has an adequate amount of free memory.

4.  Reinstall the printer drivers.

5.  Choose Print TrueType as graphics, located on the Fonts tab of the printer's Properties dialog box.

If Windows 98 doesn't immediately return control to the application, follow these steps:

1.  Reinstall the printer driver.

2.  Check and reinstall the video driver, if necessary.

3.  Check the amount of free space on the computer's disk.

4.  Remove the spool files, as described earlier in this section, and then try again.

## Fixing Problems with Specific Components

If you are having problems with printer drivers, do the following:

■  Try another driver, such as the Generic/Text Only or Generic Laser Printer driver. If this works, get another driver for your printer.

- Copy a print file directly to the printer. If this works, something is wrong with the communication between Windows 98 and the printer.

If you encounter an application that prints incorrectly, do the following:

- Try different applications with similar documents. If this works, double-check the application's configuration or check the application's manufacturer to see whether it knows of any printing problems.

If you are having problems with the print spooler, follow these steps:

1. Print directly to the printer port, as described earlier in this chapter. If this works, you might have a problem with the spooler.

2. Some applications can't handle UNC printer names. Therefore, capture the printer port. To capture a port, select the printer and choose File ⇨ Capture Printer Port from the Printers folder's main menu.

If you encounter difficulties with bidirectional communication, try the following:

- Disable bidirectional printing. Right-click the printer, choose Properties, and then click the Details tab. Click Spool Settings and choose Disable bidirectional support for this printer.

# Installing and Managing Fonts

Don't worry too much about installing fonts on your computer. Windows 98 preinstalls a large number of popular screen, TrueType, and OpenType fonts when you install it. Other applications, such as Microsoft Word, install additional fonts, which are mostly of the TrueType variety. You can also install printer-resident fonts from the printer's Properties dialog box. You can still purchase additional TrueType or OpenType collections from your closest computer retailer, or even download various public domain fonts from the Internet.

You install and otherwise mange fonts in the Fonts folder, which you can open either from the Control Panel or by going to \Windows\Fonts in Windows Explorer. The following list describes the various tasks you can perform in this folder:

- To view a sample of the font, double-click the font's icon.
- To delete a font, drag the font's icon to the Recycle Bin.
- To install a new font, drag the font file to the Fonts folder.
- To compare fonts for similarity, choose View ➪ List Fonts by Similarity from the main menu; then, pick a font from the drop-down list.

Make sure you install fonts correctly. You can install an individual font by dragging it onto the Fonts folder. If you purchase a font collection or are installing fonts that come with your printer, however, use the setup program that comes with it. This ensures that the fonts are correctly installed and makes installing a large number of fonts simpler. If your printer has printer-resident or cartridge fonts, install them via the Fonts tab of the printer's Properties dialog box. The instructions for doing so vary, depending on your printer.

# Understanding Fonts in Windows 98

Windows 98 uses fonts to print and display text. It has support for four kinds of fonts:

- **TrueType**. TrueType fonts are mathematical models that describe the outline of each character. TrueType fonts are device-independent; that is, they look the same on all output devices.

- **OpenType**. OpenType fonts are new for Windows 98. They extend the TrueType specifications by adding tables that contain advanced multilingual typesetting and typographical control information. These tables describe alternative forms for characters, baseline information for horizontal and vertical glyph positions, and explicit script/language information. OpenType fonts work with any version of Windows and any application that supports TrueType fonts. Applications that don't support OpenType read the TrueType information from the font file, ignoring the OpenType extensions.

- **Raster**. Raster fonts are *bitmaps* — arrays of dots that are rendered on the display device as they appear in the bitmap image. These fonts are not device-independent, which means they don't look the same on different devices. Raster fonts are difficult to work with, making accurate scaling, rotation, and so on, almost impossible. You know you're dealing with a raster font when the text gets "chunky" as you increase its size.

- **Vector**. Vector fonts are mathematical models that define a set of lines for each character. They're easy to scale. Windows 98 comes with only one vector font, Modern.fon, which is available to maintain compatibility with plotter devices. You find this font in \Windows\Fonts.

Windows 98 associates a font name with its font file by using the Registry. Take a look in `HKEY_LOCAL_MACHINE\Software\Microsoft\Windows\CurrentVersion\Fonts`. Each type of font has a unique file extension. Raster and vector fonts use the FON extension. TrueType fonts use the TTF extension, and OpenType fonts use the OTF extension. Windows 98 also provides a hidden file, called Ttfcache, that contains FOT type data for TrueType and OpenType fonts. This maintains compatibility with Windows 3.1, which had two font files for each TrueType font: the FOT file contained a header and pointer information, and the TTF file contained the font data.

Check to make sure you're using the correct fonts with the appropriate devices. Device fonts obviously work with the device. Raster fonts work with dot matrix devices, including dot matrix printers and displays. Vector fonts work with any printer other than dot matrix: PCL, PostScript, and plotters. TrueType and OpenType fonts work with any device, with the exception of plotters.

## Font Loading

Windows 98 stores the location of each font in the Registry. When you upgrade Windows 98 from Windows 3.1, Windows 98 automatically moves the information from the [fonts] section of Win.ini to the Registry. Windows 98 loads raster, TrueType, and OpenType fonts when it starts. Each printer driver is responsible for loading any soft fonts described in Win.ini when the driver starts.

If a font doesn't load properly, it might be corrupt. Windows 98 automatically detects when a TrueType or OpenType font file is corrupt and marks it as unavailable. Windows 98 will no longer load that font file when it starts.

You can find a list of TrueType and OpenType fonts that Windows 98 loads in the Registry key HKEY_LOCAL_MACHINE\Software\ Microsoft\Windows\CurrentVersion\Fonts; and in HKEY_CURRE-NT_CONFIG\Display\Fonts, you can find a list of resolution-dependent raster fonts. Windows 98 picks the best font resolution for the current display device from this Registry key. You find a list of every possible raster font and resolution in HKEY_LOCAL_ MACHINE\Software\Microsoft\Windows\CurrentVersion\Fontsize.

## Font Matching

Font matching is the process of finding the right font to use when an application asks for characters to print or display. Windows 98 must choose the font installed on the computer or printer that most closely matches the font requested by the application. If the exact font isn't available, or two fonts with the same name exist, Windows

98 uses font matching to find the closest font. To do so, Windows 98 uses three different methods: table mapping, numeric classification (PANOSE), and manual matching:

- **Font mapping table.** Windows 98 uses a font mapping table to map screen fonts to printer fonts. The characteristics Windows 98 uses for matching include the character set, pitch, font family, typeface name, height, width, weight, slant, underline, and strikethrough. Windows 98 uses the following search order to find a matching font:

  1. Fonts in the printer's ROM
  2. Fonts in the printer's cartridge slot
  3. Downloadable soft fonts
  4. TrueType fonts

- **Numeric classification (PANOSE).** PANOSE was created by ElseWare Corporation. It's a popular system for numerically classifying fonts by their visual characteristics. Applications can search the PANOSE database for fonts that match a classification the closest. Characteristics recorded in the PANOSE database include the following:

  - Serif
  - Proportion
  - Contrast
  - Stroke variation and arm type
  - Letterform
  - Midline
  - X-height

- **Manual matching.** Users can match fonts on their own. Open \Windows\Fonts in Windows Explorer; then, choose View ➪ List Fonts by Similarity. Pick a font from the list, and Windows 98 displays the most similar fonts at the top of the list. Windows 98 uses PANOSE information to determine font similarity for this list.

# Troubleshooting Font Problems

Many problems with fonts are actually problems with your printer; therefore, work through the troubleshooting tips you find in "Troubleshooting Printing Problems," earlier in this chapter before you try the troubleshooting steps in this section. Note also that TrueType and OpenType fonts aren't designed to work on lower-resolution (75ppi to 150ppi) printers; so, if TrueType and OpenType fonts don't render on your printer, double-check its resolution.

If a font doesn't render correctly, follow these steps:

1. Check the output in Print Preview, if the application supports it. If the font renders okay in Print Preview, the problem lies between the Windows 98 printing system and the printer.

2. Try a different font, size, face, style, and so on.

3. Try the same font in a different document or different application. If it works, the problem might be with that particular document or with the application itself.

4. Print the font from the Fonts folder in Windows Explorer. Open \Windows\Fonts in Windows Explorer, double-click the font's icon, and then click Print. If the font prints okay, the problem is likely with the document or the application.

5. Try different orientations for your output: landscape versus portrait.

6. Download TrueType fonts as bitmaps: choose Print TrueType as graphics on the Fonts tab of the printer's Properties dialog box.

7. Try each printing language supported by the printer. For example, try PostScript and PCL if the printer supports both.

8. Use a printer-resident font if you're having trouble printing TrueType or OpenType fonts.

9. Change printer resolution, because Windows 98 might require a higher printer resolution to render TrueType fonts.

10. Check the amount of memory in the printer. If the printer doesn't have enough memory, fonts might not render correctly.

# Part III

## Networking

# Chapter 10

# Using Network Resources

## Installing Network Support during Setup

If the Windows 98 Setup program doesn't find a previous network configuration but it detects a network adapter, it installs Client for Microsoft Networks and TCP/IP. You must still configure the client to connect to the appropriate domain and TCP/IP to use WINS, DHCP, and so on. If the Setup program does find a previous network configuration, it keeps your previous network settings. The Setup program also installs Dial-Up Networking. Note that the Setup program upgrades the Novell NETX client to the Client for NetWare Networks.

Windows 98 enables you to upgrade from the following network clients:

- Artisoft LANtastic version 7.0 or greater
- Banyan Enterprise Client version 7.32 or greater
- Banyan VINES version 7.0 or greater
- Digital PATHWORKS 32
- Microsoft networks such as Microsoft LAN Manager, Windows for Workgroups 3.*x*, Windows 95, and Windows NT
- Novell NETX, VLM, and IntranetWare Client for Windows 95

- IBM Networks Client for Windows 95
- Solstice NFS Client version 3.1 or greater

# Upgrading to Protected-Mode Clients

Microsoft recommends that you stick with 32-bit protected-mode clients, which include the Client for Microsoft Networks and Client for NetWare Networks. In most cases, Windows 98 automatically upgrades a real-mode component to protected-mode during the upgrade process. In other cases, you have to upgrade real-mode components manually by removing them from Config.sys and Autoexec.bat while adding the 32-bit client via the Network icon in the Control Panel. Check with the vendor to see whether updated 32-bit clients are available. The benefits are plenty, including better performance, easier maintenance, and more manageability from an administrator's perspective. More specifically, take a look at these features found only in 32-bit networking clients:

- Remote administration of clients
- Configuration stored in the Registry
- Better performance and more reliability
- System policies for more administrative control

If you allow Windows 98 to upgrade to 32-bit components from 16-bit components, it tries to keep your configuration of the real-mode components. It moves the settings it finds in files such as Autoexec.bat and Protocol.ini to the Registry, for example.

# Using a Setup Script to Install Networking Components

You use Batch 98, a program that you find on the Windows 98 CD-ROM in \Tools\Reskit\Batch, to create setup scripts that allow for unattended installations. This program creates a file called Msbatch.inf, which provides the installation options to the

Windows 98 Setup program. To install the required networking components, you can customize this file. The following listing shows an excerpt from an Msbatch.inf file that automatically configures the user's network connection. You can add this listing to your own Msbatch.inf file or create equivalent entries using Batch 98.

```
[Network]
ComputerName="Portable"
Workgroup="DOMAIN"
Description="Jerry Honeycutt"
Display=0
PrimaryLogon=VREDIR
Clients=VREDIR
Protocols=MSTCP
Security=DOMAIN
PassThroughAgent="DOMAIN"


[MSTCP]
LMHOSTS=1
LMHOSTPath="C:\WINDOWS\lmhosts"
DHCP=1
DNS=0
WINS=D


[VREDIR]
LogonDomain="DOMAIN"
ValidatedLogon=1
```

Don't specify a network adapter in Msbatch.inf; allow the Setup program to detect the adapter automatically so that the setup script works properly on a variety of different machines with different network adapters. You can still configure the networking client, protocols, and services in the setup script, though. In the prior listing, replace the user name, passthrough agent, and logon domain with the appropriate values.

# Installing Networking Support after Setup

Installing the driver for a network adapter is the same as installing one for any other device. If you're installing a Plug and Play network adapter, allow Windows 98 to detect and configure the device automatically. If you're installing a legacy network adapter, use the Add New Hardware Wizard. To install a new networking component, whether it's a client, protocol, or server, follow these steps:

1. Open the Network icon in the Control Panel.

2. Click Add to display the Select Network Component Type dialog box, from which you can choose one of the following types of components. Select the component type, and click Add to display the Select dialog box.

   - **Client**. Install a networking client, which provides access to the resources on the network and handles security. You can install any number of 32-bit clients but only a single 16-bit client.

   - **Adapter**. Install a driver from your network adapter. You should allow Windows 98 to detect Plug and Play adapters automatically, and you should use the Add New Hardware Wizard to install drivers for legacy adapters. Use this option only if you're certain of the type of adapter and its configuration.

   - **Protocol**. Install a network protocol such as TCP/IP and IPX/SPX.

   - **Service**. Install a variety of services such as the file and printer sharing service or the Microsoft Remote Registry Service.

3. On the Select dialog box, choose the vendor from the left-hand list; then, choose the component from the right-hand list. Click OK

**4.** Close the Network dialog box. Windows 98 copies the appropriate files to your computer and updates your configuration. You have to restart the computer after changing your network configuration.

If you're installing a component that's not part of the Windows 98 source files, you won't find it in any of the Select dialog boxes. Instead, click Have Disk on the Select dialog box, type the path containing the INF file for the component, and click OK. You'll see a Select dialog box that shows all the components listed in all the INF files found in that path. Select the component that you want to install, and click OK. Close the Network dialog box, and restart Windows 98 when prompted.

# Specifying the Computer Name and Workgroup

Regardless of the network client or protocol that you're using, you must provide a network name for the computer and identify the workgroup in which the computer participates. If the Windows 98 Setup program detects a network adapter during setup, it prompts you for this information. If you install an adapter later, you might have to specify these settings yourself. You can, of course, change these settings any time you like. To provide a name, workgroup, and description for a computer, follow these steps:

**1.** Open the Network dialog box from the Control Panel, and click the Identification tab.

**2.** Specify a name for the computer in Computer name, the name of the workgroup in Workgroup, and a brief description of the computer in Computer Description. Remember that the computer's name must be unique on the immediate network.

**3.** Click OK to save your changes. You have to restart the computer after you change its identity.

Make sure that the name you assign to each computer is unique on the network. It can be up to 15 characters in length and can contain only alphanumeric characters and a handful of special characters such as these:

```
! @ # $ % ^ & ( ) - _ ' { } . ~
```

The workgroup name doesn't need to be unique on the network, but it too must be no longer than 15 characters, which include the same characters available for the computer name. You can specify either a workgroup name that you already know exists or a new workgroup name in which other users will eventually participate. Wrkgrp.ini contains a list of workgroups to which you want to limit the user, which is a very good way to standardize the workgroups used throughout the organization.

# Starting the Network When Windows 98 Starts

Windows 98 automatically starts the network if you're using 32-bit networking components. Thus, you don't need to put anything in your Autoexec.bat or Config.sys files. If you're using real-mode components, however, you'll have to start them from Autoexec.bat. If you're using real-mode components to connect to a Microsoft network, for example, the Setup program puts the Net command in Autoexec.bat to start the network. In that case, you find the network settings specified in Protocol.ini in the [Proman$], [ntecard], and [Ndishlp$] sections. Don't change these settings, because Windows 98 automatically maintains them. If you're installing another type of network, the settings required in the Autoexec.bat and Config.sys files will vary; but in most cases, the client installation program adds these settings for you.

# Logging on to the Network

The first time Windows 98 starts, it prompts the user for his or her credentials. After the user provides them, Windows 98 confirms his or her password in the Set Windows Password dialog box. If a network client is not installed on the computer, Windows 98 continues booting. To log on to a network for the first time, do the following:

- **No network**. Type your name and password in the Welcome to Windows 98 dialog box.

- **Microsoft network**. Type the user name and password in the spaces provided, followed by the name of the domain validating your logon.

- **NetWare network**. Type your name and password in the spaces provided, followed by the name of the preferred server.

After the first time a user logs on to the operating system, Windows 98 displays the name of the user who last logged on in the logon dialog box. If it's the same user, the user just has to type her password. If a different user logs on, she must type her user name and password. Note that you can prevent Windows 98 from displaying the last user who logged on by using the System Policy Editor.

The user can cancel any logon dialog box. The user can cancel the Windows 98 logon dialog box, for instance, but Windows 98 will not unlock the password list; thus, the user has to retype her password for each password-protected resource. The user can cancel one of the network logon dialog boxes, but then she won't have access to those network resources.

## Unified Logon

Unified logon simplifies the logon process by relieving the user from having to retype his credentials every time he wants to access a network resource. The user logs on one time, unlocking access to other resources, including the networks. If network clients are installed on the computer, Windows 98 tries to log the user on to each network as follows:

1. Windows 98 tries to log the user on to each network automatically, using the user's Windows 98 user name and password. Microsoft calls this capability a *unified logon*. By forcing the user to use the same credentials in Windows 98 as on the network, this approach requires the user to remember fewer passwords.

2. If the user's credentials are not the same on both Windows 98 and the network, Windows 98 prompts the user for his credentials. The user can optionally save the password in his password list by selecting "Save this password in your password list" before closing the logon dialog box. From then on, the user is not prompted for network credentials.

After the first logon, Windows 98 presents the logon dialog box corresponding to the primary network logon: Windows Logon, Client for Microsoft Networks, and so on. After validating the user's credentials, Windows 98 unlocks the user's password list to retrieve the remaining passwords necessary to log the user on to any other networks for which Windows 98 finds clients. If Windows 98 can log the user on to the other networks by using the same password as for the primary network logon, it doesn't retrieve any credentials from the password list. If the primary network logon is other than Windows Logon, perhaps Client for Microsoft Networks, Windows 98 doesn't unlock the user's password list until the security provider validates the user's credentials, and the user can't create new credentials on the workstation.

## Microsoft Family Logon

The Microsoft Family Logon presents a list of users from which a user can pick when he logs on to Windows 98. This new feature keeps the user from having to retype his user name each time he logs on to the computer, especially on computers shared by multiple users. Microsoft Family Logon requires that you enable user profiles. You can enable user profiles the traditional way, using the Passwords icon in the Control Panel, but this doesn't automatically install the Microsoft Family Logon. Use the new Users icon in the Control Panel to enable user profiles and the Microsoft Family Logon at the same time. To install Microsoft Family Logon after enabling user profiles, follow these steps:

1. Open the Network Properties dialog box from the Control Panel.

2. Click the Add button to display the Select Network Component Type dialog box.

3. Select Client from the list, and click Add.

4. Select Microsoft from the Manufacturers list and Microsoft Family Logon from the Network Clients list. Click OK.

5. Close the Network dialog box to save your changes. Restart the computer after changing your network configuration.

You must select Microsoft Family Logon as your primary network logon in the Network dialog box. If you don't, the user won't see the logon dialog box that you expect.

## Login Scripts

Windows 98 runs login scripts only in the following two situations, which are also the only two times that Windows 98 downloads user profiles and system policies:

- When the operating system starts.

- When the computer's configuration includes Dial-Up Networking but not a network adapter. In this situation, Windows 98 runs the login script the first time that it connects to the network via Dial-Up Networking.

On a Windows NT network, login scripts are nothing more than batch files that Windows 98 downloads from the server and runs on the user's workstation. You can use login scripts to configure the user's computer, including such things as making network connections, setting paths, and so on. Login scripts enable the administrator to manage portions of the user's working environment without using policies. You use the User Manager for Domains to assign a login script to each user or group of users. Just remember that Windows 98 downloads login scripts from the server that validates the user's logon, the primary network logon.

Windows 98 includes a parser that can handle most statements in a NetWare login script. It can parse NDS login scripts when connecting to NDS or the bindery script when connecting in bindery mode. On NetWare 3.*x* Networks or when using the bindery, Windows 98 uses the login script called Net$log.dat that it finds in the Public directory on the server. It also downloads individual user scripts from the user's mail folder on the server. On an NDS server, Windows 98 gets the login script from the NDS database. The script parser displays the login script in a window if the script contains the keywords Write, Display, Pause, or Wait.

**Tip**

The persistent connections in Windows 98 make login scripts less useful than they used to be. Instead of connecting a network resource by mapping it in the login script, use the Map command on the network resource's property sheet. For example, right-click a network share and choose Map Network Drive. Select Reconnect at logon to make the drive mapping persistent. Windows 98 automatically connects to the device the next time the user restarts the computer.

# Browsing and Using Network Resources

Setting up the network to make browsing and using resources easy requires a bit of advance planning. The following notes describe things that you should consider prior to rolling out Windows 98:

- Plan how you want users to browse networks so that you can create a Wrkgrp.ini file beforehand that defines each workgroup. You use this file to create a list of workgroups that a user can join.

- Users who access the network over slow connections might not be able to browse resources on the network. If you have users in this situation, they can either map the network resources to a drive letter, forcing Windows 98 to verify the resource, or launch the UNC path of the network from the Run dialog box, which opens the resource in Explorer. You can force the network to send a list of names to the remote users by setting the workgroup name to the network's domain name.

- Use system policies to control what information users can browse on the network. For instance, Hide Network Neighborhood or Hide Drives in My Computer removes the Network Neighborhood from the My Computer folder.

Windows 98 networking supports the universal naming convention (UNC). You can map to network resources the old-fashioned way, either through the Net command or by mapping to the resources on their property sheets. Or you can use UNC paths. You type the UNC path to a resource anywhere that a normal path is valid as input, including in the Open or Save As dialog boxes. A UNC path has the form \\*server\share\path*, in which *server* is the name of the server that hosts the share, *share* is the name of the volume or shared resource, and *path* is the path to the resource, starting from the share. To open a folder on the Accounting server in a share called Reports in a path called Monthly, type **\\Accounting\Reports\Monthly** in the Run dialog box.

Note that the NetWare client enables you to use the traditional syntax, which looks like *server/volume:path*. You can't, however, use the NetWare 4.0 naming convention, which looks like \\\\*NDS_object\path*, in Windows 98. Most 16-bit programs and a few 32-bit programs don't support UNC paths, so you must map to the resource and then use the mapped drive letter within those programs. Alternatively, some programs provide a button on file dialog boxes that enables you to temporarily map to a network resource.

## Network Neighborhood

To open Network Neighborhood, double-click the Network Neighborhood icon on the desktop. You can also open the Network Neighborhood folder in Windows Explorer. Either way, you see a hierarchy that begins with the entire network, followed by the workgroups and domains on it. To browse a server without using Network Neighborhood, type its UNC path in the Run dialog box. For instance, type \\**MyServer** in the Run dialog box and click OK to browse the server in an Explorer window. Then, open any share or press Backspace to view the workgroup to which the user belongs.

The System Policy Editor provides a handful of policies that control the Network Neighborhood icon:

- **Hide Network Neighborhood** prevents the user from opening Network Neighborhood by removing its icon from the desktop.

- **No Entire Network in Network Neighborhood** prevents the user from accessing the Entire Network icon in Network Neighborhood.

- **No Workgroup Contents in Network Neighborhood** prevents the user from viewing workgroup contents in Network Neighborhood.

To map to a network drive, follow these steps:

1. Right-click the share in Network Neighborhood, and choose Map Network Drive. The Map Network Drive dialog box is displayed.

2. Select the drive letter that you want to assign to the share from Drive, and then select Reconnect at logon if you want Windows 98 to restore the connection after it restarts. If you have your network connection set to Quick logon, the con-

nection is not restored until you actually try to use the resource.

3. Click OK to save the drive mapping. You'll see it in Windows Explorer with the other mapped and local drives.

## Net Command

You can use the Net command to work with network resources without using Network Neighborhood. Here's an overview of three versions of the Net command that are useful for browsing and connecting to network resources:

- Type `net view \\server\` at the command prompt to view the resources shared on that particular server. To view the resources available on a workgroup, type the following: `net view/workgroup:workgroup`.

- Type `net use * \\server\share` at the command prompt to connect to a specific resource on the server. You can also append a password to the command if a password is required to connect to the resource. The asterisk specifies the next available driver letter, but you can replace it with a specific drive letter if you like.

- Type `net use drive:/delete` at the command prompt to disconnect from a mapped drive, where *drive:* is the letter of the drive to which Windows 98 mapped the resource.

# Sharing Resources on a Peer-to-Peer Network

Peer resource sharing complements the primary network server by reducing the load on the network. Instead of relying on the primary server to store everything, users can distribute the load by sharing files on their computers. This expands the network inexpensively by sharing space on each workstation. Considering that each Windows

98 workstation is rarely used to its full potential, this is a great way to leverage those resources.

Windows 98 supports only one file and printer service at a time, and each one has the following requirements:

- **File and Printer Sharing for NetWare Networks**. The computer must be using user-level security, and a NetWare server must be available on the network to act as a passthrough security provider.

- **File and Printer Sharing for Microsoft Networks**. Microsoft's file and printer sharing service can use share-level or user-level security. A Microsoft server must be available on the network to provide passthrough security if you're using user-level security.

To install file and printer sharing for either type of network, follow these steps:

1. Open the Network dialog box from the Control Panel.

2. Click the File and Printer Sharing button to display the File and Printer Sharing dialog box.

3. Select whether you want to share files and whether you want to share printers; then, close the File and Printer Sharing dialog box.

4. Click OK, and close the Network dialog box to save your settings. Restart your computer after changing your network settings.

MS-DOS mode takes complete control of the computer, preventing users from accessing shares on that computer. To prevent the user from running single-mode MS-DOS applications and thus avoid having shares unavailable, set the Disable Single-Mode MS-DOS Applications policy on that computer.

Resource security protects shared folders and printers in Windows 98. You choose between share-level security (the weaker) or user-level security (the stronger) to protect shared resources.

With share-level security, any user who knows the password can access a share. Share-level security isn't available with the file and printer sharing service for NetWare. With user-level security, a security provider validates a user's credentials before Windows 98 gives the user access to the share; and even then the share's owner must grant the user rights to the share by adding him or her to the user list.

To enable share-level security on a workstation, follow these steps:

1. Open the Network dialog box from the Control Panel, and click the Access Control tab.

2. Select Share-level access control.

3. Close the Network dialog box. Restart your computer when prompted.

To enable user-level security on a workstation, follow these steps:

1. Open the Network dialog box from the Control Panel, and click the Access Control tab.

2. Select User-level access control, and type the name of the security provider in Obtain list of users and groups from. If the network name isn't available, Windows 98 asks you what type of security provider the network name represents: NetWare, NT Domain, or NT Server or Workstation.

3. Close the Network dialog box. Restart your computer when prompted.

If you don't want users to expose files or printers on their computer, you can enable the Disable file sharing and Disable print sharing policies.

## Share-Level Security

Share-level security protects a resource by requiring users to know the password before they can access it. You can give users full access, read-only access, or both by providing a different password for each type of access. To share a folder or printer by using share-level security, follow these steps:

1. Right-click the folder that you want to share, choose Sharing, and click the Sharing tab.

2. Select Shared As, and type a name for the share in Share Name.

3. Select Read-Only, Full, or Depends on Password. Type a password in Read-Only Password if you choose Read-Only, in Full Access Password if you choose Full, or in both files if you choose Depends on Password.

4. Close the dialog box to save your changes. An open hand is superimposed over the lower-left corner of the folder's icon.

You can hide a share from Network Neighborhood by appending a dollar sign to the name: mine$. This is useful to avoid cluttering the name space with too many infrequently used shares, but be warned: some applications, particularly some Microsoft developer tools, choke on shares that are hidden in this manner. To access a hidden share, launch the share name in the Run dialog box. For example, to open the mine$ share on a computer called desktop, choose Run from the Start menu, type **\\desktop\mine$**, and press Enter. Windows 98 opens the share in a folder.

## User-Level Security

User-level security is more secure than share-level security and is therefore a bit more complicated. When a user tries to access a shared resource that's protected by user-level security, Windows 98 validates the user's credentials on the security provider. Then, it gives the user access to the resource based on the rights assigned to the user in the Sharing properties dialog box. To share a folder or printer using user-level security, follow these steps:

1. Right-click the folder or drive you want to share, choose Sharing, and click the Sharing tab.

2. Select Shared As, and type a name for the share in Share Name.

3. Give permissions to individual users and groups. Click Add to open the Add Users dialog box and add rights to each user. The rights you can assign depend on the resource you're sharing:

   - **Folders**. You can assign read-only, full, or custom access. With custom access, you can give the user read, write, create, list, delete, change file attributes, and change access rights permissions. The table at the end of this section describes the rights required for a user to perform different tasks.

   - **Printers**. You can assign the right to use the printer or not.

   - **Remote Administration**. You can assign the right to administer the workstation or not. You define this right using the Password Properties dialog box in the Control Panel.

4. Close the folder's property sheet to save your changes. An open hand is superimposed on the folder's icon, just as it is with share-level security.

After validating a user's credentials, Windows 98 checks the rights assigned to the user by the share the user is trying to access. If the user is given explicit rights to the resource (his or her name is in the access list), Windows 98 enforces those rights. If the user isn't given explicit rights, Windows 98 checks the rights of all the groups to which the user belongs. If none of these groups has explicit rights, Windows 98 denies the user access to the resource. When you share a folder and give a user rights to it, the user also gets those same rights to all the folder's child folders. These are called *implied rights*, which more formally stated are rights assigned to the nearest parent folder.

| Task | Permissions Required |
|------|---------------------|
| Change access rights | Change access control |
| Change folder or filename | Change file attributes |
| Copy files from a folder | Read and list |
| Copy files to a folder | Write, create, and list |
| Create a folder | Create |
| Create and write a file | Create |
| Delete a file or folder | Delete |
| Read from a closed file | Read |
| Rename a file or folder | Change file attributes |
| Run a program | Read and list |
| Search a folder for files | List |
| View filenames | List |
| Write to a closed file | Write, create, delete, and change |

# Securing Windows 98 on the Network

Network security is complicated; refer to your network vendor's documentation to learn how to implement it appropriately. Nevertheless, some features are common to all servers. The server maintains a user database that Windows 98 can use to validate the credentials of a user who wants to sign on to a workstation or access a shared resource protected by share-level security. When Windows 98 uses a server in this role, the server is called a *security provider*. The server also protects its resources. You assign rights to specific users or groups. The server enforces those rights, giving access to some and denying access to others, by testing the user's rights against the resource's access control list.

Alone, the server provides certain security capabilities; likewise, Windows 98 provides certain independent features. Combine the two, however, and you get capabilities such as these:

- **Policies**. System policies control what users can and can't do on their computers. Windows 98 automatically downloads policy files from the server.

- **Passwords**. By making users' Windows 98 and logon passwords identical, Windows 98 automatically logs users on to the network without requiring them to retype their credentials.

- **User-level security**. Windows 98 relies on the server to maintain an account database and provide security, which it relies on to validate a user's credentials before giving him or her access to a shared resource.

When users connect to the Internet via a dial-up connection, the Internet doesn't pose much of a threat to operating system-level security in Windows 98. That is, there aren't many ways someone can sign on to a Windows 98 workstation and access its contents without validation from a security provider. Double-check that you haven't bound the file and printer sharing service to the Dial-Up Adapter to eliminate any possibility whatsoever. This prevents access to the user's workstation from the Internet via the Dial-Up Adapter. To unbind file and printer sharing from the Dial-Up Adapter, follow these steps:

1. Open the Network dialog box from the Control Panel.

2. Select TCP/IP ⇨ Dial-Up Adapter from the list, and click Properties. If you don't have a network card installed in the computer, you see only TCP/IP. Dismiss the TCP/IP Properties Information message box, and click the Bindings tab on the TCP/IP Properties dialog box.

3. Deselect the File and Printer Sharing services. If you're connecting to a Microsoft network, deselect File and Printer Sharing for Microsoft Networks. If you're connecting to a NetWare network, deselect File and Printer Sharing for NetWare Networks.

4. Close the TCP/IP Properties dialog box and the Network dialog box. Restart your computer when prompted.

# Securing Windows 98 Passwords

Windows 98 password lists store the password for each password-protected resource the user accesses in a password list file. The password list file is in C:\Windows, and its name is *user*.pwl, where *user* is the user name. When the user accesses a password-protected resource for the first time, he or she sees the logon dialog box. Windows 98 saves the password in the user's password list if the user chooses Save this password in your password list, which is checked by default. The next time the user accesses the same resource, Windows 98 uses the password it finds in the password list. It doesn't prompt the user for the password again unless the password no longer unlocks the resource. The following list describes the types of resources for which Windows 98 stores passwords in the list:

- Any resource protected by share-level security
- Applications written using the Master Password API
- NT workstations and servers that aren't in the domain
- NT domain if the primary logon isn't Client for Microsoft Networks
- NetWare servers
- Secure Web sites

The password list is encrypted. Windows 98 unlocks the user's password list only after the user successfully logs on to the workstation. By changing the primary logon to one of the network clients, you can ensure that the password list remains locked until a security provider such as Windows NT validates the user's credentials. Note that unlocking the password list doesn't decrypt it; unlocking the list just makes the passwords available when the user accesses a password-protected resource. Passwords are always encrypted, even when transmitted over the network.

Windows 98 does not open the password cache if the user bypasses the logon by pressing Escape or clicking Cancel. In such a case, the user has to type the password each time he or she accesses a password-protected resource. For desktop users, this is usually not an issue. Mobile users deal with this all the time, however. If your portable computer is configured to log on to a network and you take the computer on the road, you'll probably cancel the logon so you can access the computer without validating your credentials on the server. If you use Dial-Up Networking to make a remote network connection, however, you have to retype your password. The solution for mobile users is to change the primary logon to Windows Logon. Doing so causes Windows 98 to open your password list when you log on with your name and password, without causing delays or problems if the security provider isn't available.

## Editing the Password List

The Password List Editor doesn't let you view the password for each resource, but it does let you remove passwords from the list. The only time you really need this utility is when you run across problems using one of the passwords. The user who owns the password list must log on to the computer to use the Password List Editor. You can't use the Password List Editor remotely; you can't even log on to the computer as Administrator to use the editor. To install the Password List Editor, follow these steps:

1. Open the Add/Remove Programs dialog box from the Control Panel, click the Windows Setup tab, and click Have Disk.

2. Type **D:\TOOLS\reskit\netadmin\pwledit\Pwledit.inf** in the space provided, where *D* is the CD-ROM's drive letter, or click Browser to locate the file. Click OK; the Have Disk dialog box is displayed.

3. Select Password List Editor from the list, and click Install.

4. Close the Add/Remove Programs Properties dialog box. You don't need to restart your computer after making this change.

To remove a password using the Password List Editor, follow these steps:

1. Start the Password List Editor. Windows 98 stores it on the Start menu in Programs ⇨ Accessories ⇨ System Tools ⇨ Password List Editor.

2. Select one or more resources from the list, and click Remove.

3. Close the Password List Editor.

# Changing or Synchronizing Resource Passwords

You can change the password of any password-protected network resource so that it's different from your Windows 98 password. If you do this, the Windows 98 password will be different from the network resource's password, so unified logon won't work, and the user will have to provide a different password to access the resource. To change a password for a password-protected network resource, follow these steps:

1. Open the Passwords Properties dialog box from the Control Panel, and click Change Other Passwords.

2. Select the resource for which you want to change the password, and click Change.

3. In the Change Password dialog box, type the old password; then, type the new password in New password and Confirm new password.

4. Close the Change Password and Passwords Properties dialog boxes to save your changes.

By synchronizing passwords, users can take advantage of the Windows 98 unified logon, accessing all network resources by typing credentials one time. Windows 98 can't synchronize NetWare passwords, but it can synchronize passwords on a Microsoft network. If the user currently has different passwords for different resources and wants to take advantage of the unified logon, she can easily change them to match the Windows 98 logon password using the Passwords Properties dialog box. To synchronize network resource passwords with the Windows 98 password, follow these steps:

1. Open the Passwords Properties dialog box from the Control Panel, and click Change Windows Password. The Change Windows Password dialog box is displayed.

2. Select the resources for which you want to synchronize the password, and click OK.

3. Close the Passwords Properties dialog box to save your changes.

# Using Policies to Tighten Up Password Security

You can use the following machine policies to enforce password security:

- **Disable automatic NetWare login**. Windows 98 doesn't automatically try to use the Windows 98 logon credentials to log the user on to a NetWare server.

- **Disable password caching**. Windows 98 doesn't store passwords in the user's password list, requiring users to retype their password every time they try to access a password-protected resource.

- **Disable passwords control panel**. This policy prevents the user from opening the Passwords Properties dialog box from the Control Panel.

■ **Hide change passwords page.** This policy prevents the user from opening the Change Passwords dialog box from the Passwords Properties dialog box.

■ **Hide share passwords with asterisks.** Windows 98 displays asterisks instead of the characters a user types when logging on to a shared resource that's protected by share-level security. Windows 98 enables this policy by default.

■ **Log on to Windows NT.** Selecting Disable caching of domain password prevents Windows 98 from storing users' domain credentials in the password list, requiring users to type their Windows 98 credentials as well as their network credentials.

■ **Minimum Windows password length.** The user must create passwords that are the minimum length specified in the policy.

■ **Require alphanumeric Windows password.** The user must create passwords that contain a combination of numbers and letters rather than letters alone. This increases password security by making passwords more difficult to guess.

■ **Require validation from network for Windows access.** Windows 98 does not give users access without first validating their credentials on the security provider.

# Chapter 11

# Installing Adapters and Protocols

## Using Microsoft's TCP/IP Protocol

Microsoft has its own implementation of the TCP/IP protocol, which is a good choice both for larger networks that span multiple segments and use routing as a means of managing data traffic and for situations in which network connectivity between different operating systems is required. Specific features of Microsoft's TCP/IP product include the following:

- Availability of common TCP/IP utilities, such as arp, ping, ftp, telnet, route, tracert, netstat, and nbtstat. (For more information on these utilities, see Appendix A, *Command Lines*.)

- A robust suite of Internet protocols, including Transmission Control Protocol (TCP), User Datagram Protocol (UDP), Internet Protocol (IP), Internet Control Message Protocol (ICMP), Address Resolution Protocol (ARP), and Domain Name System (DNS) protocol.

- Support for Windows Socket 1.1 and 2.0 API (an API used by many network and client/server programs).

- Support for the NetBIOS API (NetBIOS over TCP/IP).

- Support for Internet connectivity and connectivity to non-Microsoft operating systems, such as UNIX, Apple Systems, and various mainframe operating systems.

- Support for the asynchronous communication Point-to-Point Protocol (PPP) used in dial-up connections.

- Support for the Windows Internet Naming Service (WINS) that handles the IP address-to-NetBIOS name resolution process.

- Support for automatic TCP/IP address configuration using Microsoft's Dynamic Host Configuration Protocol (DHCP).

Microsoft's Windows 98 implementation of TCP/IP also includes the following:

- Windows Socket 2.0 support.

- IP multicasting capabilities, to enable the broadcast of data messages to a specified subset of all broadcast destinations.

- Automatic private IP addressing by the client. (For more information on private IP addressing, see the upcoming section "Understanding How TCP/IP Works.")

- *Multihoming* capabilities, by which a single system can have multiple IP addresses.

- Enhancements to DHCP to support longer time-out intervals and address-assignment conflict detection when working with leased IP addresses.

- TCP performance improvements for some types of high-bandwidth networks by supporting Fast Retransmit and Fast Recovery features, TCP Large Windows (RFC 1323), and Selective Acknowledgments (RFC 2018).

- ICMP router discovery (RFC 1256).

# Installing and Configuring TCP/IP

TCP/IP is a routed protocol that can support numerous networks with numerous network devices. Unlike NetBIOS, which relies on network node names to identify a destination on the local network, TCP/IP can be routed or sent across multiple subnets to its final destination. Data packets sent using the TCP/IP protocol can find their final destination across multiple subnets because the information necessary to determine the location of a specific network and a network device is contained within the TCP/IP address (see "IP Routing" later in this chapter). Every TCP/IP message sent across the network contains both the sender's and receiver's TCP/IP address. Thus, the TCP/IP communication protocol requires some planning before it is implemented. To configure your TCP/IP network correctly, you should understand and review the following:

- The number of networks and subnetworks that you will use.
- The number of computers that will be on each network or subnetwork.
- Whether you will use a Class A, B, or C Internet address. (See "Understanding How TCP/IP Works" later in this chapter for more information on Internet address classes.)
- Whether your network will be totally private or connect to third-party systems or the Internet.
- How you plan to manage network address changes.

To install TCP/IP on a Windows 98 computer, follow these steps:

1. Open the Network Properties dialog box from the Control Panel.
2. Click the Add button on the Configuration tab.
3. Select the protocol from the component type list.
4. Click the Add button.
5. In the Manufacturers list, select Microsoft.
6. In the Network Protocols list, select TCP/IP.
7. Click OK.

# Understanding How TCP/IP Works

TCP/IP is a full-featured protocol with many features and options for dealing with the many different types of network situations. To select the correct set of options for your particular environment, you need to understand the options and features that are available with the TCP/IP protocol and when to use them.

## Addressing

Because TCP/IP can be used to communicate with systems other than Windows and because all network addresses within a network must be unique, you must adhere to a defined set of rules when you set up your addressing scheme. These rules cover both the type of address scheme that you use and the range of address numbers that you can use.

Before you implement a TCP/IP networking environment, you must determine which addressing scheme to use. You need to choose from two types of addresses and three different classes of addresses, depending on the size and design of your network. Much as a real estate developer has to design a subdivision to accommodate traffic flow and the customer's use of the property before building any houses, you need to design your network addressing scheme before you set up your host computers.

The following are the two types of addresses that are available when you implement a TCP/IP environment:

- **Globally unique IP addresses** are assigned in blocks by the Internet Assigned Numbers Authority (IANA) to organizations, which can then assign these addresses within their organization, as needed. IANA is the organization that oversees and coordinates the assignment of every unique address on the Internet and is ultimately responsible for ensuring that these addresses are unique. Contact IANA on the Internet to obtain addresses for your organization. If you plan to make your computer or network device directly accessible via the Internet, you need unique addresses so that no address conflicts occur with any other network devices on the Internet. Visit `http://www.iana.org` and `http://www.isi.edu` for more information.

■ **Private IP addresses** can be used by an organization to configure its private internal IP networks. These addresses are useful to preserve the remaining address space on the Internet. Most computers on private networks don't need to be accessible directly from the Internet, but a need does exist for consistent IP addressing schemes. To support this consistency, IANA has reserved a number of addresses that will never be used on the Internet. These addresses may be used by organizations to configure private IP networks that are not directly accessible or visible from the Internet because these addresses are unique only within the private network and could conflict with other network devices on the Internet. The three blocks of IP addresses set aside for use in private networks are as follows:

Class A: 10.0.0.0–10.255.255.255

Class B: 172.16.0.0–172.31.255.255

Class C: 192.168.0.0–192.168.255.255

To request globally unique addresses, you can contact IANA via e-mail at `iana@isi.edu`. IANA is located at the Information Sciences Institute, University of Southern California. The Web site is `http://www.iana.org`.

## Selecting Your Addresses

The following are some tips to help you choose IP addresses:

■ If you are configuring a computer to be accessible on the Internet, use a globally unique IP address that you have obtained from IANA.

■ If you are configuring a computer that will never access the Internet, use a private IP address from the reserved numbers defined by IANA.

■ If you are configuring a computer that will access the Internet only for e-mail or Web browsing but doesn't need to be addressable from the Internet, you may use a private IP address if you use a firewall that provides proxy or Network Address Translator (NAT) capabilities when accessing the Internet.

## Proxy Servers and Network Address Translators

Many organizations need to connect private networks to the Internet to let their users send and receive Internet e-mail and browse the Internet. Two issues must be dealt with when you connect a private network to the Internet: You must ensure that private network addresses aren't used on the Internet, and you must protect the privacy of users on the private network by limiting access to their systems from the Internet. A proxy server with NAT capabilities can resolve both these issues.

A proxy server resides between users on the private network and the Internet and acts on behalf of users on the private network to access the Internet. The proxy server is configured with a valid globally unique IP address that can be used on the Internet. When a host on a private network wants to send a message to the Internet, the proxy server intercepts the message and substitutes its own valid IP source address in place of the user's private address. Thus, messages appear to originate from the proxy server rather than from the host with the private address. When incoming messages are detected, the proxy server again substitutes the local private user's destination address in place of the proxy server's address and forwards the message to the host on the private network. This provides a measure of security by preventing outside computers on the Internet from being able to communicate directly with computers on the private network. Additionally, it helps to preserve the remaining name space on the Internet — an increasingly significant issue — by requiring the use of globally unique IP addresses only by the network translation device that connects the private network to the Internet.

To configure your computer to access a gateway or proxy server, do the following:

1. Open the Network dialog box from the Control Panel.

2. Click TCP/IP in the list of components, click Properties, and click the Gateway tab.

3. Enter the IP address of the Gateway machine in the New Gateway text box.

4. Click the Add button to add the address to your Gateway list.

5. For additional gateways, repeat Steps 3 and 4. (Gateways are searched in the order in which they appear in the list, from the top to the bottom of the list.)

6. Click OK to close the Network dialog box.

## Automatic Private IP Addressing

In Windows 98, TCP/IP enables clients on a small local private network to assign themselves private IP addresses. DHCP clients can automatically assign themselves private IP addresses when the DHCP server is unavailable. (For information on other features of DHCP, see "Dynamic Address Allocation Using DHCP" later in this chapter.) When the DHCP server is unavailable during the boot process, the DHCP client uses B-node NetBIOS naming to assign itself a unique IP address from the 10.*.*.* IP address space. After assigning itself a 10.*.*.* address, the client can use TCP/IP to communicate with any other computer using a 10.*.*.* TCP/IP address on the same LAN hub. Later, when the DHCP server becomes available, the client stops using the automatically assigned private IP address and secures an IP address from the DHCP server.

## IP Address Classes

An IP address is composed of four 8-bit bytes, often referred to as *octets*. Each octet can have a value between 0 and 255. Within the IP address, octets are separated by a period, resulting in an address that looks like this: 121.10.9.117. This format is sometimes referred to as *dotted decimal notation*. Together, these four octets form a full 32-bit IP address that contains two pieces of information:

- The host ID, which identifies the specific computer or host being addressed on a network or subnetwork

- The network ID, which identifies a logical group of computers on the network, known as a *subnetwork*, or *subnet* for short

Together, the host ID and the network ID form a unique address for a host computer or network device within the network or subnetworks. Exactly how the four octets that make up the host ID and network ID are interpreted defines which class of IP address is being used. Three different classes of IP addresses have been defined for configuring an IP network: Class A, Class B, and Class C (see Figure 11-1). The size of the network, as measured by the number of subnets and end-user nodes, primarily determines which class of address should be used.

- **Class A IP address.** Use Class A addresses (0.0.0.0–127.0.0.0) when you need a larger number of host IDs and a smaller number of network IDs. A Class A IP address uses the first octet for the network IDs and the remaining three octets for the host IDs. This provides 126 values for the network IDs (octet 1) and 16,777,214 values for the host IDs (octets 2 through 4), as shown in Figure 11-1. In practice, Class A addresses are rarely used, because they provide for such a large number of host IDs that most host IDs end up being wasted.

- **Class B IP address.** Use Class B addresses (128.0.0.0–191.255.0.0) when you need a large number of host IDs and a large number of network IDs. Class B IP addresses use the first two octets for the network IDs and the second two octets for the host IDs. This provides 16,384 values for the network IDs (octets 1 and 2) and 65,534 values for the host IDs (octets 3 and 4).

- **Class C IP address.** Use Class C addresses (192.0.0.0–223.255.255.0) when you need fewer than 255 host IDs and a large number of network IDs. Class C IP addresses use the first three octets for the network IDs and the last octet for the host IDs. This provides 2,097,151 values for the network IDs (octets 1 through 3) and 254 values for the host IDs (octet 4).

|  | Octet 1: | Octet 2: | Octet 3: | Octet 4: |
|---|---|---|---|---|
| Class A | Networking ID | Host ID | Host ID | Host ID |
| Class B | Networking ID | Networking ID | Host ID | Host ID |
| Class C | Networking ID | Networking ID | Networking ID | Host ID |

**Figure 11-1** *Class A, B, and C IP addresses*

Follow these guidelines when you select your addresses:

- In practice, avoid using the Class A IP address scheme.

- If you design your network to allow for a large number of network hosts and a large number of subnets, use a Class B IP address scheme.

- If you design your network to have a smaller number of network hosts on a large number of subnets, use a Class C IP address scheme.

Some network addresses are reserved for special situations:

- Default route address (default destination for outgoing packets): 0.0.0.0

- Network addresses (to identify networks): \*.\*.\*.0

- Broadcast addresses (to broadcast to a group of computers): \*.\*.\*.255

- Multicast addresses (to broadcast to a group of networks): 224.*.*.*

- Loopback address (for loopback testing): 127.0.0.1

## Subnet Masks

As part of the definition of the address classes, a portion of the address's 32 bits is used for the network ID, and the remainder is used for the host ID. The subnet mask is used by the host computer or network device to interpret which address bits are intended for the network ID and which bits are intended for the host ID. Because each IP data packet contains the sender's and receiver's IP address, the subnet mask enables the receiving network device or computer to determine which subnet and host sent the data packet. To define the subnet mask, you specify a 1 for each bit used in the network ID and a 0 for each bit used in the host ID. Thus, the subnet mask has the following format:

Class A address: 255.0.0.0

Class B address: 255.255.0.0

Class C address: 255.255.255.0

All hosts and network devices on the same LAN must use the same subnet mask.

## IP Routing

Network architects group hosts and network devices into logical subnets when they design networks to make the network easier to maintain and to reduce network traffic. These subnets may be connected to other subnets by network devices called *routers*, which are designed to isolate the subnets from each other and to prevent the unnecessary spread of network messages. Routers attempt to route a message to the intended recipient as efficiently as possible by minimizing the number of subnets that receive the message rather than having all messages go to all hosts on all subnets, which would create a huge network traffic problem.

Basically, routers route messages by using two pieces of information: the network ID portion of the IP address and a route table. *Route tables* contain a list of addresses of other routers and the various subnets to which they can forward messages. Thus, a router doesn't need to know the address of every host on every network. Instead, when a router receives a network message, it checks whether the network ID of the address is for its own subnet (using the subnet mask), and, if so, the router delivers the message to the intended host on its own subnet. If the address is for another subnet, the router forwards the message to another router that is designated to handle messages bound for the subnet defined in the IP address.

Windows 98 automatically maintains a route table that determines where TCP/IP data packets should be sent. The route table tracks the following information, which is used to determine the routes to use when communicating over the network:

- **Network address** is the destination address. This list can have four different types of entries:
  - **Default gateway** is the route used when no match exists.
  - **Host address** is a route to a specific destination address.
  - **Network address** is a route to a specific network.
  - **Subnet address** is a route to a subnet.

- **Netmask** defines which portion of the network address must match for this route to be used (1 = must match, 0 = don't care).

- **Gateway address** is the gateway address where the packet must be sent (can be the address of either the local network card or a gateway, such as a router).

- **Interface** is the address of the network card over which the data packet should be sent.

- **Metric** is the number of "hops" needed to reach the destination. A *hop* is any other network device (router) that forwards your packet on toward its final destination. The fewer the hops, the more efficient the route is for sending the packet.

To display the route table, type route print at the MS-DOS prompt.

## Dynamic Address Allocation Using DHCP

Every device on the network must have a network address. In a Microsoft network environment, IP addresses can be allocated to network devices basically in two ways: statically and dynamically. In the early days of TCP/IP networks, IP addresses were allocated manually, and these static IP addresses were not expected to change, because updating the address lists and host addresses was time-consuming. However, with the explosion of temporarily connected users (remote users, laptop users, PCs that get shut off on a daily basis), the need to dynamically allocate IP addresses has grown, as has the problem of updating all the name and address lists that are needed for name resolution and routing purposes. To deal with these issues, Microsoft provides the Dynamic Host Configuration Protocol (DHCP).

DHCP, as defined in RFC 1541 and implemented by Microsoft, was designed to solve the problem of manually configuring TCP/IP systems. The DHCP protocol enables IP addresses to be assigned automatically from a centrally stored and managed pool of available IP addresses, which can reside on one or more servers. Other TCP/IP-related information, such as the default gateway, domain name server addresses, and the subnet mask, can also be assigned with DHCP. The IP address is "leased" to the client computer, and the address expires after a preset time limit, which can be set by the system administrator and can range from minutes to days. IP addresses are leased to enable expired addresses to be reused when they are not renewed by the requesting client. By temporarily assigning or leasing IP addresses, you can better serve computers that dynamically attach and detach from the network.

DHCP servers do not share information with other DHCP servers or with DNS servers. The IP address pool managed by a DHCP server is entirely owned by the DHCP server, and IP addresses from this pool can be assigned only by the owning DHCP server. This can cause some problems with fault tolerance. When the DHCP server is unavailable, client computers can't extend their lease on the IP address, which can cause problems in the network, because clients aren't allowed to continue using expired IP addresses.

To configure your Windows 98 computer to use DHCP, do the following:

1. From the Control Panel, open the Network dialog box.

2. Select the TCP/IP protocol that is bound to your network adapter.

3. Click the Properties button.

4. Click the IP Address tab.

5. Select the radio button labeled Obtain an IP address automatically to enable DHCP address leasing for your computer. (If you don't select this option, you must select Specify an IP address and then manually enter an IP address and subnet mask value for your computer.)

6. Click OK to retain the setting.

7. Click OK to exit the Network setup application.

DHCP servers can't detect IP addresses that are already in use on a network by non-DHCP clients. If a manually configured IP address is within the scope of IP addresses that can be assigned by the DHCP server, address conflicts can occur. To prevent this situation, exclude all manually configured IP addresses from the scope of the DHCP addresses.

## Name Resolution

Although computers can easily work with numbers, numbered IP addresses can be difficult for people to remember. For this reason, a host can be assigned a name that represents its IP address. The process of translating an IP address into a name or a name into an IP address is called *name resolution*.

In the Microsoft network environment, name resolution can be handled in several different ways, including WINS, DNS, broadcast name resolution, or through the use of the Host and LMHost files. Each of these strategies is discussed briefly in the following sections.

**Name Resolution Using Host and LMHost Files** The Host and LMHost text files contain tables of the IP addresses and the associated names of network devices and hosts that are on the network. Applications can use these tables to perform name resolution. When an application wants to resolve a NetBIOS name to an IP address, it can look up this information in the LMHost file. When an application wants to look up a DNS host name mapping to an IP address, it can use the Host file, which maintains a table of the DNS name and IP address mapping. These files can be used as an alternative to WINS and DNS when these services are unavailable. Because you must manually enter the name and IP address mappings in the Host and LMHost files, however, maintaining these files is labor-intensive and not recommended as a way to manage a network. These files are best reserved for well-known addresses that are not likely to change, such as that of a commonly used server.

**Name Resolution Using Broadcast Name Resolution** Computers that run Microsoft's TCP/IP protocol can also resolve name-to-address mappings if all network devices register their address and name on the LAN by making IP-level broadcasts. This is called Broadcast Name Resolution. All computers on the LAN are responsible for monitoring these broadcasts and responding to name queries for their own registered name. Attempts to register duplicate names are challenged by computers that monitor the broadcasts.

**Name Resolution Using Domain Name System (DNS)** The *Domain Name System* is a client/server-based naming service that is used on the Internet to provide both a standard convention for naming IP computers and a means to uniquely identify all nodes on the Internet. This service is described in Request For Comments (RFC) documents 1034 and 1035.

The client portion of the DNS software (included with Microsoft's implementation of TCP/IP) queries DNS name servers to resolve the name-to-address mappings. Multiple DNS name servers use a distributed database architecture to store information about parts of the name space, called *zones*. Each name server contains the name and address mappings for all hosts within its zone. If a DNS name server receives a query for a mapping that isn't contained in its zone, the DNS name server sends back a list of other DNS name servers that the client can query to find the correct name-to-address mapping. The client can eventually find the correct name-to-address mapping (if it is registered) by querying additional DNS name servers in this manner.

Two key components of DNS are that it requires static configuration of IP addresses for address-to-name mapping and that it uses a hierarchical structured name space called the *domain name space*. Each node or domain has a name, and each domain can contain other nodes or subdomains.

Fully Qualified Domain Names (FQDNs) also contain two key components: the domain name (plus any subdomain names) and the host name. The FQDN syntax is *host.subdomain.domain* (which may include zero, one, or more subdomains).

An example of an FQDN is bob.healthclub.com, where bob is the host name, healthclub is the subdomain, and com is the domain name, with a period separating each name part. Following the International Standard 3166, domains are allocated by country and by organizations. Two- and three-letter mnemonics are used to represent countries and organizations. The following table shows some common Internet mnemonics.

| Abbreviation | Description |
| --- | --- |
| com | Used by commercial organizations |
| gov | Used by government agencies |
| edu | Used by educational institutions |
| org | Used by various noncommercial organizations |
| net | Used by network organizations and providers |

To configure Windows 98 to use DNS name resolution, follow these steps:

1. Open the Network dialog box from the Control Panel.

2. Select the TCP/IP protocol that is bound to your network adapter.

3. Click the Properties button.

4. Select the DNS Configuration tab in the TCP/IP Properties dialog box.

5. Select the Enable DNS Server radio button if a DNS server is available.

6. Enter the host name used to identify your computer. (This is typically your computer's name, but your network administrator may assign a different name without affecting your computer's name.)

7. Enter the domain name of the Internet domain to which this computer belongs. (Note that the DNS domain name is not the same thing as an NT domain name. Typically, this Internet domain name is something similar to mycompany.com.)

8. Enter up to three IP addresses for the DNS servers that are providing name resolution services. To add a DNS IP address, enter the address in the text box, and then click the Add button. For a DNS query, Windows 98 queries the topmost DNS address first; if it doesn't receive a response, it queries the next

DNS address in the list; if it still doesn't receive a response, it queries the third (and final) DNS address to service the name resolution request.

9. Enter the Domain Suffix Search Order. You can enter multiple domain name suffixes to be searched by entering the domain suffix name in the text box and clicking the Add button. Your host name is appended to the domain suffix name to create your fully qualified Internet domain name. (When a DNS server searches for your name, it first searches its database for your host name and then for your host name combined with each domain suffix.)

10. Click OK.

You can use DNS instead of, or in conjunction with, WINS to perform name resolution. For more information on using these two products together, see *Windows NT Server 4.0 Administrator's Bible,* by Robert Cowart, published by IDG Books Worldwide.

**Name Resolution Using Windows Internet Naming Service (WINS)** The Windows Internet Naming Service is a NetBIOS name server implemented as an NT service that runs on an NT server to resolve NetBIOS names. WINS is compatible with the WINS protocol that is defined for WINS servers in RFC 1001 and RFC 1002. WINS provides a dynamic name service that tracks network names as users start and stop networked computers. Multiple WINS servers can be configured on the same network to improve the performance of name resolution and to provide redundancy. The WINS service performs this service by maintaining a distributed database for registering and querying NetBIOS name/IP address pairs. As changes occur, the WINS database can be updated automatically, which may include automatically updating multiple WINS servers when they are set up as push-and-pull partners. When set up as push-and-pull partners, one WINS server publishes or "pushes" its information to the partner WINS server, which is set up as the pull partner that requests or "pulls" information from the push partner. In this way, database updates to the WINS servers can be replicated between the partners.

WINS consists of two components: the WINS server, which runs on an NT server, and the WINS client (NetBIOS over TCP/IP), which runs under Windows 98. The WINS client is installed automatically with Windows 98 when you install TCP/IP. The server component maintains the distributed database of name-to-IP address mappings, and the client software performs the queries to resolve the IP address-to-host name mappings. Windows 98 clients can use either WINS or B-node network broadcasts to resolve NetBIOS names to IP addresses. Four node types are defined by RFCs 1001 and 1002:

- **P-node** uses point-to-point communications with a NetBIOS server to resolve names.

- **B-node** uses broadcasts to resolve host names.

- **H-node** combines the P-node and B-node techniques. It first performs a P-node query to attempt the name resolution. If this fails, H-node performs a B-node broadcast.

- **M-node** also combines the P-node and B-node techniques. It first performs a B-node broadcast to resolve the name. If this fails, M-node performs a P-node query.

A WINS-enabled Windows 98 computer defaults to using H-node for name resolutions. If WINS is not enabled, the Windows 98 computer defaults to B-node name resolution. The WINS product has greatly simplified the effort required to manage NetBIOS name mappings. Some significant advantages to using WINS are the following:

- WINS reduces the number of local broadcasts that are used for name resolution, thus improving network performance.

- WINS provides NetBIOS name-to-address mapping dynamically and requires much less administration than other forms of name resolution, such as DNS or LMHost files.

- If DHCP is used for configuration, these configuration parameters can be provided to WINS automatically; you don't have to enter them manually.

- WINS enables you to use applications that require the NetBIOS interface with the TCP/IP protocol.

To configure your computer to use the WINS protocol, follow these steps:

**1.** Open the Network dialog box from the Control Panel.

**2.** From the installed component list, select the TCP/IP protocol that is bound to your network adapter.

**3.** Click the Properties button on the Configuration tab.

**4.** Select the WINS Configuration tab from the TCP/IP dialog box.

**5.** If a DHCP server is used to provide information on WINS servers, select the radio button labeled Use DHCP for WINS resolution.

**6.** If a WINS server is available and a DHCP server is not available, select the Enable WINS Resolution radio button, and then enter the WINS server IP address for both the Primary and Secondary WINS NT servers.

**7.** If WINS has been enabled, you must also type the computer's scope identifier in the Scope ID box. This value is usually left blank or is assigned the NT domain name. The scope ID is an arbitrary ID that is used only for communications based on NetBIOS over TCP/IP. When using this protocol, all computers that use NetBIOS over TCP/IP on the same network must use the same scope ID.

**8.** Click OK.

# Using IPX/SPX-Compatible Protocol

The Internetwork Packet Exchange/Sequenced Protocol Exchange (IPX/SPX) protocol that ships with Windows 98 is compatible with the Novell NetWare implementation. Windows 98 includes both 32-bit protected-mode drivers and real-mode drivers to support IPX/SPX. This implementation of the IPX/SPX protocol supports the 32-bit Windows Socket version 1.1 API. Any Win32-based application that uses the Windows Socket 1.1 API will work with this IPX/SPX implementation.

When you install Client for NetWare Networks, Windows 98 automatically tries to install the IPX/SPX protocol because IPX/SPX is necessary for Client for NetWare Networks to communicate with a Novell NetWare server. Likewise, Client for Microsoft Networks needs the IPX/SPX protocol to communicate with any computer that runs the IPX/SPX protocol.

The IPX/SPX protocol can support the NetBIOS API (NetBIOS hosted on IPX/SPX) when the Nwnblink.vxd module is used. This hosted implementation of NetBIOS on IPX/SPX supports routing across routers configured to route IPX/SPX, or NetWare servers configured as routers.

IPX/SPX by itself is simply a protocol. It enables two computers to communicate, but it doesn't enable them to share files or printers. To perform these services, you must also have the Client for NetWare Networks software installed.

Key features of the IPX/SPX protocol are the following:

- Supports all Novell NetWare–compatible clients
- Supports the following APIs: NetBIOS, Windows Sockets, and ECB
- Supports packet-burst mode for higher network performance
- Supports automatic detection of network address, frame type, and other configuration parameters

- Provides routing across network bridges and routers that are configured for IPX/SPX routing
- Provides connectivity to NetWare networks and Windows NT networks that are running the IPX/SPX protocol and to mixed networks

To install the IPX/SPX protocol in Windows 98, follow these steps:

1. Open the Network dialog box from the Control Panel.
2. Click the Add button on the Configuration tab.
3. Select Protocol from the component type list.
4. Click the Add button.
5. In the Manufacturers list, select Microsoft.
6. In the Network Protocols list, select IPX/SPX-compatible Protocol.
7. Click OK.

Windows 98 automatically detects and sets the values for the frame type, network address, and other protocol settings, as needed. You can, however, manually configure IPX/SPX parameters as follows:

1. Open the Network dialog box from the Control Panel.
2. Open the IPX/SPX-compatible protocol that is bound to the adapter you want to configure.
3. Select the Advanced tab.
4. To change a setting, select the item to be changed in the Property list, and then enter the new setting in the Value list.
5. Click OK when you are finished.

## Addressing

Complete source and destination addresses are included in the data packets that are sent using the IPX/SPX protocol. An IPX network address consists of a 32-bit network number that is unique to each physical network (supplied by the network installer and registered with Novell) and a 48-bit node address pair. Together, these form a 10-byte network address to define a unique source and destination network device.

## IPX/SPX Routing

The IPX protocol provides connectionless datagram services that support general delivery and broadcast capabilities (much like IP) on top of the data link protocols, such as Ethernet, Token Ring, or PPP. IPX does not offer a guaranteed delivery mechanism. This service is provided by the connection-oriented SPX layer. The SPX layer builds a virtual circuit on top of the IPX protocol. This circuit handles sequencing and flow-control issues to ensure that all packets arrive and that they arrive in the correct order. With source and destination addresses that define both the network address and the host ID included in every data packet, the IPX/SPX protocol supports routing across routers and NetWare servers that are configured as IPX/SPX routers.

## Name Resolution

IPX/SPX relies on broadcasts of Service Advertising Protocol (SAP) and Routing Information Protocol (RIP) packets to access network name resolution services built into NetWare.

# Using Microsoft NetBEUI Protocol

The NetBEUI transport protocol is an extension of the original NetBIOS protocol introduced by IBM in 1985, and NetBEUI operates at the Network and Transport layers of the OSI (Open Systems Interconnection) network model. NetBEUI, which stands for *NetBIOS Enhanced User Interface,* extends the capabilities of NetBIOS by formalizing the frame format that was not specified as part of NetBIOS. NetBEUI works with networks, such as Windows for Workgroups, LAN Manager, and Windows NT server. Key characteristics of the NetBEUI protocol are the following:

- It is an efficient protocol that is optimized for smaller departmental LANs of 20 to 200 computers.

- It is a nonroutable protocol (its addresses do not contain routing information).

- It provides an API that many applications still use today.

- It is compatible with networks that still use the NetBIOS protocol.

- Window 98 provides both real-mode and protected-mode drivers for the NetBEUI protocol.

## Addressing

NetBEUI is responsible for establishing logical names on the network. NetBEUI uses a unique logical name to identify a computer on the network. This logical name can be from 1 to 15 alphanumeric characters and must be unique on the network. Generally, the network name is the same as the computer name. To communicate, two named computers on a network establish a connection, called a *session*, between themselves by using the logical names. After the session is set up, the two computers can communicate by using a reliable data transport. The NetBEUI addressing scheme does not contain any routing information (network and host IDs) and thus does not work across wide area networks (WANs) or network segments that are connected using routers. NetBEUI does, however, have a relatively low overhead, making it an efficient protocol for smaller networks. Two types of network traffic are supported with NetBEUI:

- **Connectionless traffic.** In this type, data packets are sent to the recipient without the sender's first setting up a connection.

This type of communication is less reliable than connection-oriented traffic because a logical connection between the sender and receiver is not first established. If a data packet is lost, the sender and receiver don't know about it. This type of communication usually is used to send datagrams or broadcasts.

- **Connection-oriented communications.** In this, the sender establishes a session with the receiver before sending and receiving the network messages. This type of protocol provides support for missed or lost data packets and is a reliable communication protocol.

## NetBEUI Routing

NetBEUI does not support routing across network segments through routers. For this reason, implementations of NetBEUI have been hosted on top of TCP/IP and IPX/SPX, which are both routable protocols. These hosted implementations of NetBEUI can work in a routed environment because of the routing capabilities of the underlying TCP/IP or IPX/SPX protocols.

## Name Resolution

Each networked computer has a *network interface card* (NIC) through which it connects to the network. This card's physical address is associated with the defined network name. Computers that are connected to the network listen for their address to be broadcast on the network and are responsible for identifying data packets that are addressed to them. Applications that use the NetBEUI API can use the network name instead of the address to communicate to networked computers. The NetBEUI services translate the network name to the physical address.

The Windows 98 NetBEUI is a self-tuning protocol that provides greater performance over slow links, compared with earlier implementations. If you set NetBEUI as the default protocol, Windows 98 uses NetBEUI as the default protocol to communicate with computers on the LAN and uses TCP/IP to communicate across routers to remote networks.

# Installing Network Adapters

This section discusses network adapters and the device drivers that provide an interface between the higher layers of the network architecture and the adapters. Together, the network adapters and the device drivers form the physical and data link layers of the OSI network model. Improvements in the specifications for these drivers have brought both performance gains and improved compatibility between Microsoft's desktop and server operating systems.

## Understanding How Network Adapters Work

For your computer to work in a networked environment, all software and hardware components must be installed and configured correctly. This task has become more complicated over time because of the additional features that are needed to support remote networking components. Fortunately, Windows 98 automatically detects and configures most adapter cards and installs the appropriate driver software when it is installed, based on its Plug and Play architecture. Figure 11-2 provides an overview of the software that must be configured for your network adapter card to function correctly.

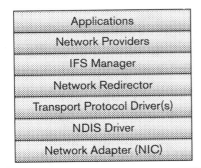

| Applications |
| Network Providers |
| IFS Manager |
| Network Redirector |
| Transport Protocol Driver(s) |
| NDIS Driver |
| Network Adapter (NIC) |

**Figure 11-2** *Microsoft Windows network architecture*

Each networked computer contains a network adapter, sometimes referred to as a NIC. A software driver that provides an interface between the card and the overlying network protocol software controls the adapter. This driver conforms to the Network Driver Interface Specification (NDIS), which describes the interface between the driver and the network adapter and the interface between the driver and the NDIS-compatible network protocols. Windows 98 supports NDIS versions 2, 3, 4, and 5. NDIS 3.0 drivers are not supported by Windows 98. Any other combination of NDIS-compatible protocols and drivers can be supported. Microsoft recommends that you use NDIS 3.1 or later drivers with Windows 98 because of the improvements introduced with NDIS 3.1.

New with the NDIS 5 specification, in addition to performance enhancements, is support for "hot" Plug and Play capabilities that enable you to install and remove most network adapters dynamically. When the adapter is shut down and removed, the power automatically shuts down, and the appropriate software is unloaded.

Two standards predominate for network adapters: NDIS, developed by Microsoft and 3Com, and the *Open Datalink Interface* (ODI), developed by Apple Computer and Novell.

NDIS continues to evolve as new features and improvements are introduced. With the release of NDIS 3.1, the model for developing NDIS drivers changed. Previous to NDIS 3.1, hardware manufacturers were free to implement the full Media Access Control (MAC) functionality. The resulting driver was dependent, however, on the operating system and the features that it supported. With NDIS 3.1 or later drivers, the half of the media access functionality that is common to all adapters is standardized and implemented by a Microsoft-provided NDIS "wrapper." These newer NDIS 3.1 or later drivers are called *miniport drivers* to distinguish them from the older *legacy* drivers.

The new Windows 98 miniport drivers are compatible with NT 3.5 and later operating systems and can run on both Windows NT and Windows 98 operating systems. These miniport drivers have .sys extensions rather than .vxd extensions. These new drivers should result in reduced support costs because supporting one common set of drivers that run on both Windows NT and Windows 98 is much easier.

# Configuring a Network Adapter

With Plug and Play adapters, Windows 98 automatically detects and configures the adapter and most of the configuration parameters. In many cases, you do not have to change these parameters. With older network adapters or adapters that are not recognized by Windows 98, you may have to configure network adapter settings manually and install vendor-supplied software.

With non–Plug and Play adapters, you need to configure Windows 98 to match the settings of the adapter card. For example, if your card has hardware jumpers that select the card's address and interrupt number, you need to configure Windows 98 to match these hardware settings. The easiest way to do this is to use the Add New Hardware Wizard in the Control Panel to enable Windows 98 to detect the new hardware and its current configuration. When you select the search and detect new hardware feature, the Add New Hardware Wizard attempts to determine the configuration of the newly installed card and install the necessary drivers. Only after trying this option and failing should you attempt to install and configure the adapter manually. If you encounter problems, be sure to read the documentation provided by the manufacturer of the adapter card for its recommendations. You might also want to check the manufacturer's Web site for updated drivers or installation notes.

The general steps to install and configure a network adapter are as follows:

1. Review any documentation that accompanies the adapter for specific installation instructions.

2. Set any hardware jumpers or configurations according to the manufacturer's recommendations.

3. Install the card in the system.

4. Read and follow any recommendations provided by Windows 98 to remove any conflicting address or interrupt settings.

5. Finally, check the device setting in Device Manager to ensure that no conflicting settings exist.

To install a network card in Windows 98, follow these steps:

1. Open the Add New Hardware Wizard from the Control Panel.

2. Click Next.

3. Select the option to search and detect new hardware.

4. Click Next until the program starts. This program may run for a long time on slower computers.

If your card is recognized, Windows 98 configures it correctly. If Windows 98 cannot configure the card, you should follow the prompts given by the system and refer to the documentation provided by the vendor to configure the card manually. Generally, you do not need to specify a network driver for your adapter, unless you're running real-mode drivers. To choose a driver for a network adapter, follow these steps:

1. Open the Network dialog box from the Control Panel.

2. Select the network adapter from the list of installed components.

3. Click the Properties button.

4. Select the Driver Type tab.

5. If applicable, select one of the following three available options:

   • Enhanced mode (32-bit and 16-bit) NDIS driver (an NDIS 3.1 or later–compliant driver)

   • Real-mode (16-bit) NDIS driver (an NDIS 2.*x*–compliant driver)

   • Real-mode (16-bit) ODI driver (Windows 3.1 ODI driver for NetWare networks)

## Configuring Resource Parameters for Network Adapters

Windows 98 does a very good job of detecting network adapters and selecting the appropriate settings. However, if you detect a conflict while using the Device Manager or need to change your adapter's resource settings manually, perform the following steps. Be aware that you cannot modify the resources of some adapters and that types of resources vary, depending on the type of adapter installed in the system. To change the resources allocated to a network adapter, do the following:

1. Open the Network dialog box from the Control Panel.

2. From the list of installed components, select the network adapter that you want to configure. (Do not select the protocol binding for the adapter by mistake!)

3. Click the Properties button.

4. If the adapter's resources can be configured, a Resource tab appears. Select the Resource tab.

5. Select the configuration to modify from the Configuration type list box. Review the current settings for this adapter, and modify them if needed.

6. To choose from available values for a specific parameter, select the arrow beside the parameter's current value. Current values are designated by a hash mark (#). If a parameter's value conflicts with another system device, that value is denoted by an asterisk (*). You should not select a value that is denoted as conflicting with other system devices. If necessary, reconfigure the appropriate conflicting system device to remove the conflict.

Some older legacy adapters have parameter settings that conflict with other system devices, but the parameter settings do not show up in the Resources tab. If you have such an adapter, you need to refer to the manufacturer's documentation to determine how to set these specific parameters on the adapter.

## Advanced Properties for Network Adapters

The advanced properties of network adapters vary, depending on the type of adapter you have installed. Windows 98 configures the advanced properties with the appropriate values when you install the adapter. To modify manually the advanced properties for network adapters, follow these steps:

1. Open the Network dialog box from the Control Panel.

2. From the list of installed components, select the network adapter that you want to configure. (Do not select the protocol binding for the adapter by mistake!)

3. Click the Properties button.

4. Select the Advanced tab.

5. Select the property to be modified from the Property list box.

6. Modify the value for the selected property in the value box, as necessary.

7. Click OK.

## Binding Protocols to Network Adapters

You must bind a protocol driver to the network adapter for the protocol to be able to communicate. Windows 98 provides great flexibility for configuring communication protocols. A protocol may be bound to more than one network adapter, and more than one protocol can be bound to any one network adapter. This enables a network adapter to support multiple protocols and enables protocols to be used over multiple communication media (modems, Ethernet adapters, Token Ring adapters, and so on). Windows 98 can automatically bind the appropriate protocols to the network adapter. To change network bindings, follow these steps:

1. Open the Network dialog box from the Control Panel.

2. From the list of installed components, select the network adapter that you want to configure. (Do not select the protocol binding for the adapter by mistake!)

3. Click the Properties button.

4. Select the Bindings tab.

5. In the list of protocols, all bound protocols for this adapter are checked. To unbind a protocol from the network adapter, clear the check box for the protocol. (If a protocol you want to use does not appear in the list, you need to go to the Configuration tab in the Network dialog box to install the protocol.)

6. Click OK.

# Chapter 12

# Installing the Client for Microsoft Networks

Configuring Windows 98 to connect to a Microsoft Network is straightforward. You install the Client for Microsoft Networks, which enables you to participate in the organization's workgroups. Optionally, you can configure the Client for Microsoft Networks to connect to a domain controller so that you can take advantage of logon security, user-level security, and more.

This chapter shows how to install and use the Client for Microsoft Networks. It describes the primary network logon, for example, as well as how to control the way in which Windows 98 restores network connections and the browse list. This chapter also recommends additional components that you might want to install. Finally, it describes how to use the Client for Microsoft Networks to work with a variety of specific Microsoft networking technologies, such as Workgroups, Windows NT Server, and LAN Manager.

## Configuring Windows NT for Windows 98

To support users who are running the Client for Microsoft Networks, you must prepare the server. These preparations are light and part of your daily routine. They include the following tasks for a Windows NT Server, which are similar on any other server:

- Add an account for the user in the User Manager for Domains
- Assign a home folder to the user if the user will be using roaming profiles
- Assign a login script that configures the computer to the user

The user must have an account on the domain controller to be able to log on to the network and access resources that are protected with user-level security. The second and third items in the preceding list are optional. Assigning a home folder to a user enables that user to use roaming profiles, assuming that you enable user profiles in Windows 98. You can use the optional login script to configure the user's workstation further, which may include making network connections, establishing settings paths to network volumes, and so on.

# Installing the Client for Microsoft Networks

The Client for Microsoft Networks provides the redirector (Vredir.vxd), which supports all Microsoft network products that use the Server Message Block (SMB) protocol. That includes LAN Manager, Windows NT, Windows for Workgroups, and Workgroup Add-on for MS-DOS. The client implements the redirector as a file system driver so that network volumes look and act like other disks mounted to the system. That is, the redirector provides Windows 98 with the capability to open, read, write, remove, and browse files on the network volume via the file system.

Aside from installing the Client for Microsoft Networks, you must take some other steps to connect to the network when using Windows 98:

- Verify that you meet the licensing requirements for NT Server.

- Install the network card and drivers using the Add New Hardware Wizard or the Network icon in the Control Panel. In most cases, Windows 98 automatically recognizes and configures a network adapter after you install it.

- Install the networking client as described in the remainder of this chapter.

- Install and configure the networking protocols: TCP/IP, NetBEUI, and so forth. You install a protocol using the Control Panel's Network icon. Click Add, and choose Protocol from the list; then, select the manufacturer on the left-hand side and the protocol on the right-hand side. Click OK, and close the Network dialog box to save your changes. Note that Windows 98 automatically installs TCP/IP when you install the Client for Microsoft Networks.

- Install any additional services, such as File and Printer Sharing for Microsoft Networks or the Microsoft Remote Registry Service. To install File and Printer Sharing for Microsoft Networks, click File and Printer Sharing on the Network dialog box, select both options, and click OK; then, close the Network dialog box to save your changes. Install the Microsoft Remote Registry Service from the Windows 98 CD-ROM; the path is \Tools\Reskit\Netadmin\Remotreg.

The Windows 98 Setup program upgrades the networking client. If it detects an existing Microsoft client when you upgrade, Windows 98 replaces it with the Client for Microsoft Networks. Otherwise, you must install this client manually:

1. Open the Network dialog box from the Control Panel.

2. Click Add to display the Select Network Component Type dialog box. From here, choose Client, and then click OK.

3. On the Select Network Client dialog box, choose Microsoft from the left-hand list; then, choose Client for Microsoft Networks from the right-hand list. Click OK.

4. Close the Network dialog box. Windows 98 copies the appropriate files to your computer and updates your configuration. You have to restart the computer after changing your network configuration.

# Configuring the Client for Microsoft Networks

The Client for Microsoft Networks isn't as configurable as some other networking clients, which makes getting it up and running a snap compared to those other clients. You must configure the following two settings to connect to a Microsoft network, which you do on the client's property sheet, but everything else is optional:

- **Primary network logon**. The primary network logon points Windows 98 to the primary security provider. Windows 98 looks to this server for login scripts, for example, as well as for system policies.

- **Logon and connection settings**. You must indicate to Windows 98 that you want it to connect to a domain controller, which you do by selecting this option and providing the name of the controller.

## Primary Network Logon

The primary network logon indicates to Windows 98 which server validates the user's logon credentials first and which server contains the network-based files required by the operating system. For example, Windows 98 looks to the client specified as the primary network logon for the following items:

- **Logon validation**. The primary network logon indicates which server is the first to validate the user's logon credentials.

- **Passthrough security**. The primary network logon indicates which server provides passthrough security to validate access to resources that are protected by user-level security.

- **System policies**. Windows 98 downloads system policies from the server that is indicated by the primary network logon.

- **User profiles**. Windows 98 downloads the user's profile from the server that is indicated by the primary network logon.

- **Login scripts**. The login script found on the server that is indicated by the primary network logon is the last login script that Windows 98 runs.

Thus, correctly setting the primary network logon is an important step in configuring the Client for Microsoft Networks. If you set the primary network logon to Windows Logon, for example, Windows 98 won't be able to handle System Policies correctly. To configure Client for Microsoft Networks as the primary network logon, follow these steps:

1. Open the Network dialog box from the Control Panel.

2. Select Client for Microsoft Networks from Primary Network Logon.

3. Click OK to save your changes. You must restart the computer after changing your network configuration for the changes to take effect.

## Logging on to the Domain

You must explicitly configure Windows 98 to log the user on to a Windows NT domain, which you accomplish by enabling this option in Client for Microsoft Networks and specifying the name of the server. You can configure Windows 98 to verify the user's credentials on an actual Windows NT domain or a Windows NT server. Regardless, users must have an account on the domain to which they're connecting. To configure the Client for Microsoft Networks to log on to a Windows NT domain, follow these steps:

1. Open the Network dialog box from the Control Panel.

2. Select Client for Microsoft Networks from the list of networking components, and then click Properties. The dialog box shown in Figure 12-1 is displayed.

3. Select Log on to Windows NT Domain if you want Windows 98 to log on to the domain automatically when it starts.

4. Type the name of the domain for which you want to validate your logon in the box labeled Windows NT Domain. This can be an actual Windows NT or LAN Manager domain, or the name of any Windows NT computer on which you have an account.

5. Click OK to save your changes; then, close the Network dialog box, and restart your computer.

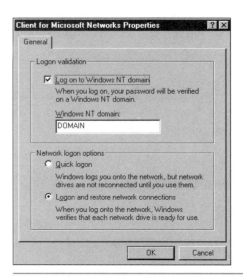

**Figure 12-1** *Logon options for the Client for Microsoft Networks*

**Tip**

The administrator optionally can require validation by a security provider before Windows 98 provides the user with access to the workstation. You can require validation by using the System Policy Editor to set the Require Validation by Network for Windows Access policy. You might also want to prevent users from setting `AutoAdminLogon` in the Registry at `HKEY_LOCAL_MACHINE\Software\Microsoft\Windows\CurrentVersion\Winlogon`, which causes Windows 98 to log the user on to the workstation, and thus the network, automatically without retyping her credentials. This setting enables anyone to walk up to the user's computer and gain access to the network without having an account on the network.

# Persistent Connections

Windows 98 enables the user to specify how the operating system restores persistent connections. The operating system can either verify each connection when it starts or merely map drive letters to connections without actually verifying them. Quick logon is the best choice for mobile users because they frequently use their computers while not connected to the network. With Quick logon, Windows 98 maps the resource but doesn't connect to it until the user tries to access it. This option also provides quicker starts but requires that you don't disable password caching in the System Policy Editor. To specify whether Windows 98 automatically restores persistent connections, follow these steps:

1. Open the Network dialog box from the Control Panel.

2. Select Client for Microsoft Networks from the list of networking components, and click Properties. The dialog box shown in Figure 12-1 is displayed.

3. Select either Quick logon, if you want Windows 98 to map drive letters without actually verifying each one, or Logon and restore network connections, if you want Windows 98 to verify each connection when it starts.

4. Click OK to save your changes; then, close the Network dialog box, and restart your computer for the changes to take effect.

# Browse Master

A *browse master* keeps a list of each workstation on the network, relieving each workstation from having to announce its presence on the network to be visible to the other workstations on the network. This results in better network performance.

Windows NT Server, Windows NT Workstation, Windows 98, Windows 95, and Windows for Workgroups can all become browse masters. Each time one of these operating systems starts, it begins an election on the network. The election determines which workstation is the browse master. On a Windows NT network, the primary domain controller (PDC) almost always is the browse master, but if the PDC isn't available, another computer can take over this role. The election process isn't actually an election. Each workstation reports its potential to act as a browse master, and the workstation with the highest potential wins the election. The most important criterion is usually the version number of the networking software in use. Because NT Server has a higher version number than Windows 98, NT server almost always wins. Other criteria include whether a workstation is running a WINS server and whether it's configured as the preferred browse master.

To change the browse master settings in Windows 98, follow these steps:

1. Open the Network dialog box, select File and Printer Sharing for Microsoft Networks, and click Properties.

2. Select Browse Master from the list shown in Figure 12-2, and then choose one of the following values:

   • **Automatic**. Windows 98 maintains the browse list if the operating system determines that it's necessary via elections.

- **Disabled**. Windows 98 never acts as the browse master. Choose this value if network performance is a problem.

- **Enabled**. Windows 98 always maintains the browse list for all computers in the workgroup. This indicates that the workstation is the preferred browse master.

3. Click OK to save your changes, and close the Network dialog box to restart your computer.

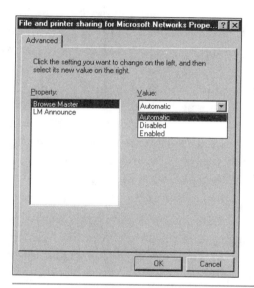

**Figure 12-2** *Choose Browse Master to change the browse master settings.*

You must designate at least one computer on a workgroup network to act as a browse master; otherwise, network browsing does not work properly. This should be a problem only if you explicitly prevent each workstation from becoming a browse master, because the default setting is to hold elections.

# Installing Complementary Components

Additional components that complement the Client for Microsoft Networks are the following:

- **Protocols**. The protocols you can install in Windows 98 include TCP/IP, IPX/SPX, and NetBEUI. I recommend that you install TCP/IP for use with the Client for Microsoft Networks because it's more robust and flexible than the alternatives. In addition, the latest version of TCP/IP that comes with Windows 98 supports automatic IP allocation on workgroup networks.

- **Remote administration**. Remote administration enables you to manage a user's computer from a remote computer. To use remote administration, you must enable it on the Passwords Properties dialog box and enable user-level security. Because user-level security requires a security provider, you won't be able to use these features on a workgroup network. You should also install the Microsoft Remote Registry Service.

- **File and printer sharing**. The file and printer sharing service enables you to share resources on the network. Many remote administration programs require that you install this server.

- **User-level security**. Windows 98 supports user-level and share-level security. User-level security requires a security provider to validate a user's credentials before the user can access resources on the computer. Another name for this is *passthrough security*. Share-level security requires only that a user know the correct password. I recommend that you enable user-level security if you have a security provider such as Windows NT or NetWare.

# Using Windows 98 with Microsoft Networks

The Client for Microsoft Networks supports Microsoft networks and works well with the following SMB (Server Message Block)–based servers:

- AT&T StarLAN
- Digital PATHWORKS
- IBM LAN Server
- LAN Manager for UNIX Systems
- Samba

By default, Windows 98 sends encrypted passwords to the server. Samba sends only plain-text passwords, however. You can force Windows 98 to send plain-text passwords by adding a DWORD value entry called `EnablePlainTextPassword` to the Registry at `HKEY_LOCAL-MACHINE\System\CurrentControlSet\Services\VxD\Vnetsup` and setting its value to 1.

## Workgroups

Workgroups arrange workstations into logical groups. Out of ten computers, five might participate in the accounting workgroup, three in the management workgroup, and two in the development workgroup. Organizing workstations into workgroups makes browsing and sharing resources easier, but it has nothing to do with security.

In a workgroup, each computer is responsible for its own security, which includes validating logon credentials and protecting access to shared resources. Workgroup networks are unlike domain-based networks, which provide central management of logon and resource access. Domain-based networks maintain a user database that each workstation on the network uses to validate logon credentials and access to shared resources. Each computer on a workgroup network contains its own accounts database and must protect its own resources.

Any computer running a Microsoft operating system, including those in the following list, can participate in a workgroup:

- Windows 98
- Windows 95
- Windows NT Workstation
- Windows NT Server

The only requirements for accessing resources on a workgroup network are that each machine use a common protocol and that the user be granted access to the resource. Because user-level security requires a security provider, such as Windows NT Server, you can protect shared resources on a workgroup network only if such a security provider also exists on the network and each workstation designates that server as the primary network logon.

## Windows NT Server

Accessing a Windows NT Server from a Windows 98 workstation requires all of the following licenses from Microsoft:

- A license for each Windows 98 workstation.
- A license for each Windows NT Server on the network.
- A client license for each workstation, Windows 98 or otherwise, that is using the Windows NT file, print, or remote access services. You can purchase licenses *per seat*, which allows a workstation to access all servers on the network, or *per server*, which allows a single connection to a particular server.

Contact the Microsoft sales office at (800) 426-9400 for more information. In Canada, you can contact Microsoft at (800) 563-0048.

## LAN Manager

Note that you can upgrade all versions of LAN Manager and IBM OS/2 LAN Server with Windows 98 or Windows NT Server. Microsoft strongly recommends that you do this upgrade, of course, because of LAN Manager's limitations compared with the other network operating systems available.

LAN Manager has a few disadvantages. Windows 98 doesn't support using a LAN Manager domain controller as a security provider, for instance; therefore, you can use only share-level security on a LAN Manager network. By default, Windows 98 can't browse LAN Manager servers. You can fix this problem by setting at least one Windows 98 workstation's workgroup name to the LAN Manager domain name. Doing so forces that Windows 98 workstation to send the names of each LAN Manager server to the other Windows 98 workstations on the network.

To enable LAN Manager workstations to see resources on Windows 98, you must meet the following requirements:

- The LAN Manager workstations must have at least one protocol in common with Windows 98.

- The Windows 98 user must provide resource access to the LAN Manager users.

- Set LM Announce to Yes on each Windows 98 computer that is using file and printer sharing. This setting ensures that each Windows 98 computer using file and printer sharing announces itself to LAN Manager workstations and servers. Windows 98 sets this property to No by default to reduce network traffic.

# Chapter 13

# Installing the Client for NetWare Networks

## Connecting to Novell NetWare

Novell NetWare comes in multiple flavors. The most popular version of Novell NetWare is version 3.1*x*; however, the most recent version is NetWare 4.*x*. The differences between these version are significant enough that you should know which version of NetWare you are connecting to before you begin to install the client software.

Windows 98 enables you to connect to NetWare versions 3.11 through 4.*x*. Versions prior to 3.11 are not supported. In addition, Windows 98 is not compatible with the Novell Client for DOS/Windows 3.*x*. If you decide to install the Novell Client for Windows 95, you should use version 2.2 or later, and update Vmlid.nlm and Odiload.vxd, which can be obtained from Novell's Web site at `http://www.novell.com`.

You can configure Windows 98 to connect to NetWare servers in five different ways:

- Use 3.*x* real-mode networking drivers that use the NETX shell.

- Use 4.*x* real-mode networking drivers that use the VLM shell.

- Use the Microsoft Client for NetWare Networks, to connect to bindery-based NetWare servers.

- Use Microsoft MS-NDS 32-bit protected-mode drivers, to connect to NDS-based NetWare servers.

- Use Novell NetWare client-32, which you must obtain from Novell.

If you upgraded from Windows 3.1*x* and were configured in Windows 3.1*x* to connect to NetWare servers, the Windows 98 installation procedure attempts to install the MS NetWare 32-bit protected-mode drivers and comment out the drivers in Autoexec.bat.

# NetWare's Protocol (IPX/SPX)

NetWare uses the Internetwork Packet Exchange (IPX) protocol to transfer requests from a client to the server. When the Microsoft Client for NetWare Networks is installed, the IPX/SPX protocol is automatically installed. Like TCP/IP's IP protocol, IPX is used as a routing mechanism and is a connectionless-based protocol. Both IPX and IP require the use of other applications that can provide a guarantee that a packet will arrive safely. (IP uses TCP, and IPX uses SPX to guarantee packet transmissions.) IPX provides services at the network and transport layers of the OSI model. IP, on the other hand, provides services only at the network layer.

Although IPX serves as the transport mechanism for data, the *NetWare Core Protocol* (NCP) communicates directly with the NetWare kernel to open, close, read, and write files. NCP is also responsible for accessing the bindery or the NDS naming services database. In Windows, these types of functions are carried out through the *Server Message Block* (SMB) protocol to perform similar functionality. Both NCP and SMB are high-level protocols that ride on top of transport protocols such as IPX or IP.

NetWare uses the *Server Advertising Protocol* (SAP) to make its presence known on networks. As the name implies, SAPs are broadcasts that occur about every minute. The broadcast packet contains information about the server name and the resources available to that server. "Installing NetWare File and Print Services," later in this chapter, explains how to configure Windows 98 to supply SAP broadcasts that emulate a NetWare file and print server.

## NDS versus Bindery

Versions of NetWare prior to version 3.1x use a flat, server-centric database called the *bindery,* which contains security and accounting information. The bindery contains user login IDs, groups, account restrictions, accounting information, queues, and printers. The bindery is referred to as a *flat, server-centric database* because security and accounting information pertains to the server on which the bindery resides. When a user needs to access resources on any particular NetWare 3.1x server, the user must log on to that particular server.

NetWare 4.x uses *Novell Directory Services* (NDS) for user authentication and contains objects within its database in a hierarchy. Objects such as servers, volumes, users, groups, printers, and queues are viewed as a tree within Network Neighborhood of Windows 98. When users log on to NetWare 4.x, they are logged on to the entire network of NetWare 4.1x servers. That doesn't necessarily mean that they have access to all the resources on a NetWare 4.x network. However, it does mean that they don't have to log on to every server to gain access to its resources.

IPX is the most commonly used protocol in NetWare environments, but a NetWare 4.x server can communicate with a workstation that is running only TCP/IP. NetWare servers that run TCP/IP are very uncommon and cause performance degradation in NetWare servers, because IP isn't native to NCP. An IP packet must be translated at the server before a request can be made to the kernel. The upcoming version of NetWare—NetWare 5—will support pure IP. Microsoft's Client for NetWare Networks does not support connectivity to NetWare servers via IP.

# Installing Microsoft's Client for NetWare Networks

Regardless of whether you are connecting to bindery-based servers or NDS-based servers, you begin the installation by adding the Microsoft Client for NetWare Networks. If you are connecting to NDS servers, you add an additional service, the Service for NetWare Directory Services.

NDS can emulate bindery services. If you are not sure which version of NetWare you are connecting to, install the Microsoft Client for NetWare Networks. Chances are good that you *may* be able to log on to a NetWare 4.*x* server and use its resources, but you won't be able to take advantage of NDS's single point of login. In addition, you may not be able to run the system login scripts created by the administrator. Both of these factors depend on the administrator's configuration of the NetWare server.

To connect to a NetWare file server using bindery services, follow these steps:

1. Open the Network dialog box from the Control Panel.

2. A working network interface card driver should already be installed. If one is not installed, you need to install one now before proceeding. After you verify that a network card driver is installed, click the Add button.

3. From the Select Network Component Type dialog box, highlight Client and then click the Add button.

4. Highlight Microsoft under Manufacturers in the left pane of the Select Network Client dialog box.

5. In the Network Clients pane, select Client for NetWare Networks and click OK.

After you click the OK button, you'll be at the Network Properties dialog box. You should see the Client for NetWare

Networks installed. Notice, too, that the IPX protocol was automatically installed and "bound" to your network interface card. If you had the dial-up adapter installed, notice that IPX is now bound to the dial-up adapter, which enables you to access NetWare servers remotely. The next step requires you to configure the Client for NetWare Networks.

# Configuring the Client for NetWare Networks

To configure the Client for NetWare Networks, follow these steps:

1. Open the Network dialog box from the Control Panel.

2. Select Client for NetWare Networks and then click the Properties button, which displays the dialog box shown in Figure 13-1.

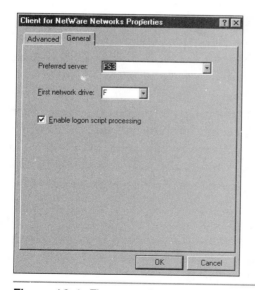

**Figure 13-1** *The properties of the Client for NetWare Networks*

3. From the General tab, type the name of your preferred server.

4. Enter the letter of your first network drive. The default is drive F, but you can set this to any letter up to Z. You can't set the first network drive letter to a drive letter lower than F.

5. Windows 98 can run the NetWare system login scripts that have been set up by the NetWare administrator. To enable this support, select the check box labeled Enable logon script processing.

6. The Advanced tab provides one option to preserve the case of files that you save to NetWare servers. By default, it's set to preserve the case of files. Rarely do you ever need to change this setting.

7. Click OK.

The preferred server (in Step 2) is the NetWare server that contains your user home directory and the system login scripts that have been configured for your user login ID. If your network has multiple NetWare servers to which you have access, you may not get the appropriate system login scripts to map drive letters and capture printer settings if you use the wrong preferred server. Check with the NetWare administrator to make sure which server you should use as the preferred server.

After you finish configuring the properties of the Client for NetWare Networks and set the primary network, click the OK button in the Network dialog box. At this point, Windows 98 installs any needed files. Then, confirm the reboot of Windows. You can choose to avoid additional reboots (and save some time) by waiting to reboot. Modifying anything in the Network dialog box requires a reboot; however, you can make all the changes to the client components now and then reboot after you complete those changes by clicking OK to close the Network dialog box.

Windows 98 requests your login ID and password for your configured client when you boot. For additional logins to other servers or operating systems, Windows 98 always tries to use the same login

ID and password that you submit when you log on. To avoid being prompted for a new login ID and password each time you connect to another server, keep all of your login IDs and passwords in synch. You can easily keep your login IDs in synch by using the Passwords option in the Control Panel.

## Caveats about the Primary Network

After you configure the NetWare client, you can select which network operating system is the primary network operating system that Windows 98 logs on to first when you boot the computer. By default, Windows 98 makes NetWare the primary network. If you use the Client for Microsoft Networking and the NetWare client, you need to take some precautions. Often, a system administrator uses a combination of permanent and automatically assigned drive mappings in a system login script. For example, the command

```
net use * \\server\ sharename
```

can be used in a system login script of a Windows NT Server to map to the next available drive. In NetWare, you can add the command

```
Map f:=sys:\users\username
```

to the login script.

Now things get kind of strange: If Client for Microsoft Networking is set as the primary network, when a user logs in, the command

```
net use * \\server\sharename
```

is executed. The * indicates that the PC will use the next available drive letter to map the directory \\server\sharename. Suppose this is drive F. After Windows NT authentication occurs, the NetWare client executes the system login script on the NetWare server. However, drive F will now be overwritten by the NetWare system login script. As mentioned, you need to take precautions, but the problem can be fixed by modifying the scripts on the NT domain servers so that, rather than using the map-next command (*), you use drive mappings that are not in use by the NetWare login scripts.

Regardless of whether the Client for NetWare Networks is your primary network operating system, you are still able to execute the system login scripts for a NetWare server. But, if you want to execute Windows NT Server login scripts, the Client for Microsoft Networking must be set to the primary network.

## Configuring MS-NDS Services

MS-NDS adds the capability for Windows 98 to access the NetWare Directory. MS-NDS is a service installation that you add to network properties, similar to installing the NetWare client. If you already installed the Client for NetWare Networks, don't remove it! It must be installed for MS-NDS to function properly. If you haven't already installed the Client for NetWare Networks, do so now. Then, use the following instructions to install Microsoft's support for NDS:

1. Open the Network dialog box from the Control Panel.
2. Click the Add button.
3. From the Select Network Component Type dialog box, highlight Service and click the Add button.
4. From the Select Network Service dialog box, choose Service for NetWare Directory Service.
5. Click OK.

After you click OK, you return to the Network dialog box. Notice that the Service for NetWare Directory Service is now installed and that the Client for NetWare Networks and the IPX protocol were automatically installed. At this point, you need to configure these clients and services.

Because MS-NDS relies on the Client for NetWare Networks, select it and click the Properties button. Then, follow the steps in the previous section, "Configuring the Client for NetWare

Networks," before you proceed to the next step. To configure the
Service for NetWare Directory Service, follow these steps:

1.  Open the Network dialog box from the Control Panel.

2.  Select Service for NetWare Directory Service in the Network
    dialog box, and click the Properties button.

3.  In the Preferred tree list box on the General tab, either type
    the known tree name or click the drop-down arrow and select
    a tree name. Note that the tree name isn't necessarily the same
    as the preferred server name.

4.  Enter the workstation default context — the container within
    the NDS tree that contains your user login ID. The default con-
    text is the path within the tree to that container; for example, a
    default container could be users.editors.idgbooks. If you're
    unsure of what to use, don't guess. Contact the NetWare NDS
    administrator to get the right answer. The context field is shown
    in Figure 13-2.

5.  Click OK.

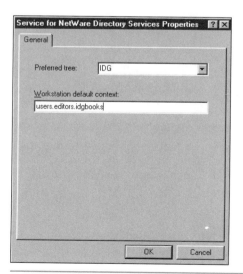

**Figure 13-2** *Configuring MS-NDS*

# Configuring the IPX/SPX-Compatible Protocol

The IPX/SPX-compatible protocol is automatically installed and configured when you install the NetWare client. You should stick with the default settings, *unless* you are also using the Client for Microsoft Networking to connect to Windows NT Server.

If you are using IPX/SPX on a Windows NT Server, you'll want to add NetBIOS over IPX/SPX. NetBIOS is an undesirable protocol because it's nonroutable. However, Windows NT uses NetBIOS to establish logical computer names on the network and to establish communications between these machines. Also, applications such as Lotus Notes use NetBIOS. To include NetBIOS over IPX/SPX, follow these steps:

1. Open the Network dialog box from the Control Panel.

2. Highlight the IPX/SPX protocol and click the Properties button.

3. Select the NetBIOS tab and select the check box labeled "I want to enable NetBIOS over IPX/SPX."

If you are using the TCP/IP protocol only to communicate with a Windows NT Server, you should modify the IPX/SPX settings so that the Client for Microsoft Networking does not bind to IPX/SPX. Having both clients bound to IPX/SPX doesn't do any harm, but configuring protocols only for the appropriate network operating system is the most efficient use of PC resources and network bandwidth. To modify the bindings, follow these steps:

1. Open the Network dialog box from the Control Panel.

2. Highlight the IPX/SPX protocol and click the Properties button.

3. Select the Bindings tab and deselect the Client for Microsoft Networking check box to unbind the client, as shown in Figure 13-3.

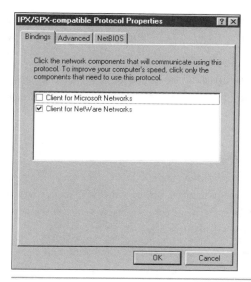

**Figure 13-3** *Selecting which networks IPX binds to*

# Other Settings in the IPX/SPX Advanced Tab

The IPX/SPX protocol supports six parameters that tune the protocol. Modify the following settings only if you know that it will resolve a problem or make better use of your network connectivity:

- **Force Even Packet Lengths**. Use this option for Ethernet 802.3 frame types where odd-length packets can cause a problem.

- **Frame Type**. Novell NetWare uses either 802.3, 802.2, Ethernet_II, Token Ring, or Token Ring Snap and it can use all of them at the same time. The preferred frame type is the Ethernet standard 802.2 frame type. You need to select the frame type only in situations in which more than one server is on the network, one server has more than one frame type loaded, and another server has only one frame type loaded. In this case, you should set the frame type to the server that has only one frame type. If the preceding conditions don't exist, set Frame Type to auto, which causes Windows 98 to find your server.

- **Maximum Connections**. Use this option to set the maximum number of connections that IPX will allow. The range is 0 through 128.

- **Maximum Sockets**. This option restricts the amount of IPX connections (sockets) that can be made concurrently to server resources. The range is 0 through 255.

- **Network Address**. Just as in IP, a NetWare server has a network address that is defined for a particular network segment. This setting never should be altered.

- **Source Routing**. In Token Ring environments, the workstation keeps track of available paths or routes. This setting enables you to set the cache between 16 and 64 paths or routes.

## Choosing Novell's Client over MS-NDS

You do have the choice to use Novell NetWare's 32-bit protected-mode client (NW32). In some cases, depending on the software and services that you're running on your network, the MS-NDS will do just fine. However, in a few other cases, listed next, you'll need to use the NetWare 32-bit client:

- If you want to use any NetWare-based utility, such as NDS Administrator utility, Novell Application Launcher, Novell IP Gateway, Remote Access Dialer, or NetWare Distributed Print Services.

- If you want to use Faxpress (a Cheyenne/Computer Associates product), which faxes directly from a client through the NetWare server. Each client using Faxpress must use the NetWare 32-bit client.

- If you decide to back up your NetWare server by using Cheyenne/CA's Arcserve product, the client software that is used to administer the tape job requires that the client be NW32.

- If you want to take advantage of NetWare NCP Packet signatures to protect your packets from being tampered with.

- If you want to use NetWare IP rather than the IPX protocol to communicate with your NetWare server.

- If you are using any application that is using a proprietary API to the NetWare client.

- If you use 3270 emulators that use TSRs or require 3270 emulation for applications in MS-DOS. In this case, you should use NETX or VLM.

If you are experiencing problems with an application, switching to a different client could potentially resolve your problems. You can download the NetWare 32-bit client (NW32) from Novell's Web site at http://www.novell.com. The installation procedures for the NW32 are menu-driven through a setup utility. If the NW32 finds the MS NetWare client, it removes it and replaces it. However, removing the client first and then rebooting and installing NW32 is the best procedure.

# Accessing Novell NetWare Servers

After you configure your client, you access NetWare servers through Network Neighborhood, just as you would any other resource. NetWare bindery servers and NetWare NDS servers appear differently in Network Neighborhood. Bindery servers appear as computers or workstations, while NDS servers appear as the three interconnected computers, identical to the Windows NT Domains or Windows Workgroups icons.

When you open NDS or bindery-based servers, you see printer resources and server volumes. You can right-click volumes to map a drive to a volume, or you can open the volume and right-click other directories deeper in the tree to map those directories. When you map a network drive on a bindery server, it uses the Universal Naming Convention (UNC), but when you map a drive in NDS, it uses NDS object mapping.

# Name-Space Support on NetWare Servers

Before Windows 98 can copy long filenames to a NetWare server, you need to modify the Windows 98 Registry and add name-space support on the NetWare server. Figure 13-4 shows the Registry modification. To modify the Registry to support long filenames, follow these steps:

1. Choose Start ⇨ Run.

2. Type **regedit** and press Enter to invoke the Registry Editor.

3. Open the key `Hkey_Local_Machine\System\CurrentControl Set\Services\VxD\Nwredir`.

4. Create a new binary value by choosing Edit ⇨ New ⇨ Binary Value.

5. Name the binary value LFNSupport and press Enter.

6. Open the LFNSupport binary key that you just created and place a 10 next to the four existing 0s.

7. Close the Registry Editor and reboot.

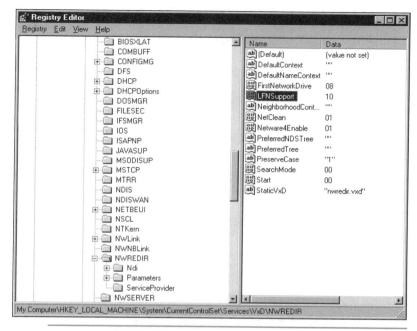

**Figure 13-4** *Adding long filename support to the Windows 98 Registry*

To add name-space support to a NetWare 3.1*x* server, follow these steps:

1.  At the NetWare command prompt, type `load os2` and press Enter. You should see the OS2 module load.

2.  Adding a name space requires free disk space. Make sure at least 10 percent of the total amount of disk space is still available before proceeding! At the NetWare prompt, type

    `add name space OS2 to1 volume xxx`

    where *xxx* is the name of the volume to which you are installing the name space. Add the name space to each volume that needs to support long filenames.

3. Load the NetWare editor and modify the Startup.cfg file, usually located on your boot drive C. At the NetWare command prompt, type `load edit` and press Enter. When you are prompted for the filename, enter `c:\startup.cfg`.

4. At the top of the Startup.cfg file, type

   `load c:\`*dir*`\os2.na`

   where *dir* is the directory in which you have your NetWare server startup files. The next time that you reboot the NetWare server, make sure that OS2.nam resides in that directory on the boot partition of your server.

NetWare 4.1*x* no longer uses the OS2 name space. It supports the LONG name space. To install long filename support in NetWare versions 4.1*x* and greater, simply follow the preceding instructions and replace `OS2` with `LONG`.

# Installing NetWare File and Print Services

NetWare file and print services require the installation of the Client for NetWare Networks. If you don't have it installed already, Windows 98 will install it for you.

You can have a Windows 98 workstation appear to be a NetWare server on the network. This functionality enables you to share printers and files and use a NetWare server as the authentication host. To workstation clients, the Windows 98 computer appears in Network Neighborhood just the same as a NetWare server. NetWare file and print services and Microsoft file and print services are very similar, because they both emulate network operating systems. However, you can't run both of these services simultaneously. Before you install NetWare file and print services, you need to remove the Microsoft file and print services. To install NetWare file and print services, follow these steps:

1. Open the Network dialog box from the Control Panel.

**2.** Click the Add button.

**3.** Select Service and then click the Add button.

**4.** From the list of manufacturers on the left side of the dialog box, choose Microsoft.

**5.** Click File and Printer Sharing for NetWare Networks.

**6.** Click the OK button.

You can modify two properties within the File and Printer Sharing for NetWare Networks service: SAP Advertising and Workgroup Advertising. To access the properties of the file and print services for NetWare, select File and Printer Sharing for NetWare Networks from the Network dialog box and click the Properties button. From the File and Print Services for NetWare properties dialog box, select the option that you want to modify:

- **SAP Advertising** supplies the network with the Server Advertising Protocol (SAP). NetWare uses this protocol to make its presence known on networks. By default, SAP Advertising is disabled on Windows-based workstations, which works just fine. If workstations are running the NETX or VLM shell, you need to enable SAP Advertising for these workstations to be able to access your file and print services.

- **Workgroup Advertising** works with the native Windows Networking protocols to make its presence known to all Windows-based workstations. By default, Workgroup Advertising is set to "Enabled: may be Master browser." Three other options are available: "Enabled — preferred master," "Enabled — will not be master," and "Disabled." Chapter 12, "Installing the Client for Microsoft Networks," describes Microsoft browsing and how workstations can store lists of shared resources that are available on Microsoft networks. With Workgroup Advertising set to Enabled, Windows workstations can access the resources located on a workstation that is running NetWare file and print services without SAP Advertising enabled. To disable Workgroup Advertising, you must enable SAP Advertising, so that the workstations that are running a NetWare client can access the resources available through NetWare file and print services. Enabling SAP Advertising makes all NetWare servers aware of your Windows 98 computer. Before enabling SAP Advertising, make sure that the computer name you are using on the Windows 98 computer is not the same as any servers on your network. If the name is the same as a server name, the NetWare server's resources could become completely unavailable.

# Enabling User-Level Security

You configure Windows 98 to use a NetWare server for passthrough user authentication, allowing access to the resources made available through File and Print Sharing for NetWare Networks. To configure Windows 98 in this manner, you use the Access Control tab in the Network dialog box. Two options are available on the Access Control tab: share-level access control and user-level access control. Share-level access control is grayed out and can't be used. In the field labeled "Obtain list of users and groups from," enter the name of a NetWare server. If the NetWare client wasn't installed before you began these installation procedures, you get an error message, but you can continue configuring these services:

1. Open the Network dialog box from the Control Panel and click the Access Control tab.

2. Select User-level access control, and type the name of the security provider in "Obtain list of users and groups from." If the network name isn't available, Windows 98 asks you what type of security provider the network name represents: NetWare in this case.

3. Close the Network dialog box, and restart your computer.

# Chapter 14

# Supporting Remote Network Connections

## Installing Dial-Up Networking

Windows 98 installs Dial-Up Networking during installation if Setup detects a modem in or attached to your computer. If Dial-Up Networking isn't installed, or you need to install another communications component, you can always add it through the Control Panel. To add additional Dial-Up Networking components to Windows 98, follow these steps:

1. Open the Add/Remove Programs Properties dialog box from the Control Panel.

2. Select the Windows Setup tab. Windows searches for the components that have already been added to your configuration and then lists the available components. Items with a checkmark have already been installed. Gray check boxes indicate that a portion of the item is installed.

3. Double-click Communications in the list of components.

4. Select the item(s) that you want to install.

5. Click Apply and then click OK.

After you click OK, Windows 98 begins copying the required installation files. If you are installing a communications component that modifies the network properties, such as the Dial-Up Networking, Dial-Up Server, or VPN components, Windows 98 prompts you to reboot, so that changed settings will take effect. Other communications applications, such as Phone Dialer, NetMeeting, or Chat, don't require you to reboot, because they don't really change any networking settings.

While Dial-Up Networking is being installed, Windows 98 configures many of the components needed for networking, such as the Dial-Up Adapter and the Microsoft TCP/IP protocol. Any other protocol found in the Network dialog box is configured to work over Dial-Up Networking. However, this may not be enough to connect to remote sites. You often need to make additional configuration changes to the network properties. For example, if you are connecting to a remote site with a NetWare server that you need access to, you need to install the Microsoft Client for NetWare Networks and the IPX/SPX protocol. If you need to use the Client for NetWare Networks, avoid selecting Enable Login Scripts, because it dramatically delays login time.

## Making a New Connection

You use the Make New Connection Wizard to create two types of connections: Dial-Up Networking connections that enable you to use a modem or an ISDN device to connect to the Internet, or VPN connections. To create a Dial-Up Networking connection, follow these steps:

1. From My Computer, select the Dial-Up Networking folder.

2. Click the Make New Connection icon.

3. Type the name of the connection — for example, My Internet or Connection to Corporate.

4. In the Select Device dialog box, choose the modem that you want to use as your connection device. If the VPN option is listed, don't select it if you are trying to create a connection to the Internet or a Dial-Up Server. Click the Next button after you select the communications device.

5. The Wizard's next dialog box lets you type the telephone numbers to your remote access servers. After entering the telephone number, select a country code if required. Then, click the Next button.

6. Complete the Dial-Up Networking connection by clicking the Finish button.

In some cases, more than one type of communications device may be installed on your computer. You may have a 28.8 Kbps modem that connects to an ISP; however, to connect to a corporate location, you may use ISDN. The Make New Connection Wizard enables you to select which modem you want to use for the specified connection.

# Modifying the Properties of the Dial-Up Connection

After you create the connection, you can modify the properties of the Dial-Up Networking connection by right-clicking the connection and choosing Properties. The properties of a Dial-Up Networking connection enable you to do the following:

- Modify the Dial-Up Networking connection telephone number, country code, and modem
- Modify the server type, protocols, and advanced options
- Enable scripting
- Enable Multilink (using multiple modems to increase connection performance)

## Configuring General Properties of Dial-Up Connections

The General tab enables you to modify the following:

- The area code and telephone number.
- The country code.
- The box labeled Use Area Code and Dialing Properties (by default this option is selected).
- The type of modem. You'll find this handy if you change modems, because the Dial-Up Networking connection is unaware of the modem change until the change is modified in the Connect Using drop-down list.

## Configuring Server Types of a Dial-Up Connection

The Server Types tab enables you to modify the options to connect to a Dial-Up Server, including the following:

- **Type of Dial-Up Server**. You can select from any of the connection-oriented protocols, such as PPP, NRN, SLIP, and Windows for Workgroups or Windows NT 3.1. Windows 98 defaults to PPP connections because that's the most widely used protocol.
- **Advanced options**. These options enable you to make the following important changes:
  - **Log on to network**. If you are logging on to an ISP, uncheck this box. Usually, this should be checked when connecting to a corporate LAN.
  - **Enable software compression**. Usually, this is turned on to increase performance in your Dial-Up Networking connection. Deselect this option only if you think it is causing problems.

- **Require encrypted password**. If this option is selected, the client uses Challenge Handshake Authentication Protocol (CHAP) and MS-CHAP only when generating a password. If this option is not selected, the client can also perform Password Authentication Protocol (PAP) if the server requests it. However, PAP is less secure than CHAP.

- **Require data encryption**. If this option is selected, the connection is refused unless the server uses data encryption. Most ISPs don't support data encryption.

- **Record a log file for this connection**. If this option is selected, Dial-Up Networking creates a log file about the connection session.

- **Allowed network protocols**. Used to connect to the target network. By default, all protocols are selected; however, select only the protocols that you need for that session. If you are connecting to an ISP for Internet access, enable only the IP protocol. If you are connecting to a remote site that uses only NetWare servers, enable only the IPX/SPX protocol. This improves your Dial-Up Networking connection performance slightly. You can also select the TCP/IP Settings button and enter additional information, such as the default gateway on remote networks, static IP addresses and DNS information for that connection, and whether you want to use IP header compression. Rarely do you need to modify any of these options, but if you do, it is because an ISP requires that these specific settings be changed.

Normally, you really don't need to modify anything on the Server Types tab in order for the Dial-Up Networking connection to work. However, you should modify the protocols settings to use the networking protocols that are required for that connection. Reducing additional protocols improves connection performance.

## Configuring the Scripting Tab

Scripts are used primarily for ISPs that require a certain logon procedure. Most ISPs provide you with the script, so that you don't have to create one manually. But if you do need to create a script, note that Windows 98 includes four sample scripts you can use as starting points. The text files are located in the \Program Files\Accessories directory. In \Windows, a document named Script.doc provides information on how to create and modify scripts. After you create a script, or are using one provided by an ISP, you need to point the Scripting tab to the file. To enable the script, follow these steps:

1. Right-click a connection that has been created by the Make New Connection Wizard and then select Properties.

2. Select the Scripting tab from the properties dialog box of your dial-up connection.

3. Click the Browse button. The Open dialog box appears.

4. Use the Open dialog box to locate the script within your directory structure and then click the Open button. This returns you to the Scripting tab.

5. From the Scripting tab, choose either Step through script or Start terminal screen minimized. Stepping through the script helps you debug and troubleshoot problems such as incorrect responses, within a script. The default option is to start with the terminal screen minimized, which displays information on-screen while you make your remote connection. Generally, this option is unchecked only when you want to see the terminal output on-screen.

6. Click OK.

## Configuring Multilink

Multilink is a Windows 98 feature that you should at least try out. *Multilink Channel Aggregation* (MLCA) enables you to combine modems or ISDN connections to increase connection performance. Furthermore, the modems don't have to be identical. Multilink can be used only as a Windows 98 client. Windows 98 Dial-Up Server can't provide MLCA. Multilink does have the following additional limitations:

- Connections can be PPP connections only.
- It must be supported by your ISP.
- It requires multiple devices to be configured to combine the logical PPP pipe over the communication link.
- MLCA works best with same-speed modems.
- It requires individual phone lines for each device.

You access the Multilink configuration utility from the Multilink tab in the properties dialog box of a Dial-Up Networking connection. To configure Multilink, follow these steps:

1. Right-click a connection that was made using the Make New Connection Wizard and then select Properties from the shortcut menu that appears.

2. Choose the Multilink tab from the Dial-Up Networking connection's properties dialog box.

3. Select the radio button labeled Use additional devices.

4. Click the Add button.

5. From the Edit Extra Device dialog box, click the Device name drop-down list and select the additional modem that you will use for your Multilink connection and then click OK. This returns you to the Dial-Up Networking connection's properties dialog box. Click OK.

6. After you configure Multilink, launch the connection. Dial-Up Networking connects the primary device first, and then the secondary device, and so on.

# Configuring Connections to Remote Servers

Connecting to a Windows NT 4.0 remote access server, Windows 98 Dial-Up Server, or any other PPP communications server is very similar to making a connection to the Internet, except that you always want to select Log on to Network. This option is turned on by default and is located on the Server Types tab of the Dial-Up Networking connection's properties dialog box.

You use the Make New Connection Wizard to specify the telephone numbers for the NT 4.0 RAS Server and to specify the appropriate modems. You really don't need to modify any of the properties of the connection, because the default parameters work well, but if you know which protocols are being used at the Windows NT 4.0 Server, you may want to enable only the necessary protocols. Then, double-click the connection that you created and enter your logon ID and password.

To set up connections to Windows NT 3.1 or Windows for Workgroups 3.11, follow these steps:

1. Create a connection by using Make New Connection Wizard.

2. Right-click the connection that you created and then select Properties.

3. Choose the Server Types tab. From the Type of Dial-Up Server drop-down list, select Windows for Workgroups and Windows NT 3.1.

4. Click OK.

# Debugging a Dial-Up Networking Connection

You can monitor PPP sessions by turning on the PPP log file. When this option is turned on, reports of PPP connections are saved to a text file. The file contains the basic layers and points of any Dial-Up Networking connection and is useful for monitoring and troubleshooting remote connections. This process is very similar to capturing packets with a network sniffer on a LAN. You can enable PPP logging for each Dial-Up Networking connection that you've created. This is a major improvement over the Windows 95 implementation of the logging capabilities.

To enable PPP logging for a connection, follow these steps:

1. Open Dial-Up Networking from My Computer.

2. Right-click one of the connection icons that you've already created and select Properties from the menu.

3. From the Dial-Up Networking connection's properties dialog box, select the Server Types tab. In the Advanced options section, select the option named Record a log file for this connection, and then Click OK.

After you initiate a session with this connection, a log file is saved to the C:\Windows directory. The log filename, called Ppplog.txt, shows all layers of connectivity to your PPP connection. Dial-Up Networking updates this file by appending new information to it.

# Creating a Secure Network Connection

Add the VPN client component to your Windows 98 configuration through the Control Panel. After installing the VPN component, you

must reboot your computer. To install the VPN component, follow
these steps:

1. Open the Add/Remove Programs Properties dialog box from
   the Control Panel.

2. Select the Windows Setup tab. Windows 98 searches for all
   installed components. After Windows completes the search,
   it places checks next to components that are already installed.

3. Choose Communications and select Virtual Private
   Networking.

4. Click OK. Windows 98 installs the component and requests
   that you reboot. The operating system might require you to
   provide the installation CD-ROM.

## Configuring VPN Access

Use the Make New Connection Wizard to configure VPN access.
You actually use the Make New Connection Wizard twice. The first
connection dials your ISP, and the second connection is the VPN
connection that establishes the tunnel to the VPN server and
authenticates the VPN server. To create the connection to the VPN
server, follow these steps:

1. After you create a connection to the Internet and verify that it
   works properly, open the Make New Connection Wizard.

2. From the Make New Connection dialog box, name the appropriate VPN connection. You can be very specific in your naming convention, for example, "VPN connection to Corporate."

3. Rather than select a modem, choose Microsoft VPN Adapter.

4. Enter the IP address to the known VPN server that resides on
   the Internet. You can also enter a DNS name.

5. Click Finish to complete the installation.

## Making a Connection to the VPN Server

You begin your virtual private network connection to the remote private network by connecting to the Internet. Launch the dial-up connection that you created to connect to your ISP. Then, after you successfully authenticate your ISP, double-click the dial-up connection that you created to use as your VPN connection. The VPN connection prompts you for a login name and password.

In the system tray, you should see two Dial-Up Networking connections and you should be able to use Network Neighborhood to browse resources on the remote network. However, because a tunnel exists between your client and the remote network, you won't be able to browse the Internet. If you want to continue browsing the Internet normally, look at the two modem icons in the system tray. One icon represents the ISP connection and the other represents the VPN connection. Double-click each of these modem icons in your system tray, find the one that's the VPN connection, and disconnect that one.

# Installing Windows 98 Dial-Up Server

To install Windows 98 as a Dial-Up Server, you may want to enable File and Printer Sharing for either Microsoft or NetWare Networks. This is necessary only if you want the remote computer to share files on the Windows 98 Dial-Up Server with the dial-up clients. If you decide to enable File and Printer Sharing for either Microsoft or NetWare Networks, you should select user-level or share-level security. This enables users to authenticate through the Windows 98 computer or through a passthrough domain or NetWare server.

To install Windows 98 as a Dial-Up Server, follow these steps:

1. Open the Add/Remove Programs Properties dialog box from the Control Panel.
2. Choose the Windows Setup tab and choose the communications option.
3. Select Dial-Up Server.
4. Click OK and exit to reboot Windows 98.

To configure Windows 98 as a Dial-Up Server, follow these steps:

1. From My Computer, open Dial-Up Networking.
2. Choose Connections ➪ Dial-Up Server.
3. Click Server Type and then choose either PPP or Windows for Workgroups or Windows NT 3.1 from the drop-down list. In most cases, leave the default of PPP. However, if you know that your client is using a different connection protocol, select the appropriate option.
4. Click OK. The Dial-Up Sever is ready to answer incoming calls.

## Configuring Security Options

Windows 98 Dial-Up Server enables clients to authenticate through the local Windows 98 computer, a NetWare server, or a Windows NT Server. How a user authenticates is determined by share-level access or user-level access settings in the Network dialog box that you access via the Control Panel.

Share-level security assigns a password to the Windows 98 Dial-Up Server through local Windows 98. After a connection is made, users browse the available resources of the Dial-Up Server and adhere to any of the share permissions that have been assigned. If the Dial-Up Server is attached to the network, and Log on to Network is enabled, the remote user can access resources connected to that network, too.

Share-level security is not as secure as user-level security, because share-level security is a single password that can be distributed easily—and because Windows 98 doesn't have much security, the password can potentially be modified by someone who knows the system is running in an office.

User-level security requires passthrough authentication to a NetWare or NT domain controller. User rights are controlled through groups that are created on these servers, and because these servers usually have network administrators, the chances of someone modifying a password are not as great.

To configure the Dial-Up Server for user-level security, follow these steps:

1. Make sure that file and printer sharing services are installed and that user-level security is enabled in the Network dialog box.

2. In the Dial-Up Networking folder, choose Connections ⇨ Dial-Up Server.

3. In the Dial-Up Server properties dialog box, click Allow caller access, then click the Add button.

4. In the Add Users dialog box, specify which users have permissions to access the Dial-Up Server. Then click OK.

5. In the Dial-Up Server properties dialog box, you can optionally click Server Type and turn on Require encrypted passwords. If you decide to use this option, your client will be required to have this option enabled also.

To configure the Dial-Up Server for share-level security, follow these steps:

1. Make sure that file and printer sharing services are installed and that user-level security is enabled in the network properties.

2. In the Dial-Up Networking folder, choose Connections ⇨ Dial-Up Server.

3. In the Dial-Up Server properties, click Allow caller access, and then click Change Password to password-protect the Dial-Up Server.

4. In the Dial-Up Server properties dialog box, optionally click Server Type and turn on Require encrypted passwords. If you decide to use this option, your client will be required to have this option enabled also.

**Tip**

If you use share-level security and forget the password that you've set, delete the Rna.pwl file located in the C:\Windows directory. To delete this file, you first must shut down RAS and restart Windows 98. After you delete the file, restart Windows 98, and then reset the password, as indicated in configuring the Dial-Up Server for share-level security. If you receive an error message that the file is corrupt or missing, this is completely normal and is resolved after the file has been created automatically by the Dial-Up Server service.

# Using Direct Cable Connection to Connect Two Computers

Before you install and configure the Direct Cable Connection (DCC), you need to establish which network protocols will be used between the host and guest computers. DCC supports the IPX/SPX and NetBEUI protocols and DCC can act as a gateway to a TCP/IP network. If you decide that you are going to use the gateway facility, you need to use the NetBEUI protocol. Decide in advance if you'll be using an infrared, a parallel, or a serial connection to create the DCC connection.

The following cables are compatible with DCC:

- Standard or basic 4-bit cable, including LapLink and InterLink cables.

- Extended capabilities port (ECP) cable. This cable works with ECP-enabled parallel ports.

■ Universal cable modem (UCM) cable. This cable supports connecting different types of parallel ports. Using this cable between two ECP ports creates the fastest possible connection.

To install Direct Cable Connection, follow these steps:

1. Open the Add/Remove Programs Properties dialog box from the Control Panel.

2. Select the Windows Setup tab. Windows searches for components. When the process is complete, any item with a check mark has been installed.

3. In the component list, double-click Communications. The Communications dialog box opens.

4. In the Components list box, click Direct Cable Connections.

5. Click OK. Windows copies setup files and requests that you reboot.

Before opening the Direct Cable Connection folder, which is located by selecting Start ➪ Programs ➪ Accessories ➪ Direct Cable Connection, connect the computers together with the cable that you're using. Windows 98 provides a Direct Cable Connection Wizard to establish the connection between the two computers. The Wizard begins when you open the Direct Cable Connection for the first time. The Wizard is very straightforward. One computer is designated as the host computer and the other is designated as the guest computer. To configure your computer as a host, follow these steps:

1. Select the Host radio button and click the Next button.

2. Select the type of cable that you are using to connect to the guest computer. At this point, you have the option to install another port if your port is not already installed. Click the Next button.

3. Click the File and Printer Sharing button only if you haven't already installed the file and printer sharing service. You must have File and Printer Sharing enabled to use DCC. If you click the File and Printer Sharing button, the Wizard launches the Network dialog box. From the Network dialog box, you can select the File and Printer Sharing button and select either "I want to be able to give others access to my files" or "I want to be able to allow others to print to my printer(s)," or select both. After you do this, you need to reboot and then begin the Wizard again. After File and Printer Sharing is enabled, you don't need to select this button again in the DCC Wizard. Click the Next button to continue the installation.

4. If you haven't shared any folders yet, DCC prompts you with a message to begin sharing a folder. Share a folder, as specified in the Wizard instructions, and then continue by clicking Next.

5. Optionally, enable password protection by selecting Use password protection. Click the Set Password button and enter the password.

6. Click Finish to complete the installation.

At this point, DCC initiates the host software. If the guest computer is already configured, the two connected workstations begin to communicate. If the guest is not connected, the host session times out and you can close it. To launch the host for connectivity later, simply select the icon from the communications folder.

To configure the guest computer, follow these steps:

1. With the cable connected, make sure that the host is ready and waiting for a guest connection.

2. Open the Direct Cable Connection from Start ➪ Programs ➪ Accessories ➪ Communications. Select the Guest radio button and then click the Next button.

**3.** Select the type of cable that you are using to connect to the guest computer. At this point, you have the option to install another port, if your port is not already installed. Click the Next button.

**4.** The guest begins to search for the host computer. When connected, authenticate with the password, if necessary.

You can't use Direct Cable and Dial-Up Networking at the same time—both applications use the same network interface (Pppmac.vxd). Before you use the DCC connection, make sure that you shut down any networking connections.

# Part IV

## Administration

# Chapter 15

# Enabling Remote Administration

## Turning on Remote Administration

To effectively administer Windows 98 using remote administration, each workstation should meet the following requirements:

- **Common network protocol**. The administrator's workstation must have at least one network protocol in common with the target workstation.

- **User-level security**. Although many remote administration tools don't require user-level security, enough do to make this a requirement.

- **Remote administration**. You enable remote administration and grant administrative privileges in the Passwords Properties dialog box.

- **Microsoft Remote Registry Service**. The Registry Editor, System Monitor, and System Policy Editor require you to install the Remote Registry Service on both the administrator's workstation and the target workstation.

■ **File and printer sharing services**. Even though Microsoft states that remote administration doesn't require file and printer sharing services on the target workstation, my experience suggests that this is also a requirement for remote administration.

Each of the following sections describes how to configure the computer to meet the requirements for remote administration. The only way for remote administration to be practical in a large organization is if you install the Microsoft Remote Registry Service, install the file and printer sharing services, and enable user-level security as you roll out Windows 98. "Enabling Remote Administration in Setup Scripts," later in this chapter, shows how to create a custom setup script that will enable remote administration on each workstation as you're installing Windows 98. Then, you can immediately begin remotely administering each workstation.

# Installing a Common Network Protocol

Both computers must have at least one protocol in common. That is, both the administrator's computer and the user's computer must have a single protocol with which the computers can communicate with each other. Having additional protocols beyond the common protocol installed is OK. To install a protocol on a Windows 98 computer, follow these steps:

1. Open the Network Properties dialog box from the Control Panel.

2. Click the Add button on the Configuration tab, select Protocol from the list of component types, and click the Add button.

3. Select the manufacturer from the left-hand list, and the name of the protocol from the right-hand list. If you don't find the protocol for which you're looking, click Have Disk to install third-party drivers.

4. Click OK to close the Select Network Protocol dialog box; then, click OK to close the Network dialog box. Windows 98 prompts you for the installation disk, if required, and you must restart the computer after making this change.

# Turning on User-Level Security

Resource security protects shared folders and printers in Windows 98. You choose between share-level security (the weaker) or user-level security (the stronger) to protect shared resources. With share-level security, any user who knows the password can access a share. Share-level security isn't available with the file and printer sharing service for NetWare. With user-level security, a security provider validates a user's credentials before Windows 98 gives him or her access to the share; and even then the share's owner must grant the user rights to the share by adding him or her to the user list. Remote administration works only with user-level security, which is easy to enable by following these instructions:

1. Open the Network dialog box from the Control Panel and click the Access Control tab.

2. Select User-level access control, and type the name of the security provider in Obtain list of users and groups from. If the network name isn't available, Windows 98 asks you what type of security provider the network name represents: NetWare, NT Domain, NT Server, or Workstation.

3. Close the Network dialog box. Restart your computer when prompted.

# Enabling Remote Administration in the Control Panel

When you enable user-level security on a Windows 98 workstation, the operating system automatically enables remote administration for the Domain Admins group in a Windows NT domain, the

Supervisor account on a NetWare 3.*x* network, or the Admin account on a NetWare 4.0 network. Thus, after enabling user-level security, you don't normally have to do anything special to enable remote administration. If you find that user-level security is enabled and remote administration is not, however, you can use the following instructions to enable remote administration using the Passwords Properties dialog box in the Control Panel:

1. Open the Passwords Properties dialog box from the Control Panel and click the Remote Administration tab. The dialog box shown in Figure 15-1 is displayed.

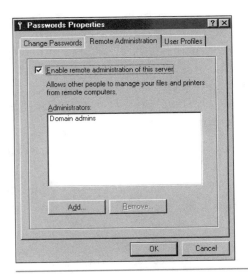

**Figure 15-1** *You'll see a different dialog box that prompts for nothing more than a password if the machine is configured for share-level security.*

2. Select Enable remote administration of this server. If this option was already selected, the computer is already configured for remote administration and you can skip these

instructions or grant administrative privileges to additional users as described in the next step.

**3.** Add the account name of each user or group to which you want to give administrative privileges. To add a name, click Add to display the Choose Administrators dialog box; then, select the users and groups you want to add, and click Add to add them to the list of administrators. Click OK to save your changes. Windows 98 assigns Domain Admins remote administration privileges by default, and, for most purposes, you should leave it at that.

**4.** Close the Passwords Properties dialog box to save your changes. You don't need to restart your computer.

# Installing the Microsoft Remote Registry Service

To install the Microsoft Remote Registry Service from the Windows 98 CD-ROM, follow these steps:

**1.** Open the Network dialog box from the Control Panel.

**2.** Click Add, select Service from the Select Network Component Type dialog box, and click Add. After a brief pause, Windows 98 displays the Select Network Service dialog box.

**3.** Specify the path to the Microsoft Remote Registry Service install files. Click Have Disk, and type *d*:\tools\reskit\ netadmin\remotreg in the space provided, where *d* is the CD-ROM's drive letter. Click OK. The Select Network Service dialog box is displayed.

**4.** Click OK to install the service. Close the Network dialog box, and restart your computer when prompted.

# Setting Up File and Printer Sharing Services

Windows 98 provides file and printer sharing services for both Microsoft and NetWare networks. It supports only one of these services at a time, and each one has the following requirements:

- **File and Printer Sharing for NetWare Networks**. The computer must be using user-level security, and a NetWare server must be available on the network to act as a passthrough security provider.

- **File and Printer Sharing for Microsoft Networks**. Microsoft's file and printer sharing service can use share-level or user-level security. A Microsoft server must be available on the network to provide passthrough security if you're using user-level security.

To install file and printer sharing for either type of network, follow these steps:

1. Open the Network dialog box from the Control Panel.

2. Click the File and Printer Sharing button to display the File and Printer Sharing dialog box.

3. Select whether you want to share files and whether you want to share printers; then, close the File and Printer Sharing dialog box.

4. Click OK and close the Network dialog box to save your settings. Restart your computer after changing your network settings.

When file and printer sharing services are installed and remote administration is enabled on a machine, Windows 98 creates a variety of hidden administrative shares whose names end with a dollar sign. You access a hidden share by launching the share name in the Run dialog box. For example, to open the ADMIN$ share on a workstation called Jerry, choose Run from the Start menu; then, type

**\\Jerry\admin$** and click OK. Windows 98 opens the share in a folder. In order to access the administrative shares, you must log on to your workstation using an account name that has administrative privileges in the Passwords Properties dialog box of the target workstation. In most cases, log on to your workstation using an account name that's a member of Domain Admins in a Windows NT domain, the Supervisor account on a NetWare 3.*x* network, or the Admin account on a NetWare 4.0 network. Here's a description of the shares Windows 98 creates when using remote administration:

- *d*$, where *d* represents each driver letter on the workstation, provides the administrator complete access to each disk on the workstation.

- ADMIN$ gives administrators access to the \Windows folder.

- IPC$ provides interprocess communication (IPC) between applications running on each computer.

# Enabling Remote Administration in Setup Scripts

Remote administration is not practical if you try physically enabling it on each computer. The best approach to remote administration is to plan well in advance of deploying Windows 98 so that you can roll the operating system out with remote administration already enabled. You do this with custom setup scripts.

The Windows 98 CD-ROM comes with a program called Microsoft Batch 98 that you can use to build a custom setup script. A setup script is nothing more than an INF file that specifies the settings that the Setup program will use while installing the operating system. A setup script is usually called Msbatch.inf. You can specify values for all the settings or just a few of them. After creating a setup script, you can push it to the user via his or her logon script, or you can allow the user to launch the Setup program with the script as its only command line parameter. You find Batch 98 and a variety of documentation about it in \Tools\Reskit\Deploy on the Windows 98 CD-ROM.

To enable remote administration using a script, add the lines shown in Listing 15-1 to Msbatch.inf after creating the file with Batch 98. If the settings in the listing already exist in the INF file, just change the existing settings in the file. Set Security to domain or server, enabling user-level security, and set PassThroughAgent to the name of the domain or server that's validating credentials for user-level security. Username indicates the group or user account that you want to have administrative rights on the computer.

**Listing 15-1** *Enabling Remote Administration in a Setup Script*

```
[Install]
AddReg=Remote.Admin

[Remote.Admin]
HKLM,"Security\Access\Admin\Remote",%Username%,1,ff,00

[Network]
Security=domain | server
PassThroughAgent=provider
services=remotereg

[strings]
Username="server\account"
```

# Editing a Remote Computer's Registry

Using the Registry Editor to edit a remote workstation's Registry requires that the remote workstation use user-level security and have remote administration enabled in the Passwords Properties dialog box. The workstation must also be running the Microsoft Remote Registry Service.

When you connect to a remote workstation's Registry, you have full access to it. Thus, be very careful with the changes that you make. And even though the changes you make are immediately reflected in the remote workstation's Registry, the user might have to reboot to reflect those changes in the rest of the operating system. In general, if the user would have to restart the workstation when making a similar change via the Control Panel, he or she will have to restart it after you change the Registry.

To connect to a remote workstation in the Registry Editor, follow these steps:

1. Open the Registry Editor.

2. Choose Registry ⇨ Connect Network Registry from the main menu. The Connect Network Registry dialog box is displayed.

3. Type the name of the remote computer, or click Browse to look for the computer. Click OK, and you should see the remote computer's Registry in the Registry Editor.

# Using the System Policy Editor Remotely

While the Registry Editor gives you full access to the remote computer's Registry, the System Policy Editor gives you access to a subset of the remote computer's Registry. It's possibly a better alternative in most cases, though, because you fill in forms and let the System Policy Editor make the changes to the Registry. You stand less chance of breaking the remote computer by using the System Policy Editor than you do by using the Registry Editor.

You can use the System Policy Editor two different ways: you can create policy files that Windows 98 automatically downloads from the network server, or you can use it in *Registry mode* to directly change a workstation's Registry. The changes you make to a remote computer can apply to the current user or the entire machine. Note also that some changes you make will not take effect until the user restarts the computer.

The System Policy Editor modifies the target workstation's Registry just like the Registry Editor; thus, it has the same requirements. It requires that the remote workstation use user-level security and have remote administration enabled in the Passwords Properties dialog box. The workstation must also be running the Microsoft Remote Registry Service.

To connect to a remote workstation in the System Policy Editor, follow these steps:

1. Open the System Policy Editor and choose File ⇨ Connect from the main menu.

2. Type the name of the computer to which you want to connect and click OK.

# Monitoring a Remote Computer's Performance

You use the System Monitor to monitor the performance of a remote workstation. System Monitor enables the administrator to track a remote computer's performance, diagnosing and fixing performance bottlenecks. It displays different performance indicators in charts that measure the computer's performance over time. You can also track the performance of multiple workstations at the same time by opening multiple instances of System Monitor. It requires that you install user-level security and the Microsoft Remote Registry Service on the remote workstation. You must also enable remote administration and install the file and printer sharing services.

To monitor the performance of a remote computer, follow these steps:

1. Open the System Monitor.

**2.** Choose File ⇨ Connect from the main menu to open the Connect dialog box. Type the name of the computer you want to monitor and click OK.

The Windows 98 CD-ROM includes the Network Monitor Agent, which provides network performance counters that you can view in the System Monitor. Network Monitor Agent is a Windows 98 service, and you use it to troubleshoot network performance on a WAN, LAN, or dial-up networking connection. After installing the Monitor Agent, you should see additional Network Monitor Performance options in the System Monitor. Install the Network Monitor Agent from \tools\reskit\netadmin\netmon on the Windows 98 CD-ROM.

# Managing a Remote Computer's Shares

You use Net Watcher to manage the shared resources on a remote computer. You can add and remove shares, for example; view connections, shared folders, and open files; close files that remote users have open; or even disconnect a remote user.

Using Net Watcher to manage the shared resources on a remote computer has similar requirements as the other remote administration tools. You must enable user-level security and remote administration. You must also install the file and printer sharing services. Net Watcher does not require Microsoft Remote Registry Service, however.

You should be aware of a few stipulations when using Net Watcher:

- If the administrator's computer is running share-level security, he or she can watch only other computers that are running share-level security.

- If the administrator's computer is using user-level security, he or she can watch computers using both types of security.

- If the administrator's computer is using File and Printer Sharing for NetWare Networks, she can watch only remote computers that are also running File and Printer Sharing for NetWare Networks.

- On a NetWare network, you can't close files on the remote computer. You can disconnect connected users, however, to close the files to which they are connected.

To connect to a remote computer using Net Watcher, follow these steps:

1. Open Net Watcher.

2. Choose Administer ⇨ Select Server from the main menu; then, type the name of the remote computer you want to administer and click OK.

3. Use Net Watcher as you would on your own computer.

If you don't log on to the administrator's workstation using an account name that has explicit administrative privileges on the target workstation, Net Watcher asks you for a password. Even if you know the magic word, you won't get access to the remote workstation unless your account name has explicit or implicit privileges to administer it. Windows 98 also prompts you for a password if the remote computer is using share-level security. In this case, you can administer the machine as long as you know the password.

# Tools Found on the Windows 98 CD-ROM

Windows 98 comes with a handful of administration tools you should know about. The Setup program doesn't install them by default, however, so you must know where to find them. The following list gives you a brief description of each tool and shows you where to find it on the CD-ROM:

- **Batch installation** is in \Tools\Reskit\Batch.
- **Long filename backup** is in \Tools\reskit\file\lfnback.
- **Network Monitor** is in \Tools\reskit\netadmin\netmon.
- **Password list editor** is in \Tools\reskit\netadmin\pwledit.
- **Remote registry** is in \Tools\reskit\netadmin\remotreg.
- **RPC print provider** is in \Tools\reskit\netadmin\rpcpp.
- **System Policy Editor** is in \Tools\reskit\netadmin\poledit.

# Chapter 16

# Implementing Profiles and Policies

## Enabling Local User Profiles

You can enable user profiles locally on each computer, or you can enable them for a group of computers by using system policies. You locally enable user profiles by using the Passwords Properties icon in the Control Panel. Aside from enabling user profiles, this dialog box allows you to determine how much information Windows 98 keeps in each profile. You can opt to include the contents of the Desktop and Network Neighborhood folders in the profile. You can also choose to include the contents of the Start menu. To enable user profiles locally after installing Windows 98, follow these steps:

1. Open the Passwords Properties dialog box from the Control Panel and click the User Profiles tab.

2. Select "Users can customize their preferences and desktop settings."

3. In the area labeled User profile settings, choose how much content you want to include in each user profile. You can choose whether to include the Desktop and Network Neighborhood folders, and whether to include the Start menu.

**4.** Close the Passwords Properties dialog box to save your changes. You have to restart the computer in order for the changes to take effect.

You find each user profile in \Windows\Profiles. This folder contains a subfolder for each user who has a profile. For example, Windows 98 stores the profile for a user who logs in using the name Jerry in \Windows\Profiles\Jerry. Here's what you find in each user's profile folder:

- **User.dat** contains the user-specific portion of the Registry.

- **\Application Data** contains user-specific data that is required by various applications. By default, the Windows Address Book, QuickLaunch toolbar, Outlook Express Mail and News, and Windows 98 Welcome store configuration data in this folder.

- **\Desktop** contains the contents of the user's desktop. In particular, any shortcuts, folders, or files the user puts on the desktop are in this folder.

- **\Cookies** contains cookies that are used by Internet Explorer. Web sites use cookies to store data persistently across connections.

- **\History** contains history data for Internet Explorer. This enables the user to see a list of Web sites he or she has visited recently.

- **\NetHood** contains any shortcuts the user adds to the Network Neighborhood folder.

- **\Recent** contains shortcuts for each document the user has recently opened. Windows 98 displays the contents of this folder on the Start menu's Documents menu. This folder is updated only by programs that are designed to add shortcuts to \Recent when a document is opened.

■ **\Start Menu** contains the contents of the Start menu. Windows 98 displays any items in \Start Menu at the top of the Start menu. It displays any shortcuts and folders under the subfolder \Programs in the submenu called Programs.

# Enabling User Profiles on the Network

Enabling user profiles on the network allows users to log on to different workstations and still use their familiar settings. Microsoft calls this capability *roving profiles*. In certain situations, this might alleviate ownership issues with regard to the organization's computing resources, allowing users to personalize their desktops and use any available workstation. To support network-based user profiles, you must make sure the infrastructure meets a few requirements:

■ **32-bit networking clients**. Each Windows 98 workstation must be using a 32-bit, protected-mode networking client.

■ **Long filename support**. To enable full support for network-based user profiles, the server must support long filenames. Without long filename support, Windows 98 stores only the User.dat file on the server. An example of a server that does *not* support long filenames is the original, unmodified NetWare 3.11.

■ **Home folders**. Each user must have a network home folder configured on the server if you're storing profiles on a Microsoft network. If you're storing profiles on a Novell NetWare network, Windows 98 stores profiles in MAIL\ *user_ID*.

■ **Primary Network Logon**. You specify the primary network logon in the Network dialog box, which you can open from the Control Panel. Windows 98 looks to the server identified by the primary network logon to find the network version of the user's profile.

- **Consistent folder names**. Make sure that each Windows 98 workstation uses consistent folder names. In particular, make sure the Windows installation folder is the same on any workstation with which you want a user to be able to access network-based profiles. If you install Windows 98 in \Windows on one workstation and in \Win on another workstation, for example, Windows 98 won't copy some components of the user's profile.

Each time the user logs off your computer, Windows 98 automatically copies the profile to the user's home folder on the network. From then on, Windows 98 uses the network version of the profile if it's more current than the local version. When copying the user's profile to the network, Windows 98 includes only the shortcuts that it finds in the \Desktop folder. It doesn't copy any folders or documents in this folder. Thus, documents and folders are only a part of the local profile, not the network version of the profile. Windows 98 uses the following process to locate the profile to use when the user logs on to the workstation:

1. **Looks for a local profile**. Windows 98 looks in the Registry key `HKEY_LOCAL_MACHINE\Software\Microsoft\Windows\CurrentVersion\Profile List` to determine whether the user has a local profile.

2. **Looks for a profile on the network**. Windows 98 looks for a user profile on the user's home folder on the network.

3. **Chooses the profile to use**. If the profile that Windows 98 finds on the network is more current than the user's local profile or if the user doesn't have a local profile, Windows 98 copies the profile from the network and loads the contents of User.dat into the Registry. If the user doesn't have a local or network profile, Windows 98 creates a profile by using default settings.

When the user logs off, Windows 98 updates both the local and network versions of the user profile. The local profile can become more current than the network version of the profile only if the user logs on to the workstation without validation from the server. That is, if Windows 98 can't validate the user's credentials because the server isn't available, it uses the local profile. However, the next time the user logs on and off the network, Windows 98 still updates the network version of the profile with the correct configuration data.

Windows 98 allows a user to log on to multiple workstations simultaneously. The situation that user profiles creates, in this case, might confuse some users. If the user is logged on to two workstations and then logs off the first, Windows 98 updates the network copy of the user's profile. Then, when the user logs off the second workstation, Windows 98 updates the network version of the user's profile again. Thus, the network version of the profile always reflects the profile of the workstation from which the user last logged off. Windows 98 does not merge changes in a user's profile when he or she is logged on to more than one Windows 98 workstation. If a user doesn't log on to the workstation—the user presses Cancel instead of providing logon credentials—Windows 98 uses the default profile.

**Tip**

To make sure that Windows 98 accurately determines whether the local profile is more current than the network profile, make sure that you update the computer's clock each time the user logs on to the network. You can accomplish this simply by adding the command

```
net time \\server /set /y
```

in which *server* is the name of the server, to the user's logon script. This command causes Windows 98 to synchronize its clock with the server's clock.

# Windows NT Networks

To use profiles with a Windows NT network, each Windows 98 workstation must meet these requirements:

- The Client for Microsoft Networks is installed.
- User profiles are enabled.
- The primary network logon is set to Client for Microsoft Networks.
- A home folder is assigned for each user on the server.

Windows 98 does not use the Winnt\Profiles folder for each user's profile. Windows NT uses this folder itself. However, you can create a folder for the user in \Winnt\Profiles and set that as the user's home folder. I recommend that you put home folders on a volume that is separate from the volume on which Windows NT is installed so that you don't risk running out of disk space if users nab too much disk space.

# NetWare Networks

To use profiles with a NetWare network, each Windows 98 workstation must meet these requirements:

- The Client for NetWare Networks is installed.
- User profiles are enabled.
- The primary network logon is set to Client for NetWare Networks.

Exactly where Windows 98 stores the user's profile depends on how you configure the network:

- **Bindery mode.** If the user logs on in bindery mode, Windows 98 stores the profile in the user's mail folder.

- **Novell Directory Services**. If the user logs on with Novell Directory Services (NDS), Windows 98 stores the user's profile in the user's home folder; thus, you must make sure that every account has a home folder associated with it.

**Tip**

In some cases, you might want to prevent a user from logging on to other computers using his or her network-based profile, even though you do want to enable user profiles for that computer. Thus, to disable roving profiles on the computer, open theRegistry key called `HKEY_LOCAL_MACHINE\Network\Logon` and add a new DWORD value entry called `UserHomeDirectory`. The value of this entry doesn't matter.

## Other Networks

Windows 98 does support network-based user profiles on networks other than Microsoft and Novell. This even includes peer-to-peer workgroup networks. To set up network-based user profiles on other networks, follow these steps:

1. Create a network folder to which all users have read-only access. Create a home folder for each user underneath that, and give all users full access to their home folders.

2. In that folder, create a text file called Profiles.ini that looks like the one shown in Listing 16-1. Each item under the `[Profiles]` section is given a name corresponding to the user's logon name and is assigned a value that is the UNC path to the user's home folder.

3. Disable roving profiles: open the Registry key called `HKEY_LOCAL_MACHINE\Network\Logon` and add a new DWORD value entry called `UserHomeDirectory`.

**4.** Open HKEY_LOCAL_MACHINE\Network\Logon and create a new string value entry called SharedProfileList. Assign to this value entry the UNC path to the Profiles.ini file that you created in Step 2.

After you configure Windows 98 by using these instructions, Windows 98 searches the text file that you specified to find the user's home folder. It uses the user's home folder for the network version of the user's profile. If Windows 98 doesn't find an entry for the user, Windows 98 doesn't load a network version of the profile and sticks with the local version.

**Listing 16-1** *Profiles.ini for Supporting Network-Based User Profiles*

```
[Profiles]
Jerry=\\server\home\jerry
Charlene=\\server\home\charlene
Lisa=\\server\home\lisa
AmyJo=\\server\home\amyjo
```

# Enabling Mandatory User Profiles

Windows 98 enables you to create mandatory user profiles for use with Microsoft or Novell networks. A *mandatory user profile* is a standard configuration that Windows 98 uses every time the user logs on to his or her computer. Essentially, the mandatory user profile is a custom User.dat file that Windows 98 copies to the user's computer each time the user logs on to the network. Windows 98 doesn't save any changes to this file, so the user starts with the same settings every time. To set up a mandatory user profile for a specific user, follow these steps:

**1.** Enable user profiles on the user's workstation.

**2.** Create a profile on any Windows 98 workstation and customize the user preferences to suit your needs.

3. Copy the files and folder that you want to include in the profile to an appropriate folder on the network.

4. Rename User.dat to User.man.

If Windows 98 detects User.man when the user logs on to the workstation, Windows 98 automatically copies User.man to the user's computer and loads it into the Registry, instead of loading any other copy of User.dat. During the course of the user's session, Windows 98 does save changes to the local User.dat file, but it never copies those changes back to the network. Thus, Windows 98 doesn't save configuration changes to the network copy of User.man so that the user gets the same settings the next time the user logs on to the workstation.

Both mandatory user profiles and system policies enable you to enforce settings for the user. They do so a bit differently, however. Mandatory user profiles work only with user-specific settings and require that you control every single setting. System policies work with both machine-specific and user-specific settings. You can also use system policies to choose the settings that you want to control. In most cases, you want to use system policies to lightly enforce certain settings for the user. If you use mandatory user profiles, the user pays a performance penalty when Windows 98 starts, and you pay a productivity penalty, because users will nag you to death every time they want to change something in their configuration.

# Understanding System Policies

System policies enable the administrator to override certain settings in the Registry. These settings can be machine- or user-specific. You store system policies in a file called Config.pol, which you put on the server specified as the user's primary network logon. System policies have several characteristics that make them the single most useful administration tool that Windows 98 provides:

- **Restrictions**. You can restrict the user in numerous ways. For example, you can restrict the user to running only a handful of programs, disable certain icons in the Control Panel, or enforce a certain desktop configuration. The possibilities are limitless.

- **Individuals and Groups**. You can apply policies to individual users or to groups defined on a Microsoft or Novell network. For example, you can apply one set of policies to the Accounting group while using a different set of policies for the Development group.

- **Customizable**. Windows 98 provides a default set of policies that you can use, or you can define your own policies, using policy templates, for any application that uses the Windows 98 Registry.

**Tip**

If you want to set policies that relate directly to Internet Explorer or any application in the Internet Explorer suite, use the Profile Manager, which is part of the Internet Explorer Administration Kit (IEAK).

# Templates, Policies, and the Registry

Before you go on, you must understand how each component in the policies process relates to the other components. Basically, you need to be concerned with the following three components:

- **Templates**. Templates are text files, which have the ADM file extension, that describe the policies you want to set. You can think of a template as defining forms and relating each field in the form to a particular value entry in the Registry. Templates are extremely flexible and, as is usually the case, sometimes difficult to create.

- **Policy files**. Policy files, which are binary files that you create by using the System Policy Editor, have the POL file extension. You open one or more policy templates in the System Policy Editor, define values for one or more policies described in the template, and then save the result in a policy file. Windows 98 loads into the Registry the values that the policy file describes.

- **Registry**. When Windows 98 loads a policy file, it overwrites the values in the Registry with the values it finds in the policy file. Each entry in the policy file is an order pair, containing a name and a value, just like the Registry. Windows 98 first loads the Registry from the user's profile, as normal, and then updates the Registry with the values found in the policy file. This assures that the policy always overrides the Registry.

# Requirements for Using System Policies

To use system policies, you must configure each workstation correctly. To avoid having to perform these tasks on each individual workstation, consider adding them to a custom setup script that will correctly configure each workstation when you roll out Windows 98. Such a script can do the following:

- Install the System Policy Editor on each administrator's workstation.

- Enable user profiles on each Windows 98 workstation (without user profiles, system policies work with machine-specific settings only).

- Install support for group policies on every workstation that will use system policies.

- Create the policy files. You can create default user and default machine policies; user- and machine-specific policies; and group policies.

- Copy the policy files into the Netlogon folder of a Windows NT server or the Public folder of a NetWare server. The Netlogon share is usually \Winnt\System32\Repl\ Import\Scripts on the Windows NT server. This also happens to be the same folder in which you store logon scripts.

# Configuring System Policies on the Network

You'll better understand how to configure your network for using system policies if you take a look at the process Windows 98 uses to download policies. *Downloading policies* means that Windows 98 copies the settings it finds from the policy file to the user's Registry, overwriting whatever values it finds there already. Here's the process Windows 98 uses to identify and download the appropriate policy files:

1. **User policies**. If user profiles are enabled, Windows 98 looks for a policy with the same name as the user's logon name. If Windows 98 finds such a policy, it loads the settings from it; and, regardless, it loads the default user policy.

2. **Group policies**. If you install support for group policies, Windows 98 creates a list of any groups to which the user belongs; then, Windows 98 looks for policies named with the same name as the group. The System Policy Editor allows you to prioritize groups, so Windows 98 downloads the groups with the lowest priority first, ending with the groups that have the highest priority. This ensures that higher-priority policies overwrite lower-priority policies. Note that Windows 98 does not copy group policies for a user if a user policy file exists for that user.

3. **Machine Policies**. Windows 98 looks for a policy that matches the computer's name. If it finds one, it uses the settings found in it; and, regardless, it loads the default computer policies.

If you have a large network with thousands of users logging on to it simultaneously, you have a potential bottleneck, because by default Windows 98 loads policies only from the primary domain control of a Windows NT network. However, you can enable load balancing for system policies to cause Windows 98 to look in alternative locations for the policy file. To enable load balancing, select the Load balance option in the Remote Update policy for Windows 98 Networking. This is a machine setting, so you find it in the Local Computer, Default Computer, or a machine-specific policy. For load balancing to work, you must copy the policy file to the Netlogon share of each backup domain control and any other server participating in the network. You can make this much easier on yourself by using replication.

# Automatic Downloading

Windows 98 automatically downloads the appropriate policy file from the Netlogon folder of a Windows NT server or the Public folder of a NetWare server. The server on which Windows 98 looks for policies depends on which server you identify as the primary network logon in the Network dialog box, which you open from the Control Panel. To configure Windows 98 to download system policies automatically, follow these steps:

1. On each Windows 98 workstation, set the primary network logon to either Client for Microsoft Networks or Client for NetWare Networks, whichever is appropriate.

2. Copy the policy file — Config.pol in most cases — to the Netlogon folder of a Windows NT server or the Public folder of a NetWare server. If you're copying files to a NetWare server, make sure that you copy the file to the user's preferred server; Windows 98 won't copy a policy file stored on other NetWare servers or from computers running File and Printer Sharing for NetWare Networks.

# Manual Downloading

If Windows 98 automatically downloads policies from the server, why would you want to manually download them? First, by manually downloading policies, you can control where you store each user's policies. Second, some network clients don't support policies, particularly 16-bit clients; thus, in such cases you have no choice but to use manually downloaded policies if you want to use policies with such a networking client. Note also that Windows 98 does not automatically load a policy file on stand-alone workstations, so you must use manual downloading if you want to load a policy file from the local computer. To configure Windows 98 to download system policies manually, follow these steps:

1. Open the System Policy Editor and choose File ➪ Open Registry to open the local computer's Registry. If you want to configure a remote computer, choose File ➪ Connect from the main menu, type the name of the computer in the space provided, and then close the dialog box.

2. Open the Local Computer icon, or the icon representing the remote computer, and expand the Windows 98 Network folder, followed by the Update folder.

3. Select Remote Update and then type the UNC path and filename of the system policy file in Path for manual update.

4. Save your changes and close the System Policy Editor.

If you've installed a 32-bit networking client on each Windows 98 workstation, but you still want to use manual downloading, an alternative approach is available that saves you from having to configure each workstation individually. Go ahead and allow each Windows 98 workstation to download policies from the server automatically; then, use the Remote Update policy to have Windows 98 load policies from additional servers, as appropriate for your organization. If you installed a 16-bit networking client, however, you have no choice but to enable manually downloaded policies on each workstation. To enable manual downloading when automatic downloading is enabled, follow these steps:

1.  Open Config.pol in the System Policy Editor.

2.  Open the Default Computer icon; expand the Windows 98 Network item, followed by Update.

3.  Select the Remote Update check box and select Manual in Update Mode. Type the UNC path and filename of the system policy file in Path for manual update.

4.  Save your changes and close the System Policy Editor.

# Installing the System Policy Editor

The System Policy Editor is a powerful tool that you should keep out of users' hands. To keep users from accessing this tool, don't install it on their computers.

You use the System Policy Editor to create policy files from templates. You can find it on the Windows 98 CD-ROM in \TOOLS\reskit\netadmin\poledit. Don't try to copy the files from this folder to your computer, as Microsoft suggests. Use the steps outlined in this section to install it. Windows 98 copies Windows.adm (which provides the template for creating Config.pol files) and Common.adm to \Windows\Inf folder. The remaining ADM files are custom templates from which you can create additional policies. To install the System Policy Editor, follow these steps:

1.  Open the Add/Remove Programs Properties dialog box in the Control Panel and click the Windows Setup tab.

2.  Specify the location of the System Policy Editor's INF file. To do so, click Have Disk and type the path to the \TOOLS\reskit\netadmin\poledit folder on the Windows 98 CD-ROM. You can click Browse to locate this folder. Close the Install from Disk dialog box; and the Have Disk dialog box appears, which contains a single entry for the System Policy Editor.

3. Select System Policy Editor, click Install, and Windows 98 installs the System Policy Editor. Provide the Windows 98 CD-ROM, if requested. You don't have to restart your computer for these changes to take effect.

After you install the System Policy Editor, you start it from the Start menu by choosing Programs ⇨ Accessories ⇨ System Tools ⇨ System Policy Editor.

If you want to use group policies, you must install support for group policies on each Windows 98 workstation. You can install this support via a custom setup, or you can install it on individual workstations via the Add/Remove Programs Properties dialog box. To install support for group policies via Add/Remove Programs, follow these steps:

1. Open the Add/Remove Programs Properties dialog box from the Control Panel and click the Windows Setup tab.

2. Select System Tools and click Details. Select Group policies and click OK to close the System Tools dialog box.

3. Close the Add/Remove Programs Properties dialog box. Windows 98 installs support for group policies on the workstation, copies Grouppol.dll in \Windows\System, and updates the Registry.

# Using the System Policy Editor to Set Restrictions

The System Policy Editor operates in the following two modes:

- **Registry mode.** In this mode, you edit the local or remote computer's Registry directly. This is much like using the Registry Editor, except that you're using a policy template to edit the Registry by using forms.

- **Policy file**. In this mode, you create policy files (POL) that you copy to the server, as described earlier in "Configuring System Policies on the Network." Windows 98 automatically downloads the policy files to the Registry when a user logs on to the network.

To open a computer's Registry in the System Policy Editor, follow these instructions:

- **Open the local computer's Registry**. Choose File ⇨ Open Registry from the main menu.

- **Open a remote computer's Registry**. Choose File ⇨ Connect and type the name of a remote computer in the space provided, and then click OK to open a remote computer's Registry in the System Policy Editor.

To create or open a policy file by using the System Policy Editor, follow these instructions:

- **Create a new policy file**. Choose File ⇨ New Policy. Choose File ⇨ Save As to save the policy file. You typically save to a file called Config.pol.

- **Open an existing policy file**. Choose File ⇨ Open Policy. Choose File ⇨ Save to save changes to the policy file.

When you use the System Policy Editor in policy file mode, the icons are different. Instead of an icon called Local User, you see an icon called Default User. Likewise, you see an icon called Default Computer instead of an icon called Local Computer.

# Defining Default Policies for Users and Computers

The System Policy Editor enables you to define policies such as what features are available to the user for the default user and default computer. These polices apply to every user and every computer. To define default policies for all users and computers, follow these steps:

1. Open the Policy Editor and either create a new policy file or open an existing policy file. In most cases, the filename should be Config.pol.

2. Define default policies for all users. To do so, open the Default User icon. Select the policies that you want to enforce and then close the Default User Properties dialog box.

3. Define default policies for all computers. To do so, open the Default Computer icon, and a dialog box similar to the one for Default User appears; select the policies that you want to enforce and then close the Default Computer Properties dialog box.

**Tip**

To make administering policies as easy on yourself as possible, define as much as you can for the default user and default computer. Then, if you have user- or group-specific needs, define those as described in the next section. In other words, use default policies to define the rules; use user and group policies to define exceptions to those rules.

# Creating Policies

You can define policies for groups as defined on a Windows NT or NetWare server. It works the same as creating groups for individual users or computers, except that you pick a server-defined group instead of a specific user or computer. Incidentally, this means that you can't create new groups, but instead have to rely on the groups defined by the server. You must install this support on every Windows 98 workstation on which you want to use group policies. Your best bet is to install group policy support as part of a custom setup script. To add a user, computer, or group to the policy file, do the following:

- **Add a user**. Choose Edit ⇨ Add User from the main menu. Type the name of the user in the space provided or click Browse to pick a user name; then click OK.

- **Add a computer**. Choose Edit ⇨ Add Computer from the main menu. Type the name of the computer in the space provided or click Browse to pick a computer; then click OK.

- **Add a group**. Choose Edit ⇨ Add Group from the main menu. Type the name of the group in the space provided or click Browse to pick a group; then click OK.

**Caution**

Defining policies for a specific user prevents Windows 98 from applying any group policies to that user.

Users can belong to more than one group, and the System Policy Editor makes special provisions for handling that situation. You can prioritize groups so that the policies in one group have priority over the settings in another group. Windows 98 loads the policies in the lower-priority groups first and loads the policies in the higher-priority groups last. By doing so, Windows 98 always ensures that the highest priority policies are written to the Registry last, overwriting any conflicting policies defined in lower priority groups. To set the priority level for a group, follow these steps:

1.  Choose Options ⇨ Group Priority from the main menu. The Group Priority dialog box appears.

2.  Sort the list by order of priority, with items at the top of the list having higher priority than items below. To move an item in the list, select it and click Move Up or Move Down.

3.  Close the Group Priority dialog box to save your changes.

# Using Custom Policy Templates

A policy template defines the structure and input forms that are used to define policies. It associates the input you provide with actual settings in the Registry. The Windows 98 default policies are actually defined in two template files called Windows.adm and Common.adm that you find in \Windows\Inf. Windows 98 provides additional templates in \Windows\Inf that define a variety of other policies:

| Template | Policies For |
| --- | --- |
| Chat.adm | Microsoft Comic Chat |
| Conf.adm | NetMeeting |
| Inetresm.adm | Internet Explorer |
| Inetsetm.adm | Internet Explorer |
| Oem.adm | Outlook Express |
| Pws.adm | Personal Web Server |
| Shellm.adm | Additional shell policies |
| Subsm.adm | Internet Explorer Channels |

Aside from the additional templates that Windows 98 provides, you can create your own custom templates. If you have an internal application for which you want to define policies, for instance, create a template. To do so, the application must load its configuration data from the Registry. You're limited to defining policies that act on the configuration data found in the Registry; in other words, you can't define a policy that disables an application's menu if the application doesn't already have a Registry setting that does exactly that. To use an additional template with the System Policy Editor, follow these steps:

1. Close any open policy files.

2. Choose Options ⇨ Policy Template from the main menu; the Policy Template Options dialog box appears. The list box shows all the policy templates that you've loaded into the System Policy Editor.

3. Add the template. To do so, click Add, specify the path to the policy file (ADM), and then close the Open Template File dialog box.

4. Close the Policy Template Options dialog box to start working with the additional policy template.

The policy template that you add doesn't replace your existing templates; it complements them. That is, when you add the Shellm.adm policy template from \Windows\Inf, you see additional policies for each user and machine that give you more control over the Windows 98 shell.

The language used to create policy template files is straightforward, but putting the keywords together to make anything meaningful is a bit more complicated. The Windows 98 Resource Kit contains additional information about building templates. The online version of the resource kit is on the Windows 98 CD-ROM in \Tools\Reskit\Help. Your best bet for understanding how to create template files is to study the templates that the System Policy Editor provides in \Windows\Inf.

# Troubleshooting System Policies

To help you troubleshoot problems with system policies, enable error messages. You can do this by enabling the Remote Update policy, and selecting Display error messages. Armed with error messages that help you diagnose problems with system policies, you can try the following general troubleshooting steps before moving on to the steps contained in the rest of this section:

■ Make sure that the Registry key used in the policy file is correct and that you've correctly set the policy.

- If you're using a custom policy template, make sure the application actually uses the Registry settings that you define in the template.

- Double-check that you haven't cleared an option that you actually intended to leave undefined.

- Make sure that you've copied the policy file, Config.pol, to the correct network location and that each user can access that path.

**Caution**

Windows 98 is plagued with a large number of problems and nuances that can make getting profiles and policies to work correctly challenging in some circumstances. Briefcases don't work well when storing them on a desktop that's contained in a profile, for instance. You can find a list of similar issues by searching Microsoft's Knowledge Base at `http://support.microsoft.com`. Use the keyword **user profiles** to look up articles about user profiles and the keywords **policy** or **policies** to look up articles about system policies.

If group policies don't work for a particular user or computer,

- See whether you've defined a policy for the user that overrides any other policies, including default and group policies.

- Verify that you have configured the Windows 98 workstation to support group policies.

- Verify that the user is actually a part of the group for which you've defined the policies.

- Double-check that you've enabled user profiles on the user's computer.

If Windows 98 loads computer policies, but not user policies,

- User profiles must be enabled on the computer for Windows 98 to load user policies.

If Windows 98 doesn't load policies from the Windows NT network,

- Verify that Config.pol is in the Netlogon folder of the primary domain controller. If you've enabled load balancing by selecting the Load-balance option of the Remote Update policy, copy Config.pol to the Netlogon folder of any other server participating on the network as well.

- Verify that the workstation is configured correctly for the network. In particular, make sure the user can log on to the domain.

- Verify that Windows 98 is configured to download policies automatically.

If Windows 98 doesn't load policies from the NetWare network,

- Verify that Config.pol is in the Public folder on the SYS: volume of a NetWare server.

- Check that Preferred Server on the Windows 98 workstation is set to the NetWare server containing the Config.pol file.

- Verify that the workstation is configured correctly for the network. In particular, make sure the user can log on to the preferred server.

- Verify that Windows 98 is configured to download policies automatically. See "Automatic Downloading," earlier in this chapter, for more information.

If Windows 98 doesn't download policies when using manual downloading,

- Make sure the path that you specify in Path for manual update, which is described in "Manual Downloading," contains the name of the policy file: \\\\*server*\\Netlogon\\ Config.pol, for example.

- Verify that the user has read access to the folder in which you stored the Config.pol file.

# Chapter 17

# Scheduling Tasks and Running Scripts

## Automatically Scheduling Common Tasks

The Windows Tune-Up Wizard provides an umbrella for a variety of Windows 98 support tools. For example, Tune-Up Wizard automatically runs Disk Defragmenter, ScanDisk, Disk Cleanup, and Compression Agent (only if a DriveSpace 3 volume is present) on a schedule created by answering a few simple questions.

Choose Start ➪ Programs ➪ Accessories ➪ System Tools ➪ Windows Tune-Up to launch the Windows Tune-Up Wizard. You can use Tune-Up Wizard in either of two ways. The first dialog box gives you the choice of either using the most common tune-up settings or customizing each setting. If you choose to use the most common tune-up settings, the Tune-Up Wizard asks you whether you want to schedule the tasks at Night, Midnight to 3:00 AM; Days, Noon to 3:00 PM; or Evenings, 8:00 PM to 11:00 PM. If you choose to customize the tune-up settings, you have complete control over which utilities Tune-Up Wizard schedules and the time for which it schedules them.

To create customized settings for the Windows Tune-Up Wizard, follow these steps:

1. Start the Windows Tune-Up Wizard.

2. Select Custom – Select each tune-up setting myself, and then click Next.

3. Choose a schedule. You can pick between Nights, Days, Evenings, or Custom. Even if you pick one of the suggested schedules, you can still customize it; therefore, you should pick one of the predefined schedules and then fine-tune it later. Click Next.

4. Select the programs that you want to keep in your StartUp folder. By default, Windows Tune-Up Wizard selects all the programs. If you want to remove a program from the StartUp folder, deselect it. Click Next.

5. Select Yes, speed up my programs regularly, if you want to schedule Disk Defragmenter. Then, click Reschedule to change the schedule, and Settings to change Disk Defragmenter's settings. If you don't want to schedule Disk Defragmenter, select No, do not speed up my programs. Click Next.

6. Select Yes, scan my hard disk for errors regularly, if you want to schedule ScanDisk. Then, click Reschedule to change the schedule, and Settings to change ScanDisk's settings. If you don't want to schedule ScanDisk, select No, do not scan my hard disk for errors. Click Next.

7. Select Yes, delete unnecessary files regularly, if you want to schedule Disk Cleanup. Then, click Reschedule to change the schedule, and Settings to change Disk Cleanup's settings. If you don't want to schedule Disk Cleanup, select No, do not delete unnecessary files. Click Next.

**8.** If you want to run each scheduled utility immediately, select When I click Finish, perform each scheduled tune-up for the first time.

**9.** Click Finish to close the Windows Tune-Up Wizard.

After scheduling tasks such as ScanDisk and Disk Defragmenter via the Windows Tune-Up Wizard, you can adjust each task's settings manually to better suit the user's needs. Other than in very specialized situations, the tasks scheduled by the wizard are the only ones required by most users.

# Scheduling a Task

The Task Scheduler is a feature that enables you to create jobs that run at scheduled times and intervals. It's ideal for running regular disk maintenance and other types of maintenance. You can even schedule scripts to perform various administrative tasks and then schedule them to run periodically.

Windows 98 stores all jobs, or tasks, in the Scheduled Tasks folder. To open the Scheduled Tasks folder, you can either choose Programs ➪ Accessories ➪ System Tools ➪ Scheduled Tasks or open the Scheduled Tasks icon in My Computer. Even better, you can select the Scheduled Tasks folder in Windows Explorer. When you open the Scheduled Tasks folder, you see the Advanced menu option added to Explorer's menu bar. This option enables you to stop and start the Task Scheduler, receive notification of missed tasks, or view the Task Scheduler's log file.

You add tasks in either of two ways: (1) Drag-and-drop any executable file onto the Scheduled Tasks folder, which creates a default schedule for the program (daily at 9:00 a.m.). (2) Use the Scheduled Task Wizard, which is the best way to add a task because the Wizard prompts you for all the pertinent information at one time, avoiding the need to go back and reedit the task after creating it. The Scheduled Task Wizard displays different dialog boxes, depending on the type of task you're creating: Daily, Weekly, Monthly, Once, At System Startup, At Logon, or When idle. The following sections provide more details about creating each type of task, and the following instructions provide a general overview for creating any type of task:

1. Open the Add Scheduled Task icon in the Scheduled Tasks folder. A dialog box explaining the purpose of the Wizard is displayed. Click Next.

2. Select the program you want to schedule. The Scheduled Task Wizard shows you a list of registered applications and their version numbers. Pick an application from the list, or click Browse to locate an EXE file on the computer. Click Next.

3. Type a name for the scheduled task in the space provided, and describe the frequency at which you want the program to run by selecting Daily, Weekly, Monthly, One time only, When my computer starts, or When I log on. Click Next to continue, and the Scheduled Task Wizard opens a different dialog box, the nature of which depends on the task's frequency you selected.

4. Describe the schedule for the task, as described in the following sections. The Scheduled Task Wizard doesn't display a dialog box when you choose When my computer starts or When I log on. Click Next to continue.

5. Click Finish to save your new task. Optionally, select Open advanced properties for this task when I click Finish, and the Scheduled Task Wizard opens the task's property sheet for you. You see a new icon for the task in the Scheduled Tasks folder. Note that the icon you see in the folder is the program's icon with a small clock superimposed over the bottom-left corner of it.

**Tip**

To use the Task Scheduler effectively, you must make sure that the computer's clock is correct. You can periodically update the time by double-clicking the time in the taskbar. Better yet, you can automatically update the time from a network server by typing net time \\*servername* /set at the DOS prompt. This automatically adjusts your computer's clock so that it matches the server's. If you schedule this command to run once or twice a day, you can be sure that your clock is always correct, assuming of course that the server's clock is correct. If you don't have a network server available, try one of the shareware clock programs you find at http://www.hotfiles.com. Search for the keywords **windows** and **clock**. Programs such as Bruce Adelsman's AtomTime adjust the computer's clock to match one of the many time servers on the Internet.

# Daily

Set the daily start time in Start time, and then choose from one of the following options:

- **Every Day** runs the task every day of the week at the start time.
- **Weekdays** runs the task Monday through Friday at the start time.
- **Every** runs the task every specified number of days at the start time.

Set the date on which you want the task to first start running by choosing a date from Start date. If you want the task to start immediately, leave Start date set to the default value, which is the current date.

## Weekly

Not only do you specify the start time, you specify the weekly interval: every week, every other week, and so on. You must choose the days of the week that you want to run the task: any combination of Monday through Sunday. You can run the same task every Wednesday and Friday, for instance.

## Monthly

The Scheduled Task Wizard gives you a number of different ways to schedule monthly tasks. You specify the starting time for the task, as usual, which is the time the task runs on the scheduled day. You also select one of the following options:

- **Day**. Pick the exact day of the month you want to run the task: 1 through 31.
- **The**. Choose first, second, third, fourth, or last from the first drop-down list; then, choose a day of the week from the second drop-down list.

After you choose the day of the month that you want to run the task, pick the months on which you want the task to run. Normally, you'd select all the months. There aren't many good reasons to run a task just a few months out of the year.

## One Time Only

Pick the start date and time for the task. The task runs one time, at the date and time you specify.

# Changing a Scheduled Task

Anytime after creating a task, either by dropping an EXE file on the Scheduled Tasks folder or by using the Scheduled Task Wizard, you can change the task's settings. If you create a task by using drag-

and-drop, you must schedule and set options for it. Likewise, if you used the Scheduled Task Wizard, you might want to set additional options or further refine the schedule. You do so by right-clicking the task's icon in the Scheduled Tasks folder and then choosing Properties.

The Scheduled Task Wizard doesn't give you the opportunity to specify a program's command line. You can, however, change the command line in the task's property sheet. If that doesn't help, you can usually discover a program's command line options by looking in its online help file or running the program with the /? parameter. The /? parameter causes most command-line-oriented programs to display a list of options. Try this, for example: dir /?. To change the command line options for a scheduled program, follow these steps:

1. Open the task's property sheet from the Scheduled Tasks folder.

2. Type a new command line in Run. Make sure that you enclose long filenames containing spaces within a pair of double quotation marks. The Scheduler uses 8.3 filenames by default, and you should consider doing so as well.

3. In the box labeled Start, type in the name of the folder in which you want the program to start. This is the first folder in which the application will look for data or target files.

4. Close the task's property sheet to save your changes.

Some programs integrate directly into the Task Scheduler, eliminating the need to specify command line options. You recognize that you're scheduling such a program because you see the Settings button just below the command line on the Task tab of the task's property sheet. Click this button to set options for the program. For example, if you schedule ScanDisk, click the Settings button to display options that are specific to ScanDisk. Schedule Disk Defragmenter, and you see options specific to it. Disk Cleanup also integrates into the Task Scheduler. The Task Scheduler stores the options in the task's JOB file.

# Changing a Task's Schedule

Working with the Schedule tab of a task's property sheet is similar to using the Scheduled Task Wizard, but the property sheet gives you much finer control over how and when the Task Scheduler runs the program. The forms you see for each type of schedule are slightly different from what you find in the Scheduled Task Wizard, though, as pointed out here:

- **Daily**. You don't see the Every Day or Weekdays option on a task's property sheet, as you did when setting a daily schedule with the Scheduled Task Wizard. You can implement a weekdays schedule by selecting Monday through Friday on a weekly schedule, however.

- **Weekly**. The form for a weekly schedule is the same in a task's property sheet as it is in the Scheduled Task Wizard.

- **Monthly**. The form for a monthly schedule is roughly the same in both a task's property sheet and in the Scheduled Task Wizard, the one exception being that you click Select Months in a task's property sheet to choose the months in which you want the schedule to run.

- **Once**. The Scheduled Task Wizard calls this type of schedule "One time only." Otherwise, no difference exists between the two forms.

- **At System Startup**. The Scheduled Task Wizard calls this type of schedule "When my computer starts." Otherwise, no difference exists between the two forms.

- **At Logon**. The Scheduled Task Wizard calls this type of schedule "When I log on." Otherwise, no difference exists between the two forms.

- **When idle**. The Scheduled Task Wizard doesn't offer this option. It causes a task to run after your computer sits idle for a certain period of time. For example, you can schedule ScanDisk to run after your computer has been idle for more than an hour.

To change a task's schedule on the Schedule tab of its property sheet, follow these steps:

1. Open the task's property sheet from the Scheduled Tasks folder, and click the Schedule tab.

2. Select the type of schedule you're creating from Schedule Task. You'll notice that the contents of the Schedule Task group change, depending on the type of schedule you select.

3. Set a start time in Start time, which indicates the time at which the Scheduler runs the program on the appropriate days. You can edit each portion of the time — hour, minute, and AM/PM indicator — or you can use the spinner buttons to change the time.

4. Set your schedule in the Schedule Task group; then, close the task's property sheet to save your changes.

## Deferring a Task until a Later Date

You can schedule a task so that it doesn't start running until some future date. If you want to run ScanDisk on a daily basis but don't want to start until next week, for instance, you can create the task and change its start date to the following week. To defer a task until a later date, follow these steps:

1. Open the task's property sheet, and click the Schedule tab; then, click the Advanced button. You see the Advanced Schedule Options dialog box.

2. Select a starting date from Start Date.

3. Optionally, select End Date, and pick a date for the task to stop running. If you want to run a task only between 9/15 and 10/15, for example, pick 9/15 from Start Date and 10/15 from End Date.

4. Close the task's property sheet to save your changes.

Although deferring a task has limited usefulness for an individual user, an administrator with enterprise-wide responsibility might appreciate it. Consider a situation in which you're scheduling tasks on hundreds of computers in the organization. You might want all the scheduled tasks to start running on the same day, but you can't get all the computers set up in time to keep them synchronized. If you defer the task to the same future date on all the computers — say, one week in the future — you have more than enough time to distribute the JOB files, using any means necessary.

## Repeating a Task at Specific Intervals

You can cause a task to run repeatedly at specific intervals, starting at the task's start time. This isn't the same as scheduling a task to run at periodic intervals, such as every day. It's more of a second-level schedule, in which the task repeats every so many minutes at each scheduled time. You can limit the length of time during which the task repeats, too. For example, you can have a program that checks for available disk space run every five minutes for one hour at each scheduled time. To repeat a task at specific intervals, beginning at the task's start time, follow these steps:

1. Open the task's property sheet, go to the Schedule tab, and click the Advanced button. You see the Advanced Schedule Options dialog box.

2. Select Repeat task, and specify the repeat interval. You can select minutes or hours from the drop-down list.

3. Select Time and specify the time, if you want to be explicit about the time at which you want the task to stop repeating, or select Duration and specify the duration, if you want to specify a duration for repeating the task.

4. Close the Advanced Schedule Options dialog box to save your changes.

If you're overlapping schedules for a program, make sure that you select "If the task is still running, stop it at this time" so that the program isn't still running when the next scheduled time rolls around.

# Creating Multiple Schedules for a Task

When you select Show multiple schedules, at the bottom of the Schedule tab, the schedule shown at the top of the tab changes to a drop-down list. Select a schedule from the list to change it. Click New to create a new schedule as well, or click Delete to remove the selected schedule. To create a new schedule for an existing task, follow these steps:

1. Open the task's property sheet, and select the Schedule tab.

2. Select Show multiple schedules to see the drop-down list, New button, and Delete button at the top of the dialog box.

3. Click New to create a new schedule. Then, fill in the schedule.

4. Close the task's property sheet to save your changes.

# Making a Task Wait until the Computer Is Idle

Regardless of a task's schedule, you don't want some programs to run while the user is trying to get real work done. A good example is a task that runs Microsoft Backup. If you happen to be working when the task is scheduled to launch Backup, you don't want to be interrupted while it takes over your computer. You'd rather have the task wait until you finish your work. The Task Scheduler enables you to specify that a scheduled task isn't to start unless your computer has been idle for a given period of time. To make a task wait until your computer is idle for a period of time, follow these steps:

1. Open the task's property sheet to the Settings tab.

2. Select Only start the scheduled task if computer is idle for, and type the number of minutes for which you want the Task Scheduler to wait before launching the program. This is the number of minutes the computer must be idle before launching the program.

3. Type the number of minutes for which you want the Task Scheduler to retry launching the program. This is the total amount of time, beginning with the task's start time, that you want the Task Scheduler to try launching the program.

4. If you want the Task Scheduler to stop the program when you start using your computer again, select Stop the scheduled task if computer is in use.

5. Close the task's property sheet to save your changes.

Beyond delaying a task until your computer is idle, the Task Scheduler gives you two other options:

- You can specify a period of time during which the Task Scheduler will continually retry the task, waiting for the computer to become idle.

- You can specify that the Task Scheduler is to stop the program if you start using your computer while the program is running.

## Making a Task Work with Power Management

The Task Scheduler gives you several options to determine how a task operates when power management is involved. If you look at the Settings tab of a task's property sheet, you notice three power-management options at the bottom:

- **Don't start scheduled task if computer is running on batteries** helps prevent a disk-intensive program, such as ScanDisk, from draining your battery power.

- **Stop the scheduled task if battery mode begins** determines what happens to the task if you unplug your computer from the power source, resorting to battery power.

- **Wake the computer to run this task** causes the Task Scheduler to turn on your computer, if it's suspended, to run the task. Note that this requires a computer that supports this feature. You don't see this option if APM is disabled in CMOS.

# Pausing or Stopping the Task Scheduler

You might pause the Task Scheduler if you don't want any tasks to launch while you're installing a program. To pause the Task Scheduler, choose Advanced ➪ Pause Task Scheduler from the main menu while you're viewing the Scheduled Tasks folder. When you pause the Task Scheduler, it's still running in the background, and its icon is still in the taskbar. Any tasks that would have launched will not do so until their next scheduled time. To restart the Task Scheduler, choose Advanced ➪ Continue Task Scheduler from the Scheduled Tasks folder's main menu.

When you stop the Task Scheduler, it stops running in the background and won't start when you restart Windows 98. The difference between that and pausing the Task Scheduler is subtle. Choose Advanced ➪ Stop Using Task Scheduler from the Scheduled Tasks folder's main menu. To start using the Task Scheduler again, choose Advanced ➪ Start Using Task Scheduler.

# Troubleshooting with the Task Scheduler's Log

The Task Scheduler keeps a log of everything it does. To view the log in Notepad, choose Advanced ➪ View Log from the Scheduled

Tasks folder's main menu. The most recent entry is at the bottom of the file. The log contains a date-and-time entry for each time the Task Scheduler stops, starts, pauses, or continues. It also contains an entry for each time the Scheduler launches a program and for each time a program finishes. The following listing shows you what the log looks like when the Task Scheduler launches ScanDisk:

```
"ScanDisk.job" (SCANDSKW.EXE)
     Started 1/21/98 3:48:59 AM
"ScanDisk.job" (SCANDSKW.EXE)
     Finished 1/21/98 3:50:32 AM
     Result: No errors found (0).
```

Here are some additional notes about using the Task Scheduler's log file:

- If you try to view the log file and get an error message that says it's in use by another program, make a copy of C:\Windows\SchedLog.txt. View the copy.

- You can't clear out or remove the log file while the Task Scheduler is running. Stop the Task Scheduler by choosing Advanced ➪ Stop Using Task Scheduler from the main menu; then, remove the log file. After removing the log file, restart the task scheduler by choosing Advanced ➪ Start Using Task Scheduler from the main menu.

# Launching Scripts from the Task Scheduler

Scheduled scripts are useful for performing a variety of functions in Windows 98 on a regular basis. For example, you can use a script to launch a program only when a certain file is available on a network share. Here are some ideas to get you going (the possibilities are endless):

- Once a day, synchronize the contents of a briefcase folder.

- When your computer is idle, copy important documents on which you're working to a backup folder.

- Every Friday morning, build a compound document in Microsoft Word that contains a summary of your schedule from Outlook and an excerpt from a budget spreadsheet; then, automatically mail it to your boss.

- On the first of every month, scan the hard disk of every Windows 98 workstation on the network, looking for and removing Sol.exe.

- Once a week, copy new JOB files to the Scheduled Tasks folder on each user's computer to update the scheduled tasks.

- Twice a week, download the boot log files from all the Windows 98 workstations on the network, and examine each of them for errors. Create a text document showing each workstation that has errors.

- Once each week, check a network share for updated copies of important files, and copy newer files to your computer.

To schedule a task that launches a script, you use a command that looks like `wscript.exe` *scriptname*. Wscript.exe is the Windows Scripting Host. If you want to launch an MS-DOS script, use `cscript.exe` *scriptname*, instead.

# Working with Schedules on Remote Computers

As an administrator, you want to work with scheduled tasks on other Windows 98 workstations in the organization. You can do so by meeting the following conditions:

- The computer must have the Remote Registry Service installed. This enables you to remotely administer the computer's Registry. Install the Remote Registry Service via the Network icon in the Control Panel; the manufacturer is Microsoft.

- The Windows 98 workstation must explicitly identify your user name as having administrative responsibility for the computer. By default, Windows 98 gives Domain admins administrative rights in the Remote Administration tab of the Passwords Properties dialog box, which you open from the Control Panel.

- The computer must provide an administrative share for the disk on which the Scheduled Tasks folder resides. The administrative share looks like *D*$, where *D* is the drive letter (C$, for example).

After a workstation meets these requirements, you can open the remote computer's Scheduled Tasks folder via Network Neighborhood. Open the computer in Network Neighborhood to see an icon for the Scheduled Tasks folder. Open the folder. It functions exactly like the Scheduled Tasks folder on your own computer.

The Scheduled Tasks folder is just a folder like any other. It's actually located in C:\Windows\Tasks. What makes it special is the hidden Desktop.ini file. This file links the folder to a Windows 98 shell extension, giving the folder its special behaviors, which depend on what the shell extension does. If in doubt, display a DOS directory of C:\Windows\Tasks. Each scheduled task is nothing more than a JOB file that contains the task's specifications, such as the command line, schedule, and advanced options. You can copy these JOB files like any other file. Thus, you can define JOB files on your computer and then distribute them to the C:\Windows\Tasks folders on other networked Windows 98 workstations. Because you're an administrator who is using an administrative share, you actually copy the file to \\*computer*\c$\Windows\Tasks, where *computer* is the name of each computer to which you're copying the JOB file. By default, you must be a member of the Domain admins group or be identified in the Password Properties dialog box on each computer as having administrative rights.

You can add the Task Scheduler to Windows NT 4.0 and Windows 95, too. Internet Explorer 4.0 includes this option. Although the Windows 95 version of Internet Explorer implicitly provides the Task Scheduler, you must add the Task Scheduler to Windows NT 4.0 by updating it from Microsoft's Web site after installing Internet Explorer 4.0. The JOB files you create in Windows NT 4.0 or Windows 95 are compatible with Windows 98 JOB files. You can thus create tasks on your server and distribute them to each workstation.

# Automating Administrative Tasks with Scripts

Administrators can use scripts to automate administrative tasks such as connecting to a network or updating the user's Registry. The Windows 98 CD-ROM documents how to write scripts for the Windows Scripting Host. Look in \Tools\Reskit\Scrpting. You can also learn from the material that you find at Microsoft's Windows Scripting Host site: http://www.microsoft.com/management. The Windows 98 Setup program installs several examples to get you started. Look in \Windows\Samples\WSH to find the following:

- **Chart.vbs** shows how to control an application by using VBScript. This example works with charts in Microsoft Excel.

- **Excel.vbs** shows how to control an application by creating a spreadsheet in Microsoft Excel.

- **Network.vbs** shows how to perform network tasks by using a script, including reading network properties, connecting and disconnecting, and listing the available network drives.

- **Registry.vbs** shows how to update the Registry by using a script.

- **Shortcut.vbs** shows how to create shortcuts by using a script.

- **Showprop.vbs** shows how to display properties for a script.

- **Showvar.vbs** shows how to collect system information by using a script, including iterating through environment variables.

To launch a script, double-click it in Windows Explorer; or type its filename in the Run dialog box, and press Enter. Scripts are text files that use the JS extension for JScript and VBS extension for VBScript. Microsoft associates both types of files with Notepad, but you can associate them with WordPad, instead, which makes editing scripts easier. To associate either file extension with WordPad, use Windows Explorer's Folder Options dialog box to change the command executed for either file extension's Edit command.

Windows 98 provides two different script interpreters: one DOS-based and one Windows-based. The DOS-based interpreter is Cscript.exe, and the Windows-based interpreter is Wscript.exe. Wscript is the interpreter that Windows 98 uses if you double-click a script in Windows Explorer or launch a script from the Run dialog box. If you want to launch a script using the DOS-based interpreter, you must run Cscript.exe and pass it the path and filename of the script:

```
cscript.exe script.vbs
```

Both versions of the interpreter support a variety of command line options. With the DOS-based interpreter, you specify each option via the command line. Each of the following options begins with two forward slashes, not one, because any options specified with a single slash are passed directly to the script:

```
cscript filename [host options] [script options]
```

- //? displays help for command line options.

- //i enables the interpreter to display prompts and script errors.

- //b prevents the interpreter from displaying prompts and script errors.

- //T:nn kills the script if it runs for longer than nn seconds. This is good for debugging.

- //logo displays an execution banner.

- //nologo prevents the execution banner from being displayed.

- //H:Cscript registers Cscript.exe as the default script interpreter in the Registry.

- //H:Wscript registers Wscript.exe as the default script interpreter in the Registry.

- //S saves the current options as the default.

With the Windows-based interpreter, you specify options via a WSH file. Right-click a script file, choose Properties, and click the Script tab. The Script tab contains options similar to those you specify on the command line of the DOS-based interpreter. As a result, Windows 98 creates a WSH file. WSH files look like INI files, behave similarly to PIF files, and contain options for the script with which they are associated. Once you've created a WSH file, you can launch the script by double-clicking either the WSH file or the script file. Make sure you keep the script and WSH files together in the same folder.

# Chapter 18

# Administering the Registry

The Registry is the central configuration database for Windows 98. The operating system and most applications with the Windows logo store their configuration data in this hierarchical database.

This chapter describes the technologies — such as user profiles and Plug and Play — that the Registry makes possible. It also shows you how to back up and restore the Registry, how to edit the Registry with the Registry Editor, and how to troubleshoot the Registry.

## Limiting the Risk

Editing the Registry is risky because you can cause an application or hardware device to stop working properly. Worse yet, you can prevent Windows 98 from starting altogether. In many cases, you won't even know that you've created a problem until much later; this is a terrible situation because you likely won't connect the recent problem to the earlier changes that you made in the Registry.

The Registry Editor invites many of these problems itself. It packs a lot of power in that it gives you total control of the system, but it has a very weak user interface. Using it is almost like editing your configuration with a text editor. It has no Undo feature, so changes are immediate and irrevocable. It doesn't validate your changes as a property sheet does, either, so you can put a bad value in a setting without ever knowing it. Many values in the Registry are related — changing one requires you to change the other. The Registry Editor doesn't know about these relationships, so you're on your own. The fact that no standard exists for naming or storing values in the Registry leads to obscure names and values that are, at best, difficult to understand.

Scare you? Yes, editing the Registry is risky, but you can significantly minimize that risk. As you work with the Registry, pledge to observe the following bits of advice, and you'll never irreparably damage your configuration by editing the Registry:

- **Back up the Registry before you make any changes**. Windows 98 makes a daily backup of the Registry. In many cases, this is fine. If you're doing extensive work in the Registry, however, back it up again using the tools described in this chapter. If nothing else, back up the particular branch of the Registry in which you're working.

- **Make one change at a time**. Make a change and test it, make another change and test it, and so on. In other words, don't confuse yourself by making too many changes at one time. You're more likely to figure out what went wrong and less likely to render your system impotent if you can always pinpoint the culprit.

- **Don't delete configuration data without testing**. By renaming configuration data to some obscure name, you effectively delete it. After you are sure that removing the data doesn't harm your configuration, permanently delete it.

- **Record the original value before changing configuration data**. You can rename a value to an obscure name and then add a new value using the original name. This keeps the original configuration data handy so that you can quickly restore it by deleting the new value and renaming the old value to the original name. At the very least, write down the original value on a piece of paper so that you can recall it, if necessary.

One final comment about the risk of editing the Registry: don't overreact to these disclaimers. I can quote a variety of sources that say editing the Registry is like walking through quicksand with cement shoes. No matter how wise these sources seem, *the Registry still makes a better friend than enemy.* The Registry is an invaluable administration and configuration tool that you must use to leverage Windows 98 fully in the enterprise. Of course, being an intelligent person who understands the risk, you'll do just fine.

# Pinpointing the Registry Files

Windows 98 divides the Registry into two binary files: System.dat and User.dat. In a normal installation without user profiles, you find both of these files in \Windows. You can't view either file using a text editor, as you can with INI files, so you must use the Registry Editor to work with them. Windows 98 turns on the read-only, system, and hidden attributes to prevent mishaps from occurring, which also prevents defragmenting utilities from consolidating or relocating either file. System.dat contains machine-specific settings, and User.dat contains user-specific settings.

Dividing the Registry into two files makes sense when you consider that user profiles enable each user to keep his own settings. Nothing changes in System.dat; Windows 98 stores it in \Windows. Windows 98 creates a separate User.dat for each user who has a profile on the computer. You find each user's User.dat file in his profile folder under \Windows\Profiles. My profile folder is \Windows\Profiles\Jerry, for instance. You still find a User.dat file in \Windows, mind you, which Windows 98 uses when a user does not log on with valid credentials or when Windows 98 creates a profile for a new user. Windows 98 also supports *roaming profiles,* which are copies of the user's profile that it copies to the server. The user can log on to any other appropriately configured Windows 98 workstation, and Windows 98 copies the user's User.dat file to that workstation.

By now, you've caught on to the fact that System.dat always comes from \Windows because it contains configuration data that's particular to that computer, but User.dat can come from a variety of different places. Use the following table to determine which User.dat Windows 98 uses in different situations. The first column describes the folder that contains User.dat, and the second column describes conditions in which Windows 98 uses the User.dat file in that location. \Windows always contains a User.dat file. You find a User.dat file in \Windows\Profiles\*User* only if user profiles are enabled on the computer and the user has a profile. \\*Server\Home* contains a User.dat file only if you create a home folder for the user on the network and enable Windows 98 to support roaming users.

| Location | Used When |
| --- | --- |
| \Windows | User profiles are not enabled. |
| | User doesn't log on with valid credentials. |
| | Windows 98 creates a new user profile with default settings. |
| \Windows\Profiles\*User* | User profiles are enabled and user logs on with credentials. \Windows\Profiles\*User* is more current than either \\*Server*\Netlogon or \\*Server*\Public, or the network server is not available. |
| \\*Server*\*Home* | User profiles are enabled and \Windows\Profiles\*User* is not more current than \\*Server*\*Home*. |

The Registry consists of one other optional file, called Config.pol, which is a system policy file. System policies enable the administrator to define machine- and user-specific settings that override System.dat and User.dat. The administrator can apply those settings to all computers or users, to a specific computer or specific user, or to a group of users. The administrator uses the System Policy Editor to create the Config.pol file and then posts this file to the server. Each time a user logs on to the network, Windows 98 downloads the settings from Config.pol to the

Registry. As you can see, system policies give the administrator a good amount of control over each user and each computer's configuration. If this file exists, you find it in the Netlogon share of a Windows NT network or the Public folder on a NetWare network.

# Backing Up and Restoring the Registry

Avoid problems — back up the Registry. You can correct most any Registry problem with a recent, good backup. Backing up the Registry is good protection, but you must do it wisely. If you back up your system about once a month, you might be forced to roll your system back a month to recover from more serious problems. On the other hand, if you back up every day with the same tape, you might propagate a serious Registry error onto the tape before you ever realize a problem exists; then, you're left without a good backup at all. Your best plan is to back up the Registry as part of a regular backup strategy that rotates full weekly backups once a month and keeps an incremental or differential backup throughout each week.

If you're a laggard when it comes to performing regular backups, you'll find comfort in knowing that Windows 98 automatically backs up the Registry once each day. The first time you start Windows 98 each day, it runs the Windows Registry Checker (Scanregw.exe in \Windows), which scans the Registry for errors, repairs any errors it finds, and makes a backup copy of the Registry. Registry Checker stores each backup copy of the Registry in CAB files that you can find in \Windows\Sysbckup. The first backup is RB000.cab, the second is RB001.cab, and so forth. The file with the highest number is the most recent backup. You can view the contents of a CAB file by right-clicking it and choosing View to see its contents. In it, you see System.dat, System.ini, User.dat, and Win.ini.

**Caution**

The Windows Registry Checker keeps only five backup copies of the Registry. That's just not enough. If you consider that most Registry problems can go undetected for several days, especially by novice users, all five backup copies might already contain an error before you realize that a problem exists. You can increase the number of backup copies that Windows Registry Checker keeps, however, by changing the `MaxBackupCopies` settings in \Windows\Scanreg.ini to a higher number. I recommend that you change this setting to a value greater than 10.

# Copying the Files Using Windows Explorer

The most straightforward way to make a quick backup copy of the Registry is to copy the files by using Windows Explorer. Display hidden and system files; then, drag a copy of System.dat from \Windows and User.dat from \Windows or \Windows\Profiles to a backup folder.

If you want to make these backups even easier, create a batch file that you can launch from the Start menu. Use `Xcopy.exe` with the /h and /r switches. /h copies hidden and system files. /r replaces read-only files. Listing 18-1 shows what the batch file should look like. This batch file keeps only one backup copy of the Registry, incidentally, so it's good only for a quick backup before changing the Registry, not as a part of a regular backup plan. Note that if you've enabled user profiles, you should modify the batch file slightly so that it copies User.dat from the user's profile folder to a backup folder contained within the profile folder, like this:

```
xcopy %WinDir%\Profiles\User\User.dat
%WinDir%\Profiles\User\Registry\User.dat /h /r
```

**Listing 18-1** *Regback.bat*
```
xcopy %WinDir%\System.dat %WinDir%\Registry\ /H /R
xcopy %WinDir%\User.dat %WinDir%\Registry\ /H /R
```

To restore this backup, simply reverse the procedure. Windows 98 can't be running when you restore this backup, however, so you first must shut down Windows 98 to MS-DOS mode or boot to MS-DOS mode. Then, copy System.dat and User.dat from their backup locations to their original locations.

### Caution

Never restore a backup copy of the Windows 95 Registry after you upgrade to Windows 98. Doing so renders your machine absolutely useless. Windows 98 stores more information in the Registry than required by its predecessor, and restoring the Windows 95 Registry leaves Windows 98 without information that it requires to start. Just to be safe, go ahead and remove your old Windows 95 Registry backups now.

# Creating Backups Using the Registry Checker

The Windows Registry Checker should be your primary means for backing up and restoring the Registry. Windows Registry Checker automatically backs up the Registry once each day. You can also force Windows Registry Checker to make additional backups. If you're sitting down to do some major work on the Registry, for instance, you can pop up Windows Registry Checker, make a quick backup, and go about your business. To force Windows Registry Checker to make an additional backup, follow these steps:

1. Start the Windows Registry Checker by running \Windows\ Scanregw.exe. Windows Registry Checker scans the Registry for errors and notifies you that it has already backed up the Registry today.

2. Click Yes. Windows Registry Checker creates a new CAB file containing the current Registry files in \Windows\Sysbckup.

3. Close the dialog box that tells you the backup is complete.

You restore the Registry by using Microsoft Registry Checker. The name of the program is different, and it's an MS-DOS program. Regardless, it's the complementary program to Windows Registry Checker, which restores a backup copy of the Registry from a CAB file, \Windows\Sysbckup. You can't run this program from Windows, so you must either start your computer to the command prompt or shut down Windows 98 to the command prompt. To restore a Registry backup made by Windows Registry Checker, follow these steps:

1. Start Windows 98 in MS-DOS mode. To do so, choose Command Prompt Only from the boot menu; or choose Start ⇨ Shut Down ⇨ Restart in MS-DOS mode, and then click OK.

2. At the command prompt, type scanreg /restore, and then press Enter to start Microsoft Registry Checker.

3. Select a backup from the list. Microsoft Registry Checker displays the date, status, and filename of each Registry backup. In most cases, pick the most recent backup that does not contain errors.

4. Press Enter to restart your computer.

Run Scanreg.exe in \Windows to start the Microsoft Registry Checker. If you're starting this program from a batch file, note that it returns 0 if it completes with no errors; otherwise, it returns one of the error codes shown in the following table. With the exception of /restore and /fix, the following command line options work with both Scanregw.exe and Scanreg.exe:

- /backup backs up the Registry.
- /restore restores the backup copy of the selected Registry.
- "/comment" associates a comment with a backup copy of the Registry.
- /fix fixes any errors it finds in the Registry.

- /autoscan scans the Registry for errors and backs up the Registry.

- /scanonly scans the Registry for errors without backing it up.

| Error Level | Describes This Error |
| --- | --- |
| 0 | No errors were found. |
| 2 | The Registry is corrupted. |
| -2 | Not enough memory is available to run the Registry Checker. |
| -3 | Registry Checker couldn't find one or both of the Registry files. |
| -4 | Registry Checker was unable to create one or both Registry files. |

# Backing Up the Computer Using Microsoft Backup

Windows 98 comes with an improved backup utility called Microsoft Backup. Windows 98 doesn't install Microsoft Backup in a typical installation, but you can install it using the Add/Remove Programs Properties dialog box in the Control Panel. Then, start Microsoft Backup by choosing Start ⇨ Programs ⇨ Accessories ⇨ System Tools ⇨ Backup. To back up the Registry with Microsoft Backup, follow these steps:

1. Click the Backup tab.

2. Choose Job ⇨ Options, and click the Advanced tab to display the Backup Job Options dialog box.

3. Select Back up Windows Registry, and then click OK to save your changes.

4. Continue your backup routine as usual.

Microsoft Backup is better suited to full-system backups. That is, if you restore the Registry with Microsoft Backup, you should consider restoring the full system to make sure the files on your system match the settings stored in the Registry. If you restore an older version of the Registry without restoring the remaining files, a good chance exists that the Registry will be out of kilter with the rest of the system. For example, any applications that you installed since the last Registry backup will lose their Registry settings, even though the application is still installed on your computer. Plus, if you removed an application since your last Registry backup, restoring the backup will replace that application's settings in the Registry. To restore the Registry from a backup made by Microsoft Backup, follow these steps:

1. Click the Restore tab.
2. Choose Job ⇨ Options, and click the Advanced tab to display the Job Options dialog box.
3. Select Restore Windows Registry, and click OK to save your changes.
4. Continue the restore operation, as normal.

## Exporting a Portion of the Registry

You took a pledge earlier in this chapter never to edit the Registry without first backing it up. Exporting a portion of the Registry might be the way to go, though, instead of doing a full backup. If you're changing a particular key, for example, export the branch starting at that key. The Registry Editor creates a REG file. If the changes you're making get out of hand, you can import the REG file to restore the branch to its original condition. "Importing and Exporting the Registry," later in this chapter, describes how to use the Registry Editor to back up a portion of the Registry.

## System.1st: A Last Resort

Look in the root folder of your boot disk, and you should see a file called System.1st. This is a copy of System.dat that Windows 98 made immediately after you successfully installed Windows 98 and the operating system started for the first time. It contains no custom settings nor the slightest bit of information about the applications that you installed. It's the original Registry.

If none of your backup copies of the Registry is helping and your system isn't starting at all, you might have to restore System.1st. Make a backup copy of \Windows\System.dat, just in case you change your mind. Then, start Windows 98 to the Command Prompt by using the boot menu, and copy \System.1st to \Windows\System.dat. This gets your computer up and running, but, as noted earlier, without any of the changes that you've made to the Registry.

# Understanding What's in the Registry

The Registry contains most of the configuration data for Windows 98 and any applications that you install. Acting as the central repository for configuration data, the Registry essentially ties together all the bits and pieces of the operating system so that the system behaves as a cohesive unit. For example, imagine installing an application that performs some task on your documents — prints them, perhaps. When you install the application, it adds entries to the Registry that enable it to work seamlessly with the operating system, making any determination of where the application ends and Windows 98 begins a difficult task. For example, the application can register the following:

- Additional commands that appear on the context menu when you right-click the file
- Extensions that add tabs to the property sheet when you right-click the document and choose Properties
- An uninstaller so that you can easily remove the application from your computer by using the Add/Remove Programs Properties dialog box

- OLE components that enable the application to support drag-and-drop and other OLE technologies

The Windows 98 Registry is equally useful as an administration tool or a configuration tool. You don't have to scour hundreds of INI files to look for configuration data. You can access the data remotely because the Registry can act as an RPC server for remote administration.

Windows 98 makes the following small improvements to the Registry over the Windows 95 version:

- **Smaller footprint.** The Registry uses less real-mode and protected-mode memory, enabling Windows 98 to start faster and improving performance across the board.

- **Better caching.** Microsoft improved the Registry's caching so that you can look up values in the Registry in less time. Again, this improves performance across the board.

- **More robustness.** The Registry now detects many types of errors and automatically repairs them. It does so via the Windows Registry Checker. You're much less likely to see Registry errors when you start Windows 98 than you were when you started Windows 95.

- **Better backups.** The Windows Registry Checker is a vastly improved backup utility over the utilities that Microsoft provided for Windows 95. Registry Checker is quicker, makes more sense, and is easier to use.

- **Higher limits.** The Registry removes the limit of 64K for data in a value entry.

# Exploring the Contents of the Registry

The organization of the Registry hasn't changed much since Windows 95. It's still a hierarchical database of configuration data, organized similarly to the file system. Keys can contain any number of subkeys and value entries. *Keys* are analogous to folders, and *values* are analogous to files.

You generally can use the terms *key* and *subkey* interchangeably, as this book does. Most often, this book uses the term *key* to refer directly to any key in the Registry. It uses the term *subkey* to refer to any child of the particular key being discussed. Thus, when you are working with the key called `Software\Classes`, any discussion of the child key called `.bmp` refers to it as a subkey. This book also uses the term *subkey* to refer to all of a key's children in a general sense.

Whereas keys define the overall structure of the Registry, value entries store the actual configuration data. Each value entry has the following three parts:

- **Name**. The name identifies the value entry within its parent key.

- **Type**. The type indicates what type of data the key contains. Type can be one of three things: binary, string, or DWORD. Table 18-1 describes each data type. The first column shows the icon that is displayed next to the value entry to identify the type.

- **Data**. The data stored in the value entry can be up to 16K in size and usually conforms to the value entry's data type.

**Table 18-1** *Value Entry Types*

| Icon | Type | Description |
|------|------|-------------|
| 🔲 | String | Text. The Registry Editor displays strings within quotation marks, but the string doesn't actually contain the quotation marks. |
| 🔲 | Binary | Binary values up to 16K in size. The Registry Editor accepts and displays binary values in hexadecimal notation. |
| 🔲 | DWORD | 32-bit binary values. The Registry Editor accepts and displays DWORD values in hexadecimal notation. |

Key and value entry names can contain any alphanumeric character, spaces, and the underscore (_). March 3rd is a valid value entry name, but 3/3 is not. Names must also be unique within their scope, which means that within a particular Registry key, each value entry's name must be unique. A value entry with the same name can exist in any other key, however, even within a subkey.

Every Registry key has at least one value entry called default, which looks like (Default) in the Registry Editor. Windows 98 provides this value entry to maintain backward compatibility with Windows 3.1 applications. This is always a string value and, in many cases, is null because no value has ever been assigned to it. Some applications that need to store only one value in a key assign that value to the default value entry instead of creating a new one. Other applications use the default value entry to store a selector, which names a particular value entry in the key.

The organization of the Registry looks like an upside-down tree, with the computer at the very top. Just below the computer, you find six *root keys*, so named because they root a Registry branch at the very top of the hierarchy. Think of them as top-level categories. The two primary root keys are HKEY_LOCAL_MACHINE and HKEY_USERS. HKEY_LOCAL_MACHINE represents the machine-specific portion of the Registry and is stored in System.dat. HKEY_USERS roughly represents the user-specific portions of the Registry and is stored in User.dat. The remaining root keys are either dynamic keys or *aliases*, which are shortcuts to branches within the two primary root keys. Windows 98 provides some aliases for compatibility with Windows 3.1 and others just for programming convenience.

## HKEY_LOCAL_MACHINE

HKEY_LOCAL_MACHINE contains machine-specific configuration data for the computer on which Windows 98 is installed. This data is stored in System.dat. The information in this key applies to the computer itself rather than to any user who might log on to it. The following list gives you an overview of each subkey that you find under this root key:

- **Config**. This subkey contains information about each hardware profile configured on the system. Windows 98 assigns an ID to each configuration and creates a subkey for it under `Config`. The alias called `HKEY_CURRENT_CONFIG` is mapped to one of the configurations in `Config`.

- **Enum**. This subkey contains information collected by the Windows 98 bus enumerators. Under `Enum`, you find configuration data for each device that Windows 98 finds on your computer. The organization and contents of this subkey depend on the hardware installed on the computer.

- **Hardware**. Windows 98 doesn't do much with this subkey; it's provided more for compatibility with Windows NT.

- **Network**. This subkey contains information about the current user, including details about the current session and the user's account name.

- **Security**. This subkey contains information about the network security provider, public shares, and private administrative shares. Windows 98 also keeps track of all incoming connections in this subkey.

- **Software**. This is by far one of the most interesting subkeys in the Registry. Applications, including Windows 98, store configuration data that's specific to the computer in this subkey. Each application stores its configuration data in a branch that looks like \*Company\Product\Version*, where *Company* is the name of the company, *Product* is the name of the product, and *Version* is the version number of the product.

- **System**. Control sets determine which drivers and services Windows 98 loads and how to configure them. The subkey called `CurrentControlSet` contains all the data that controls how Windows 98 starts. Within a control set, you find two interesting subkeys. `Control` describes how Windows 98 starts, and `Services` contains information about the device drivers and services that Windows 98 loads.

The single largest branch of the Registry is `HKEY_LOCAL_MACHINE\` `SOFTWARE\CLASSES`. It contains all the associations between programs and document types. It also contains configuration data, such as OLE registration, shell extensions, and so forth. The bottom line? This branch represents about 50 percent of the entire Registry, as measured by exporting both the entire Registry and the branch to a REG file and comparing the results.

# HKEY_USERS

`HKEY_USERS` contains configuration data that's specific to each user. A subkey called `.DEFAULT` represents the default user, which corresponds to the User.dat file in \Windows. If you've enabled user profiles, an additional subkey exists for each user who has a profile on the computer. Each of these subkeys has the same organization. The alias called `HKEY_CURRENT_USER` is mapped to the subkey under `HKEY_USERS` that belongs to the current user.

Underneath each subkey in `HKEY_USERS`, you find the following subkeys:

- **AppEvents**. The configuration data in `AppEvents` associates sound files with various sound events, such as minimizing a window.

- **Control Panel**. `Control Panel` contains settings that normally are changed in the Control Panel. Such settings include the appearance of the desktop, cursors, international settings, and power-management settings.

- **Keyboard layout**. This subkey contains information about the current keyboard layout and is related to the international settings found under `Control Panel`.

- **Network**. `Network` describes any persistent and temporary network connections.

- **RemoteAccess**. This subkey contains information that is used for remote network access via Dial-Up Networking.

- **Software**. The configuration data contained in `Software` is similar to that contained in `HKEY_LOCAL_MACHINE\Software`, except that the data in `Software` applies specifically to the user. The configuration data is organized the same, too, with a subkey for each vendor, followed by a subkey for each product, followed by a subkey for each version.

The Registry has an order of precedence, much like the order of operations in mathematics. Windows 98 and other applications sometimes store the same value in both `HKEY_LOCAL_MACHINE` and `HKEY_USERS`. More likely, an application might store a value in `HKEY_LOCAL_MACHINE` and, if the user customizes a setting, the user's preference in `HKEY_USERS`. In such cases, the value stored in `HKEY_USERS` overrides the value stored in `HKEY_LOCAL_MACHINE`.

## Aliases and Dynamic Root Keys

`HKEY_LOCAL_MACHINE` and `HKEY_USERS` are the primary keys in the Registry. Their data is stored in the two Registry files, System.dat and User.dat, that you find on the disk. The remaining root keys are aliases or dynamic keys. *Aliases* are shortcuts to other branches within the two primary root keys. Change any value in the aliases, and the identical value changes in the primary root key. Dynamic keys look and act like the two primary root keys, but they're memory-resident. When you shut down Windows 98, they disappear because Windows 98 doesn't write them to the Registry. Dynamic root keys exist for such things as performance monitoring, which requires that Windows 98 have fast access to the data.

Here's an overview of each of the remaining four root keys:

- **HKEY_CURRENT_CONFIG**. This subkey is an alias for one of the configurations stored under `HKEY_LOCAL_MACHINE\Config`. It refers to the current hardware configuration.

- **HKEY_DYN_DATA.** This is a dynamic subkey that contains configuration data to which Windows 98 must have fast access. It includes information about the status of each device and records performance information for use by System Monitor.

- **HKEY_CLASSES_ROOT.** This subkey is an alias for HKEY_LOCAL_MACHINE\Software\Classes, which contains configuration data that associates programs with documents. It also contains registration information for OLE, including shell extensions. The alias is primarily for compatibility with Windows 3.1 programs.

- **HKEY_CURRENT_USER.** This subkey is an alias for one of the subkeys under HKEY_USERS. It refers to the subkey that contains the profile for the current user.

# Abbreviations for Root Keys

You frequently see the following abbreviations used for the Registry's root keys:

HKCR for HKEY_CLASSES_ROOT

HKCU for HKEY_CURRENT_USER

HKLM for HKEY_LOCAL_MACHINE

HKU for HKEY_USERS

HKCC for HKEY_CURRENT_CONFIG

HKDD for HKEY_DYN_DATA

# Using the Registry Editor

Windows 98 doesn't put the Registry Editor on the Start menu. You launch it by running Regedit.exe from \Windows. You can also copy a shortcut to the Registry Editor on the Start menu, if you like.

Windows 98 doesn't necessarily make a provision for securing the Registry. You can disable the user's ability to use the Registry Editor by setting the policy in the System Policy Editor. The Registry

Editor and System Policy Editor both cooperate with system policies, but the various shareware programs that you can use don't necessarily cooperate. Similarly, the user can still change the Registry by
creating and importing a REG file. In most cases, you don't need to
worry about users' editing the Registry, because they probably won't
even know that it or the Registry Editor exists. If you support users
who know just enough to be dangerous, however, the only thing that
you can do is declare psychological warfare and scare them to death.

Figure 18-1 shows the Registry Editor. The left pane contains
each Registry key. An icon representing the computer is at the top.
Below that is a folder for each key and, within each folder, subfolders for each subkey. Click the plus sign next to a key to expand it;
click the minus sign to collapse it. The right pane shows the value
entries for the selected key. The icon indicates the type of value.
Following the icon, you see the value entry's name and value.

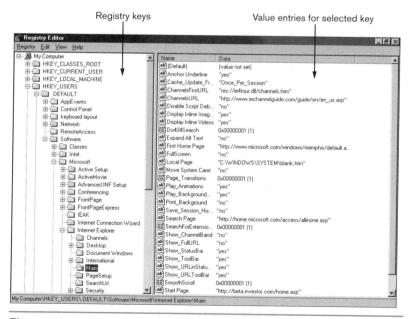

**Figure 18-1** *The status bar contains the full path of the Registry, in case
you can't see it in the left pane.*

# Adding a Key or Value Entry

To add a new key or value entry, follow these steps:

1.  Right-click the Registry key in which you want to create a new key or value entry. From the context menu, choose New ⇨ Key to create a new key; or choose New followed by String Value, Binary Value, or DWORD Value to create a new value entry. The Registry Editor creates a new entry and highlights it so that you can rename it.

2.  Type a name for the new key or value entry, and press Enter. If you created a new key, you're finished. Otherwise, use the instructions for changing a value entry to change the new value entry.

# Changing a Value Entry

To change a value entry, follow these steps:

1.  Double-click the value entry. You should see a different dialog box, depending on the value entry's type.

2.  Change the value entry, as described in the following list, and click OK to save your changes.

    -   **String**. You edit a string value in the Edit String dialog box. Type the new string in the space provided, and click OK to save your changes.

    -   **Binary**. You edit a binary value in the Edit Binary Value dialog box. Type the new value in hexadecimal notation, and click OK to save your changes.

    -   **DWORD**. You edit a DWORD value in the Edit DWORD Value dialog box. Select either Hexadecimal or Decimal, type the value in the space provided, and click OK to save your changes.

The system might not recognize your changes immediately. In many cases, you might have to restart Windows 98 or the application for it to recognize a change. This is definitely the case if the application loads the configuration data that you're changing when it starts and doesn't reload the data during normal execution. Windows 98 does notify each of its subsystems and each application when the Registry changes, giving them a chance to recognize those changes, but most applications don't take advantage of this facility to update their configuration.

## Searching for Data in the Registry

The Registry Editor enables you to search value strings in the key names, value entry names, and value entry data. This can help you quickly locate configuration data without wasting a lot of time browsing the Registry. In particular, if you're searching for configuration data that belongs to a particular application, try searching for a portion of the application's name or its installation path. Another quick way to find most applications is to search in the key HKEY_LOCAL_MACHINE\ Software, where the programs are kept by manufacturer name. To find a string in the Registry, follow these steps:

1. Move the cursor to the top of the left pane. Because the Registry Editor begins the search at the current cursor location, you are assured that you're searching the entire Registry.

2. Choose Edit ⇨ Find from the main menu. The Find dialog box is displayed.

3. Type the string for which you're looking in the space provided, and press the Enter key. The Registry Editor searches for the string and highlights the next occurrence, if found. Otherwise, it displays a dialog box letting you know that it finished the search.

After you search the Registry, you can repeat the last search from the current cursor location by pressing F3. If the Registry Editor finds a match, it highlights the next occurrence. Otherwise, it lets you know that it finished the search without finding anything.

The Registry Editor supports incremental searches, too. It works only on the visible portion of the Registry tree, not on any subkeys hidden under collapsed branches. To use the incremental search, put the cursor in the left pane, and start typing the name of the key for which you're searching. As you type, the Registry Editor highlights the first key that matches what you've typed thus far.

## Importing and Exporting the Registry

You can export any branch of the Registry to a REG file, which is a text file that looks similar to an INI file. The first line of a REG file is always REGEDIT4, which indicates the version of the Registry Editor that created the file, and the second line must always be blank. Key names look similar to section names in INI files, except the key name represents the entire path of the key. Listing 18-2 shows several lines exported from a current Registry.

**Listing 18-2** *An Example REG File*

```
REGEDIT4

[HKEY_CLASSES_ROOT\.bmp]
@="Paint.Picture"
"Content Type"="image/bmp"

[HKEY_CURRENT_USER\InstallLocationsMRU]
"a"="E:\TOOLS\ADMIN\POLEDIT\"
"b"="A:\"
"MRUList"="ab"
```

In a REG file, value entries look much like items do in INI files. Names are quoted, however, with the exception of the default value entry for a key. A REG file uses the at-sign (@) to represent the default value entry. The three different types of data are written to the Registry, as shown in the following list:

String: *"String"*

Binary: HEX: 00 FF 00 FF 00 FF

DWORD: DWORD: 00000001

## Exporting a Registry Branch

Exporting a particular branch is a great short-term backup when you're working in the Registry. You're more likely to back up the branch this way because it's much quicker than launching one of the backup utilities described in this chapter. Before you make a change, export the branch that you're changing to a REG file. Then, if you make a mistake or things get a bit out of hand, import the REG file back into the Registry to restore it to its original condition.

To export a particular Registry branch to a REG file, follow these steps:

1. Select the key at the top of the branch that you want to export.

2. Choose Registry ⇨ Export Registry File from the main menu.

3. Select the path and type a filename for the REG file in the space provided. Click Save. The Registry Editor exports that branch to the specified REG file.

## Importing a REG File into the Registry

Don't accidentally import a REG file. The default action for REG files is Merge. Thus, when you open a REG file (single-click it in single-click mode), Windows 98 automatically merges that file into the Registry. To import a REG file into the Registry, follow these steps:

1. Choose Registry ⇨ Import Registry File from the main menu. The Import Registry File dialog box is displayed.

2. In the space provided, type the full path of the REG file that you want to import, or browse for the file.

3. Click Open. The Registry Editor imports the REG file.

## Performing Other Common Tasks

The Registry Editor enables you to perform a variety of other tasks, each of which is listed here:

- **To remove a value key or value entry**, right-click the key or value entry, and choose Delete.

- **To rename a key or value entry**, right-click the key or value entry, and choose Rename. Type a new name for the item, and press Enter.

- **To copy the fully qualified path of a key**, right-click the key, and choose Copy Key Name. The Registry Editor copies the full path name of the key, including the root key, to the clipboard.

- **To print a particular branch of the Registry**, select the key representing the top of the branch that you want to print; then, choose Registry ⇨ Print from the main menu. Click OK to print the branch to the printer. Don't even think about trying to print the entire Registry, because it consumes hundreds of pages of text.

# Manually Removing a Program from the Registry

Not all applications have uninstall programs, and even the programs that do have one sometimes leave a lot of junk behind in the Registry. Fortunately, most programs predictably store configuration data in the same places, making their removal from the Registry much easier. Before you try to remove a program manually from the Registry, make sure that you get a good backup copy. Though these steps won't remove every last bit of a program from the Registry, they clean up quite a bit of the mess that it might leave behind.

1. Remove any key or value that contains references to the program's EXE and DLL files. Make a note of each EXE and DLL file that you see in the program's installation paths. Then, search the Registry for each file, one by one, and remove each key or value entry containing the file. Use good judgment; don't remove a key that obviously contains entries used by other programs. One such common entry is Ctrl3d.dll, several of which exist; many programs use this DLL for display resources.

2. Remove any key or value entry containing the program's installation path. Search the Registry for all the program's installation paths. If the program has subfolders in its installation path, for example, search for the full path of every subfolder. Remove any keys or value entries that contain the path. Use good judgment; don't remove a key that obviously contains entries used by other programs.

3. Remove any key or value entry that contains the program's name. Search for the program's name. Just to be sure, search for a portion of, or a single word contained in, the application's name, too. Delete any keys or value entries containing the name of the program. Again, use good judgment when you are deciding whether to remove a key. Don't remove a key that obviously contains entries used by other programs.

# Editing the Registry on Multiple Computers

Multi-Remote Registry Change is a shareware product that you can download from `http://www54.pair.com/eytch`. It costs $25 to register and is well worth the price if it keeps you at your desk during lunch.

Multi-Remote Registry Change is an administrator's power tool. It enables you to change a Registry value on any number of remote computers, all at one time. Select the computers that you want to change from the list of network names, and specify the key and value that you want to change. For example, you can use this utility to customize every computer on the network so that they all use a standard desktop wallpaper, or maybe you want to customize the user interface by using a Registry tweak similar to what Tweak UI provides.

# Troubleshooting the Registry

To prevent users from accessing the Registry, do the following:

**1.** Don't install the Registry Editor when you roll out Windows 98.

**2.** Set the Disable Registry Editing Tools system policy.

If you get a Registry error when Windows 98 starts, do the following:

- If you see a message that says `Windows encountered an error accessing the system Registry: Windows will restart and repair the system Registry for you now`, permit Windows 98 to restart and repair the Registry in MS-DOS mode. This should fix the problem.

- If you see a message that says `Windows was unable to process the registry`: This may be fixed by rebooting to `Command Prompt Only` and running `SCANREG /FIX`. Otherwise, there may not be enough conventional memory to properly load the registry, run the DOS version of the Registry Checker to scan and fix any errors that it finds. If that doesn't work, try optimizing your memory so that you load a minimum number of drivers in low memory.

If Add/Remove Programs reports an error when it is removing a program, do this:

- If you see an error message that says `An error occurred while trying to remove program. Uninstallation has been canceled`, you probably have manually removed the program. Remove any entries that you find in `HKEY_LOCAL_MACHINE\Microsoft\Windows\CurrentVersion\Uninstall` that belong to the application.

If Windows 98 reports missing device drivers when it starts, do the following:

- If you recently removed a program, reinstall the program, and use the appropriate uninstaller to remove it.

- If the missing driver has a VXD extension, remove all references to the file from the Registry.

- If the missing driver is a 386 file, disable the line in System.ini by putting a semicolon in front of it.

# Appendixes

# Appendix A

# Command Lines

## Commands for Batch Files

You can include any command in a batch file (BAT or CMD files), including EXE and COM programs. Some intrinsic commands enable you to process statements conditionally or repetitively, though. Most of the commands in the following list are intrinsic and, with the exception of `for`, are useful only in a batch file. For a description of most of the command lines, take a look at the following sections.

| | | |
|---|---|---|
| call | for | pause |
| choice | goto | rem |
| echo | if | shift |

## call

Invokes another batch file without stopping the first batch file.

### Syntax

`call filename [parameters]`

| | |
|---|---|
| *filename* | Specifies the name of the batch file to invoke. |
| *parameters* | Specifies optional parameters to pass to the batch file. |

# choice

Waits for the user to make a choice and sets ERRORLEVEL to the offset in *choices* of the key that the user presses.

## Syntax

choice [/c [:] *choices*] [/n] [/s] [/t [:] *c,nn*] [*text*]

| | |
|---|---|
| /c [:] *choices* | Specifies the keys the user can press. The default is *"YN"*. |
| /n | Specifies not to display the choices at the end of the prompt. |
| /s | Treats the choices as case-sensitive. |
| /t [:] *c,nn* | Specifies the default choice is *c* after *nn* seconds. |
| *text* | Specifies the prompt to display. |

# echo

Displays a message on the screen or disables command echoing from the batch file. Displays status (on or off) if used with no options.

## Syntax

echo *text*
echo [on | off]

| | |
|---|---|
| *text* | Specifies the text to display on the screen. |
| on | Enables command echoing. |
| off | Disables command echoing. |

# for

Repeats a command for each file in a set specified by a wildcard.

## Syntax

for %*var* in (*wildcard*) do *command* [*command parameters*]

| | |
|---|---|
| %*var* | Specifies an alphanumeric variable such as %i or %file. |
| *wildcard* | Specifies a file mask, such as j*.txt, which can include a path. |

| | |
|---|---|
| `command` | Specifies the command to execute for each file in the set. By including the variable in the command, you can execute the command on the file – as in `for %f in (*.tmp)` `do del %f`, which deletes every file that matches `*.tmp` in the set specified by `%f`. |
| `command parameters` | Specifies additional parameters for the command. |

# goto

Branches to another labeled location in the batch file.

## Syntax

`goto label`

| | |
|---|---|
| `label` | Specifies the label to which you want to branch. You insert the label, which looks like `:label`, on a line by itself. |

# if

Tests a condition and executes a command if the condition is true. Three forms exist. The first executes a command, such as `goto`, if the ERRORLEVEL environment variable contains a certain value. The second executes a command if two strings, both of which can be an environment variable, are equal. The third executes a command if a file exists.

## Syntax

```
if [not] ERRORLEVEL number command
if [not] string1==string2 command
if [not] EXIST filename command
```

| | |
|---|---|
| `not` | Negates the result of the condition. |
| `number` | Specifies the error level for which you're testing. |
| `command` | Specifies the command to execute if the condition is true. |
| `string1` | Specifies an environment variable or a string. |
| `string2` | Specifies an environment variable or a string. |
| `filename` | Specifies the name of a file or folder. |

## shift

Shifts the position of the batch file's parameters. Each batch file parameter is identified as %0, %1, %2, and so on. Shift would put %2 into %1 and %1 into %0, and would drop %0.

### Syntax

shift

# Commands for Config.sys

The intrinsic commands in this section are available for use in Config.sys. This section briefly describes the commands and many of their command lines. For more detailed information, consult the Config.txt file in C:\Windows. The sections that follow describe the command lines for many of the following commands:

| | |
|---|---|
| accdate | lastdrive/lastdrivehigh |
| break | menucolor |
| buffers/buffershigh | menudefault |
| country | menuitem |
| device/devicehigh | numlock |
| dos | rem |
| drivparm | set |
| fcbs/fcbshigh | shell |
| files/fileshigh | stacks/stackshigh |
| include | submenu |
| install/installhigh | switches |

## accdate

Specifies whether to record the date that files are last accessed for each drive.

## Syntax

```
accdate=drive1+|- [drive2+|-] ...
```

| | |
|---|---|
| *drive1* | Specifies the drive letter. |
| + | Records the date each file on that drive was last accessed. |
| - | Does not record the date each file on that drive was last accessed. |

# break

Sets or clears Ctrl+C checking. Enabling Ctrl+C checking allows you to stop a program at times other than when it's checking the keyboard. Provides a status (on or off) if typed with no command line options.

## Syntax

```
break on | off
```

| | |
|---|---|
| on | Enables Ctrl+C checking. |
| off | Disables Ctrl+C checking. |

# buffers/buffershigh

Allocates memory for the specified number of disk buffers.

## Syntax

```
buffers=n[,m]
buffershigh=n[,m]
```

| | |
|---|---|
| *n* | Specifies the number of disk buffers, between 1 and 99, to allocate. The default is 30. |
| *m* | Specifies the number of disk buffers, from 0 to 8, to allocate in the secondary buffer cache. The default is 0. |

# country

Enables country-specific settings for dates, times, and so on.

## Syntax

```
country=xxx[,[yyy][,[drive:][path]filename]]
```

| | |
|---|---|
| *xxx* | Specifies the country code. |
| *yyy* | Specifies the character set for the country given in *xxx*. |
| *drive:path* | Specifies the path to the file containing country information. |
| *filename* | Specifies the name of the file containing country information. |

# device/devicehigh

Loads a device driver into memory.

## Syntax

```
device=[drive:][path]filename [parameters]
devicehigh=[drive:][path]filename [parameters]
```

| | |
|---|---|
| *drive:path* | Specifies the path to the device driver file. |
| *filename* | Specifies the name of the device driver file. |
| *parameters* | Contains any additional parameters for the device driver. |

# dos

Specifies whether MS-DOS should maintain a link to the upper memory area, load itself into the high memory area, or both.

## Syntax

```
dos=high|low[,umb | ,noumb] [,auto | ,noauto]
dos=[high, | low,] umb | noumb [,auto | ,noauto]
dos=[high, | low,] [umb, | noumb,] auto | noauto
```

| | |
|---|---|
| high\|low | Specifies whether MS-DOS should load into low memory or high memory. The default is *low*. |
| umb\|noumb | Specifies whether MS-DOS should manage the upper memory blocks created by a program, such as EMM386. The default is *noumb*. |

auto|noauto            Specifies whether MS-DOS should automatically load HIMEM.SYS.
                       The default is `auto`.

# drivparm

Defines parameters for disks and other devices.

## Syntax

```
drivparm /d:number [/c] [/f:factor] [/h:heads] [/i] [/n]
[/s:sectors] [/t:tracks]
```

| | |
|---|---|
| `/d:number` | Specifies the physical drive number in the range of 0 to 255. |
| `/c` | Specifies whether the drive can detect if the drive door is open. |
| `/f:factor` | Specifies the drive type: |

|   |   |
|---|---|
| 0 | 160K/180K or 320K/360K |
| 1 | 1.2MB |
| 2 | 720K 3.5-inch disk |
| 5 | Hard disk |
| 6 | Tape |
| 7 | 1.44MB 3.5-inch disk |
| 8 | Read/write optical disk |
| 9 | 2.88MB 3.5-inch disk |

| | |
|---|---|
| `/h:heads` | Specifies the maximum number of heads on the disk, ranging from 1 to 99. |
| `/i` | Specifies a device that's electronically compatible with a 3.5-inch floppy disk. |
| `/n` | Specifies a nonremovable block device. |
| `/s:sectors` | Specifies the number of sectors per track that a block device supports, ranging from 1 through 99. |
| `/t:tracks` | Specifies the number of tracks per side that the block device supports. |

# fcbs/fcbshigh

Specifies the number of file control blocks to allocate.

## Syntax

```
fcbs=n
fcbshigh=n
```

n       Specifies the number of file control blocks to allocate, ranging from 1 through 255. The default is 4.

# files/fileshigh

Specifies the number of file handles to allocate.

## Syntax

```
files=n
fileshigh=n
```

n       Specifies the number of file handles to allocate, ranging from 8 through 255. The default is 8.

# install/installhigh

Loads a memory-resident program into memory.

## Syntax

```
install=[drive:][path]filename [parameters]
installhigh=[drive:][path]filename [parameters]
```

drive:path      Specifies the path to the program file.
filename      Specifies the name of the program file.
parameters      Contains any additional parameters for the program.

# lastdrive/lastdrivehigh

Specifies the maximum number of drives available on the system.

## Syntax

```
lastdrive=n
lastdrivehigh=n
```

n            Specifies the highest drive letter to allocate.

# numlock

Specifies whether Num Lock is on or off when the computer starts.

## Syntax

`numlock=[on|off]`

on          Turns on Num Lock when the computer starts.

off         Turns off Num Lock when the computer starts.

# set

Sets an environment variable from within the Config.sys file. Displays all the current environment variables if executed with no command line options.

## Syntax

`set var=string`

*var*         Specifies the name of the variable.

*string*      Contains the value to assign to the variable.

# shell

Specifies the program to use as the command interpreter.

## Syntax

`shell=[[drive:]path]filename [parameters]`

drive:path          Specifies the location of the command interpreter.

*filename*          Specifies the filename of the command interpreter.

*parameters*        Contains additional parameters for the command interpreter. See "Command" under "Commands for Launching Programs" later in this appendix.

## stacks/stackshigh

Specifies the number of data stacks to allocate for hardware interrupts.

### Syntax

```
stacks=n,s
stackshigh=n,s
```

| | |
|---|---|
| n | Specifies the number of stacks to allocate, ranging from 8 to 64 and including 0. |
| s | Specifies the size of each stack, ranging from 32 to 512. |

## switches

Specifies special options for starting the operating system.

### Syntax

```
switches=[/f] [/k] [/n] [/e[:n]]
```

| | |
|---|---|
| /f | Skips the two-second delay after displaying "Starting MS-DOS." |
| /k | Forces enhanced keyboards to behave like conventional keyboards. |
| /n | Prevents you from using F5 or F8 to skip startup commands. |
| /e | Indicates that Io.sys should not relocate the EBIOS. |
| /e[:n] | Indicates that Io.sys should relocate n bytes of the EBIOS, ranging from 48 to 1024 in multiples of 16. |

# Commands for Device Drivers

Windows 98 includes a number of MS-DOS device drivers that you can use to configure your computer. This appendix describes the command lines for the following commands, but you can find more information in Msdosdrv.txt in C:\Windows. Here are the device drivers that come with Windows 98; you find the command lines for many of these described in the following sections:

Ansi.sys

Dblbuff.sys

Emm386.exe

Himem.sys

Display.sys

Ramdrive.sys

Drvspace.sys/Dblspace.sys

Setver.exe

Ega.sys

# Dblbuff.sys

Performs double buffering, which enables hard-disk controllers that don't work properly with memory provided by EMM386 or Windows 98 to work properly. Windows 98 automatically determines whether you need this device driver and installs it in Config.sys.

## Syntax

```
device=[drive:][path]dblbuff.sys [/d+]
```

drive:path        Specifies the location of Dblbuff.sys.

/d+               Specifies that Dblbuff.sys will double-buffer all disk I/O all the time.
                  Dblbuff.sys normally stops double-buffering if it appears unnecessary.

# Display.sys

Enables an EGA, VGA, or LCD monitor to display international character sets.

## Syntax

```
device=[drive:][path]display.sys
con[:]=(type[,[hwcp][,n]])
device=[drive:][path]display.sys
con[:]=(type[,[hwcp][,(n,m)]])
```

drive:path        Specifies the location of Display.sys.

type              Specifies the adapter in use: EGA or LCD. Use EGA for both EGA and
                  VGA monitors.

hwcp              Specifies the character set used by the hardware:

                  437       United States

| 850 | Multilingual (Latin I) |
| 852 | Slavic (Latin II) |
| 860 | Portuguese |
| 863 | Canadian-French |
| 865 | Nordic |
| *n* | Specifies the number of character sets the hardware supports, ranging from 0 to 6, in addition to the primary character set. |
| *m* | Specifies the number of subfonts the hardware supports for each code page. The default for LCD monitors is 1 and for EGA monitors is 2. |

# Drvspace.sys/Dblspace.sys

Determines the final memory location of Drvspace.bin or Dblspace.bin. These files provide access to your compressed drives.

## Syntax

```
device=[drive:][path]drvspace.sys /move [/nohma] [/low]
devicehigh=[drive:][path]drvspace.sys /move [/nohma]
       [/low]
device=[drive:][path]dblspace.sys /move [/nohma] [/low]
devicehigh=[drive:][path]dblspace.sys /move [/nohma]
       [/low]
```

| *drive:path* | Specifies the location of Drvspace.sys or Dblspace.sys. |
| */move* | Moves the BIN file to its final location in memory. |
| */nohma* | Prevents Drvspace.sys or Dblspace.sys from locating the BIN file in the high memory area. |
| */low* | Prevents Drvspace.sys or Dblspace.sys from locating the BIN file in conventional memory. |

# Emm386.exe

Provides access to the upper memory area and uses extended memory to emulate expanded memory. You can use this device driver only with 386 processors or better. You must install Himem.sys before installing Emm386.exe.

## Syntax

```
DEVICE=[drive:][path]EMM386.EXE [ON|OFF|AUTO] [memory]
        [MIN=size] [W=ON|OFF] [Mx|FRAME=address|/Pmmmm]
        [Pn=address] [X=mmmm-nnnn] [I=mmmm-nnnn]
        [B=address] [L=minXMS] [A=altregs] [H=handles]
        [D=nnn] [RAM=mmmm-nnnn] [NOEMS] [NOVCPI]
        [HIGHSCAN] [VERBOSE]
[WIN=mmmm-nnnn] [NOHI] [ROM=mmmm-nnnn] [NOMOVEXBDA]
        [ALTBOOT] [NOBACKFILL]
```

| | |
|---|---|
| *drive:path* | Specifies the location of EMM386.exe. |
| ON \| OFF \| AUTO | **ON** activates EMM386, **OFF** suspends it, and **AUTO** puts it in auto mode. Auto mode enables expanded-memory and UMB support when a program requires it. You can use Emm386.exe at the DOS prompt to change this value. |
| *memory* | Specifies the maximum amount of extended memory to allocate for expanded memory. This amount is over and above the memory the operating system uses for UMBs and the device driver itself. Valid values are from 64 to 32768 in multiples of 16, and the default value is the total amount of free extended memory. If you use **noems**, the default is 0. |
| MIN=*size* | Specifies the minimum amount of expanded memory that EMM386 provides, if available. Valid values are from 0 to the memory specified in *memory*. The default value is 256. If *size* is greater than *memory*, EMM386 uses *MIN*. |
| W=ON \| OFF | Enables or disables support for the Weitek coprocessor. The default is **OFF**. Most computers no longer use the Weitek coprocessor. |
| M*x* | Specifies the page frame address: |
| | 1    C000h |
| | 2    C400h |
| | 3    C800h |
| | 4    CC00h |
| | 5    D000h |
| | 6    D400h |

| | |
|---|---|
| 7 | D800h |
| 8 | DC00h |
| 9 | E000h |
| 10 | 8000h |
| 11 | 8400h |
| 12 | 8800h |
| 13 | 8C00h |
| 14 | 9000h |

**FRAME=**address — Specifies the page frame segment base address directly. Valid values range from 8000h to 9000h and C000h to E000h in increments of 400h. To provide expanded memory while disabling the page frame, use **none**. Doing so might cause some programs that use expanded memory to work incorrectly.

**/P**mmmm — Specifies the address of the page frame. Valid values are from 8000h to 9000h and C000h to E0000h in increments of 400h.

**P**n=address — Specifies the page frame segment base address for a specific page. Valid values for n range from 0 to 255. Valid values for the address range from 8000h to 9000h and C000h to E000h in increments of 400h. The addresses for pages 0 to 3 must be contiguous to maintain compatibility with LIM EMS 3.2. If you use /mx, frame, or /pmmmm, you can't specify the address of pages 0 to 3.

**X=**mmmm-nnnn — Prevents EMM386 from using a range of addresses as a page frame or for UMBs. Valid values are from A000h to FFFFH, rounded to the nearest 4K boundary. This switch takes precedence over /i.

**I=**mmmm-nnnn — Specifies a range of addresses to use as a page frame or for UMBs. Valid values are from A000h to FFFFH, rounded down to the nearest 4K boundary.

**B=**address — Specifies the lowest segment available for EMS banking. Valid values are from 1000h to 4000h. The default is 4000h.

**L=**minXMS — Specifies the amount of memory that must remain available after EMM386 is loaded. The default is 0.

**A=**altregs — Specifies the number of fast alternate register sets to allocate to EMM386. Valid values are from 0 to 254, and the default is 7. Each alternate register adds about 200 bytes of overhead to EMM386.

**H=**handles — Specifies the number of handles EMM386 uses. Valid values are from 2 through 255. The default is 64.

| | |
|---|---|
| D=*nnn* | Specifies the amount of memory to reserve for buffered DMA. This value should reflect the largest DMA transfer that will occur while EMM386 is active. Valid values are from 16 to 256, and the default is 16. |
| RAM=*mmmm–nnnn* | Specifies a range of addresses to use for UMBs and enables EMS support. If you don't specify a range, EMM386 uses all the available adapter space to create UMBs and a page frame for EMS. |
| NOEMS | Provides access to the upper memory area without providing access to expanded memory. |
| NOVCPI | Disables VCPI support. Use this switch in conjunction with **NOEMS**. Specifying both switches causes EMM386 to disregard the *memory* parameter and the /MIN switch. |
| HIGHSCAN | Specifies that EMM386 will scan upper memory for extra UMBs or EMS windows. Use this switch with care because EMM386 might find memory areas that don't really exist, causing the computer to stop responding. |
| VERBOSE | Displays status and error messages when EMM386 loads. |
| WIN=*mmmm–nnnn* | Specifies a range of memory addresses to reserve for Windows. Valid values are from A000h to FFFFH, rounded to the nearest 4K boundary. /x takes precedence over /win, and /win takes precedence over /ram, /rom, and /i. |
| NOHI | Prevents EMM386 from loading into the upper memory area, increasing the amount of upper memory available for UMBs and decreasing the amount of conventional memory available to applications. |
| ROM=*mmmm–nnnn* | Specifies a range of addresses that EMM386 uses to shadow ROM. Valid values are from A000h to FFFFH, rounded to the nearest 4K boundary. |
| NOMOVEXBDA | Prevents EMM386 from moving extended BIOS information from conventional to upper memory. |
| ALTBOOT | Specifies that EMM386 should use an alternate handler to restart the computer when you press Ctrl+Alt+Delete. |
| NOBACKFILL | When you use **noems** or **ram**, specifies that EMM386 should automatically backfill conventional memory if less than 640K exists. Use this switch only if your computer has less than 640K of conventional memory, as Windows 98 doesn't support backfilled memory. |

# Himem.sys

Manages the use of extended memory, including the high memory area (HMA). When using both Himem.sys and Emm386.exe, load Himem.sys before loading Emm386.exe.

## Syntax

```
device=[drive:][path]himem.sys [/a20control:on|off]
      [/cpuclock:on|off] [/eisa] [hmamin=m]
      [/int15=xxxx] [/machine:xxxx] [/noabove16]
      [/noeisa] [/numhandles=n] [/shadowram:on|off]
      [/testmem:on|off] [/verbose] [/x]
```

| | |
|---|---|
| *drive:path* | Specifies the location of Himem.sys. |
| /a20control: | Specifies whether Himem.sys takes control of the A20 line. |
| on\|off | The A20 handler gives Himem.sys access to HMA. The default value is ON. |
| /cpuclock:on\|off | Specifies whether Himem.sys affects the computer's clock speed. Set to ON if Himem.sys seems to change your clock speed; doing so slows down Himem.sys, though. |
| eisa | Specifies that Himem.sys should allocate all extended memory. Use this switch only with EISA computers that contain more than 16MB of memory. |
| hmamin=*m* | Specifies in K how much memory a program must require before Himem.sys gives the program use of the HMA. Valid values are from 0 to 63. Omitting this switch allocates the HMA to the first program that requests it. |
| /int15=*xxxx* | Specifies in K how much extended memory to allocate for the interrupt 15h interface. Some programs use this interface rather than the XMS method used by Himem.sys. Valid values are from 64 to 65535, and the default is 0. |
| /machine:*xxxx* | Specifies the type of computer you're using. You don't normally need to specify this switch, because Himem.sys correctly identifies most computers. Here are the codes you use with /machine: |
| | at          IBM AT or 100% compatible |
| | ps2        IBM PS/2 |
| | ptlcascade    Phoenix Cascade BIOS |

| | |
|---|---|
| hpvectra | HP Vectra (A & A+) |
| att6300plus | AT&T 6300 |
| acer1100 | Acer 1100 |
| toshiba | Toshiba 1600 & 1200XE |
| wyse | Wyse 12.5 Mhz 286 |
| tulip | Tulip SX |
| zenith | Zenith ZBIOS |
| at1 | IBM PC/AT (alternative delay) |
| at2 | IBM PC/AT (alternative delay) |
| css | CSS Labs |
| at3 | IBM PC/AT (alternative delay) |
| philips | Philips |
| fasthp | HP Vectra |
| ibm7552 | IBM 7552 Industrial Computer |
| bullmicral | Bull Micral 60 |
| dell | Dell XBIOS |

| | |
|---|---|
| `/noabove16` | Specifies not to use interrupt 15h Compaq Bigmem support to scan for extended memory. |
| `/noeisa` | Prevents Himem.sys from doing EISA scanning for extended memory. |
| `/numhandles=`*n* | Specifies the maximum number of EMB handles that can be used at the same time. Valid values range from 1 to 128, and the default is 32. Each handle has an overhead of 6 bytes of memory. |
| `/shadowram:`<br>`on|off` | Specifies whether to shadow the ROM in RAM. |
| `/testmem:on|off` | Specifies whether Himem.sys performs a memory test when you start your computer. The default is **ON**. |
| `/verbose` | Specifies that Himem.sys display status and error messages. |
| `/x` | Specifies not to use interrupt 15h. |

# Ramdrive.sys

Uses a portion of your computer's memory to emulate a disk drive. Ramdrive.sys creates a virtual disk for each time it appears in Config.sys.

## Syntax

```
device=[drive:][path]ramdrive.sys [disk sector [entries]]
        [/e | /a]
```

| | |
|---|---|
| *drive:path* | Specifies the location of Ramdrive.sys. |
| *disk* | Specifies in K how much memory to allocate for the disk. Valid values are from 4 to 32767. |
| *sector* | Specifies the size of the disk sector. Valid values are 128, 256, or 512. Specifying *sector* requires that you specify *disk*. |
| *entries* | Specifies the maximum number of files and folders you can create on the disk's root folder. Valid values are from 2 to 1024. The default is 64. |
| */e* | Creates the drive in extended memory. |
| */a* | Creates the drive in expanded memory. |

## Setver.exe

Loads the MS-DOS version table into memory. See "Setver" under "Commands for Files and Disks" later in this appendix.

## Syntax

```
device=[drive:][path]setver.exe
```

| | |
|---|---|
| *drive:path* | Specifies the location of Setver.exe. |

# Commands for the Registry

The following two programs are useful for working with the Registry:

- Regedit
- Scanreg

# Regedit

Imports values into or exports values out of the Registry.

## Syntax

```
regedit [/l:system] [/r:user] filename1 ...
regedit [/l:system] [/r:user] /e filename [regkey]
regedit [/l:system] [/r:user] /c filename
```

| | |
|---|---|
| /l:system | Specifies the name of the file containing the system hive. |
| /r:user | Specifies the name of the file containing the user hive. |
| filename1 | Specifies the REG file from which Regedit will import Registry keys, without replacing the entire contents of the Registry. |
| /e filename | Specifies the REG file into which Regedit will export. |
| /c filename | Specifies the REG file from which Regedit will import Registry keys, replacing the entire contents of the Registry. |

## Scanreg

Scans, backs up, or restores the Windows 98 Registry.

## Syntax

```
scanreg [/backup | /restore] [/autorun]
   [/comment="comment"] [/fix] [/opt]
```

| | |
|---|---|
| /backup | Backs up the current Registry. |
| /restore | Restores the Registry. |
| /autorun | Displays a dialog box only when an error occurs. |
| /comment | Adds a comment to the CAB file when backing up. |
| /fix | Repairs the Registry. |
| /opt | Optimizes the Registry. |

# Commands for Launching Programs

You use the following commands to launch command interpreters (shells) or to work with applications in general:

| | |
|---|---|
| Command | Loadhigh/lh |

```
Doskey          Mem
Explorer        Start
```

# Command
Starts a new command interpreter (shell).

## Syntax
```
command [[drive:]path] [device] [/e:nnnn] [/l:nnnn]
    [/u:nnn] [/p]
[/msg] [/low] [/y [/[c|k] command]]
```

| | |
|---|---|
| `drive:path` | Specifies the folder containing Command.com. |
| `device` | Specifies the device to use for input and output. |
| `/e:nnnn` | Sets the initial environment to *nnnn* bytes, between 256 to 32,768. |
| `/l:nnnn` | Specifies internal buffer lengths (requires `/p`). |
| `/u:nnn` | Specifies the input buffer length (requires `/p`), between 128 and 255. |
| `/p` | Makes the new command interpreter permanent. |
| `/msg` | Specifies to store all error messages in memory (requires `/p`). |
| `/low` | Forces Command.com to keep all its resident data in low memory. |
| `/y` | Single steps through the batch program specified by `/c` or `/k`. |
| `/c command` | Command returns after executing the command specified in `command`. |
| `/k command` | Command continues running after executing the command specified in `command`. |

# Doskey
Enables you to recall and edit DOS command lines.

## Syntax
```
doskey [/bufsize:size] [/echo:on|off] [/file:file]
    [/history]
[/insert] [keysize:size] [/line:size] [/macros]
    [/overstrike]
```

```
[/reinstall] [macroname=[text]]
```

| | |
|---|---|
| `/bufsize:size` | Sets the size of the macro and command buffer. The default is 512. |
| `/echo:on\|off` | Enables or disables echo of macro expansions. The default is **on**. |
| `/file:file` | Specifies a file containing a list of macros. |
| `/history` | Displays all commands stored in memory. |
| `/insert` | Inserts new characters into a line when typing. |
| `/keysize:size` | Specifies the size of the keyboard type-ahead buffer. The default is 15. |
| `/line:size` | Sets the maximum size of the line-edit buffer. The default is 128. |
| `/macros` | Displays all DOSKEY macros. |
| `/overstrike` | Overwrites new characters on a line when typing (default). |
| `/reinstall` | Installs a new copy of DOSKEY in memory. |
| `macroname` | Specifies a name for a macro that you create. |
| `text` | Specifies the commands to assign to `macroname`. |

# Explorer

Launches a new instance of Windows Explorer.

## Syntax

```
explorer [/n] [/e][,/root,object][[,/select],subobject]
```

| | |
|---|---|
| `/n` | Opens a new window, even if the folder is already open. |
| `/e` | Uses the Explorer view. The default is the folder view. |
| `/root,object` | Specifies the object to use as the root of the Windows Explorer window. The default is the desktop, but you can make any folder the root. |
| `/select` | Opens the parent folder and selects `object`. |
| `subobject` | Specifies the object that receives the initial focus. The default is the root folder. |

# Loadhigh/lh

Loads an application into the upper memory area.

## Syntax

```
loadhigh [drive:][path]filename [parameters]
loadhigh [/l:region1[,minsize1];region2[,minsize2]...]
    [/s]] [drive:][path]filename [parameters]
```

| | |
|---|---|
| `drive:path` | Specifies the location of the program. |
| `filename` | Specifies the name of the program file. Passes any parameters to the program. |
| `parameters` | Contains any additional parameters for the program. |
| `/l:region` | Specifies the memory region into which you want to load the program. |
| `minsize` | Specifies the minimum size for the region specified using `/l`. |
| `/s` | Shrinks the UMB to its smallest size when the program is running. |

# Mem

Displays information about the used and free memory in the computer.

## Syntax

```
mem [/c | /d | /f | /m module] [/p]
```

| | |
|---|---|
| `/c` | Classifies programs by memory usage. |
| `/d` | Displays the status of all modules in memory. |
| `/f` | Displays information about the free memory left in both conventional and upper memory. |
| `/m module` | Displays detailed information about the memory used by `module`. |
| `/p` | Pauses after each screen of information. |

# Start

Launches a program in Windows 98, giving you control over how it starts.

## Syntax

```
start [/m | /max | /r] [/w] program
```

```
start [/m | /max | /r ] [/w] document
```

| | |
|---|---|
| /m | Starts the program in a minimized window. |
| /max | Starts the program in a maximized window. |
| /r | Starts the program in a normal window. |
| /w | Does not return until the other program exits. |
| *program* | Specifies the name of the program to run. |
| *document* | Specifies the name of a document to launch. Start opens the document in the program that's associated with its file extension. |

# Commands for Files and Disks

The following commands are available for working with files and disks in Windows 98. The command lines for most of these programs are described in the following sections.

| | | |
|---|---|---|
| attrib | fc | setver |
| cd/chdir | fdisk | sort |
| chkdsk | find | smartdrv |
| copy | format | subst |
| del/erase | label | sys |
| deltree | md/mkdir | type |
| dir | more | verify |
| diskcopy | move | vol |
| edit | rd/rmdir | xcopy |
| extract | ren/rename | |

## attrib

Displays or changes file attributes.

### Syntax

```
attrib[+r|-r][+a|-a][+s|-s][+h|-h]
    [drive:][path]filename] [/s]
```

| | |
|---|---|
| +r | Sets the read-only attribute. |

| | |
|---|---|
| -r | Clears the read-only attribute. |
| +a | Sets the archive attribute. |
| -a | Clears the archive attribute. |
| +s | Sets the system attribute. |
| -s | Clears the system attribute. |
| +h | Sets the hidden attribute. |
| -h | Clears the hidden attribute. |
| *drive:path* | Specifies the location of *filename*, or the path on which `attrib` operates. |
| *filename* | Specifies the name of the file whose attributes `attrib` will change. *filename* can include wildcards. |
| /s | Processes files in all folders within the specified path. |

# cd/chdir

Switches to a different folder. If you type `cd` without any parameters, it reports the current folder.

## Syntax

```
cd [drive:][path]
cd [..]
```

| | |
|---|---|
| *drive:path* | Specifies the location to which you want to change. |
| .. | Specifies to change to the parent of the current folder. |

# chkdsk

Checks a disk and displays a status report. Consider using ScanDisk instead of Chkdsk because ScanDisk is more reliable.

## Syntax

```
chkdsk [drive:] [[path]filename] [/f] [/v]
```

| | |
|---|---|
| *drive* | Specifies the drive to scan. |
| *path* | Specifies the path containing a file to scan; must be used with *filename*. |

| | |
|---|---|
| *filename* | Specifies the name of a file to scan. |
| /f | Fixes errors on the disk. |
| /v | Displays the full path of every file on the disk. |

# copy

Copies one or more files from one location to another.

## Syntax

```
copy [/a | /b] source [[/a | /b] [+source ...]
    [destination [/a | /b]] [/v] [/y | /-y]
```

| | |
|---|---|
| /a | Specifies that the file is a text file. |
| /b | Specifies that the file is a binary file. |
| *source* | Specifies the file or files to copy. |
| *destination* | Specifies the destination or filename for the new files. |
| /v | Verifies new files as they are written. |
| /y | Prevents **copy** from prompting you when overwriting existing files. |
| /-y | Prompts you when overwriting existing files. |

# del/erase

Deletes one or more files from the computer.

## Syntax

```
del [drive:][path]filename [/p]
```

| | |
|---|---|
| *drive:path* | Specifies the location of the file or files to delete. |
| *filename* | Specifies the name of the files to delete. You can use wildcards. If you omit *filename*, *del* removes all the files from the designated folder. |
| /p | Prompts for confirmation before deleting each file. |

# deltree

Deletes one or more files and folders, including subfolders.

## Syntax

```
deltree [/y] [drive:]path [[drive:]path[...]]
```

| | |
|---|---|
| `/y` | Suppresses prompts that confirm you want to delete the folder. |
| `drive:path` | Specifies the location of the folder you want to delete. |

# dir

Displays a listing of the files and subfolders in the given folder.

## Syntax

```
dir [drive:][path][filename] [/p] [/w] [/a[[:attributes]]
    [/o[[:]sortorder]] [/s] [/b] [/l] [/v] [/4]
```

| | |
|---|---|
| `drive:path` | Specifies the drive or folder for which you want to list the files. |
| `filename` | Specifies an optional file mask to use when displaying the list. |
| `/p` | Pauses after each screen of information. |
| `/w` | Uses the wide list format, which fits more filenames on the screen with less information about each file. |
| `/a` | When used with no attributes, displays hidden and system files. Otherwise, displays files with the specified attributes: |

| | |
|---|---|
| D | Directories |
| H | Hidden files |
| S | System files |
| R | Read-only files |
| A | Files with the archive attribute |
| - | Prefix attribute to D, H, S, R, and A to reverse meaning |

| | |
|---|---|
| `/o` | Lists files sorted in one of these orders: |

| | |
|---|---|
| N | By name (alphabetic) |
| E | By extension (alphabetic) |
| G | Group folders first |
| A | By last access date (earliest first) |
| S | By size (smallest first) |
| D | By date and time (earliest first) |
| - | Prefix to reverse the order |

| | |
|---|---|
| /s | Displays files in the given folder and all subfolders. |
| /b | Uses a bare format with no headings or summaries. |
| /l | Uses lowercase letters. |
| /v | Uses verbose mode. |
| /4 | Displays years with four digits. |

# diskcopy

Copies the contents of a floppy disk to another floppy disk.

## Syntax

```
Diskcopy [drive1: [drive2:]] [/1] [/v] [/m]
```

| | |
|---|---|
| *drive1* | Specifies the floppy drive containing the disk to copy. |
| *drive2* | Specifies the floppy drive containing the destination disk. If *drive2* is missing, Diskcopy assumes you are copying to *drive1* and asks you to swap disks. |
| /1 | Copies the first side of the disk. |
| /v | Verifies that the disk is copied correctly. |
| /m | Forces a multipass copy using memory only. |

# edit

Is the text-only text editor that comes with Windows 98.

## Syntax

```
edit [/b] [/h] [/r] [/s] [/nnn] [file ...]
```

| | |
|---|---|
| /b | Opens Edit in monochrome mode. |
| /h | Displays the maximum number of lines possible. |
| /r | Loads file in read-only mode. |
| /s | Forces Edit to use short filenames. |
| /nnn | Loads a binary file, wrapping lines to *nnn* characters wide. |

| | |
|---|---|
| `file` | Specifies the file to load. Wildcards are allowed, and you can specify multiple filenames. |

# extract

Extracts files from Microsoft CAB files. It's particularly useful for restoring files from the Windows 98 CD-ROM.

## Syntax

```
extract [/y] [/a] [/d | /e] [/l dir] cabinet filename
extract [/y] source [newname]
extract [/y] /c source destination
```

| | |
|---|---|
| `/y` | Doesn't prompt before overwriting files. |
| `/a` | Processes all cabinet files, following cabinet chain. |
| `/d` | Displays a directory of the cabinet file. |
| `/e` | Extracts files specified in `filename` from `cabinet`. |
| `/l dir` | Specifies the folder in which to store extracted files. |
| `cabinet` | Specifies the cabinet file containing two or more files. |
| `filename` | Specifies the name of the file to extract from the cabinet. |
| `source` | Specifies the name of a compressed file, which is a cabinet file containing only one file. |
| `newname` | Specifies a new filename to give to the extracted file. |
| `/c` | Copies the source file from a DMF disk to the destination. |
| `destination` | Specifies the destination to copy a source file from a DMF disk. |

# fc

Compares two sets of files and displays the differences between them.

## Syntax

```
fc [/a] [/b] [/c] [/l] [/lbn] [/n] [/t] [/w] [/nnnn]
[drive1:][path1]filename1 [drive2:][path2]filename2
```

| | |
|---|---|
| `/a` | Displays only the first and last line for each set of differences. |

| /b | Performs a binary comparison. |
| /c | Specifies that a text comparison is case-insensitive. |
| /l | Performs a text comparison. |
| /lbn | Specifies that the maximum number of mismatches is $n$. |
| /n | Displays line numbers in a text comparison. |
| /t | Does not expand tab characters. |
| /w | Compresses white space before performing the comparison. |
| /nnnn | Specifies that $nnnn$ lines must match after a mismatch. |
| drive1:path1 | Specifies the drive or folder of the first file. |
| filename1 | Specifies the optional name of the first file. |
| drive2:path2 | Specifies the drive or folder of the second file. |
| filename2 | Specifies the optional name of the second file. |

# fdisk

Prepares a hard disk for use with MS-DOS and Windows 98. This is not the same as formatting.

## Syntax

```
fdisk /status /x [/mbr]
```

| /status | Displays partition information for the hard disk. |
| /x | Ignores support for extended disk access. |
| /mbr | Rewrites the master boot record. |

# find

Searches files containing a text string.

## Syntax

```
find [/v] [/c] [/n] [/i] "string"
    [[drive:][path]filename[ ...]]
```

| /v | Displays all lines that don't contain the string. |
| /c | Displays only the number of lines containing the string. |

| | |
|---|---|
| /n | Displays line numbers with displayed lines. |
| /i | Specifies that the search is case-insensitive. |
| "string" | Specifies the string for which to search in the files specified. |
| drive:path | Specifies the drive and path in which to search. If filename isn't present, find looks at every file in the path. |
| filename | Specifies the name of the file in which to search. |

# format

Formats a disk for use with MS-DOS and Windows 98. A hard disk generally must be fdisked before it can be formatted.

## Syntax

```
format drive: [/v[:label]] [/q] [/f:size] [/b | /s] [/c]
format drive: [/v[:label]] [/q] [/t:tracks /n:sectors]
    [/b | /s] [/c]
format drive: [/v[:label]] [/q] [/1] [/4] [/b | /s] [/c]
format drive: [/q] [/1] [/4] [/8] [/b | /s] [/c]
```

| | |
|---|---|
| /v[:label] | Specifies the volume label. |
| /q | Performs a quick format. |
| /f:size | Specifies the size of the floppy disk to support: 160, 180, 320, 360, 720, 1.2, 1.44, or 2.88. |
| /b | Allocates space on the disk for system files. |
| /s | Copies the system files to the disk. |
| /c | Tests disk clusters that are marked as bad. |
| /t:tracks | Formats the disk with the specified number of tracks. |
| /n:sectors | Formats the disk with the specified number of sectors. |
| /1 | Formats a single side of the floppy disk. |
| /4 | Formats a 5.25-inch 360K floppy disk in a high-density drive. |
| /8 | Formats eight sectors per track. |

# label

Changes the label for a disk volume.

## Syntax

```
label [drive:] [label]
```

*drive*          Specifies the drive containing the disk.

*label*          Specifies the label. If *label* is missing, `label` removes the label from
                 the disk.

# md/mkdir

Makes a new folder.

## Syntax

```
md [drive:]path
```

*drive:path*          Specifies the name of the new folder to create.

# move

Moves or renames files and folders.

## Syntax

```
move [/y | /-y] [drive:][path]filename1[,...] destination
move [/y | /-y] [drive:][path]dirname1 dirname2
```

*/y*                   Suppresses prompts to create folders or overwrite files.

*/-y*                  Does not suppress prompts to create folders or overwrite files.

*drive:path*           Specifies the drive and path of the files to move or rename. If no
                       filenames are given, **move** operates on the entire path.

*filename1*            Specifies one or more filenames to move.

*destination*          Specifies the destination into which you want to move the files.

*dirname1*             Specifies the folder you want to rename.

*dirname2*             Specifies the new name of the folder.

# rd/rmdir

Removes an empty folder from the computer.

## Syntax

```
rd [drive:]path
```

*drive:path*  Specifies the location of the folder to delete.

# ren/rename

Renames one or more files or folders.

## Syntax

```
ren [drive:][path][folder1 | file1] [folder2 | file2]
```

*drive:path*  Specifies the location of the folder or file you're renaming.
*folder1|file1*  Specifies the folder or file you're renaming.
*folder2|file2*  Specifies the new name of the folder or file.

# setver

Sets the MS-DOS version number that Windows 98 reports to programs. The first form displays the current version table. The second adds an entry to the table, and the third deletes an entry. You must load Setver.exe in Config.sys first.

## Syntax

```
setver [drive:path]
setver [drive:path] filename n.nn
setver [drive:path] filename /d [/q]
```

*drive:path*  Specifies the path of the Setver.exe file.
*filename*  Specifies the filename of the program.
*n.nn*  Specifies the MS-DOS version to report to the program.
*/d*  Deletes a version-table entry for the program specified in *filename*.
*/q*  Hides messages normally generated while deleting a table entry.

# smartdrv

Installs and configures the SmartDrive disk-caching utility. This program normally is not required when running Windows 98.

## Syntax

```
smartdrv [/x] [[drive[+|-]]...] [/u] [/c | /r] [/f | /n]
    [/l] [/v | /q | /s]
[initsize [winsize]] [/e:element] [/b:buffer]
```

| | |
|---|---|
| /x | Disables write-behind caching for all drives. |
| drive | Sets caching options for the drives specified. |
| + | Enables write-behind caching for the specified drive. |
| – | Disables all caching for the specified drive. |
| /u | Does not load the CD-ROM caching module. |
| /c | Writes all information in the write-cache to the hard disk. |
| /r | Clears the cache and restarts SmartDrive. |
| /f | Flushes the cache before the command prompt returns. |
| /n | Doesn't flush the cache before the command prompt returns. |
| /l | Prevents SmartDrive from loading itself into upper memory. |
| /v | Displays a status message when loading. |
| /q | Does not display a status message when loading. |
| /s | Displays additional information about SmartDrive's status. |
| initsize | Specifies the amount of XMS memory in K for the cache. |
| winsize | Specifies the amount of XMS memory in K for the cache for use with Windows. |
| /e:element | Specifies how many bytes to move at one time. |
| /b:buffer | Specifies the read-ahead buffer size. |

# sys

Copies the MS-DOS system files and command interpreter to a formatted disk.

## Syntax

```
sys [drive1:][path] drive2:
```

*drive1:path*      Specifies the path containing the system files.

*drive2*      Specifies the drive to which you want to copy the system files.

# xcopy

Copies files and folders from one location to another, replicating the structure.

## Syntax

```
xcopy source [destination] [/a | /m] [/d[:date]] [/p] [/s
    [/e]] [/w] [/c] [/i] [/q] [/f] [/l] [/h] [/r] [/t]
    [/u] [/k] [/n] [/y | /-y]
```

| | |
|---|---|
| *source* | Specifies the location of the source files or source path. |
| *destination* | Specifies the location to which you want to copy the source folders or the new name of the files you're copying. |
| /a | Copies only files that have the archive attribute set, without turning off the archive attribute. |
| /m | Copies only files that have the archive attribute set, turning off the archive attribute after copying them. |
| /d[:date] | Copies files changed on or after the specified date. If no date is given, copies only files whose source time is newer than the destination time. |
| /p | Prompts you before creating each folder or file. |
| /s | Copies folders and subfolders, except empty ones. |
| /e | Copies folders and subfolders, including empty ones. |
| /w | Prompts you to continue before copying files. |
| /c | Continues copying files, even after an error occurs. |
| /i | Assumes the destination is a folder if you're copying more than one file and the destination doesn't exist. |
| /q | Does not display filenames while copying them. |
| /f | Displays the full source and destination while copying files. |
| /l | Displays files that would be copied, without actually copying them. |

| | |
|---|---|
| /h | Copies hidden and system files in addition to other files. |
| /r | Overwrites read-only files. |
| /t | Creates the folder structure, but doesn't actually copy files. |
| /u | Updates only files that already exist at the destination. |
| /k | Copies attributes for each file. |
| /n | Copies using short filenames. |
| /y | Overwrites existing files without prompting you first. |
| /-y | Prompts you before overwriting existing files. |

# Commands for TCP/IP

Windows 98 provides the following utilities for use with TCP/IP, installing them on your computer when you install the TCP/IP network protocol via the Network Properties dialog box in the Control Panel. The command lines for all these utilities are in the following sections.

| | | |
|---|---|---|
| Arp | Nbstat | Route |
| Ftp | Netstat | Telnet |
| Ipconfig | Ping | Tracert |

## Arp

Displays or changes the IP-to-Ethernet or IP-to-Token Ring address translation tables used by the address resolution protocol (ARP).

### Syntax

```
arp -a [addr] [-N [if_addr]
arp -a addr [if_addr]
arp -s addr ether_addr [if_addr]
arp -d addr
```

| | |
|---|---|
| a | Displays current ARP entries; if **addr** is specified, it displays only the IP and physical address of the specified computer. |

| | |
|---|---|
| `addr` | Specifies an IP address in dotted decimal notation. |
| N | Displays the ARP entries for `if_addr`. |
| `if_addr` | Specifies the IP address of the interface for which the address translation table should be modified. The first interface is used if `if_addr` is missing. |
| s | Adds an entry to the ARP cache table that associates `addr` with the physical address `ether_addr`. |
| `ether_addr` | Specifies the physical address as 6 hexadecimal bytes separated by hyphens. |
| d | Deletes the entry specified by `addr` from the ARP cache table. |

# Ftp

Transfers files between the client computer and a host running the FTP service.

## Syntax

`ftp [-v] [-n] [-i] [-d] [-g] [host] [-s: filename]`

| | |
|---|---|
| v | Suppresses responses from the remote host. |
| n | Suppresses autologon when connecting. |
| i | Turns off interactive prompts during multiple file transfers. |
| d | Enables debugging, displaying all FTP commands. |
| g | Prevents use of wildcard characters in local filenames. |
| `host` | Specifies the name or IP address of the host to connect to. |
| `s: filename` | Specifies a response file containing FTP commands that `ftp` will execute automatically after it starts. |

# Ipconfig

Configures the IP in Windows 98. Try also Winipcfg.exe.

## Syntax

```
ipconfig [/all] [/batch [file]] [/renew_all]
    [/release_all]
[/renew nnn] [/release nnn]
```

| /all | Displays detailed information about the local host. |
| /batch [*file*] | Writes to the given file or to Winipcfg.out. |
| /renew_all | Renews all adapters. |
| /release_all | Releases all adapters. |
| /renew *nnn* | Renews the adapter identified as *nnn*. |
| /release *nnn* | Releases the adapter identified as *nnn*. |

# Nbtstat

Displays protocol statistics and current TCP/IP connections using NetBIOS over TCP/IP.

## Syntax

```
nbtstat [-a host] [-A ip_addr] [-c] [-n] [-R] [-r] [-S]
     [-s] [interval]
```

| a *host* | Lists the remote computer's name table, given its name. |
| A *ip_addr* | Lists the remote computer's name table, given its IP address. |
| c | Lists the contents of the NetBIOS name cache. |
| n | Lists local NetBIOS names. The word *Registered* in the listing indicates the name is registered on this network node by b-node broadcast or a WINS server. |
| R | Reloads LMHOSTS after purging the NetBIOS name cache. |
| r | Lists name resolution statistics for Windows network. |
| S | Displays workstation and server sessions, listing remote hosts by IP address. |
| s | Displays workstation and server sessions, converting remote host IP addresses to a name, if possible, using the HOSTS file. |
| *interval* | Repeatedly displays the selected statistics, pausing at *interval* seconds. Without this parameter, Nbtstat displays the statistics once. |

# Netstat

Displays protocol statistics and current TCP/IP connections.

## Syntax

```
netstat [-a] [-ens] [-p protocol] [-r] [interval]
```

| | |
|---|---|
| a | Displays all connections, including server connections. |
| e | Displays Ethernet statistics. |
| n | Displays addresses and port numbers as numbers, rather than trying to look up names. |
| s | Displays statistics per each protocol. |
| p *protocol* | Shows connections for the specified protocol: `tcp`, `udp`, `icmp`, or `ip`. |
| r | Displays the routing table. |
| *interval* | Repeatedly displays the selected statistics, pausing at `interval` seconds. Without this parameter, Netstat displays the statistics once. |

# Ping

Verifies that a remote host is responding.

## Syntax

```
ping [-t] [-a] [-n count] [-l length] [-f] [-i ttl] [-v
    tos] [-r count]
[-s count] [[-j host-list] [-k host-list]] [-w timeout]
    destinations
```

| | |
|---|---|
| t | Pings the host until you interrupt it. |
| a | Specifies not to resolve addresses into host names. |
| n *count* | Sends the number of echo packets given by `count`. The default is 4. |
| l *length* | Sends echo packets containing an amount of data specified by `length`. The default is 64 bytes, and the maximum is 8192 bytes. |
| f | Sends a **Do Not Fragment** flag in the packet. The packet will not be fragmented by routers along the way. |
| i *ttl* | Sets the **Time to Live** field to `ttl`. |
| v *tos* | Sets the **Type of Service** field to `tos`. |

| | |
|---|---|
| r count | Records the route of the packet, coming and going, in the Record Route field. Specify the number of hosts in count, which can range from 1 to 9. |
| s count | Specifies the number of hops in count. |
| j host-list | Routes packets through the hosts listed in host-list. Intermediate gateways may separate consecutive hosts. |
| k host-list | Routes packets through the hosts listed in host-list. Intermediate gateways may not separate consecutive hosts. |
| w timeout | Specifies a timeout in milliseconds. |
| destinations | Specifies the remote host to ping. |

# Route

Manipulates the network routing tables.

## Syntax

route [-f] [command [destination] [METRIC metric] [MASK mask] [gateway]]

| | | |
|---|---|---|
| f | Clears all gateway entries from the routing tables. | |
| command | Specifies one of the following commands: | |
| | print | Print a route |
| | add | Add a route |
| | delete | Delete a route |
| | change | Change a route |
| destination | Specifies the host to send command. | |
| METRIC metric | Specifies a cost for this destination. | |
| MASK mask | Specifies the network mask. | |
| gateway | Specifies the gateway. | |

# Telnet

Provides terminal emulation, connecting to a remote host running a Telnet server. Telnet supports DEC VT 100, DEC VT 52, or TTY over TCP/IP.

## Syntax

```
telnet [host [port]]
```

| | |
|---|---|
| *host* | Specifies the host to which Telnet should connect. Specify either a host name or an IP address. |
| *port* | Specifies the port on which to connect. This enables you to open a connection with servers that listen on ports other than 23, such as HTTP or Gopher. |

## Tracert

Traces the route a packet travels from the local host to the remote host.

## Syntax

```
tracert [-d] [-h max_hops] [-j host-list] [-w timeout]
    target
```

| | |
|---|---|
| d | Specifies not to resolve IP addresses into host names. |
| h *max_hops* | Specifies the maximum number of hops to reach the target. |
| j *host-list* | Specifies a source route in *host-list*. |
| w *timeout* | Specifies the timeout in milliseconds for each hop. |
| *target* | Specifies the name of the destination host. |

# Commands for Networks (NET)

The NET command is a command-line driven utility that provides a rich set of commands to perform many network maintenance functions. The general syntax of the command is NET, followed by a command type, followed by specific options for that command type. Some of these command functions include logging on and off a workgroup, sharing and unsharing network resources, accessing network resources, and displaying information about resources and the connections to those resources. Some of the commands are server-specific and may not be available from a workstation, and others are designed for a workstation and may not make sense when used from a server. An overview of the most useful commands follows.

# NET CONFIG

Displays your current workgroup settings.

## Syntax

NET CONFIG [/YES]

/YES                Executes the **NET CONFIG** command without prompting you to provide information or confirm actions.

# NET DIAG

Runs Microsoft's network diagnostics program. This program tests the hardware connection between computers and displays information about a computer.

## Syntax

NET DIAG [/NAMES | /STATUS]

/NAMES           Is a diagnostic server name used to avoid conflicts when multiple users are running **NET DIAG** on the network. This option works only if the NetBIOS protocol is being used.

/STATUS         Enables you to specify a computer for which you want to display network diagnostic information.

# NET INIT

Loads protocols and network adapter drivers without binding them with the Protocol Manager. You may find this command helpful when you are using third-party drivers.

## Syntax

```
NET INIT [/DYNAMIC]
```

`/DYNAMIC`        Loads the Protocol Manager dynamically.

# NET LOGOFF

Removes the connections between your computer and any shared resources that you are accessing. This command logs you out of the workgroup.

## Syntax

```
NET LOGOFF [/YES]
```

`/`        Executes the **Tracert** command without first prompting you to provide information or confirm actions.

# NET LOGON

Identifies you as a member of a particular workgroup and gives you access to shared resources for that workgroup. If you type NET LOGON without options, you are prompted for your logon name and password during the logon process.

## Syntax

```
NET LOGON [user [password | ?]] [/DOMAIN:name] [/YES]
    [/SAVEPW:NO]
```

| | |
|---|---|
| `user` | Specifies the logon name that identifies you as a member of the workgroup. |
| `password` | Specifies your logon password that gains you access to your password-list file. |
| `?` | Causes you to be prompted for your password. |
| `/DOMAIN` | Indicates that you want to log on to a Microsoft NT or LAN Manager domain. |
| `name` | Specifies the name of the domain you want to log on to. |

| /YES | Executes the **NET LOGON** command without first prompting you to provide information or confirm actions. |
|------|------|
| /SAVEPW:NO | Executes the **NET LOGON** command without prompting you to create a password-list file. |

# NET PRINT

Controls printer jobs and displays information about print queues on shared printers. When you specify the name of a computer with the NET PRINT command, information is displayed regarding the print queues for all the shared printers on that computer.

## Syntax

```
NET PRINT \\computer[printer] | port [/YES]
NET PRINT \\computer | port [job# [/PAUSE | /RESUME
   | /DELETE]] [/YES]
```

| computer | Specifies the name of the computer whose print queue's information will be displayed. |
|------|------|
| printer | Specifies the name of the shared printer whose information will be displayed. |
| port | Specifies the name of your computer's parallel port (LPT#) that is connected to the printer you want information about. |
| /YES | Executes the **NET PRINT** command without first prompting you to provide information or confirm actions. |
| job# | Specifies the number assigned to a queued print job. |
| /PAUSE | Pauses the print job. |
| /RESUME | Resumes a paused print job. |
| /DELETE | Deletes a print job from the queue. |

# NET USE

Connects and disconnects your computer to or from a shared network resource. It can also be used to display your current connections. This command has a different syntax, depending on whether you are accessing a shared port or shared drive.

## Syntax

```
NET USE [drive: | *] [\\computer\directory
[password | ?]] [/SAVEPW:NO] [/YES] [/NO]
NET USE [port:] [\\computer\printer [password | ?]]
    [/SAVEPW:NO] [/YES] [/NO]
NET USE drive: | \\computer\directory /DELETE [/YES]
NET USE port: | \\computer\printer /DELETE [/YES]
NET USE * /DELETE [/YES]
NET USE drive: | * /HOME
```

| | |
|---|---|
| *drive* | Specifies the drive letter to be assigned to a shared directory. |
| * | Indicates to use the next available drive letter. When this option is used with the /DELETE parameter, it forces a disconnect of all your current connections. |
| *computer* | Specifies the name of the host computer sharing the resource on the network. |
| *directory* | Specifies the directory name of the shared directory. |
| *password* | Specifies the password to be used for the shared resource, if any. |
| ? | Indicates that you want to be prompted for the shared resource password. |
| /SAVEPW:NO | Causes the password that you type not to be saved in the password-list file. When you use this option, you are required to reenter the password the next time that you connect to this resource. |
| /YES | Executes the NET USE command without first prompting you to provide information or confirm actions. |
| /NO | Executes the NET USE command, automatically responding with NO when you are prompted to confirm actions. |
| *port* | Specifies the LPT printer port name that you assign to a shared printer. |
| *printer* | Specifies the name of the shared printer. |
| /DELETE | Removes your current connection to a shared resource. |
| /HOME | Establishes a connection to your home directory, as specified in your LAN Manager or NT user account. |

To display help on the NET USE command, enter NET USE /?. To display information on your current connections, enter NET USE without any options.

# NET VER

Displays the type and version information for the current workgroup redirector.

## Syntax

```
NET VER
```

# NET VIEW

Displays the computers in a specified workgroup or a list of the shared resources on a specific computer.

## Syntax

```
NET VIEW [\\computer] [/YES]
NET VIEW [WORKGROUP:workgroupname] [/YES]
```

| | |
|---|---|
| computer | Is the name of the computer whose shared resources you want to view. |
| YES | Executes the **NET VIEW** command without first prompting you to provide information or confirm actions. |
| /WORKGROUP | Lists the names of computers in another workgroup that share resources. |
| workgroupname | Specifies the name of the workgroup whose computers you want to list. |

# Commands for International Settings

Windows 98 provides the following commands to change international settings, such as country codes, keyboard layouts, and code pages. The following sections describe some of these commands in more detail.

```
chcp
country
```

```
keyb
mode
nlsfunc
```

# keyb

Configures the keyboard for use with a specific language.

## Syntax

```
keyb [xx[,[yyy][,[drive:][path]filename]]] [/e] [/id:nnn]
```

| | |
|---|---|
| *xx* | Specifies a two-letter keyboard code. |
| *yyy* | Specifies the code page for the character set. |
| *drive:path* | Specifies the path to the keyboard definition file. |
| *filename* | Specifies the filename of the keyboard definition file. |
| */e* | Specifies that you've installed an advanced keyboard. |
| */id:nnn* | Specifies the keyboard that's in use. |

# nlsfunc

Loads country-specific information into memory.

## Syntax

```
nlsfunc [[drive:] [path]filename]
```

| | |
|---|---|
| *drive:path* | Specifies the drive and path to the file containing country-specific information. |
| *filename* | Specifies the name of the file containing country-specific information. |

# Appendix B

# Keyboard Shortcuts

This appendix describes the shortcuts that you can use with a variety of objects in Windows 98. These include both mouse and keyboard shortcuts for objects such as dialog boxes, files, and so on.

## Files and Objects

Table B-1 describes keyboard shortcuts that you can use on a selected object.

**Table B-1** *Keyboard Shortcuts for Objects*

| Press | To |
| --- | --- |
| F2 | Rename the selected object |
| Ctrl+X or Shift+Delete | Cut the selected object to the clipboard |
| Ctrl+C or Ctrl+Insert | Copy the selected object to the clipboard |
| Ctrl+V or Shift+Insert | Paste the contents of the clipboard as an object in the selected folder |
| Delete | Delete the object to the Recycle Bin |
| Shift+Delete | Permanently delete the object without storing it in the Recycle Bin |
| Shift+F10 | Open the object's context menu |
| Alt+Enter or Alt+double-click | Open the object's properties dialog box |
| Shift+double-click | Explore the object if it has an Explore command |
| Shift+right-click | Open the alternative context menu (Open With) |

# Windows Explorer Trees

Table B-2 describes keyboard shortcuts that you can use to work with the tree view in Windows Explorer.

**Table B-2** *Keyboard Shortcuts for Explorer Trees*

| Press | To |
| --- | --- |
| + on keypad | Expand selection |
| * on keypad | Expand everything under selection |
| - on keypad | Collapse selection |
| Ctrl+arrow | Scroll without moving the selection |
| Left arrow | Collapse selection if expanded; otherwise, move to parent |
| Right arrow | Expand selection if collapsed; otherwise, move to first child |

# Windows Explorer Folders

Table B-3 describes keyboard shortcuts that you can use when working with a folder.

**Table B-3** *Keyboard Shortcuts for Explorer Folders*

| Press | To |
| --- | --- |
| F3 | Find files in the selected folder |
| F4 | Open the combo box in the Address toolbar |
| F5 | Refresh the folder's contents |
| F6 | Switch between the tree pane, folder pane, and address bar |
| Ctrl+Z | Undo the previous operation |
| Ctrl+A | Select all files in the folder |
| Alt+left arrow | Move to the previous folder in the folder's history list |
| Alt+right arrow | Move to the next folder in the folder's history list |
| Backspace | Display the parent folder |

# Applications

Table B-4 describes keyboard shortcuts that you can use when working with most applications in Windows 98.

**Table B-4** *Keyboard Shortcuts for Applications*

| Press | To |
|---|---|
| F1 | Display help |
| Alt or F10 | Open the menu bar |
| Ctrl+Esc | Display the Start menu |
| Alt+Tab | Switch to the running application that was previously active |
| Alt+Tab+Tab | Choose from a list of running applications |
| Alt+Esc | Switch to next running application |
| Alt+F4 | Close the active window or close Windows 98 if no windows are on the desktop |
| Print Scrn | Copy an image of the entire screen to the clipboard |
| Alt+Print Scrn | Copy an image of the active window to the clipboard |
| Alt+Spacebar | Open a window's system menu |

# MDI Applications

Table B-5 describes keyboard shortcuts that you can use when working with an MDI application's child windows.

**Table B-5:** *Keyboard Shortcuts for MDI Windows*

| Press | To |
|---|---|
| Ctrl+F4 | Close the active child window |
| Alt+hyphen | Open the system menu of the active child window |
| Ctrl+Tab or Ctrl+F6 | Switch to the next child window |

# Dialog Boxes

Table B-6 describes keyboard shortcuts that you can use when working with most dialog boxes in Windows 98.

**Table B-6** *Keyboard Shortcuts for Dialog Boxes*

| Press | To |
|---|---|
| Enter | Activate the default button (OK) |
| Space | Simulate a left-click on the active control |
| Tab | Move to the next control in the dialog box |
| Shift+Tab | Move to the previous control in the dialog box |
| Alt+down arrow | Open the drop-down list of a combo box |
| Ctrl+Tab | Move to the next tab in the Properties dialog box |
| Shift+Ctrl+Tab | Move to the previous tab in the Properties dialog box |

# Common Dialog Boxes

Table B-7 describes keyboard shortcuts that you can use when working with the common Open and Save As dialog boxes in Windows 98.

**Table B-7** *Keyboard Shortcuts for Common Dialog Boxes*

| Press | To |
|---|---|
| F4 | Open the Save In or Look In combo box |
| F5 | Refresh the dialog box's contents |
| Ctrl+Z | Undo the previous operation |
| Ctrl+A | Select all files in the folder if the application supports opening multiple files |
| Backspace | Display the parent folder |

# Drag-and-Drop

Table B-8 describes keyboard shortcuts that you can use when using drag-and-drop to copy and move files in Windows 98.

**Table B-8** *Keyboard Shortcuts for Drag-and-Drop*

| While Dragging, Press | To |
|---|---|
| Ctrl | Copy |
| Shift | Move |
| Ctrl+Shift | Create shortcut |

# Accessibility Emergency Keys

Table B-9 describes the emergency keys that you can use to enable quickly the Windows 98 accessibility features.

**Table B-9** *Emergency Keys for Accessibility*

| Press | To |
|---|---|
| Press Shift five times | Toggle StickyKeys |
| Right Shift for eight seconds | Toggle FilterKeys |
| Num Lock for five seconds | Toggle ToggleKeys |
| Left Alt+left Shift+Num Lock | Toggle MouseKeys |
| Left Alt+left Shift+Print Scrn | Toggle HighContrast |

# Microsoft Natural Keyboard Keys

Table B-10 describes keyboard shortcuts that you can use with Microsoft's Natural Keyboard. Note that these shortcuts actually work with any keyboard that has the Windows key on it.

**Table B-10** *Keyboard Shortcuts for Natural Keyboards*

| Press | To |
| --- | --- |
| Win+R | Open the Run dialog box |
| Win+M | Minimize all open windows |
| Shift+Win+M | Undo Minimize All |
| Win+F1 | Start Windows Help |
| Win+E | Start Windows Explorer |
| Win+F | Use Find in files or folders |
| Ctrl+Win+F | Find computer on the network |
| Win+Tab | Cycle through taskbar buttons |
| Win+Break | Open System Properties dialog box |

# Windows 98 Startup

Table B-11 describes keyboard shortcuts that you can use to change how Windows 98 starts.

**Table B-11** *Keys for Starting Windows*

| Press | To |
| --- | --- |
| F4 | Start the previous operating system |
| F5 | Start Windows 98 in Safe mode |
| Shift+F5 | Boot to the DOS 7.0 command line |
| Ctrl+F5 | Start without compressed drives |
| Shift+F8 | Confirm each command step by step |
| F6 | Start in Safe mode with networking support |
| F8 | Load the Startup menu |

# Index

*(continued)*

*(continued)*

# my2cents.idgbooks.com

## Register This Book — And Win!

Visit **http://my2cents.idgbooks.com** to register this book and we'll automatically enter you in our fantastic monthly prize giveaway. It's also your opportunity to give us feedback: let us know what you thought of this book and how you would like to see other topics covered.

## Discover IDG Books Online!

The IDG Books Online Web site is your online resource for tackling technology — at home and at the office. Frequently updated, the IDG Books Online Web site features exclusive software, insider information, online books, and live events!

### 10 Productive & Career-Enhancing Things You Can Do at www.idgbooks.com

1. Nab source code for your own programming projects.

2. Download software.

3. Read Web exclusives: special articles and book excerpts by IDG Books Worldwide authors.

4. Take advantage of resources to help you advance your career as a Novell or Microsoft professional.

5. Buy IDG Books Worldwide titles or find a convenient bookstore that carries them.

6. Register your book and win a prize.

7. Chat live online with authors.

8. Sign up for regular e-mail updates about our latest books.

9. Suggest a book you'd like to read or write.

10. Give us your 2¢ about our books and about our Web site.

You say you're not on the Web yet? It's easy to get started with IDG Books' *Discover the Internet*, available at local retailers everywhere.